The Special Educator's BOOK OF LISTS

Second Edition

Roger Pierangelo, Ph.D.

JOSSEY-BASS
A Wiley Imprint
www.josseybass.com

Published by Jossey-Bass
A Wiley Imprint
989 Market Street, San Francisco, CA 94103-1741   www.josseybass.com

Jossey-Bass books and products are available through most bookstores. To contact Jossey-Bass directly, call our Customer Care Department within the U.S. at (800) 956-7739, outside the U.S. at (317) 572-3993 or fax (317) 572-4002.

Jossey-Bass also publishes its books in a variety of electronic formats. Some content that appears in print may not be available in electronic books.

Permission granted by Allyn and Bacon for use of material from *Assessment in Special Education: A Practical Approach* (4th ed.) by Roger Pierangelo and George Giuliani.

Much of the clip art in this book is from Art Explosion by Nova Development.

Library of Congress Cataloging-in-Publication Data

Pierangelo, Roger.
    The special educator's book of lists / Roger Pierangelo.—2nd ed.
        p.   cm.
    Rev. ed. of: The special education teacher's book of lists. c1995.
    Includes bibliographical references.
        ISBN 0-7879-6593-6 (pbk. : alk. paper)
        1. Special education—Handbooks, manuals, etc.   2. Special education teachers—Handbooks, manuals, etc.   I. Pierangelo, Roger. Special education teacher's book of lists.   II. Title.
        LC3965.P54 2003
        371.9—dc21
                                                        2002155181

Printed in the United States of America

SECOND EDITION

PB Printing 10 9 8 7 6 5 4 3

DEDICATION

To my loving wife, Jackie, and our two beautiful children, Jacqueline and Scott, I dedicate this book and all the work that went into it. To my parents who got so much pleasure from being parents, my sister, Carol, who would make any brother proud, and my brother-in-law, Dr. George Giuliani, who throughout our relationship has always been there unconditionally.

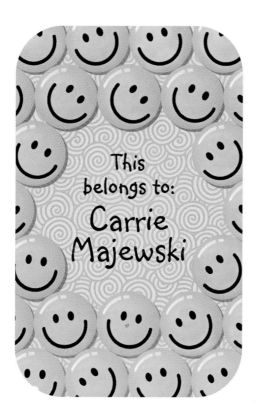

ACKNOWLEDGMENTS

Ollie Simmons, an absolutely exceptional individual and personal friend who always helps me start the day with a smile.

Helen Firestone, one of the most instrumental individuals in my career who always believed in me.

Charlotte Podolsky, head of Pupil Personnel Services in Herricks for many of my years in the district before her retirement, who always showed a genuine support and confidence in my work.

In memory of Bill Smyth, a truly "extraordinary ordinary" man and one of the best guidance counselors and individuals I have ever known.

All the students, parents, and teachers of the Herricks Public School District whom I have had the pleasure of meeting, knowing, and helping in my 28 years in the district.

Bernice Golden, my editor, whose organization, efficiency, and dedication made the writing of this book a pleasurable experience.

Susan Kolwicz, editor of my five books published by Prentice Hall Direct, I wish all the best in her new endeavor.

PROFESSIONAL ACKNOWLEDGMENT

While I used many worthwhile sources and sites, I would like to take this opportunity to acknowledge and thank the National Information Center for Children and Youth with Disabilities (NICHCY) for its outstanding contributions to the field of special education.

ABOUT THE AUTHOR

Roger Pierangelo, Ph.D., is a New York State licensed clinical psychologist with over 30 years' experience related to the field of special education. He has been a regular classroom teacher; school psychologist in the Herricks Public School District (New Hyde Park, New York); Associate Visiting Professor at Long Island University; Full Adjunct Professor in the Graduate Education Department at Long Island University; Associate Adjunct Professor in the Graduate Special Education Department at Hofstra University; Administrator of Psychology Programs and member of Committees on Psychology; evaluator for the New York State Education Department; director of a private clinic; and consultant to numerous private and public schools, PTA, and SEPTA groups.

Dr. Pierangelo earned his B.S. from St. John's University, an M.S. from Queens College, Professional Diploma from Queens College, a Ph.D. from Yeshiva University, and is a Diplomate Fellow in Forensic Sciences from the International College of Professional Psychology.

Dr. Pierangelo is a member of the American Psychological Association, New York State Psychological Association, Nassau County Psychological Association, New York State Union of Teachers, and Phi Delta Kappa.

Dr. Pierangelo is the author of *The Survival Kit for the Special Education Teacher* and *The Special Education Teacher's Book of Lists* (The Center for Applied Research in Education). He is also co-author of *The Parent's Complete Guide to Special Education, The Complete Guide to Transition Services*, and *The Special Educator's Complete Guide to 109 Diagnostic Tests* (The Center for Applied Research in Education); *301 Ways to Be a Loving Parent* (Shapolsky Publishers); *Why Your Students Do What They Do and What to Do When They Do It—Grades K–5, Why Your Students Do What They Do and What to Do When They Do It—Grades 6–12, Creating the Confident Child in the Classroom—The Use of Positive Restructuring*, and *What Every Teacher Needs to Know About Children With Special Needs* (Research Press); *The Special Education Yellow Pages* (Merrill Publishers); and *Assessment in Special Education: A Practical Approach* and *Transition Services in Special Education— A Practical Approach* (Allyn and Bacon).

ABOUT THIS RESOURCE

The field of special education is constantly changing and more is expected and demanded from the education of this exceptional population. Today's special educators must be familiar with the academic, legal, medical, psychological, social, environmental, and perceptual aspects of an exceptional child's life. Without this knowledge or quick access to resources that hold it, professionals are at a disadvantage. Having the right "tool" at the right time can only enhance teaching and result in success.

The Special Educator's Book of Lists is such a tool. This unique information source and timesaver for preK–12 special educators contains ready-to-use lists to help you make important decisions and to assist you in every phase of the special education process.

Included are a broad range of lists conveniently organized into ten sections that contain the most current research on all types of disabilities, including identification, assessment, and remediation . . . simplified explanations of special education practices and procedures, laws, regulations, and rights . . . and numerous definitions, organizations, journal publications, parent resources, and practical tools for parents. This is an all-inclusive reference guide for special and regular educators, administrators, physicians, professors, tutors, parents, and anyone else interested in or involved with the field of special education.

HELPFUL AND UNIQUE FEATURES

This book, which contains the most up-to-date information possible, is a unique guide because it provides:

- a variety of practical lists, charts, tables, references, and forms that can be used on a daily basis in all areas involving children with disabilities.

- legal, medical, and psychological facts, references, and lists that can enhance your understanding of the many factors that affect children with disabilities.

- useful and reproducible forms that can save time, enhance instruction, and reinforce concepts.

- practical and step-by-step lists for identification, assessment, and practical remediation of all disabilities.

- vast references, forms, lists, charts, and tables that can be reproduced and handed out to assist parents in their everyday activities with their children who have disabilities.

HOW TO USE THIS BOOK

The Special Educator's Book of Lists assists you through every phase of child development and can be referred to by anyone seeking assistance with children from birth to adulthood. Each section enables you to feel more secure and aware about the sometimes overwhelming process of special education.

Part 1, **Legal Issues in Special Education**, presents an overview of the laws and landmark court cases that govern the special education process. In a time when understanding the laws and proper procedures is crucial, you will find these lists indispensable in making professional decisions.

Part 2, **Foundations of the Special Education Process**, provides a summary of preventive and diagnostic measures to help identify students with disabilities. It contains descriptions of signs and characteristics to look for and offers tips on what to do when presented with children with high-risk symptoms. This section also provides extensive information on understanding the steps in the overall special education process.

Part 3, **Specific Exceptionalities**, contains numerous descriptive lists, information, facts, and suggestions for dealing with more than 20 exceptionalities. From developmental concerns to causality, this section provides a good base of information on each category.

Part 4, **Special Education Assessment**, takes you through the various tools and procedures used in diagnosing and identifying special education students. It provides a wealth of resources covering hundreds of specific evaluation measures used to measure strengths and weaknesses in all areas.

Part 5, **IEP Information**, provides up-to-date information on how to develop an Individualized Education Plan, explanations of the various sections of the IEP, and considerations for making test-modification recommendations.

Part 6, **Eligibility Committee**, presents an overview of the responsibilities and requirements necessary for a successful referral to this committee.

Part 7, **Classroom Instruction Techniques for Children with Disabilities and Special Needs** contains numerous practical tips and materials. These alternate learning activities will facilitate instruction of children with developmental, emotional, and learning disabilities.

Part 8, **Transition Services**, contains more than 45 lists providing you with a complete overview of this very important period in the child's life when he or she moves from school to the adult world. The lists cover everything from the role of the family in the transition process to residential models and employment.

Part 9, **Parent Education**, contains practical parenting suggestions for helping children with homework, improving self-esteem, communicating better, using discipline effectively, and spotting possible signs of learning disabilities. When both teachers and parents have this knowledge, they can discuss diagnosis, behavior-management techniques, and remediation, and help children at school and at home.

Part 10, **Appendices**, features special education, psychological, and medical terminology and definitions as well as a list of key abbreviations in the field of special education. It also provides you with lists of organizations and publishers of resources on topics related to special education as well as a comprehensive list of references and suggested readings.

The Special Educator's Book of Lists places in your hands an unparalleled up-to-date reference packed with valuable information and materials that might otherwise take years and much effort to acquire! Teachers, parents, administrators, counselors, physicians, and college students who are interested in a child's educational process from preschool through adulthood will find this guide to be an invaluable resource.

Roger Pierangelo

TABLE OF CONTENTS

Part 3: Specific Exceptionalities 83

DEVELOPMENTAL INFORMATION

AUTISM/PERVASIVE DEVELOPMENT DISABILITY

ADHD

GIFTED

VISUALLY IMPAIRED

BILINGUAL AND CULTURALLY DISADVANTAGED

PHYSICALLY DISABLED

TRAUMATIC BRAIN INJURY

OTHER SPECIAL EDUCATION EXCEPTIONALITIES

WRITTEN LANGUAGE

MATHEMATICS

SPELLING

COMPREHENSIVE TESTS OF EDUCATIONAL ACHIEVEMENT

ASSESSMENT OF BEHAVIOR

Early Childhood Assessment

Other Areas of Assessment

Writing a Professional Report

PART 1

Legal Issues in Special Education

1.1   Landmark Court Cases in Special Education

Listed below in order of occurrence are some of the most significant court decisions affecting special education in the United States.

Brown v. *Board of Education* (1954): In *Brown*, the U.S. Supreme Court ruled that, under the 14th amendment to the U.S. Constitution, it was illegal practice to arbitrarily discriminate against any group of people. The Court then applied this principle to the schooling of children, holding that a separate education for African American students is not an equal education. Because of its famous ruling, "separate but equal" is no longer accepted.

> *Brown* set the precedent for future discrimination cases in education. People with disabilities were recognized as another group whose rights had been violated because of arbitrary discrimination. For children, the discrimination occurred when they were denied access to schools because of their disabilities. Using *Brown* as their legal precedent, students with disabilities claimed that their segregation and exclusion from school violated their opportunity for an equal education under the 14th amendment—the equal protection clause. Since *Brown* established that school districts should not segregate by race, then it was argued that schools should also not be able to segregate or otherwise discriminate by ability and disability.

Hobson v. *Hansen* (1967): A U.S. district court declared that the District of Columbia school system's tracking system was invalid. However, special classes were allowed, provided that testing procedures are rigorous and that retesting is frequent (Sattler, 1992).

Diana v. *State Board of Education* (1970): In this case, California was mandated by the court to correct bias in assessment procedures used for Chinese American and Mexican American students. *Diana* had three very important holdings that would later influence the enactment of federal special education laws:

1. If a student's primary language is not English, he or she must be tested in both English and the primary language;

2. Culturally unfair items must be eliminated from all tests used in the assessment process; and

3. If intelligence tests are used in the assessment process, they must reflect Mexican American culture (*Diana* v. *State Board of Education*, C-70: 37RFT N.D. Cal., 1970).

PARC v. *Commonwealth of Pennsylvania* (1972): In this case, a U.S. federal court in Pennsylvania ratified a consent agreement assuring that schools may not exclude students who have been classified as mentally retarded. Also, the court mandated that all students must be provided with a free public education. Both of these rulings would play a fundamental role in the enactment of future federal special education laws (*PARC* v. *Commonwealth of Pennsylvania*, 343 F. Supp. 279, E.D. PA, 1972).

Wyatt v. *Stickney* (1972): In Alabama, a federal court ruled that mentally retarded children in state institutions have a constitutional right to treatment as institutionalized patients (*Wyatt* v. *Stickney*, 344 F. Supp. 387 M.D. Ala 1972).

Guadalupe v. *Tempe Elementary School* (1972): In Arizona, a U.S. district court ratified a stipulated agreement that children cannot be placed in educable mentally retarded classes unless they score more than two standard deviations below the population mean on an approved IQ test administered in the child's primary language. It also stipulated that other assessment procedures must be used in addition to intelligence tests and that parental permission must be obtained for such placements (Sattler, 1992, p. 779).

Mills v. *Board of Education of District of Columbia* (1972): This case set forth future guidelines for federal legislation, including the rights of students with disabilities to have access to a free public education and due process protection, as well as a mandated requirement to receive special education services regardless of the school district's financial capability.

PASE (Parents in Action on Special Education) v. *Joseph P. Hannon* (1980): In this case regarding bias in IQ testing, an Illinois judge found that on the IQ tests he examined, only 9 of the 488 test questions were racially biased. Consequently, IQ tests were found not to be discriminatory. Furthermore, the judge indicated that clinical judgment also plays a large role in interpreting IQ test results. Therefore, the decision in *PASE* resolved some of the controversy about the use of IQ tests for special education classification. As a result, the use of intelligence tests was acceptable in psychoeducational assessment as long as the assessors follow all other procedural safeguards under federal law (No. 74 C 3586 N.D. Ill. 1980).

Luke S. & Hans S. v. *Nix et al.* (1982): In the state of Louisiana, all evaluations had to be completed within a 60-day time period. The plaintiffs in this case argued that thousands of students were not being appropriately evaluated within this time period. The court ruled in favor of the plaintiffs and informed the state of Louisiana that greater pre-referral assessment should be done before a referral is made.

Board of Education of Hendrick Hudson School District v. *Rowley* (1982): In this case, the parents of Amy Rowley, a deaf student with minimal residual hearing and excellent lip reading skills, sought the services of a full-time signing interpreter in her regular classes. Amy had been provided with an FM trainer (a piece of assistive technology which increases the level of sound input), a teacher of the deaf for one hour per day, and a speech instructor for three hours per week. Even though Rowley was missing about half of what was being discussed in class, she was very well adjusted, was performing better than the average child in the class, and was "advancing easily from grade to grade."

Based on these facts, the U.S. Supreme Court determined that Rowley was receiving an "appropriate" education without the sign interpreter. In reaching this opinion, the Court concluded that the obligation to provide an appropriate education does not mean a school must provide the "best" education or one designed to "maximize" a student's potential. However, the program must be based on the student's unique individual needs and be designed to enable the student to benefit from an education. In other words, the student must be making progress (Hager, 1999, p. 5).

Jose P. v. *Ambach* (1983): In this case, the plaintiffs filed suit against New York City. Their complaint involved the inappropriate delivery of services. The plaintiffs argued that many students in special education were not receiving services in an appropriate time frame. The court ruled in favor of the plaintiffs and stated that a maximum of 30 days can elapse

1.1 continued

from the time of referral to evaluation. The court informed the defendants that all evaluations must be "timely evaluations."

Larry P. v. *Riles* (1984): In this California case, using IQ tests as the assessment measure for placing African American students in special education as mentally retarded was found to be discriminatory. Schools in California were mandated by the court to reduce the disproportionate representation of African American students in special education.

In *Larry P*, the court determined that IQ tests were discriminatory against African Americans for three reasons:

1. IQ tests actually measure achievement rather than ability. Because African Americans throughout their educational history had been denied equal educational opportunities through schools segregated by race, they would inevitably have achievement scores lower than the norms and thus be discriminated against in testing.

2. IQ tests rest on the plausible, but unproven, assumption that intelligence is distributed in the population in accordance with a normal statistical curve (bell-shaped); thus, the tests are artificial tools unsuitable for ranking individuals.

3. IQ tests lead to the classification of more African American students than white students in dead-end classes for students with mild to moderate disabilities (No. C-71-2270 RFP [1979] and No. 80-4027 DC No. CV 71-2270 in the US Court of Appeals for the Ninth Circuit [1984]).

Georgia State Conference of Branches of NAACP v. *State of Georgia* (1984): A U.S. court of appeals ruled that African American children schooled in the state of Georgia were not being discriminated against solely because there was a disproportionate number of them in classes for low achievers. The court explained that there was no evidence of differential treatment of African American and white students (Sattler, 1992).

Daniel R. R. v. *State Board of Education* (1989): *Daniel R. R.* is one of the leading cases that helped open the door to increased inclusion of children with disabilities in regular education classes. The court noted that Congress created a strong preference favoring mainstreaming—i.e., educating the student in the regular education classroom with supports. Ironically, the court determined that it was not appropriate to include the child in this case in fulltime regular education. However, the court's analysis of the least restrictive environment requirement, especially its interpretation of what is meant by providing supplementary aids and services in the regular classroom, has been followed by a number of other courts (Hager, 1999, p. 6).

In determining whether it is appropriate to place a student with disabilities in regular education, the student need not be expected to learn at the same rate as the other students in the class. In other words, part of the required supplementary aids and services must be the modification of the regular education curriculum for the student, when needed. The court in *Daniel R. R.* noted, however, that the school need not modify the program "beyond recognition." Also, in looking at whether it is "appropriate" for the child to be in regular education—in other words, whether the student can benefit educationally from regular class placement, the school must consider the broader educational benefit of contact with students who do not have disabilities, such as opportunities for modeling appropriate behavior and socialization (Hager, 1999, p. 6).

Gerstmeyer v. *Howard County Public Schools* (1994): In this case, the Howard Schools district had been told that a child needs to be evaluated for the first grade four months before entering the first grade. The evaluation was not done prior to entering the first grade. The parents sent their child to private school, and the evaluation was only done six months after the initial referral. The parents sued the district for the costs of private schooling and tutoring caused by the delay. The court ruled in favor of the parents and ordered the Howard Schools district to reimburse them for all associated costs (Taylor, 1997).

1.2 Federal Legislation for Individuals with Disabilities

SECTION 504 OF THE VOCATIONAL REHABILITATION ACT

Section 504 of the Vocational Rehabilitation Act is a civil rights law enacted in 1973. It was created to prevent discrimination against all individuals with disabilities in programs that receive federal funds. For children of school age, Section 504 ensures equal opportunity to all school activities for all students.

Section 504 plays a very important role in assessment, especially for those students who do not meet the criteria to be classified for special education. It provides that some students not eligible for services in special education may be entitled to receive accommodations to help them in school. For example, a child with Attention Deficit Disorder (ADD) may meet the criteria for special accommodations under Section 504 even though Attention Deficit Disorder is not a classification covered under federal law. Other students who might be helped under Section 504 are those with asthma, allergies, arthritis, or diabetes, to name just a few.

P.L. 93-380: THE FAMILY EDUCATION RIGHTS AND PRIVACY ACT (FERPA)

The Family Education Rights and Privacy Act (FERPA), often called the Buckley Amendment, gives parents of students under the age of 18, and students age 18 and over, the right to examine records kept in the student's personal file. The FERPA was passed in 1974 to cover all students, including those in postsecondary school. According to the National Information Center for Children and Youth with Disabilities (NICHCY, 1997):

- Parents and eligible students have the right to inspect and review the student's educational records.

- Schools must have written permission from the parent or eligible student before releasing any information from a student's records.

- Parents and eligible students have the right to have the records explained and interpreted by school officials.

- School officials may not destroy any education records if an outstanding request to inspect and review them exists.

- Parents and eligible students who believe that information in the education records is inaccurate or misleading may request that the records be amended. The parent or eligible student must be advised if the school decides not to amend the records, and they have a right to a hearing.

Finally, each school district must give parents of students in attendance, or students age 18 or over, an annual notice that informs them of their rights under this law and the right of parents or eligible students to file a complaint with the U.S. Department of Education.

P.L. 94-142: THE EDUCATION OF ALL HANDICAPPED CHILDREN'S ACT (EHA)

Because of the victories that were being won for students with disabilities in the early 1970s, parents and student advocates began to lobby Congress for federal laws and money to ensure that students with disabilities receive an education that meets their needs. In 1975, the stage was clearly set for a national special education law. Years of exclusion, segregation, and denial of basic education set in motion an imperative for civil rights laws that would guarantee these students with disabilities access to the education system (Smith, 1998, p. 21).

Although it was clear that advancement was being made in providing services to students with disabilities, Congress found in 1975 that:

- More than 1.75 million children with disabilities were being excluded entirely from receiving a public education solely on the basis of their disability.

- More than four million of the estimated eight million children with disabilities in this country were not receiving the appropriate educational services they needed and were entitled to receive.

- Many children with disabilities were still being placed in inappropriate educational settings because their disabilities were undetected or because of violations of their individual rights.

- One million children with disabilities in the United States were excluded entirely from the public school system and did not go through the educational system with their peers.

- Because of the lack of adequate services within the public school system, families were frequently forced to find services outside the public school system, often at great distance from their residences and at their own expense.

- State and local educational agencies have a responsibility to provide education for all children with disabilities.

- It was in the national interest for the federal government to assist state and local efforts to provide programs to meet the educational needs of children with disabilities in order to assure equal protection under the law.

Based on these findings, it is evident that Congress recognized the necessity for special education for children with disabilities and was concerned about the widespread discrimination. In response, Congress enacted into federal law the Education of All Handicapped Children's Act (EHA), Public Law (P.L.) 94-142. This law set forth federal procedural safeguards for children with disabilities and their parents. It outlined the entire foundation upon which current special education practices rest. The major provisions of P.L. 94-142 are:

1.2 continued

Before any evaluations, testing, and/or placement can be done, there must be parental informed consent. Informed consent is defined as the following:

1. The parent must be fully informed of all information relevant to the activity for which consent is sought, in his or her native language, or by another mode of communication.

2. The parent must understand and agree in writing to the carrying out of the activity for which consent is sought; the written agreement must describe the activity and list the records (if any) which will be released and to whom.

3. The parent must be informed that the giving of consent is voluntary and may be revoked at any time.

All students in special education must be placed in the least restrictive environment. Students with disabilities need to be placed in the environment that is most suited for their educational needs, or, as it is termed, the Least Restrictive one. Under federal law, schools must, to the maximum extent possible, ensure that individuals with disabilities, including individuals in public and private institutions or other care facilities, are educated with individuals who are not disabled. This is known as mainstreaming, although the federal law did not define this term. Also, special classes and separate schooling are to be used only when the nature or severity of the disability is such that education in regular classes with the use of supplementary aids and services cannot be achieved satisfactorily. The settings for placement and service delivery were envisioned to fall on a continuum of least restrictive to most restrictive.

All students in special education must have an individualized education plan (IEP). All students in special education are required to have an individualized education program designed to meet their needs. The IEP includes both short-term and long-term goals, along with information on how and where services will be provided. (See Part 5 for a comprehensive discussion of the components of an IEP.)

The evaluation for placement in special education must be nondiscriminatory. Under federal law, the following requirements must be adhered to in order for an evaluation to be considered nondiscriminatory:

- All instruments used in the evaluation of a student for determination of a disability should be free from bias.

- When considering eligibility for special education, a multidisciplinary team must do the evaluation.

- All testing materials and procedures used for the purposes of evaluation and placement of children with disabilities must be selected and administered so as not to be racially or culturally discriminatory.

- All tests and other evaluation materials must have been validated for the specific purpose for which they are used.

- Tests and other evaluation materials must be administered by trained personnel in conformance with the instructions provided by the producers of the materials.

- No single procedure can be used as the sole criterion for determining an appropriate educational program for a child.

- The individual must be assessed in all areas related to the suspected disability, including—where appropriate—health, vision, hearing, social and emotional status, general intelligence, academic performance, communicative status, and motor abilities.

Tests must be given and reports must be written in the student's native language. When conducting assessments, the tester must give the test in the child's native language, and all reports must be written in the parent's native language.

Students and parents are entitled to due process. All students and their parents must be afforded due process. This means that if a conflict or disagreement ensues concerning a student's eligibility for special education placement or services, no changes can be made until the issue has been settled at an impartial hearing.

Zero rejections are allowed for all students. All students have the right to a public school education and cannot be excluded because of a disability. Students are entitled to a free and appropriate public school education; they have the right to a public school education at no cost to the parents regardless of the extent of the disability. Also, it is the responsibility of each state to identify children who may need and be entitled to special education services.

P.L. 98-524: THE VOCATIONAL EDUCATION ACT OF 1984 (THE PERKINS ACT)

The Vocational Education Act of 1984, often referred to as the Carl D. Perkins Act or the Perkins Act, authorizes federal funds to support vocational education programs. One of the goals of the Perkins Act is to improve the access of those who either have been underserved in the past or who have greater-than-average educational needs. Under the act, "special populations" includes those who have a disability, are disadvantaged, or have limited English proficiency. This law is particularly important because it requires that vocational education be provided for students with disabilities. The regulations based on this law can be found in C.F.R: Title 34; Parts 400–499 (NICHCY, 1997).

The Perkins Act states that individuals who are members of special populations (including individuals with disabilities) must be provided with equal access to recruitment, enrollment, and placement activities in vocational education. In addition, these individuals must be provided with equal access to the full range of vocational education programs available to others, including occupationally specific courses of study, cooperative education, apprenticeship programs and—to the extent practical—comprehensive guidance and counseling services. Under the law, vocational education planning should be coordinated among public agencies, including vocational education, special education, and the state vocational rehabilitation agencies. The provision of vocational education to youth with disabilities should be monitored to ensure that such education is consistent with objectives stated in the youth's IEP (NICHCY, 1997).

1.2 continued

P.L. 99-457: EDUCATION OF THE HANDICAPPED ACT AMENDMENTS OF 1986

In 1983, Congress amended the Education of All Handicapped Children's Act to expand incentives for preschool special education, early intervention, and transition programs. All programs under EHA became the responsibility of the Office of Special Education Programs (OSEP). In 1986, P.L. 99-457 was passed, requiring all states to provide free and appropriate public education to children with disabilities of ages 3 to 5. It differs primarily from P.L. 94-142 in that the focus of services is on the entire family. For infants and toddlers, services are often provided through home visits; for preschoolers, services may occur in special classes in regular schools or special schools. In addition, a new Part H was added to the law, serving infants and toddlers with special needs. In 1991, P.L. 102–19 reauthorized and amended both Part H (Infant and Toddler) and Part B (Preschool) legislation.

Under P.L. 102-19, infants and toddlers up to age 3 qualify for EHA benefits if they are either experiencing a developmental delay or have a diagnosed physical or mental condition with a high probability of resulting in a developmental delay. The areas of delay that P.L. 102-19 covers include:

- Cognitive development
- Physical development
- Language and speech development
- Psychosocial development
- Self-help skills

Finally, whereas P.L. 94-142 mandated IEPs, P.L. 99-457 mandated Individualized Family Service Plans (IFSPs) for infants and toddlers.

1.3 The Individuals with Disabilities Education Act— 1997 (IDEA '97)

In 1990, the reauthorization of P.L. 94-142 was enacted and became Public Law 101-476. (Reauthorization is simply the act of amending and renewing a law.) Public Law 101-476 is widely known as IDEA—The Individuals with Disabilities Education Act. IDEA continued to uphold the provisions set forth in 94-142. It was amended to P.L. 105-17 on June 4, 1997 and is now often referred to as IDEA '97. Some of the changes made were substantial; others fine-tune processes already in place for schools and parents to follow in planning and providing special education and related services for children with special needs (Venn, 1994).

Under IDEA, most of the mandates under 94-142 remained intact. However, IDEA also included some important revisions and additions.

- IDEA added significantly to the provisions for very young children with disabilities and for students preparing to leave secondary school.

- IDEA added two new categories in special education: Autism and Traumatic Brain Injury.

- Under IDEA, the term *handicap* was removed from the law and the preferred term, *disability*, was substituted.

- IDEA mandated transition services no later than the age of 16 years of age.

- IDEA required further public commenting re a legal definition of deficit disorder.

- IDEA stated that states can be sued in federal courts for violating its propositions.

In addition to the guidelines and procedures set forth in 94-142 and IDEA of 1990, IDEA '97 added many provisions.

IDEA '97 strengthened the least restrictive environment mandate.

IDEA '97 fostered increased efforts to educate students with disabilities in the Least Restrictive Environment (LRE). For example, if a child were to be placed in special education, it must be considered whether and how the child can participate in the general curriculum, and the IEP is to indicate the extent to which the student will not be with peers without disabilities [20 U.S.C. 1414(d)(1)(A)(i)-(iv)]. Prior to IDEA '97, the IEP was to indicate the opposite—i.e., the extent to which the student would be educated with peers without disabilities.

IDEA '97 strengthened parents' roles further. Perhaps only making explicit what should already have been obvious, it required that schools consider the results of evaluations, the strengths of the child, and the concerns of the parents for enhancing the child's education when developing the IEP [20 U.S.C. 1414(d)(3)(A)]. Under IDEA '97, parents are to be a part of the group that determines their child's eligibility [(Section 300.534.535(a)(1)]. IDEA '97 also stated that parents should have the opportunity to examine all records pertaining to their child, not just "relevant" records as stated in the old law.

IDEA '97 added related services to the types of services to be provided for transition services. Services are to be based on the individual student's needs, taking into account the student's preferences and interests.

IDEA '97 enlarged the scope of an appropriate education by requiring that not only should it meet students' unique needs, but it should also "prepare them for employment and independent living" [20 U.S.C. 1400(d)(1)(A)].

11

1.3 continued

IDEA '97 strengthened the obligations of other agencies to provide services to students while they are in school. All states now must have interagency agreements to ensure fulfillment of responsibilities by all public agencies that are responsible for providing services that are considered special education services. The agreements must also specify how the various agencies will cooperate to ensure the timely and appropriate delivery of services to students [20 U.S.C. 1412(a)(12)].

IDEA '97 emphasized assistive technology. The need for assistive technology must now be considered for *all* students when developing the Individualized Education Plan.

IDEA '97 expands the number of members of the IEP team. This will be discussed in detail in Chapter 10. In addition to parents, the team must include at least one special education teacher and at least one teacher from the regular education classroom if the child participates in regular education.

IDEA '97 gives school authorities several options in disciplining a student with a disability. Schools can suspend a child for up to ten days or order a change in the child's education setting for up to ten days if they discipline students without disabilities in the same way.

IDEA '97 changed Part H, serving young children, to Part C. In doing so, IDEA '97 expanded to include provisions for "at-risk" children from birth to 5 years old, in addition to children already being served.

Finally, IDEA '97 mandated that children and youth receiving special education have the right to receive the related services necessary to benefit from special education instruction. Related services include: transportation and such developmental, corrective, and other supportive services as are required to assist a child with a disability to benefit from special education. This includes speech pathology and audiology, psychological services, physical and occupational therapy, recreation (including therapeutic recreation), early identification and assessment of disabilities in children, counseling services (including rehabilitation counseling), medical services for diagnostic or evaluation purposes, school health services, social work services in schools, and parent counseling and training (C.F.R: Title 34; Education; Part 300.16, 1993).

As they currently stand, IDEA '97and Section 504 of the Rehabilitation Act of 1973 strengthen each other in important areas. For example, they both:

- Call for school systems to carry out a systematic search for every child with a disability who is in need of a public education.

- Mandate a Free and Appropriate Education (FAPE) regardless of the nature and severity of an individual's disability.

- Make it clear that education and related services must be provided at no cost to parents.

- Have similar requirements to ensure that testing and evaluation of a child's needs are not based on a single testing instrument.

- Emphasize the importance of educating children and youth with disabilities with their peers who do not have disabilities to the maximum extent appropriate (NICHCY, 1997).

1.4 The Americans with Disabilities Act, P.L. 101-336

In July 1990, President George H. W. Bush signed into law Public Law 101-336—The Americans with Disabilities Act (ADA). He said, "Let the shameful walls of exclusion finally come tumbling down." Senator Tom Harkin, the chief sponsor of the act, spoke of this law as the emancipation proclamation for people with disabilities. This civil rights law is based on Section 504 of the Vocational Rehabilitation Act of 1973, but it further extends the rights of individuals with disabilities. It protects all individuals with disabilities from discrimination and it requires most employers to make reasonable accommodations for them. The ADA plays a very important role in transitional services for students with disabilities. It also plays a significant role in making sure that all school buildings are accessible to people with disabilities. For example, a school would be in violation of the ADA if it is not accessible for wheelchairs, does not have emergency exits for all, or does not have ramps.

IDEA and ADA differ in certain important areas (Turnball et al., 1995, p. 55).

- IDEA benefits only those who are between certain ages (birth to 21 years). By contrast, ADA benefits all people with disabilities without regard to age.

- IDEA benefits only those people in school. By contrast, ADA benefits people in employment and in a wide range of public and private sectors.

- IDEA provides money to state and local agencies to help educate students with disabilities and defines the rights and services afforded by law. By contrast, ADA prohibits discrimination, but it does not provide money to help anyone achieve compliance with its mandates.

But despite their differences, IDEA and ADA work together. IDEA helps state and local education agencies create services to educate students with disabilities; ADA protects students against discrimination when they are not in school.

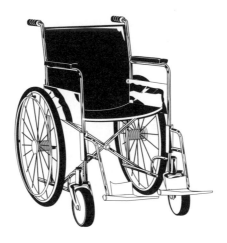

1.5   Least Restrictive Educational Placements

The concept of Least Restrictive Environment (LRE) applies to the placement of students with disabilities in the most advantageous educational environment suitable for their needs. Contrary to the beliefs of many teachers and parents, LRE does not mean every student with a disability should be placed in a regular classroom. The concept must be fully understood by special education teachers so that they can relieve the anxiety of teachers, parents, and students when it comes to appropriate educational placement.

The placement of a student with a disability is the responsibility of the Eligibility Committee on Special Education, with the input of staff and the consent of parents. The Eligibility Committee, a state-required school district committee assigned to oversee and monitor all children with disabilities, must analyze all available information and determine the "starting placement" for the child that will most likely ensure success and provide the child with the highest level of stimulation and experience for his or her specific disability and profile of strengths and weaknesses.

In order to accomplish this task, the Eligibility Committee has a variety of placements from which to choose. These placements range in levels of restriction—including class size, student-teacher ratio, length of program, and degree of mainstreaming,

In the normal course of events, it is hoped that children would only be placed in a more restrictive environment if it is to their educational advantage. However, they should be moved to a less restrictive setting as soon as they are capable of being educated in that environment.

The placements below follow a path from least restrictive to most restrictive.

1. *Regular class placement*—This placement is the least restrictive placement for all children without disabilities. However, without some type of special education supportive services, this placement would not be suitable for a child with a disability and is usually not considered suitable by the Eligibility Committee.

2. *Regular class placement with consulting teacher assistance*—A consultant teacher model is used when supportive special education services are required but the Eligibility Committee feels that the child will be better served by remaining in the classroom rather than by being pulled out for services. Because the child remains within the class even though he or she is receiving services, this placement is considered the second LRE setting.

3. *Regular class placement with some supportive services*—This placement may be used with a student who has a mild disability and requires supportive services but can remain in the regular classroom for the majority of the day. The services that may be applied to this level include adaptive physical education, speech and language therapy, in-school individual or group counseling, physical therapy, occupational therapy, etc.

4. *Regular class placement with itinerant specialist assistance*—Itinerant services are sub-contracted by the district and provided by outside agencies. These services are usually provided for students when the disability is such that the district wishes to maintain the child in the district, but there are not a sufficient number of students with that disability to warrant hiring a teacher. An example of this may be a hard-of-hearing child who can maintain a regular class placement as

long as supportive itinerant services are provided by a teacher specializing in hearing impairments.

5. *Regular class placement with resource room assistance*—This placement is usually provided for students who need supportive services but can successfully remain within the regular classroom for the majority of the day. This type of program is a "pull out" program, and the services are usually provided in a separate room. The teacher-student ratio with this type of service is usually 5:1 and the amount of time spent within the resource room cannot exceed 50 percent of the child's day.

6. *Part-time mainstreaming*—This placement is for students who need a more restrictive setting for learning, behavioral, or intellectual reasons. These students cannot be successful in a full-time regular class or with a "pull-out" supportive service, but they can be successfully mainstreamed for a part of the school day. The special education teacher determines the nature of the mainstream experience.

7. *Full-time special class in a regular school*—This placement is viewed as the LRE setting for students whose disability does not permit successful participation in any type of regular classroom setting, even for part of the day. These are students who usually require a very structured, closely monitored program on a daily basis but not so restrictive a program as to warrant an out-of-district placement. These students can handle the rules and structure of a regular school building, but not the freedom or style of a less-restrictive setting within the school.

8. *Special day school outside the school district*—This type of restrictive educational setting is a desirable placement for students whose disability is so severe that they may require a more totally therapeutic environment and closer monitoring by specially trained special education teachers or staff members. The child is transported by district expense to the placement. Many state policies try to limit travel time on the bus to less than one hour.

   These programs may have student/teacher/assistant ratios of 6:1:1, 6:1:2, 9:1:1, 9:1:2, 12:1:1, or 15:1:1, depending upon the severity of the child's disability. (The first number in the ratio refers to the mandated number of students allowed in the class; the second number refers to the number of teachers assigned to the class; and the last number refers to the number of assistants.) The more severe the disability, the lower the student/teacher/assistant ratio. These programs can run 10 or 12 months, depending upon the severity of the disability and the individual needs of the child.

9. *Residential school*—Residential placements are considered the next most-restrictive placement. Not only does the student with a disability receive his or her education within this setting, but he or she usually resides there for the school term as well. The nature and length of home visits depend upon several factors that are usually determined by the residential school staff after evaluation and observation. For some students, home visits may not take place at all; however, others may go home every weekend.

   Some students are placed in residential placements by the court. In this case, the child's local school district is only responsible for providing the costs of the educational portion, including related services if needed.

1.5 continued

10. *Homebound instruction*—This very restrictive setting is usually provided for students who are in the process of transition between programs and have yet to be placed. It should never be used as a long-term placement because of the social restriction and limitations.

    This option is also used when a child is restricted to his or her residence because of an illness, injury, etc., and if it remains the only realistic educational service until the child recovers. Homebound instruction requires an adult at home until the teacher arrives, or it can be held at a community center, library, or some other site deemed appropriate by the Eligibility Committee.

11. *Hospital or institution*—The most restrictive setting used is a hospital or institutional setting. Although this is the most restrictive overall, it may be the LRE setting for certain students (e.g., those who have attempted suicide, those who have experienced pervasive clinical depression, or those who are severely or profoundly retarded).

1.6   Conditions of Public Law 504

Coverage extends to persons who have, have a record of having, or are regarded as having:

- A physical or mental impairment substantially limiting one or more major life activity(ies) but not severe enough to warrant classification under IDEA (Individuals with Disabilities Education Act)

Entitlement:

- Regular or special education and related services

Students covered under Section 504 but not covered under IDEA:

- Do not have one of the 13 disabilities under IDEA. (Note: Children with ADD may have a health impairment under IDEA.)
- Do not need special education but need related services or accommodations to benefit from an education.

Students covered under IDEA but not covered under Section 504:

- Unilateral placements in private schools when the local educational agency has made available (not denied) a free appropriate public education to a child

Funding:

- No federal funds are available specifically for Section 504.
- All agencies receiving any federal funds must comply with Section 504.

Procedural requirements similar to IDEA:

- Free education
- Evaluation
- Least Restrictive Environment
- Procedural due process
- 504 Individualized Education Plan

Some equal educational opportunity issues pertinent solely to Section 504:

- Access to magnet schools
- Program accessibility
- Access to school activities (e.g., parent conferences, board meetings, etc.) for parents/community members with disabilities

Enforcement:

- Office for Civil Rights, U.S. Department of Education

1.7 Parents' Rights in the Special Education Process

1. Your child is entitled to a free, appropriate public education that meets the unique educational needs of your child at no cost to you.

2. You must be notified whenever the school wishes to evaluate your child, wants to change your child's educational placement, or refuses your request for an evaluation or a change in placement.

3. You may request an evaluation if you think your child needs special education or related services.

4. You should be asked by your school to provide "parent consent." This means that you understand and agree in writing to the evaluation and initial special education placement for your child. Your consent is voluntary and may be withdrawn at any time.

5. You may obtain an independent, low-cost evaluation if you disagree with the outcome of the school's evaluation. The school district will supply you with the names of such agencies.

6. You may request a reevaluation if you suspect your child's current educational placement is no longer appropriate. The school must reevaluate your child at least once every three years, but your child's educational program must be reviewed at least once during each calendar year.

7. You may have your child tested in the language he or she knows best. For example, if your child's primary language is Spanish, he or she must be tested in Spanish. Students who are hearing impaired also have the right to an interpreter during their testing.

8. The school must communicate with you in your primary language. The school is required to take whatever action is necessary to ensure that you understand its oral and written communication, including arranging for an interpreter if you are hearing impaired or if your primary language is not English.

9. You may review all of your child's records and obtain copies of these records, but the school may charge you a reasonable fee for making copies. Only you, as parents, and those persons directly involved in the education of your child will be given access to personal records. If you feel any of the information in your child's records is inaccurate, misleading, or violates the privacy or other rights of your child, you may request that the information be changed. If the school refuses your request, you then have the right to request a hearing to challenge the questionable information in your child's records.

10. You must be fully informed by the school of all the rights provided to you and your child under the law. You may participate in the development of your child's Individualized Education Plan (IEP) or, in the case of a child who is below school age, the development of an Individualized Family Service Plan (IFSP). The IEP and IFSP, both written statements of the educational program, are designed to meet your child's unique needs. The school must make every possible effort to notify you of the IEP or IFSP meeting and to arrange it at a time and place agreeable to you. As an important member of the team, you may attend the IEP or IFSP meeting and share your ideas about your child's special needs, the type of program appropriate to meeting those needs, and the related services the school will provide to help your child benefit from his or her educational program.

11. You may have your child educated in the least restrictive school setting possible. Every effort should be made to develop an educational program that will provide your child with the greatest amount of contact with children who are not disabled.

12. You may request a due process hearing to resolve differences with the school that could not be resolved informally.

1.8   The Concept of Procedural Due Process

Due process, as it applies to special education, includes the legal procedures and requirements developed to protect the rights of children, parents, and school districts. For children suspected of having a disability, due process guarantees a free and appropriate public education in the least restrictive educational setting. For parents, due process protects their rights to have input into the educational program and placement of their child, and to have options in cases of disagreement with the recommendations of the school district. For school districts, due process offers recourse in cases of parent resistance with a request for evaluation, challenges to an independent evaluation sought by parents at public expense, or unwillingness of parents to consent to the Eligibility Committee recommendation.

The components of due process include procedural safeguards such as:

Appropriate written notice—Notice to parents is required in the following situations:

1. Actions proposed by the Eligibility Committee to evaluate the existence of a suspected disability.

2. Meetings by the Eligibility Committee to discuss the results of the evaluation to determine a suspected disability.

3. Meetings to discuss the planning of an Individualized Education Plan.

4. Proposed actions to review an Individualized Education Plan.

5. Proposed actions to reevaluate a child's classification or placement.

6. Aging-out notification for children with disabilities who are no longer eligible for tuition-free educational services.

Written consent from parents—Written consent is required in these four specific situations:

1. Consent for an initial evaluation of a child not previously classified as having a disability.

2. Consent allowing for the provisions recommended by the Eligibility Committee with regard to classification and special education placement.

3. Notification prior to providing services in a 12-month program for the first time for a child with disabilities.

4. Notification prior to aging out of public education by a child with a disability.

Confidentiality of records—The confidentiality of a student's records is protected under due process. Confidentiality ensures that only parents and educational institutions or agencies that have legitimate interest in the child's education will be permitted to see the records. However, written consent from parents is required for the release of any information on their child other than in the following instances:

1. Release of information to staff members or school officials within the school district in which the child is a resident if they have a legitimate interest in the child's education.

2. Release of information to other school districts in which the child with a disability may enroll. In this case, the parents are notified of the transfer of information. They may request copies of the information sent and may contest, through a hearing, the content of the transferred information.

Surrogate parents—In most cases, the parents of the child with a suspected disability represent him or her at Eligibility Committee meetings. However, if the parents are unknown or unavailable, or if the child is a ward of the state, the Eligibility Committee must determine if there is a need for the assignment of a surrogate parent to represent the child. When this happens, the Board of Education chooses a surrogate from a list of eligible individuals.

Impartial hearings—An impartial hearing is a procedure used to resolve disagreements between parents and the school district. This due process procedure can be utilized when:

1. A parent disagrees with an Eligibility Committee recommendation.

2. A parent disagrees with a Board of Education determination.

3. The Eligibility Committee fails to evaluate and recommend a program within 30 days of the signed consent by the parents.

4. The Eligibility Committee fails to implement its recommendations within the 30-day requirement period.

5. The school district fails to administer a triennial evaluation.

6. The school district fails to hold an annual review of a child with a disability.

7. The parent or parents are unwilling to give consent for an evaluation.

8. Parents are unwilling to consent to the recommendations of the Eligibility Committee concerning the classification or special education placement of a child with a disability.

Appeals to the Commissioner of Education—This option provides another level of resolution for parents and school districts when an impartial hearing cannot resolve the disagreement. This is a legal process, and the procedures are usually outlined in state manuals of the Commissioner's regulations.

1.9 Disability Categories Requiring Special Education Services

- *Autistic*—This disorder is characterized by difficulty in the child's ability to respond to people, events, and objects. Responses to sensations of light, sound, and feeling may be exaggerated, and delayed speech and language skills may be associated features. The onset of this condition is usually observed before two-and-one-half years of age.

- *Blind*—The student who is classified as blind exhibits vision that requires special Braille equipment and reading materials. The condition is so severe that he or she does not have what is considered functional sight.

- *Deaf*—The individual classified as deaf has a loss of hearing so severe, usually above an 80-decibel loss, that it hinders effective use of the sense of hearing. This disability usually necessitates the use of specialized services or equipment in order for the child to communicate.

- *Emotionally disturbed*—Students classified with this disability have behavior disorders over a long period of time and to such a degree that they are unable to function well in school. These disturbances may interfere with developing meaningful relationships, may result in physical symptoms or irrational fears, and may limit the individual's overall productivity.

- *Hard of hearing*—A student in this category has a hearing loss that may or may not be permanent, and has some sense of hearing with or without an aid. However, this student still requires specialized instruction and special education assistance.

- *Learning disabled*—These students have a disability in receiving, organizing, or expressing information. They are of at least average intelligence but have difficulty listening, thinking, speaking, reading, writing, or doing arithmetic; this results in a significant discrepancy between ability and school achievement. This disability is not the result of emotional, mental, physical, environmental, or cultural factors.

- *Mentally disabled*—These students have a developmental delay that causes them to learn at a slower pace. They also exhibit a significantly lower level of intelligence and marked impairment in social competency skills. This category includes Educable Mentally Disabled (IQ usually between 55 and approximately 80) and Trainable Mentally Disabled (IQ below 55).

- *Multiply disabled*—This category is for students who have disabilities in more than one category, such as both deafness and blindness.

- *Orthopedically impaired*—These students have a physical disability, and their educational performance is directly affected by this condition. Such conditions as cerebral palsy and limb amputation fall into this category.

■ *Other health impaired*—Students who are classified in this category have limited strength, vitality, or alertness due to chronic or acute health problems. Conditions that fall into this area include heart conditions, asthma, Tourette's syndrome, attention deficit hyperactive disorder, diabetes, and so on.

■ *Partially sighted*—Children classified in this area have some functional sight, usually 20/70 or better with best correction. This student may be able to learn to read regular print with glasses or to read special books that are printed with large type.

■ *Speech impaired*—These students have a communication disorder. They are unable to produce speech sounds correctly, have difficulty in understanding or using words and forming sentences, or exhibit stuttering or some other voice impairment.

PART 2

Foundations of the Special Education Process

2.1   Questions to Consider When Doing a Classroom Observation

Basic behaviors need to be observed when conducting a classroom observation (e.g., attention, focus, aggressiveness, compliance, flexibility, rigidity, oppositional behavior, shyness, controlling behavior, distractibility, impulsivity, social interaction, and so on). Here are questions to consider:

1. Is there a difference between the nature of behaviors in a structured setting (e.g., classroom) and an unstructured setting (e.g., playground)? This factor may shed light on the child's need for a more structured environment in which to learn. Children who do not have well-developed internal control systems need a highly structured environment to maintain focus and appropriate behavior. Some children cannot shift between structured and unstructured situations. They may not possess the internal monitor that regulates conformity and logical attendance to rules. These children may be more successful in a structured play setting that is set up and organized by teachers during the lunch hour.

2. Does the child seem to respond to external boundaries? The child's ability to respond to external boundaries is important to the teacher because it is a monitor of his or her potential learning style. If a child who lacks internal controls does conform to external boundaries (e.g., time-out, teacher proximity during work time), then this factor needs to be taken into consideration when prescribing classroom management techniques. When a child conforms to such boundaries, then his/her behavior is a message of what works for him/her.

3. What is the child's attention span during academic tasks? Attention span at different ages is measured normally in minutes or hours. You should become aware of the normal attention span for children of all ages and compare the child over several activities and days to see if a pattern of inattention is present. If the attention span is very short for someone of his/her age, then modifications to work load (i.e., shorter, but more frequent assignments) may have to be included.

4. Does the child require constant teacher supervision or assistance? A child who requires constant teacher supervision or assistance is a child who may be exhibiting a possible symptomatic behavior. This behavior may result from attention deficit disorder, processing problems, emotional difficulties involving need for attention or control, high anxiety, internal stress, limited intellectual capacity, hearing problems, etc. All of these areas need to be checked out, and a good evaluation should determine the root of such behavior. However, the key is always the frequency, intensity, and duration of such symptoms.

5. Does the child interact appropriately with peers? Observing children at play can tell us a great deal about self-esteem, tension levels, social maturity, physical development, and many other factors. Social interaction is more common in children over the age of 6 or 7, but parallel play is still common in younger children.

Appropriate social interaction gives us insight into the child's own internal boundaries and organization. A child who always needs to control may really be masking high levels of tension. The more controlling children are, the more out of control they are feeling. A child who can appropriately conform to group rules, delay his/her needs for the good of the team, and conform to rules and various changes or inconsistencies in rules, may be a child who is very self-assured and has low anxiety levels. The opposite is almost always typical of children at risk. However, one should always consider developmental stages since certain behaviors, such as control, might be more typical at early ages.

6. Is the child a high- or low-status child? Observing a child in different settings allows us the opportunity to see the social status of the child and its impact on his or her behavior. Low-peer-status children are often more apt to feel insignificant and therefore fail to receive positive social cues that help reinforce feelings of self-esteem. This behavior is often seen in children with learning disabilities. Having the psychologist begin a counseling group of five or six low-status children may enable them to feel empowered, with feelings of connection.

2.2   Observation Report Form

The following type of unstructured checklist allows the observer to fill in any information that he/she feels is important. As seen by the example below, any of a number of general areas can and should be observed. This checklist can also serve to fulfill the district Eligibility Committee's requirement for a classroom observation that must be part of the packet when a review for classification is required.

Name of Student Observed: _____   Observer: _____

Date of Observation: _____   Place of Observation: _____

	Classroom	Playground	Lunchroom	Gym

Behaviors to Observe:

- Impulsivity
- Attention to task
- Attention span
- Conformity to rules
- Social interaction with peers
- Aggressiveness
- Level of teacher assistance required
- Frustration levels
- Reaction to authority
- Verbal interaction
- Procrastination
- Organizational skills
- Developmental motor skills

2.3   How to Interpret and What to Look for in Group Achievement Test Results

There is a great deal of information that can be gleaned from group achievement test results. Although individual tests should only be administered when evaluating a child's suspected disability, group achievement test results may reflect certain very important patterns. Most schools administer group achievement tests or group intelligence tests yearly or every few years. If these results are available for a student, the teacher may want to explore the various patterns that exist. It is helpful if there are several years' results to analyze. A pattern over time can be more reliable for interpretation.

The first thing the teacher may need to know is the meaning of the many abbreviations that exist on group achievement test results. These include:

NP or NPE—National percentile

LP or LPE—Local percentile

S—Stanine

GE—Grade Equivalent

RS—Raw score

SS—Standard Score

SAI—School Abilities Index (new term for IQ)

GP—Grade Percentile

AP—Age Percentile

2.3 continued

NORMAL PATTERN

John: Age 14, Grade 8, SAI-115 (80th percentile)

3rd grade

	Reading Comprehension	Vocabulary	Applications	Computation	Total Reading	Total Math
RS	32	24	35	36	56	71
NP	75	68	76	87	72	82
LP	56	53	65	76	61	75
GE	4-3	3-9	4-3	4-9	4-5	4-8
S	7	6	7	8	7	8

5th grade

	Reading Comprehension	Vocabulary	Applications	Computation	Total Reading	Total Math
RS	37	28	39	39	65	78
NP	73	65	72	84	70	79
LP	58	56	66	78	64	72
GE	6-3	5-9	6-3	6-9	6-5	6-8
S	7	6	7	8	7	8

7th grade

	Reading Comprehension	Vocabulary	Applications	Computation	Total Reading	Total Math
RS	32	24	35	36	56	36
NP	79	69	78	88	75	86
LP	60	58	66	79	68	77
GE	8-3	7-9	8-3	8-9	7-1	8-8
S	8	7	8	8	7	8

Profile Interpretation

- Look at the consistency of scores from year to year in the same test area. In this profile, there is very little scatter, and the test results parallel the child's intellectual ability level (approximately 80th percentile).
- There is no discrepancy between ability and achievement.

POSSIBLE LD PATTERN

Mary: Age 11, Grade 5, SAI-102 (51st percentile)

Grade 2

	Reading Comprehension	Vocabulary	Applications	Computation	Total Reading	Total Math
RS	12	14	26	26	26	52
NP	18	12	48	51	16	52
LP	6	3	39	41	6	45
GE	K-5	K-5	2-3	2-6	K-5	2-4
S	1	1	4	4	1	4

Grade 3

	Reading Comprehension	Vocabulary	Applications	Computation	Total Reading	Total Math
RS	12	13	25	27	25	52
NP	14	11	49	52	14	54
LP	5	2	35	43	5	46
GE	1-1	1-0	3-3	3-4	1-0	2-5
S	1	1	4	5	1	4

Grade 4

	Reading Comprehension	Vocabulary	Applications	Computation	Total Reading	Total Math
RS	12	14	35	36	26	71
NP	15	18	46	50	16	52
LP	11	13	35	46	11	45
GE	2-3	1-9	4-3	4-4	1-9	4-5
S	1	1	4	5	1	5

Profile Interpretation

■ In this profile, we notice that Mary is consistently and severely below expected level in the areas of comprehension, vocabulary, and total reading.

■ This consistency is a pattern over the years and never shows any scatter.

■ The results in reading show a severe discrepancy from ability (approximately 51st percentile).

2.3 continued

POSSIBLE EMOTIONAL PATTERN

Billy: Age 15, Grade 8, SAI-120 (90th percentile)

3rd grade

	Reading Comprehension	Vocabulary	Applications	Computation	Total Reading	Total Math
RS	18	34	45	16	52	61
NP	25	68	76	27	72	52
LP	16	53	65	22	61	45
GE	2-3	4-2	4-7	2-9	4-5	3-5
S	7	6	7	2	7	5

5th grade

	Reading Comprehension	Vocabulary	Applications	Computation	Total Reading	Total Math
RS	37	18	39	39	55	78
NP	73	22	72	84	30	79
LP	58	16	66	78	24	72
GE	6-4	2-9	6-3	6-9	2-6	6-8
S	7	2	7	8	3	8

7th grade

	Reading Comprehension	Vocabulary	Applications	Computation	Total Reading	Total Math
RS	12	39	15	36	51	51
NP	29	89	28	88	35	46
LP	20	68	16	79	28	37
GE	5-3	9-9	5-3	9-9	4-5	6-8
S	3	8	2	8	3	4

Profile Interpretation

- This profile presents a possible emotional pattern in that there is a great deal of scatter within the same skill area over the three years.
- The profile presents a "roller coaster" pattern.
- There is no clearly consistent deficit area, and the child's true ability, although not consistent, is observed in specific years.

2.4   How to Examine School Records

The school usually has a wealth of information about all children, distributed among a number of people and a number of records. Gathering this information after a referral and prior to evaluation may reduce the need for testing and will provide a very thorough picture of the child and his/her abilities and patterns. Investigating the following areas will contribute to the overall "picture" of the child:

Prior teacher reports: Comments written on report cards or in permanent record folders may provide a different view of the child under a different style of teaching. Successful years with positive comments may be a clue to the child's learning style and may provide information about the conditions under which the child responds best.

Reports of prior parent–teacher interviews: Prior conferences between previous teachers and parents may provide information that may be important in understanding the child's patterns and history.

Cumulative school record: This particular file may contain information from standardized achievement test results, group IQ results, teacher comments dating back to kindergarten, records from previous schools, individual reading test results, and family information.

Group IQ test information: This information is usually found in the permanent record folder. Many schools administer this type of test (e.g., Otis Lennon, Henmon Nelson) in grades 3, 6, and 9, so look carefully. Within the past year or so, the term "School Abilities Index" (SAI) has replaced the term "IQ" or Intelligence Quotient.

Standardized test scores: These scores should be analyzed for patterns of strengths and deficiencies. The older the child, the greater the number of scores there are to examine.

Report card grades: These materials can be reviewed for comments and for patterns of productive and difficult years.

Attendance records: These records should be reviewed for patterns of lateness and/or absence. If such patterns exist, the reasons should be investigated to rule out medical causes (hospital stays, illnesses), psychological causes (dysfunctional family patterns, school phobia, etc.) or social causes (peer rejection or isolation).

Number of schools attended: There are instances when a child is enrolled in several schools over a period of several years. The reasons for the many moves should be investigated because they may have added to the child's adjustment difficulties.

Prior teacher referrals: Investigate school records for prior referrals from teachers. There are times when a teacher will refer, but no action may have been taken due to time of year, parent resistance, delay in evaluation procedures, etc. These referrals may still be on file and may reveal information that can be useful.

33

2.4 continued

Medical history in the school nurse's office: Investigate these records for indications of visual or hearing difficulties, prescribed medication that may have an effect on the child's behavior (e.g., antihistamines), or medical conditions in need of attention that might be contributing to the child's present situation.

Whatever the situation, the special education teacher should review all the available records in the school building.

2.5 Pupil Personnel or Child Study Team Guidelines

When a Pupil Personnel Team (PPT) or Child Study Team first receives a referral from a teacher, it must consider many issues. Here are questions to be considered:

1. Has this child ever been referred to the PPT? Prior referral may indicate a historical disturbance or long-term problem—and therefore a more serious situation—especially if the same pattern exists. Situational disturbances with no prior problems usually have a better prognosis.

2. Do we have any prior psychological, educational, language, etc., evaluations? This information is very important so that child is not put through unnecessary testing. These reports also offer the team another perspective on the problem.

3. Is anyone familiar with other family members? Family patterns of behavior may help define contributing factors to the child's problem. They may also offer the team some insights to the best approach to take with this family.

4. Are there any medical issues we need to be aware of that might impact on this case? These issues are crucial, and the existence of medical problems should always be determined first. Difficulties with hearing, eyesight, taking medication, severe allergies etc., may be significant contributors to poor performance and may be masked in descriptions such as "unmotivated," "lazy," "stubborn," and so on.

5. What do his or her report cards look like? What patterns are exhibited? Some children have trouble starting off in a new situation and play catch up the entire year. Others do well the first marking period and slowly decline to a pattern of poor grades. Still others exhibit the "roller coaster" effect, consistently receiving grades that fluctuate from failing to passing and vice versa. Knowing the child's report card "style" may help with the type of support, remediation, and program offered.

6. What are his/her group achievement test score patterns? Achievement test scores can offer a great deal of useful information about a child's patterns. If the team suspects a learning disability, then the areas affected should be consistently low from year to year. Many fluctuations of scores and wide ranges of results may be more indicative of an emotional issue than a learning disability.

7. If no prior testing is available, is there any group IQ test information to give us some general idea of his/her ability? Although group IQ tests should never be used to determine a high-risk child's true intellectual potential, they may offer a general idea of ability.

8. Has anyone observed this child? This piece of information is required if the team is considering referring the child to the Eligibility Committee. In any case, observation should always be a piece of the contributing information presented to the PPT. It is very important for the team to know how this child functions in structured and unstructured settings.

2.5 continued

9. Do we have samples of his/her class work? Samples of class work over a period of time offer a clearer overview of the child's abilities and attitudes toward class work.

10. Have the parents been notified of the teacher's concerns? It is the responsibility of the classroom teacher to alert the parents that she or he is concerned and would like the PPT to take a closer look. A parent does not have a legal right to refuse such a request, as it is considered a normal school procedure.

2.6   Pre-Referral Strategies Recommended by the Child Study Team Prior to Formal Evaluation

1. When a child displays problem behaviors in the classroom, the cause may not be inherent within the child, but rather, the classroom teacher's style (e.g., unrealistic, unclear, or overly demanding expectations; excessive criticism, etc.). If this is the case, then help for the teacher can come in the form of classroom management techniques. These include:

Meeting with teacher teams.

Conducting parent interviews.

Displaying the class schedule with times.

Changing the child's seating.

Seating the student with good role models.

Using peer tutors when appropriate.

Limiting number of directions.

Simplifying complex directions.

Giving verbal as well as written directions.

Providing extra work time.

Shortening assignments.

Modifying the curriculum.

Identifying and addressing preferred learning styles.

Providing manipulatives.

Providing examples of what is expected.

Using color coding of materials to foster organizational skills.

Developing a homework plan with parental support.

Developing a behavior modification plan if necessary.

Using positive reinforcement.

Using technology as an aid.

Providing extra-help classes.

Extending remedial reading or math services.

Suggesting in-school counseling.

Preparing daily/weekly progress reports.

2. It is important to determine whether a medical condition, such as a visual or hearing impairment, is causing or compounding a child's poor performance in school.

Symptoms that may require a hearing test include:

Child asks you to repeat frequently.

Child consistently misinterprets what he/she hears.

Child does not respond to auditory stimuli.

Child slurs speech, speaks in a monotone voice, or articulates poorly.

2.6 continued

Symptoms that may require a vision test include:

Child turns head when looking at board or objects.

Child squints excessively.

Child rubs eyes frequently.

Child holds books and materials close to the face or at unusual angles.

Child suffers frequent headaches.

Child avoids close work of any type.

Child covers an eye when reading.

Child consistently loses place when reading.

3. Other areas to investigate include:

- Disciplinary action
- Medical exam
- Change of program
- Consolidation of program
- Referral to child protective services
- Portfolio assessment

According to Venn (2000), portfolio-based assessment provides several distinct advantages and disadvantages. The *advantages* include:

Student self-evaluation, reflection, and critical thinking.

View of performance based on genuine samples of student work.

Flexibility in measuring how students accomplish their learning goals.

Shared responsibility between teachers and students for setting learning goals and for evaluating progress toward meeting those goals.

Extensive student input into the learning process.

Cooperative learning activities, including peer evaluation and tutoring, cooperative learning groups, and peer conferencing.

Structuring learning in stages.

Opportunities for students and teachers to discuss learning goals and progress toward those goals in structured and unstructured conferences.

Measurement of multiple dimensions of student progress by including different types of data and materials.

The *disadvantages* of portfolio assessment include:

Extra time is needed to plan an assessment system and conduct the assessments.

Gathering all of the necessary data and work samples can make portfolios bulky and difficult to manage.

Developing a systematic and deliberate management system is difficult, but this step is necessary in order to make portfolios more than a random collection of student work.

Scoring portfolios involves the extensive use of subjective evaluation procedures such as rating scales and professional judgment; this limits reliability.

Scheduling individual portfolio conferences is difficult, and the length of each conference may interfere with other instructional activities.

2.7 Responsibilities and Roles of the Special Education Teacher

The special education teachers in today's schools play a very critical role in the proper education of exceptional students. Teachers are unique in that they can play many different roles in the educational environment. For instance, the special education teacher can be assigned as:

1. *A teacher in a self-contained special education classroom in a regular school.* This role involves working with a certain number of students with disabilities in a special education setting. This type of setting allows for mainstreaming, the involvement of a child with disabilities in a regular classroom for a part of the regular school day—when the student is ready for this type of transitional technique. A teaching assistant usually assists the teacher in a self-contained classroom.

2. *A resource teacher in a categorical resource room.* This type of resource room, found in a special school, deals with only one type of exceptionality.

3. *A teacher in a non-categorical resource room.* This type of resource room is usually found in a regular mainstream school where many children with exceptionalities are educated. This type of setting necessitates close involvement with each child's homeroom teacher and the transfer of practical techniques and suggestions to facilitate the child's success while in the regular setting.

4. *An educational evaluator on the Child Study Team or Pupil Personnel Team.* This is a school-based support team that discusses and makes recommendations for high-risk students. This role requires a complete and professional understanding of testing, other evaluation procedures, and diagnosis and interpretation of test results.

5. *A member of the Committee on Special Education.* This is a district-based committee mandated by federal law. Its responsibilities include the classification, placement, and evaluation of all children with disabilities within the district. This role involves interpreting educational test results, making recommendations, and diagnosing strengths and weaknesses for the Individualized Education Plan—a list of goals, needs, and objectives required for every student with a disability.

6. *A member of a multidisciplinary team.* Team members are responsible for educating secondary students in a departmentalized program.

7. *A consultant teacher.* This position requires a special education teacher to work in the regular classroom with a child who has a disability.

8. *An itinerant teacher.* In this type of arrangement, a special education teacher is hired to work with children who have disabilities in several districts. In this way, children are provided with the required auxiliary services, and districts are able to meet requirements without having a program of their own.

9. *A private practitioner.* Children are evaluated and remediation is provided as an auxiliary service after school.

Whatever the role, the special education provider will always encounter a variety of situations that require practical decisions and relevant suggestions. No matter what role you play in special education, there is always a need to fully understand symptoms, causality, evaluation, diagnosis, prescription, and remediation of disabilities and to be able to communicate vital information to other professionals, parents, and students.

2.8 Symptomatic Behaviors Exhibited by High-Risk Students

A high-risk student is usually a student who is experiencing severe emotional, social, environmental, or academic stress. As a result of this intense turmoil, many behaviors can be exhibited in a dynamic attempt to alleviate anxiety. Behaviors can show up in many different patterns. Some of the more common characteristics that can be observed in either elementary or secondary high-risk students are:

- A history of adequate or high first-quarter grades followed by a downward trend leading to failures in the final quarter.

- A history of excessive absences.

- A history of excessive lateness.

- A history of difficulty separating from parents at the start of the school day. While this can be normal behavior in very young children, it is considered a more serious symptom after age 6 or 7.

- High achievement scores and a high school abilities index coupled with a history of low academic performance.

- Consistent failure in at least two subjects for two or more quarters.

- A history of parent "coverage" for a student's inappropriate behavior, poor work performance or failure, poor attitude, and/or absences.

- A student's tendency to wander the halls after school with no direction or purpose.

- A history of projecting reasons for one's own poor performance—such as handing in work late, failures, or cutting school—onto others.

- A history of the student's feeling powerless to deal with his/her approach to problems.

- A recent stress-related experience such as divorce, separation, death of a parent, or a parent's loss of employment.

- A history of unusually frequent visits to the nurse.

- Social withdrawal from peers with an emphasis on developing relationships with adults.

2.9 How to Determine the Severity of a Problem

While many symptoms may indicate a problem, several of the following guidelines should be used to determine the severity of the situation:

1. *Frequency of symptoms*—Consider how often the symptoms occur. The greater the frequency, the greater the chance of a serious problem.

2. *Duration of symptoms*—Consider how long the symptoms last. The longer the duration, the more serious the problem.

3. *Intensity of symptoms*—Consider how serious the reactions are at the time of occurrence. The more intense the symptom, the more serious the problem.

Dynamic problems—conflicts, fears, and insecurities—create tension. The more serious the problem, or the greater number of problems experienced by a child, the greater the level of tension. When tension is present, behavior is used to relieve the tension. When serious problems exist, the behavior required to relieve this tension becomes more immediate. As a result, the behavior may be inappropriate and impulsive rather than well thought out.

When tension is very high, it may require a variety of behaviors to relieve the dynamic stress. These behaviors then become symptoms of the seriousness of the problem. That is why the frequency and intensity of the symptomatic behavior reflects the seriousness of the underlying problem(s).

As the child becomes more confident or learns to work out his or her problems, for example, through therapy, the underlying problems are reduced. As a result, they generate less tension and consequently, less inappropriate, impulsive, or self-destructive behavior patterns.

2.10 Symptomatic Behaviors Possibly Indicating More Serious Problems

Examples of typical symptomatic behavior that may be indicative of more serious concerns may include the following:

- impulsivity
- frequently hands in incomplete work
- gives excuses for inappropriate behavior
- constantly blames others for problems
- panics easily
- distractible
- short attention span
- over-reactive
- physical with others
- intrusive
- unable to focus on tasks
- procrastinates
- squints
- turns head while listening
- disorganization
- inflexibility
- irresponsibility
- poor judgment
- denial
- forgetful
- daydreams
- unwillingness to venture a guess
- unwillingness to reason
- social withdrawal
- extreme use of self criticism
- bullies other children
- needs constant reassurance
- poor reader
- argumentative
- tells lies excessively
- awkward gait
- fearful of adults
- fearful of new situations
- verbally hesitant
- hypoactive
- hyperactive
- fears criticism
- rarely takes chances
- moody
- defies authority
- anxious
- unable to generalize
- insecure
- has trouble starting work
- tires easily
- controlling
- overly critical
- painfully shy
- overly social
- slow starter
- destroys property
- lazy
- inconsistency of behavior
- poor spelling

2.11 Common Avoidance Behavior Patterns Exhibited by Children with Suspected Learning Problems

Avoidance behaviors are tools used by children who are experiencing problems learning. Children will often exhibit these symptoms at home and at school to avoid loss of parental approval, peer humiliation, or fear of failure. Examples include:

- *Selectively forgets.* The selectivity of the forgetfulness usually centers on areas of learning that may be creating frustration.

- *Forgets to write down assignments day after day.* The avoidance of a perceived failure experience is satisfied through the use of this behavior.

- *Takes hours to complete homework.* This symptom also occurs if a child is under tension and cannot concentrate for long periods of time. He or she will tend to "burn out" quickly and daydream the afternoon or night away.

- *Finishes homework very quickly.* With this symptom, the child's major objective is to get the ego-threatening situation (homework) over as quickly as possible. Every attempt is made to "rush" through the assignments with little if any care or patience.

- *Can't seem to get started with homework.* When children's anxiety levels are very high it makes it very difficult to "start the engine." They may spend a great deal of time "getting ready" to do the homework by arranging their books, sharpening pencils, getting out paper, opening the textbooks, getting a glass of water, going to the bathroom, and so on, but they never really seem to get their assignments started.

- *Frequently brings home unfinished class work.* Students frequently exhibit this symptom for three reasons:

  1. The student has a low energy level and, therefore, has problems dealing with tasks involving sustained concentration.

  2. The student might be reacting to a parent who constantly sits next to a child when he or she is doing homework. The child then becomes conditioned to this assistance and learns to be helpless without it.

  3. The student might have a need for attention. Bringing home unfinished class work may prompt some parents to sit with their child and complete the work. This "captive audience" of parent attention is reinforced when a parent tries to leave.

- *Consistently leaves long-term assignments until the last minute.* Avoidance of school-related tasks, especially long-term ones, is a frequent symptom of children with low energy levels

2.11 continued

▪ *Complains of headaches, stomachaches, and other physical ailments before or after school.* Very high-tension levels over an extended period of time may result in somatic (bodily) complaints. These complaints, while real to the child, may indicate an avoidance of an uncomfortable or ego-deflating situation. When a child has a pattern of these types of complaints, then the teacher needs to see this "signal" as a symptom of a more serious problem.

▪ *Exhibits "spotlight" behaviors.* "Spotlight" behaviors are any behaviors that bring the focus of attention to the child—calling out, laughing out loud, getting up out of seat, annoying other children. When this occurs, it is usually a release of tension.

1. Some children use "spotlight" behaviors to alleviate the tension of academic inadequacy and may even hope to get into trouble so he or she is able to leave the room.

2. Another reason for "spotlight" behaviors is a need to be in control. Keep in mind, however, that the more controlling a child is, the more out of control he or she feels.

3. The third reason for "spotlight" behaviors is for the sole purpose of gaining the teacher's attention. However, in this way, the child is determining when he or she gets attention, not the teacher.

2.12 Energy Drain and Its Effect on Behavior and Learning

NORMAL DEVELOPMENT—DIVISION OF ENERGY

Everyone has a certain amount of psychic energy to use in dealing with the everyday stresses of life. In normal development there is a certain amount of stress but because of an absence of major conflicts that tend to drain energy, the individual has more than enough reserve to keep things in perspective. Consequently, the division of energy and the symptoms that result (more often than not), when a child is relatively "conflict free," may look like this:

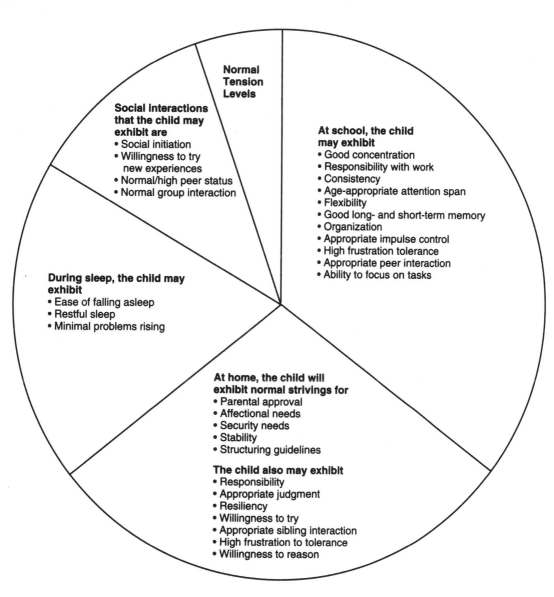

Normal Tension Levels

Social interactions that the child may exhibit are
• Social initiation
• Willingness to try new experiences
• Normal/high peer status
• Normal group interaction

At school, the child may exhibit
• Good concentration
• Responsibility with work
• Consistency
• Age-appropriate attention span
• Flexibility
• Good long- and short-term memory
• Organization
• Appropriate impulse control
• High frustration tolerance
• Appropriate peer interaction
• Ability to focus on tasks

During sleep, the child may exhibit
• Ease of falling asleep
• Restful sleep
• Minimal problems rising

At home, the child will exhibit normal strivings for
• Parental approval
• Affectional needs
• Security needs
• Stability
• Structuring guidelines

The child also may exhibit
• Responsibility
• Appropriate judgment
• Resiliency
• Willingness to try
• Appropriate sibling interaction
• High frustration to tolerance
• Willingness to reason

2.12 continued

HIGH TENSION LEVEL—DIVISION OF ENERGY

However, when serious conflicts arise, the available energy must be "pulled" to deal with the conflicts—like white blood cells to an infection. Since energy must be drained away, there is less available energy to keep things in perspective. In this case the resulting symptoms and behaviors take on a different look.

When a parent or teacher observes a pattern of behaviors similar to these, he or she should automatically become aware that some serious problem might exist. These symptoms are not the problems, but an outgrowth of a serious problem. It is therefore very important for the teacher or team to try to identify what the problem or problems are so that treatment can be initiated.

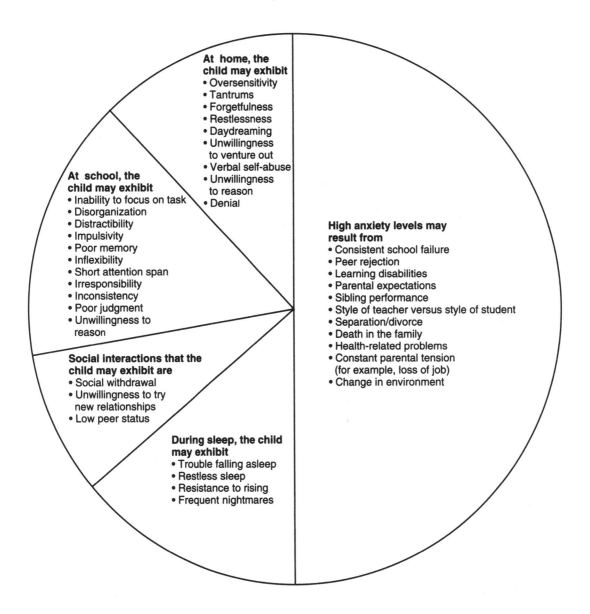

At home, the child may exhibit
• Oversensitivity
• Tantrums
• Forgetfulness
• Restlessness
• Daydreaming
• Unwillingness to venture out
• Verbal self-abuse
• Unwillingness to reason
• Denial

At school, the child may exhibit
• Inability to focus on task
• Disorganization
• Distractibility
• Impulsivity
• Poor memory
• Inflexibility
• Short attention span
• Irresponsibility
• Inconsistency
• Poor judgment
• Unwillingness to reason

Social interactions that the child may exhibit are
• Social withdrawal
• Unwillingness to try new relationships
• Low peer status

During sleep, the child may exhibit
• Trouble falling asleep
• Restless sleep
• Resistance to rising
• Frequent nightmares

High anxiety levels may result from
• Consistent school failure
• Peer rejection
• Learning disabilities
• Parental expectations
• Sibling performance
• Style of teacher versus style of student
• Separation/divorce
• Death in the family
• Health-related problems
• Constant parental tension (for example, loss of job)
• Change in environment

2.13   Examples of Structured Referral Forms

Many schools use a referral form procedure that teachers submit, indicating the possibility of a high-risk student. This is usually the first step in the referral process. The form then goes to the Pupil Personnel Team for discussion and future direction. The initial sections of these forms are usually the same, containing basic identifying information. The differences are usually in the body of the form. Following are three examples of these forms.

REFERRAL FORM

Student Name:_____   Date of Referral:_____

Grade Level:_____   Date of Birth:_____

Teacher Name:_____   Chronological Age:_____

Parent's Names:_____   Phone:_____

Please answer the following questions using behavioral terms:

What symptoms is the child exhibiting that are of concern at this time?

What have you tried that has worked?

What have you tried that does not seem to work toward alleviating these symptoms?

What are the child's present academic levels of functioning?

What is the child's social behavior like?

Have the parent(s) been contacted? yes_____ no_____ If no, why not?

Further comments?

REFERRAL FORM

Student Name:_____   Date of Referral:_____

Grade Level:_____   Date of Birth:_____

Teacher Name:_____   Chronological Age:_____

Parent's Names:_____   Phone:_____

Grades Repeated (if any):

Current Academic Performance Levels:

Math:_____   Reading:_____   Spelling:_____

Any observable behavioral or physical limitations:

Reasons for referral:

List specific academic and behavioral strengths:

List academic and behavioral weaknesses:

What have you tried to help remedy the problem?

Have the parent or parents been notified of this referral? yes____ no____

What was their reaction?

REFERRAL FORM

Student Name:_____   Date of Referral:_____

Grade Level:_____   Date of Birth:_____

Teacher Name:_____   Chronological Age:_____

Parent's Names:_____   Phone:_____

Why is this pupil being referred?

How have you attempted to deal with these problems?

Have you discussed this referral with the student? What was his or her reaction?

What is the child's perception of the situation?

Current performance estimates (below, on, or above grade level)

Math:_____   Reading:_____   Spelling:_____

Describe the child's current social behavior with peers:

Is there any relevant history that may assist in the understanding of this child?

Have the parent/s been contacted about this referral? yes____ no____

What was their reaction?

2.14   Examples of Student Rating Scales

Some schools will use a student rating scale along with or instead of a referral form. The purpose of a rating scale is to get a more objective level on a student's behavior, performance, and characteristics. Such forms do not force the referring teacher to generalize comments, but instead allow for a more accurate appraisal of the student. The teacher is usually asked to rate the student along some continuum determined by the frequency and intensity of the behavior being rated. Following are two examples of such scales.

Student Rating Scale

	Never	Seldom	Sometimes	Most of the time	Always

Academic Behavior
 1. Has trouble comprehending what he or she reads.
 2. Uses adequate word attack skills.
 3. Loses his or her place while reading.
 4. Slows down when reading aloud.
 5. Exhibits good sight word vocabulary.
 6. Shows adequate math computational skills.
 7. Understands word problems.
 8. Applies mathematical skills in solving problems.
 9. Exhibits appropriate handwriting for age.
10. Exhibits adequate spelling skills.

Classroom Behavior
 1. Exhibits impulsivity.
 2. Exhibits distractibility.
 3. Gets along with peers.
 4. Follows rules of a game.
 5. Is willing to reason.
 6. Conforms to boundaries and rules in the classroom.
 7. Attends to task.
 8. Completes homework.
 9. Completes classwork in allotted time.
10. Listens carefully.
11. Becomes easily frustrated.
12. Cooperates with others.

Language Behavior
 1. Exhibits adequate vocabulary.
 2. Exhibits limited verbal fluency.
 3. Exhibits faulty articulation.

Pupil Behavior Rating Scale

Please rate the behaviors listed below according to the following scale:

Rating
1. The behavior does not apply to this child and is never observed.
2. The behavior is rarely exhibited.
3. The behavior occurs some of the time.
4. The behavior occurs most of the time.
5. The behavior always occurs.

____Anxious

____Disruptive

____Fights frequently

____Unhappy

____Withdrawn

____Moody

____Distractible

____Impulsive

____Does not complete work

____Short attention span

____Daydreams

____Argumentative

____Disorganized

____Easily confused

____Poor speller

____Poor reader

____Limited reading comprehension

____Faulty articulation

____Poor grammar

____Problems judging time

____Poor fine-motor skills

____Slow in completing tasks

____Poor logical reasoning and thinking

____Poor number concepts

____Tires easily

____Defies authority

____Fears criticism

____Critical of others

____Controlling

____Painfully shy

____Slow starter

____Inconsistent

____Hyperactive

____Hypoactive

____Fearful of new situations

____Procrastinates

____Rarely takes chances

____Overreactive

____Problems with writing

____Problems with math

____Poor vocabulary usage

____Poor expressive language ability

____Inadequate word attack skills

____Poor balance and coordination

____Poor gross-motor skills

____Tracing and drawing difficulties

____Difficulty with abstract concepts

____Problems with auditory memory tasks

2.15   Procedures to Follow
If You Suspect Abuse or Neglect

Remember, if you suspect abuse or neglect, you are obligated by law to report the case. If you suspect possible abuse or neglect, follow the following steps:

1. Gather all the information you can about the suspected incident or incidents and write it up in factual and behavioral terminology. (This means no opinions, interpretations, assumptions, or guesses should be given, just factual observations or information. Some examples: "The child said," "I directly observed," "There were black and blue marks on his or her legs.")

2. Notify your direct administrator (usually the building principal) of the information you have that caused you to suspect abuse or neglect. Here again, verbalize only facts. At this point, the administrator will usually call the Child Abuse Hotline or assign someone to call. If you are assigned to call, keep the following in mind:

- Make sure you call the mandated reporters' hotline. Many states have two lines—one for the public to report cases and one for mandated reporters. The numbers can be found in the phone book or by calling 800-555-1212 and asking for the State Child Abuse and Neglect Hotline for Mandated Reporters, since most of these hotlines are 800 numbers.

- Once you have a counselor on the phone, immediately ask for his or her name and note the time and date of your call.

- Inform the counselor that you believe you have a suspected case of abuse or neglect. He or she will ask you some basic questions for their records and then ask you what evidence you have to suspect that something has taken place.

- Again, report only facts and direct observations. At this point, the counselor may indicate that this case is either reportable or not reportable.

- If the case is reportable, the counselor will ask you more questions, so be prepared with the following information: the child's full name, the address of the child, the child's birth date, the parent's/guardian's first and last names (if different), the child's telephone number, the parent's/guardian's work number (if known), other siblings in the house and their ages, the grade of the child, the school and school district of the child, number and nature of any previous reports.

3. After the counselor gathers all the information, he or she may assign a case number so be prepared to jot this down. He or she will inform you that the case will be passed onto a local caseworker who will be in touch with the school.

4. Ask the counselor if he or she feels that the child can go home or if the school should retain the child until the caseworker appears. The school has this right if the child's health or safety will be compromised in any way by returning home. Many times, the caseworker will come immediately if it is deemed a serious case and will speak with the child before the end of the school day. A home visit is usually made within 24 hours or less if the case is considered serious.

5. The school nurse, under the direction of the building administrator, may photograph any obvious marks or contusions for evidence.

6. Once the case is reported, you will probably receive a Report of Suspected Child Abuse or Maltreatment form from the Department of Social Services. The school must fill this out and return it within 24 hours. Here again, the person who made the original contact with the state counselor may be the one who fills out the form. An example of this type of form appears in List 2.17. Keep in mind that this is a legal requirement.

7. In some instances, the counselor may indicate that a case does not sound reportable as abuse or neglect. He or she may indicate that it does represent poor judgment on the part of parents but does not constitute abuse or neglect. At this point, you can ask why and solicit advice for the next step. However, if the case is judged as not reportable, write your administrator a letter indicating the time and date as well as the name of the counselor to whom you spoke, and the reasons why the case was not accepted as reportable. Your legal responsibilities are now covered. However, your moral responsibilities have just begun.

8. In some instances, your administrator will listen to the facts but will not see the case as reportable. If this occurs, you should ask the reasons why and suggest that the case be presented to the Child Abuse counselor for input. However, if the administrator continues to indicate that he or she does not feel it needs to go any further, inform him or her that as a mandated reporter you feel a responsibility to call the Child Abuse Hotline and ask the counselor on call if he or she feels it is a reportable case. If an administrator does not want to report a case and you agree with this decision, and it is later determined that abuse or neglect was taking place, you may find yourself in very serious trouble. It is not acceptable to use the excuse "I told my administrator." Remember, you are a mandated reporter and directly responsible for actions taken or not taken.

2.16   Clinical and Behavioral Clues to Possible Child Abuse or Neglect

Because special education teachers are mandated reporters, you should be aware of clinical and behavioral clues to possible abuse. Try to keep in mind that you should use common sense and proper judgment prior to reporting suspected abuse. Such reports are a serious matter. On the other hand, never hesitate to report suspected abuse because you believe that "such a family could never do such things." Remember that, as a mandated reporter, you are really an advocate for children in cases of suspected abuse or neglect. Never assume that something is so obvious that someone must have called it in. It is always better to be safe than sorry.

PHYSICAL ABUSE

Some Possible Behavioral Signs of Physical Abuse:

1. Child shows fear of or resistance to going home.
2. There is a past history of self-injurious behavior.
3. Child exhibits extreme neurotic conditions such as obsessions, compulsions, and phobias.
4. Child often wears clothing that is inappropriate for the season—long sleeves in the summertime, possibly to cover up bruises.
5. Child exhibits extreme mood changes and periods of aggressive behavior.
6. Child seems apprehensive or afraid of adults.
7. Child flinches or reacts defensively to nonthreatening adult gestures or behavior.
8. Child communicates that his or her bruises are due to constantly falling or hitting things.

Some Possible Physical Signs of Physical Abuse:

1. Unexplained marks, welts, bites, or bruises on the body.
2. Unexplained burns.
3. Unexplained injuries to the head area.

SEXUAL ABUSE

Some Possible Behavioral Signs of Sexual Abuse:

1. Child acts in an infantile manner and exhibits frequent withdrawal and fantasy.
2. Child has difficulties maintaining peer relationships.
3. Child engages in sexual activities with other children.
4. Child exhibits frequent lateness or absences from school.

5. Child resists physical examinations.

6. Child has a history of running away.

7. Child may have a history of self-injurious behavior.

8. Child demonstrates sophisticated, bizarre, or unusual knowledge of sexual acts or behavior and expresses these to other children or adults.

Some Possible Physical Signs of Sexual Abuse:

1. Child mentions the presence of or exhibits bruise in genital areas.

2. Child has difficulty walking or sitting for long periods of time because of pain.

3. Child exhibits bruise in the mouth area.

4. Child exhibits extreme pain, itching, or discomfort in the genital area.

5. Child has a history of urinary tract infections.

6. Child has developed sexually transmitted diseases, especially in the pre-adolescent period.

NEGLECT OR MALTREATMENT

Some Possible Behavioral Signs of Neglect:

1. Child is frequently caught taking food from other children.

2. Child arrives at school much earlier than the other children.

3. Child seems to hesitate going home at the end of the day and is seen wandering the halls.

4. Child exhibits constant fatigue.

5. Child frequently falls asleep in class.

6. Child develops habit disorders (e.g., tics and other signs of tension).

7. Child exhibits symptoms typical of conduct disorders, i.e., antisocial behavior.

8. Child frequently uses drugs or alcohol.

9. Child develops clinging behavior patterns toward other adults.

Some Possible Physical Signs of Neglect:

1. Child seems to have medical or physical conditions that go untreated.

2. Child exhibits severe lags in physical development as a result of malnutrition.

3. Child expresses constant hunger.

4. Child comes to school exhibiting poor hygiene.

5. Child comes to school inappropriately dressed for the particular weather conditions.

6. Child mentions that he or she is left home alone a great deal.

7. Child exhibits chronic absences from school.

8. Child has a history of lateness to school.

2.17   Example of a Report Form for Suspected Child Abuse or Neglect

Subjects of Report

List all children in household, adults responsible for household, and alleged perpetrators.

	Last Name	First Name	M.I.	Aliases	Sex M or F	Birth date or age	Ethnic Code	Suspect or Relationship Code	Check if alleged Perpetrator Code
1.									
2.									
3.									
4.									
5.									
6.									
7.									

If known, list addresses and telephone numbers:

Basis of Suspicions

Alleged consequences or evidence of abuse or maltreatment. Place the above line numbers next to the appropriate area. If all children, write "LL."

_____Sexual abuse   _____Drug withdrawal

_____Emotional neglect   _____Child's drug/alcohol

_____Abandonment   _____Lack of medical care

_____Lack of supervision   _____Malnutrition

_____DOA/Fatality   _____Failure to thrive

_____Fractures   _____Educational neglect

_____Lacerations, bruises, welts   _____Lack of food, clothing, shelter

_____Excessive corporal punishment _____Internal injuries

_____Other; Specify_____

State reason for suspicion. If possible, include type and extent of the child's injury or abuse and if known, give time and date of maltreatment in each case. Further, if known, list any evidence of prior injuries, abuse, or alleged incidents of maltreatment to the child or any siblings. Also, list suspicions of any behavior on the part of the parent/s that may contribute to the problem.

Month_____Date____Year____   Time_____AM___PM____

(continued)

Sources for the Report

People Making This Report

Name   Telephone
Address

Agency/Institution

Source of This Report if Different

Name   Telephone
Address

Agency/Institution

Relationship (mark X for Reporter and * for Source)

___Medical examiner/coroner   ___Physician   ___Hospital staff   ___Law enforcement

___Neighbor   ___Relative   ___Social services   ___Public health

___Mental health   ___School staff ___Other (specify)_____

This Section for Physicians Only

Medical diagnosis of child:

Signature of physician who examined or treated child:

Telephone number:

Hospitalization required: ___None   ___Less than one week   ___1–2 Weeks   ___More than 2 Weeks

Actions Taken or about to be Taken:

___Medical examination   ___Hospitalization   ___Notified D.A.   ___Notified medical examiner

___Notified coroner   ___Returned home   ___Removal/Keeping   ___X-Ray   ___Photographs

Signature of person making this report: Title: Date Submitted

2.18   Steps in the Special Education Process

The process of identifying a student with a suspected disability is referred to as the special education process. This process involves a variety of steps that must follow district, state, and federal guidelines. These guidelines have been created to protect the rights of students, parents, and school districts. Working together within these guidelines allows for a thorough and comprehensive assessment of a student and the proper special education services and modifications, if required. When a student is having difficulty in school, the professional staff frequently makes many attempts to resolve the problem. When these interventions do not work, a more extensive look at the student is required.

The remaining lists in this section will outline, in detail, the step-by-step process that is normally followed in special education. A brief explanation of the step-by-step continuum follows. Each step will be covered in depth in the chapters noted.

STEPS IN THE ASSESSMENT CONTINUUM

Step I—Pre-Referral: When concerns are realized by the classroom teacher, an attempt is made for simple classroom interventions. These may include meeting with the child, providing extra help, simplified assignments, parent conferences, peer tutoring, etc. If these attempts are unsuccessful, then Step II is indicated.

Step II—Child Study Team and Pre-Referral Strategies: Referral to a school-based Child Study Team, Pre-Referral Team, Pupil Personnel Team, etc., for a pre-referral intervention plan is made by the classroom teacher. More involved pre-referral strategies are considered, such as direct classroom management interventions and modifications, observations by professional staff, observations and analysis of teaching methods, in-school counseling, assessment of environment, extra help, change of program, consolidation of program, disciplinary action, further parent conferences, medical referral, etc. If these strategies prove unsuccessful, then Step III is needed.

Step III—Screening: Screening the child for a suspected disability by members of the school staff (e.g., psychologist, educational evaluator, speech and language clinician) is done. If screening reveals a possible disability, then a referral is made for a more comprehensive assessment to the Step IV team.

Step IV—Multidisciplinary Team: This team, made up of members of the school staff, parents, and other professionals when required, decides which evaluations and professionals will be involved in this specific assessment. The team then provides a thorough and comprehensive evaluation for possible special education services. Assessments may include standardized tests, portfolio assessments, curriculum-based assessments, criterion-referenced assessments, etc. If the findings of this team indicate the existence of a disability, then the process continues with Step V.

Step V—Putting it all together: Once the MDT team completes the assessment, members of the team will determine the strengths and weaknesses of the student; a possible diagnostic category; the level of severity of the problem; recommendations to the school, the teachers, and the parents; and other information that will later be used to determine the appropriate, if any, special education recommendations. The process continues with Step VI.

Step VI—Writing a professional report: Once the members of the team establish the above, they should write up a professional report that clearly outlines their findings. This report will be part of the materials that go to the Eligibility Committee.

Step VII—Preparation for presentation to the Eligibility Committee: The MDT puts together the information packet for presentation to the Eligibility Committee. This packet will contain all the necessary forms, reports, and results of assessments that will be used to determine possible classification and special education services. Step VIII is next.

Step VIII—Eligibility Committee meetings: Once the packet is complete, an Eligibility Committee meeting (that is, Committee on Special Education, IEP Committee, Eligibility Committee) is scheduled. The results of this meeting will determine whether or not the student meets the criteria for a disability and for a special education program and/or services. If the student is so classified, then the process moves to Step IX.

Step IX—IEP development: Final IEP development occurs, and placement is instituted. If eligibility is not accepted, then Step X is indicated.

Step X—Alternate planning: Alternate planning is formulated and suggested by the Eligibility Committee to the local school.

2.19   The Multidisciplinary Team (MDT)

Many schools are moving toward a more global approach to the identification of students with suspected disabilities through the development of a district-based team. This team may be referred to as the *Multidisciplinary Team (MDT)*, *Multifactor Team (MFT)*, or *School-Based Support Team (SBST)*, depending on the state in which the student resides. Throughout this text, we will refer to this team as the Multidisciplinary Team. This team usually comes into operation when the local school-based team (Child Study Team) has conducted a screening and suspects a disability. Once that is determined, the MDT takes over. This team is mandated by IDEA, so that the child and his or her parents are guaranteed that any comprehensive evaluation will be conducted by a multitude of professionals to decrease the possibility of subjective and discriminatory assessment. To further comply with IDEA, the MDT must follow the following guidelines:

■ Testing and assessment materials and procedures used for the purposes of assessment and placement of individuals with exceptional needs are selected and administered so as not to be racially, culturally, or sexually discriminatory.

■ Tests and other assessment materials are provided and administered in the pupil's primary language or other mode of communication—unless the assessment plan indicates reasons why this provision and administration are not feasible.

■ Tests and other assessment materials have been validated for the specific purpose for which they are used.

■ Tests and other assessment materials are administered by trained personnel in conformance with the instructions provided by the producer of the tests and other assessment materials, except that individually administered tests of intellectual or emotional functioning are administered by a credentialed school psychologist.

■ Tests and other assessment materials administered to a pupil with impaired sensory, manual, or speaking skills are selected and administered so as to ensure that they produce results that accurately reflect the pupil's aptitude, achievement level, or any other factors that they purport to measure and do not reflect the pupil's impaired sensory, manual, or speaking skills unless those skills are the factors purportedly being measured.

■ No single procedure is used as the sole criterion for determining an appropriate educational program for an individual with exceptional needs.

■ The pupil is assessed in all areas related to the suspected disability including, where appropriate, health and development, vision (including low vision), hearing, motor abilities, language function, general ability, academic performance, self-help, orientation and mobility skills, career and vocational abilities and interests, and social and emotional status. A developmental history is obtained, when appropriate. For pupils with residual vision, a low vision assessment is provided.

■ Persons knowledgeable about the particular disability conduct assessments of students suspected of having that disability, including suspected low-incidence disabilities. For instance, if the screening reveals a suspected learning disability, then a learning disabilities specialist becomes part of the team. If the child is suspected of having a hearing impairment, then an audiologist becomes a member of the team. Special attention is given to unique educational needs—including but not limited to skills and the need for specialized services, materials, and equipment.

The role of the MDT is to work as a single unit in determining the possible cause, contributing behavioral factors, educational status, prognosis (outcome), and recommendations for a student with a suspected disability. Bringing together many disciplines and professional perspectives to help work on a case is the major objective of the MDT, so that a single person is not required to determine and assimilate all of the factors having an impact on a particular child. The MDT is responsible for gathering all the necessary information on a child in order to determine the most effective and practical direction for him or her in special education. In many states, the findings of the MDT are then reviewed by another committee (e.g., Eligibility Committee, IEP Committee, Committee on Special Education etc.) whose role is to determine whether or not the findings of the MDT fall within the guidelines for classification and special education services. In accomplishing this task, the team members will employ several types of assessments and collect data from many sources.

2.20 Membership of the Multidisciplinary Team

Although specific state regulations on the membership of the MDT may differ, the members are usually drawn from the following within the school and community:

■ *School psychologist:* The role of the school psychologist on the MDT involves the administration of individual intelligence tests, projective tests, personality inventories, and the observation of the student in a variety of settings.

■ *School nurse:* The role of the school nurse is to review all medical records, screen for vision and hearing, consult with outside physicians, and refer to outside physicians, if necessary.

■ *Classroom teacher:* The teacher works with the local school-based Child Study Team to implement pre-referral strategies and plans, and he or she implements—along with the special education team—classroom strategies that create an appropriate working environment for the student.

■ *School social worker:* The social worker's role on the MDT is to gather and provide information concerning the student's family. This may be accomplished through interviews, observations, conferences, etc.

■ *Special Education teacher:* The role of this individual includes consultation with parents and classroom teachers about pre-referral recommendations. This person also administers educational and perceptual tests; may be called upon to observe the student in a variety of settings; may be involved in the screening of students with suspected disabilities; writes IEPs, including goals and objectives; and recommends intervention strategies to teachers and parents.

■ *Educational diagnostician:* This person administers a series of evaluations including norm-referenced and criterion-referenced tests, observes the student in a variety of settings, and makes educational recommendations that are incorporated in the IEP as goals and objectives.

■ *Special Education supervisor:* This person provides expertise on the district's procedures, local policies, federal laws, and assessment procedures.

■ *Physical therapist:* The physical therapist is called upon to evaluate a child who may be experiencing problems in gross motor functioning, living and self-help skills, and vocational skills necessary for functioning in certain settings. This professional may screen, evaluate, provide direct services, or consult with the teacher, parent, or school.

■ *Behavioral consultant:* This individual works closely with the team in providing direct services or consultation on issues involving behavioral and classroom management techniques and programs.

■ *Speech/language clinician:* This professional will be involved in screening for speech and language developmental problems, be asked to provide a full evaluation on a suspected language disability, provide direct services, and consult with staff and parents.

- *Audiologist:* This professional will be called upon to evaluate a student's hearing for possible impairments and, as a result of the findings, may refer the student for medical consultation or treatment. The audiologist may also assist in helping students and parents obtain equipment (e.g., hearing aids) that may have an impact on the child's ability to function in school.

- *Occupational therapist:* The occupational therapist is called upon to evaluate a child who may be experiencing problems in fine-motor skills and/or living and self-help skills. This professional may screen; evaluate; provide direct services; consult with the teacher, the parent, or the school; and assist in obtaining the appropriate assistive technology or equipment for the student.

- *Physician's assistant:* This person provides medical knowledge to the team.

- *Regular teacher:* This person provides anecdotal information on the child's performance and behavior.

- *Guidance counselor:* This individual may be involved in providing aptitude test information; providing counseling services; working with the team on consolidating, changing, or developing a student's class schedule; and assisting the Child Study Team in developing pre-referral strategies.

- *Parents:* The parent(s) play an extremely important role on the MDT in providing input for the IEP; working closely with members of the team; and carrying out, assisting, or initiating academic or management programs within the child's home.

2.21 Formal Referral for a Suspected Disability

Once the Child Study Team (CST) determines that a suspected disability may exist, a formal referral is made to the multidisciplinary team. A *formal referral* is nothing more than a form that starts the special education process. A referral for evaluation and possible special education services is initiated by a written request. However, you should understand that people other than the CST have the right under due process to initiate a formal referral for a child with a suspected disability. Depending on state regulations, these could include:

- The child's parent, an advocate, or a person in parental relationship.

- A classroom teacher.

- Any professional staff member of the public or private school district.

- A judicial officer—A representative of the court.

- A student on his or her own behalf if he or she is 18 years of age or older, or an emancipated minor (i.e., a person under the age of 18 years of age who has been given "certain adult rights" by the court).

- The Chief School Officer of the state or his/her designee who is responsible for welfare, education, or health of children.

2.22 Initial Referral to the MDT from the School Staff

Once the CST has determined that a suspected disability may exist, the team must alert the chairperson of the MDT that a child with a suspected disability is being referred for review. At this time the MDT may fill out a form similar to the one below.

Initial Referral to the MDT from the School Staff

To: _____

From: _____ School: _____ Date: _____

Name/Title: _____

The following student is being referred to the CST for suspicion of a disability:

Student Name: _____ Sex: ____ Grade:____ Ethnicity: _____

Parent/Guardian Name: _____

Address: _____

City: _____ State: _____ Zip: _____

Telephone: _____ Date of Birth: _____

Current Program Placement: _____

Teacher (Elem): _____ Guidance Counselor (Secondary): _____

Reasons for Referral: Describe the specific reason and/or needs that indicate the suspicion of a disability. Specify reason why referral is considered appropriate and necessary.

(continued)

Describe recent attempts to remediate the pupil's performance prior to referral, including regular education interventions such as remedial reading and math, teaching modifications, behavior modifications, speech improvement, parent conferences, etc., and the results of those interventions.

Do you have a signed Parent Assessment Plan? Yes ____ No ____ (If yes, send copy attached)

Is there an attendance problem? Yes ____ No ____

Language spoken at home? _____

Did student repeat a grade? Yes ____ No ____ If yes, when?

Is an interpreter needed? Yes ____ No ____ Deaf:

Is a bilingual assessment needed? Yes ____ No ____ If yes, what language?

Is student eligible to receive ESL (English as a Second Language) services?
Yes ____ No ____

If yes, how many years receiving ESL services? _____ If yes, determine how student's educational, cultural, and experiential background were considered to determine if these factors are contributing to the student's learning or behavior problems.

TEST SCORES WITHIN LAST YEAR
(E.g., Standardized Achievement, Regents Competency, etc.)

TEST NAME	AREA MEASURED	PERCENTILE SCORE	COMMENT

(continued)

Has school staff informed parent/guardian of referral to CST? Yes _____ No _____

By whom? _____

What was the reaction of the parent/guardian to the referral? _____

To be completed by school nurse:

Medical Report Summary

Any medication? Yes _____ No _____ If yes, specify:

Health problems? Yes _____ No _____ If yes, specify:

Scoliosis screening: Positive _____ Negative _____

Date of last: Physical: _____ Vision results: _____ Hearing Results: _____

Relevant medical information: _____

Nurse's signature: _____

Principal's signature: _____

To be completed by the appropriate administrator:

Date received: _____ Signature: _____

Chairperson: _____

Date notice and consent sent to parent/guardian: _____

Parent consent for initial evaluation received: _____

Date agreement to withdraw referral received: _____

Projected Eligibility Meeting date: _____

If eligible, projected date of implementation of services: _____

Projected Eligibility Board of Education Meeting date: _____

2.23 Initial Referral to the MDT from a Parent/Guardian

The Initial Referral to the MDT from the school staff alerts the chairperson of the MDT that the local school has made every attempt to resolve the student's difficulties prior to the formal referral. The form also informs the chairperson that the parents' rights have been followed. In other cases, a student's parent or guardian may initiate a referral to the MDT due to suspicion of a disability under special education laws or Section 504 of the Rehabilitation Act. A fully completed referral form and any relevant information are sent to the appropriate special education administrator. Usually upon the receipt of the parent's referral, the chairperson of the MDT will send to the parent/guardian an assessment plan (discussed below) and the parent's due process rights statement. The building principal is also notified of the referral.

If for some reason a child's suspected disability is brought to the school's attention by the parent, then a form similar to the one below is filled out and forwarded.

Initial Referral to the MDT from a Parent/Guardian

Date: _____

To: _____

Re: _____   Date of Birth: _____

I am writing to refer my child, _____, for consideration of an educational disability under special education laws and/or under Section 504 of the Vocational Rehabilitation Act (mental or physical impairment that substantially limits one or more life functions). I am concerned about my child's educational difficulties in the following areas:

Parent Name/Signature: _____

Address: _____

_____

Telephone No.: _____

Date of Referral:_____

Child's Birth Date:_____

School: _____   Grade: ____

Please attach any relevant evaluations or documents or information that support the referral.

Date received by MDT Chairperson: _____

Note: If a release for testing (assessment plan) is not secured at a separate meeting, the chairperson of the MDT will mail one to the parent along with the letter indicating that a referral has been made. However, no formal evaluations may begin until the district has received signed permission from the parent or guardian.

2.24   Assessment Plans/Consent for Evaluation

Prior to any assessment, the MDT must secure an agreement from the parent to allow the members of the team to evaluate the child. This release is part of the assessment plan and should meet the following requirements:

- Be in a language easily understood by the general public.

- Be provided in the primary language of the parent or other mode of communication used by the parent, unless to do so is unfeasible.

- Explains the types of assessments to be conducted.

- State that no Individualized Education Plan (IEP) will result from the assessment without the consent of the parent.

- State that no assessment shall be conducted unless the written consent of the parent is obtained prior to the assessment. The parent shall have at least 15 days (may vary from state to state) from the receipt of the proposed assessment plan to arrive at a decision. Assessment may begin immediately upon receipt of the consent.

- Include a copy of the notice of parent rights, including the right to electronically record the proceedings of the Eligibility Committee meetings.

- State that the assessment shall be conducted by persons competent to perform the assessment, as determined by the school district, county office, or special education local plan area.

- State that any psychological assessment of pupils must be conducted by a qualified school psychologist.

- State that only a credentialed school nurse or physician who is trained and prepared to assess cultural and ethnic factors appropriate to the pupil being assessed shall conduct any health assessment of pupils.

2.25   Assessment Options of the MDT

Only when the parents have been informed of their rights, a release is obtained, and the assessment plan is signed, can assessment begin. The MDT has several evaluation options from which to choose. The areas most often considered by the MDT to assess a child with a suspected disability include:

Achievement Evaluation

Such an evaluation is frequently recommended when a child's academic skill levels (reading, math, writing, and spelling) are unknown or inconsistent and when his or her learning process shows gaps (e.g., in memory and expression). The evaluation will determine if a discrepancy exists between intellectual potential and academic achievement as required for the classification of Learning Disabled (LD), and it will determine strengths and weaknesses in the child's academic and processing levels. The objectives of an academic evaluation are:

- To help identify the child's stronger and weaker academic skill areas. The evaluation may provide this information which is very useful when making practical recommendations to teachers about academic expectations, areas in need of remediation, and how best to input information to assist the child's ability to learn.

- To help the teacher gear the educational materials to the learning capacity of the individual child. For example, a child reading two years below grade level may require modified textbooks or greater explanation prior to a lesson.

- To develop a learning profile that can help the classroom teacher understand the best ways to present information to the child and therefore increase his or her chances of success.

- To help determine, along with other information and test results, if the child's academic skills are suitable for a regular class or are so severe that he or she may require a more restrictive educational setting (i.e., an educational setting or situation best suited to the present needs of the student—e.g., resource room, self-contained classroom, special school, etc.).

Whatever achievement battery the special educator chooses, it should be one that covers enough skill areas to make an adequate diagnosis of academic strengths and weaknesses.

Some symptoms that might justify the recommendation for an academic evaluation are:

- Consistently low test scores on group achievement tests.
- Indications of delayed processing when faced with academic skills.
- Labored handwriting after grade 3.
- Poor word recall.
- Poor decoding (word attack) skills.
- Discrepancy between achievement and ability.
- Consistently low achievement despite remediation.

In most cases of a suspected disability, the academic evaluation is always a part of the formal evaluation.

Language Evaluation

This recommendation usually occurs when the child is experiencing significant delays in speech or language development, problems in articulation, or problems in receptive or expressive language. Some symptoms that might warrant such an evaluation include:

- Difficulty pronouncing words through grade 3.
- Immature or delayed speech patterns.
- Difficulty labeling thoughts or objects.
- Difficulty putting thoughts into words.

Psychological Evaluation

This recommendation is appropriate when the child's intellectual ability is unknown or when there is a question about his or her ability to learn. It is useful when the CST suspects potential learning, emotional, or intellectual problems. The psychological evaluation can rule out or rule in emotionality as a primary cause of a child's problem; ruling this factor out is necessary before the diagnosis of LD can be made. Some symptoms that might signal the need for such an evaluation are:

- High levels of tension and anxiety exhibited in behavior.
- Aggressive behavior.
- Lack of motivation or indications of low energy levels.
- Patterns of denial.
- Oppositional behavior.
- Despondency.
- Inconsistent academic performance, ranging from very low to very high.
- History of inappropriate judgment.
- Lack of impulse control.
- Extreme and consistent attention-seeking behavior.
- Pattern of provocative behavior.

Objectives of the psychological assessment include:

- to determine the child's present overall levels of intellectual ability.
- to determine the child's present verbal intellectual ability.
- to determine the child's non-language intellectual ability.
- to explore indications of greater potential.
- to find possible patterns involving learning style (e.g., verbal comprehension, concentration).
- to ascertain possible influences of tension and anxiety on testing results.

2.25 continued

- to determine the child's intellectual ability to deal with present grade-level academic demands.

- to explore the influence of intellectual ability as a contributing factor to a child's past and present school difficulties (e.g., limited intellectual ability found in retardation).

As with the academic assessment, the psychological evaluation is a normal part of every referral for a suspected disability.

Perceptual Evaluation

A perceptual evaluation is suggested when the team suspects discrepancies in the child's ability to receive and process information. This assessment may focus on a number of perceptual areas including, but not limited to:

1. *Auditory Modality*—the delivery of information through sound.

2. *Visual Modality*—the delivery of information through sight.

3. *Tactile Modality*—the delivery of information through touching.

4. *Kinesthetic Modality*—the delivery of information through movement.

5. *Reception*—the initial receiving of information.

6. *Perception*—the initial organization of information.

7. *Association or Organization*—relating new information to other information and giving meaning to the information received.

8. *Memory*—the storage or retrieval process that facilitates the associational process to give meaning to information or help in relating new concepts to other information that might have already been learned.

9. *Expression*—the output of information through vocal, motoric, or written responses.

The objectives of the perceptual assessment are:

- To help determine the child's stronger and weaker modalities for learning. Some children are visual learners, some are auditory, and some learn best through a combination of modalities. However, if a child is a strong visual learner in a class where the teacher relies on auditory lectures, then it is possible that his or her ability to process information may be hampered.

- To discover information that is very useful when making practical recommendations to teachers about how to best input information to assist the child's ability to learn.

■ To help determine a child's stronger and weaker processing areas. A child having problems in memory and expression will fall behind the rest of the class very quickly. The longer these processing difficulties continue, the greater the chance that secondary emotional problems—emotional problems resulting from continued frustration with the ability to learn—will develop.

Occupational Therapy Evaluation

The team may consider this evaluation when the child is exhibiting problems involving fine-motor and upper body functions. Examples of these would include abnormal movement patterns, sensory problems (sensitivity to sound, visual changes, etc.), hardship with daily living activities, organizational problems, attention-span difficulties, interpersonal problems, and problems with assistive technology equipment.

Physical Therapy Evaluation

The team may consider this evaluation when the child is exhibiting problems with lower body and gross motor areas. Examples of these include range-of-motion difficulties, architectural barrier problems, problems using special equipment, problems with posture, gait, endurance, joint abnormalities, manual dexterity, and checking prosthetic and orthotic devices.

2.26 Parental Participation in the Assessment Process

Once the Child Study Team (CST) has made a formal referral for assessment to the Multidisciplinary Team (MDT) for a child with a suspected disability, the parents need to be called in to provide pertinent background information that will assist in the assessment process. The participation of the parents is crucial to this process.

While designing, conducting, interpreting, and paying for the assessments are the school system's responsibilities, parents have an important part to play before, during, and after the evaluation. There is a range of ways in which parents may involve themselves in the assessment of their child. The extent of their involvement, however, is a personal decision and will vary from family to family.

Waterman (1994) lists parental options, responsibilities, and expectations prior to an assessment for a suspected disability:

- Parents may initiate the assessment process by requesting that the school system evaluate their child for the presence of a disability and the need for special education.

- Before any initial evaluation of the child may be conducted, the school must notify parents and obtain their written consent.

- Parents may wish to talk with the person responsible for conducting the evaluation to find out what the evaluation will involve.

- Parents may find it very useful to become informed about assessment issues in general and any specific issues relevant to their child (e.g., assessment of minority children, use of specific tests or assessment techniques with a specific disability).

- Parents should advocate a comprehensive evaluation of their child—one that investigates all skill areas apparently affected by the suspected disability and that uses multiple means of collecting information (e.g., observations, interviews, alternative approaches).

- Parents may suggest to the MDT specific questions they would like to see addressed through the assessment.

- Parents should inform the MDT of any special accommodations the child will need (e.g., removing time limits from tests, conducting interviews/testing in the child's native language, or adapting the testing environment to the child's specific physical and other needs).

- Parents should inform the MDT if they themselves need an interpreter or other special accommodations during any of their discussions with the school.

- Parents may prepare their child for the assessment process, explaining what will happen and, where necessary, reducing the child's anxiety. It may help the child to know that he or she will not be receiving a "grade" on the tests he or she will be taking.

- Parents need to share with the MDT their insights into the child's background (developmental, medical, and academic) and past and present school performance.

- Parents may wish to share with the MDT any prior school records, reports, tests, or evaluation information available on their child.

- Parents may need to share information about cultural differences that can illuminate the MDT's understanding of the student.

- Parents need to make every effort to attend interviews the MDT may set up with them and provide information about their child.

2.27   How to Conduct Parent Intakes

A parent intake should be done with sensitivity and diplomacy. Keep in mind that while some questions may not offend most parents, some parents may perceive them as intrusive. The questions should be specific enough to help in the diagnosis of the problem, but not so specific as to place the parent in a vulnerable and defensive position. There are four main areas usually covered in a parent intake. They are as follows:

1. Identifying Data and Family Information

2. Developmental History

3. Academic History

4. Social History

Examples of specific information that may need to be provided for each of the above areas include:

■ *Identifying Data and Family Information:* Confirmation of names, addresses, phone numbers, ages and dates of birth for the child, siblings, and parents; parents' occupations; other adults residing within the home; marital status of parents.

■ *Developmental History:* Length of delivery, type of delivery, complications (if any), approximate ages of critical stages (e.g., walking, talking), hospital stays, illnesses other than normal ones, sleeping habits, eating habits, high fevers, last eye exam, last hearing exam, falls or injuries, traumatic experiences, medications, prior testing.

■ *Academic History:* Number of schools attended, types of schools attended, adjustment to kindergarten, best school years, worst school years, best subjects, worse subjects, prior teacher reports, prior teacher comments, homework, behavior.

■ *Social History:* Groups or organizations, social behavior in a group situation, hobbies, areas of interest, circles of friends, sports activities.

EXAMPLE OF PARENT INTAKE FORM

Identifying Data

Name of Student: *Tyrome Marshall*

Address: *12 Court Street*

Phone: *675-7863*

Date of Birth: *3/4/93*

Age: *9–1*

Siblings:

(Brothers—names and ages): *Mohammed, age15*

(Sisters—names and ages): *Sari, age 4*

Mother's Name: *Halle*   Father's name: *Benjamin*

Mother's occupation: *Medical Technician*

Father's occupation: *Accountant*

Referred by: *Teacher*

Grade: *4*

School: *Holland Avenue*

Developmental History

Length of pregnancy: *full term*

Type of delivery: *forceps*

Complications: *Apgar score 7, jaundice at birth*

Long hospital stays: *None*

Falls or injuries: *None*

Allergies: *Early food allergies, none recently*

Medication: *None at present*

Early milestones (e.g., walking, talking, toilet training): *According to parent, Tyrome was late in walking and talking in comparison to brother. He was toilet trained at 3. Parent added that he seemed to be slower than usual in learning things.*

Traumatic experiences: *None*

Previous psychological evaluations or treatment (Please explain reasons and dates): *None. However parent indicated that 1st grade teacher suggested it but the teacher never followed through.*

Previous psychiatric hospitalizations: *No*

(continued)

Sleep disturbances: *Trouble falling asleep, somnambulism at age 5 but only lasted a few weeks. Talks a great deal in his sleep lately.*

Eating disturbances: *Picky eater, likes sweets*

Last vision and hearing exams and results: *Last eye test in school indicated 20/30. Last hearing test in school was inconclusive. Parent has not followed through on nurse's request for an outside evaluation.*

Excessively high fevers: *No*

Childhood illnesses: *Normal ones*

Academic History

Nursery school experience: *Tyrome had difficulty adjusting to nursery school. The teacher considered him very immature, and his skills were well below those of his peers. He struggled through the year.*

Kindergarten experience (adjustment, comments etc.): *Tyrome's difficulties increased. According to the parent, he had problems with reading and social difficulties. His gross and fine motor skills were immature.*

First grade through sixth grade (teacher's comments, traumatic experiences, strength areas, comments, etc): *According to past teachers, Tyrome struggled through the years. He was a nice boy and polite and at times tried hard. But in the later grades 2 and 3, his behavior and academics began to falter. Teachers always considered referral but felt he might grow out of it.*

Subjects that presented the most difficulty: *Reading, math, spelling*

Subjects that were the least difficult: *Science*

Most recent report card grades (if applicable): *Tyrome has received mostly NEEDS TO IMPROVE on his report card.*

Social History

Groups or organizations: *Tried Boy Scouts but dropped out. Started Little League but became frustrated.*

Social involvement as perceived by parent: *Inconsistent. He does not seem to reach out to kids, and lately he spends a great deal of time alone.*

Hobbies or interests: *Baseball cards, science.*

2.28   Confidentiality

Information about the child collected through the assessment automatically becomes a part of a child's school records. The school district should establish policies regarding confidentiality of information contained in the school record, such as informing the parent and the child (above 18) of their right to privacy, of who has access to the information, and of their right to challenge those records should they be inaccurate, misleading, or otherwise inappropriate. To communicate this information to the parent, handouts describing the district's policy on confidentiality of school records are usually given out on the day of the intake.

Because persons conducting the evaluation are involved in collecting confidential information about a child's health status and educational development, it is very important that verbal as well as written accounts of the child's performance be held in the strictest confidence. Personnel involved in the evaluation should treat their own impressions and concerns about the children they see in a confidential manner and should refrain from talking about children and their performance with people not directly involved with conducting the evaluation. If parents ask how their child is doing during the evaluation, explain that the screening results are meaningful only after all the testing has been completed and their child's performance in all areas has been recorded. You should also inform them at this time that they are entitled to receive a complete typed report from the evaluation personnel. The person in charge of evaluation may choose to designate certain persons responsible for answering specific questions about the evaluation instruments, children's responses, and reports.

At this point and with the written consent of the parent or legal guardian, the MDT will move to the evaluation phase of the assessment process. The next several chapters will address the various evaluation instruments available to the MDT in the formal evaluation of a child with a suspected disability.

2.29   Other Specialists and Their Roles in Helping Children

▪ *Audiologists* are trained to identify and measure types and degrees of hearing loss, assess how disabling the condition is, recommend rehabilitation, fit hearing aids, and counsel parents on how to help their child adjust to a hearing loss.

▪ *Learning Disability Teacher Consultant (LDTC)* is an individual with a graduate degree that enables him or her to assess a student's learning and performance and consults with teachers on issues pertaining to the education of a child with disabilities, the theoretical and physiological basis of learning and remediation of basic skills, as well as the diagnosis and correction of learning problems.

▪ *Occupational Therapists* are trained to build or rehabilitate the basic skills involved in everyday living by developing treatment activities and by adapting materials to suit the special needs of the child who is disabled. They focus on fine-motor activities—especially the use of hands and fingers, on coordination of movement, and on self-help skills.

▪ *Ophthalmologists* are physicians who specialize in the diagnosis of the eye and structures related to it.

▪ *Orthopedists* are surgeons who specialize in preserving and restoring the function of the skeletal system, as well as muscles, joints, tendons, ligaments, nerves, and blood vessels.

▪ *Pediatricians* are physicians who specialize in the treatment of children, their development and care, and their diseases.

▪ *Physical Therapists* are skilled in the techniques of treatment to rehabilitate and restore fundamental body movements after illness or injury. PTs work under the supervision of a physician. Their focus is on large muscle and gross motor activities.

▪ *Psychiatrists* are physicians who specialize in the diagnosis and treatment of emotional problems and mental disorders. They are trained in psychotherapy.

▪ *Psychologists* are trained in the assessment and treatment of people with emotional, interpersonal, or behavioral problems. They work in a variety of settings—schools, clinics, mental health centers, and hospitals. School psychologists specialize in counseling students and their families and work with families, teachers, and other school staff to improve the child's ability to function in a school setting. Only psychologists conduct psychological testing done in schools. A behavioral psychologist specializes in the objective observation and analysis of behavior and in developing behavior management programs.

▪ *Speech Pathologists* are trained in the study of human communication, its normal development, and its disorders. They evaluate the reception, integration, and expression of speech and language of children or adults, and assist in treating whatever problems exist.

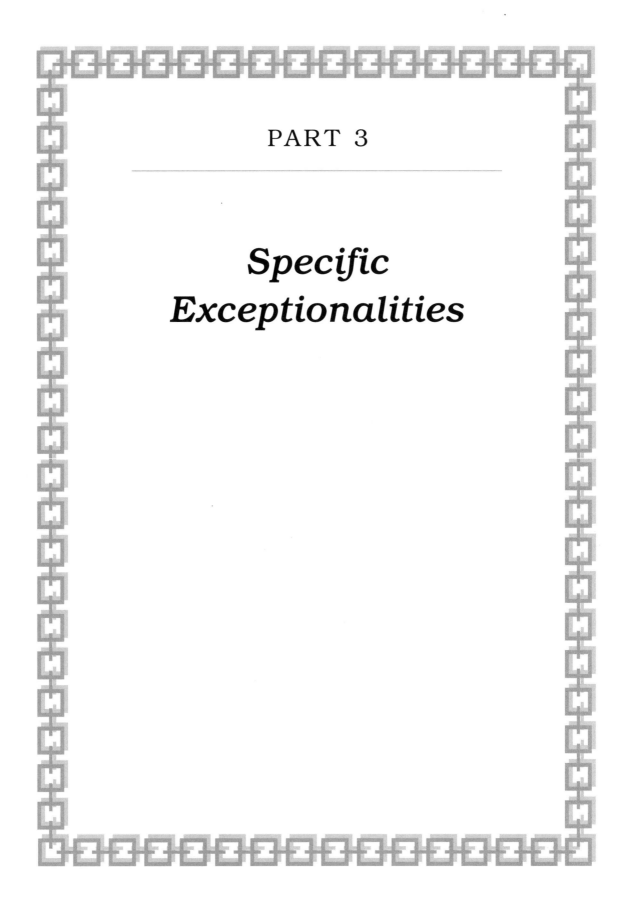

PART 3

Specific Exceptionalities

3.1   Principles of Normal Development

- The sequence of development is, in general, the same for all children, but each child develops at his/her own rate and to his/her own level.

- Rates of growth and development vary between individuals and between different developmental areas within the same individual.

- Children progress step-by-step in orderly sequences of development. Each accomplishment prepares the way for the next one.

- Individual differences are apparent in young children at a very early age; they also tend to remain apparent over time.

- Early development proceeds by process of increasing differentiation and integration whereby early mass responsiveness (e.g., a startled newborn's whole body tenses) develops into a more localized and specific type of responsiveness (e.g., an older child may just turn his/her head or shut eyes when startled).

- As development proceeds, small units of behavior (e.g., hand movements) are combined and integrated into larger, functional behaviors (e.g., reaching and grasping objects).

- Progress in development is often uneven; the rate of change in one skill area may vary while other skills are being learned.

- Motor development and voluntary movements progress from the head downward and from the trunk outward.

- There are times during which children show that they are ready for new learning. These periods are called critical learning periods. Prior to and after such periods, learning may prove to be more difficult.

- Most children give their caregivers subtle behavioral cues about their needs and readiness for new learning. Progress is best when the stimulation provided matches the child's readiness to learn.

- As children develop increasing capacities for learning and doing, they tend to use these capacities.

- All areas of development (e.g., motor development, conceptual developments) are interrelated.

- A child's genetic factors, social and cultural background, and family influence the processes and outcome of development.

- Development results from both growth and learning, each of which continually influences the other.

3.2 Gross Motor Developmental Milestones

Activity	Approximate age
Child raises chin while lying on stomach.	1 month
Child raises chest while lying on stomach.	2 months
Child reaches for objects, but misses them.	3 months
Child's head is set forward, steady, lumbar curvature.	4 months
Child turns over.	4–6 months
Child sits on lap and grasps object.	5 months
Child sits in high chair and grasps dangling object.	6 months
Child sits with good posture.	10 months
Child creeps and crawls.	11 months
Child pulls to standing position.	11 months
Child climbs stairs and steps.	13 months
Child walks alone unsupported, seldom falls.	18 months
Child sits self in small chair.	18 months
Child walks carrying large objects.	20 months
Child raises self from sitting position with hips first.	22 months
Child runs well without falling.	2 years
Child kicks ball without overbalancing.	2 years
Child jumps with both feet in place.	2½ years
Child picks up objects from floor without falling over.	2½ years
Child stands on one foot, even momentarily.	3 years
Child pedals tricycle.	3 years

3.3 Receptive Language Milestones

Activity	Approximate age
Child understands a few words.	11 months
Child points to one named body part on request.	1 year
Child stops activity to name.	1 year
Child stops activity to "no."	1 year
Child points to familiar persons, animals, toys on request.	15 months
Child follows one-step simple commands.	15 months
Child points to three named body parts on request.	17 months
Child follows two-step command.	20 months
Child points to five or six pictures of common objects on request.	21 months
Child points to five body parts on self or doll.	22 months
Child follows three-step command given in one long utterance.	2 years
Child understands 200–400 words.	2 years
Child understands 800 words.	3 years
Child verbalizes past experiences.	3 years
Child points to big, little, soft, loud.	3 years
Child follows commands with 2–3 actions.	4 years
Child understands approximately 1,500 words.	4 years

3.4 Expressive Language Milestones

Activity	Approximate age
Child says first word.	10 months
Child shakes head and says "no-no."	11 months
Child imitates the sounds of others (e.g., "mama").	1 year
Child uses three words in speaking vocabulary.	13 months
Child uses verbs.	14 months
Child uses at least six words.	17 months
Child refers to self by name.	21 months
Child uses "me" and "you."	23 months
Child says 50–200 words.	2 years
Child knows full name.	2 years
Child uses plurals.	2 years
Child asks questions.	2½ years
Child uses negatives in speech.	2½ years
Child enunciates vowel sounds.	3 years
Child enunciates consonant sounds.	3 years
Child speaks with 75–80 percent intelligibility.	3 years
Child uses three- and four-syllable words.	4 years
Child says six- to eight-word sentences.	4 years
Child's speech is about 90–95 percent intelligible.	4 years

3.5   Milestones for Dressing Skills

Activity	Approximate age
Child pulls and tugs at clothing.	3–4 months
Child cooperates in dressing by holding out limbs.	1 year
Child removes shoes by self.	14 months
Child places socks on feet by self.	18 months
Child puts on own hat.	18 months
Child pulls up pants.	18 months
Child unzips.	18–20 months
Child attempts to put on own shoes.	19 months
Child can dress self partially.	2 years
Child pulls up pants, unassisted.	2 years
Child undresses self.	2½ years
Child puts on shirt and coat.	2½ years
Child attempts to place shoes on feet.	2½ years
Child chooses own outfit.	3 years
Child unbuttons clothes.	3 years
Child puts on clothing in the correct direction.	3½ years
Child dresses and undresses with supervision (not including shoe laces and so on).	4 years
Child buttons front buttons on clothing.	52–56 months
Child zips up and down and snaps simple snaps.	5 years
Child ties shoes with bows.	5½ years
Child unlaces bows on shoes.	5½ years
Child dresses self completely.	5½ years

3.6   Milestones for Eating Skills

Activity	Approximate age
Child sucks and swallows liquids.	Birth
Child has gagging reflex.	Birth
Child sucks and swallows liquids supplied from spoons.	2 months
Child eats strained baby foods from spoon.	3 months
Child brings hand against bottle when eating.	3 months
Child sips from a cup that is held for him or her.	4 months
Child becomes excited when hearing sounds of food preparation.	4 months
Child holds spoon but needs assistance.	5 months
Child feeds self soft food.	6 months
Child begins to bite and chew food.	6 months
Child holds own baby bottle.	7 months
Child chews small lumpy food.	8 months
Child takes bottle out of mouth and replaces it.	9 months
Child uses fingers to feed self.	10 months
Child holds cup with two hands.	1 year
Child chews table food.	13–15 months
Child grasps spoon and places in mouth with some spilling.	15 months
Child manages spoon without assistance with little spilling.	1½ years
Child requests food when hungry.	23 months
Child requests liquids when thirsty.	23 months
Child holds a small glass with one hand, unassisted.	2 years
Child uses a fork to grab food.	3 years
Child spreads butter on bread.	3 years
Child helps set table.	4 years
Child uses a fork to separate food.	4 years
Child pours water from a pitcher into a glass.	4 years
Child uses a knife to cut food.	5 years
Child sets the table without assistance.	6 years

3.7   Milestones for Toileting and Grooming Skills

Grooming Activity

	Approximate Age
Child holds on to side of tub and cries when removed.	5 months
Child splashes water with hands and feet.	6 months
Child grimaces when face is washed with cloth.	6 months
Child exhibits resistance to washing face.	8 months
Child opens and pulls out drawers.	1½ years
Child washes hands and face by self, but not well.	2 years
Child washes front of body while in bath.	2 years
Child runs a brush through hair.	2½ years
Child brushes teeth with assistance.	3½ years
Child washes and dries face with towel by self.	4 years
Child brushes teeth with no assistance.	4 years
Child puts away own toys by self with supervision.	4 years
Child hangs up coat by self on hook.	4 years
Child brushes hair independently.	5 years
Child hangs up own clothes without supervision.	5 years
Child washes self alone.	6 years

Toileting Activity

	Approximate Age
Child has about four bowel movements a day associated with waking up.	1 month
Child has two bowel movements a day, either at waking or after being fed.	2 months
Child shows some delay between feeding and elimination.	4 months
Child stays dry for one- to two-hour intervals.	7 months
Child may awaken at night and cry to be changed.	1½ years
Child may indicate wet pants.	1½ years
Child has an occasional accident.	22 months
Child uses same word for both functions of elimination.	22 months
Child begins to differentiate between elimination functions.	2 years
Child climbs onto toilet by self.	2½ years
Child can control bladder for up to 5 hours.	2½ years
Child begins to develop a routine for elimination.	3 years
Child attempts to wipe self but not successful.	3½ years
Child stays dry at night.	4 years
Child toilets self without assistance.	5 years
Child washes and dries own hands after toileting.	5 years
Child has bowel movement a day.	5 years

3.8   Fact Sheet on Autism

DEFINITION

Autism and Pervasive Developmental Disorder NOS (not otherwise specified) are developmental disabilities that share many of the same characteristics. Usually evident by age 3, autism and PDDNOS are neurological disorders that affect a child's ability to communicate, understand language, play, and relate to others.

In the diagnostic manual used to classify disabilities, the DSM-IV-TR (American Psychiatric Association, 2000), "autistic disorder" is listed as a category under the heading of "Pervasive Developmental Disorders." A diagnosis of autistic disorder is made when an individual displays 6 or more of 12 symptoms listed across three major areas: social interaction, communication, and behavior. When children display similar behaviors but do not meet the criteria for autistic disorder, they may receive a diagnosis of Pervasive Developmental Disorder NOS. Although the diagnosis is referred to as PDDNOS, in this fact sheet, we refer to the diagnosis as PDD, as it is more commonly known.

Autistic disorder is one of the disabilities specifically defined in the Individuals with Disabilities Education Act (IDEA), the federal legislation under which children and youth with disabilities receive special education and related services. IDEA, which uses the term "autism," defines the disorder as "a developmental disability significantly affecting verbal and nonverbal communication and social interaction, usually evident before age 3, that adversely affects a child's educational performance. Other characteristics often associated with autism are engagement in repetitive activities and stereotyped movements, resistance to environmental change or change in daily routines, and unusual responses to sensory experiences." (In keeping with the IDEA and the way in which this disorder is generally referred to in the field, we will use the term autism throughout the remainder of this fact sheet.)

Due to the similarity of behaviors associated with autism and PDD, use of the term pervasive developmental disorder has caused some confusion among parents and professionals. However, the treatment and educational needs are similar for both diagnoses.

INCIDENCE

Autism and PDD occur in approximately 5 to 15 per 10,000 births. These disorders are four times more common in boys than girls.

The causes of autism and PDD are unknown. Currently, researchers are investigating areas such as neurological damage and biochemical imbalance in the brain. These disorders are not caused by psychological factors.

CHARACTERISTICS

Some or all of the following characteristics may be observed in mild-to-severe forms:

- Communication problems (e.g., using and understanding language, gestures, and facial expressions);
- Difficulty in relating to people, objects, and events;

3.8 continued

- Unusual play with toys and other objects;
- Difficulty with changes in routine or familiar surroundings; and
- Repetitive body movements or behavior patterns.

Children with autism or PDD vary widely in abilities, intelligence, and behaviors. Some do not speak; others have limited language that often includes repeated phrases or conversations. Those with more advanced language skills tend to use a small range of topics and have difficulty with abstract concepts. Repetitive play skills, a limited range of interests, and impaired social skills are generally evident as well. Unusual responses to sensory information—for example, loud noises, lights, and certain textures of food or fabrics—are also common.

EDUCATIONAL IMPLICATIONS

Early diagnosis and appropriate educational programs are very important to children with autism or PDD. Public Law 105-17, the Individuals with Disabilities Education Act (IDEA), formerly the Education of the Handicapped Act, includes autism as a disability category. From the age of 3, children with autism and PDD are eligible for an educational program appropriate to their individual needs. Educational programs for students with autism or PDD focus on improving communication, social, academic, behavioral, and daily living skills. Behavior and communication problems that interfere with learning sometimes require the assistance of a knowledgeable professional in the autism field who develops and helps to implement a plan that can be carried out at home and school.

The classroom environment should be structured so that the program is consistent and predictable. Students with autism or PDD learn better and are less confused when information is presented visually as well as verbally. Interaction with nondisabled peers is also important, for these students provide models of appropriate language, social, and behavior skills. To overcome frequent problems in generalizing skills learned at school, it is very important to develop programs with parents, so that learning activities, experiences, and approaches can be carried over into the home and community.

With educational programs designed to meet a student's individual needs and with specialized adult support services in employment and living arrangements, children and adults with autism or PDD can live and work in the community.

3.9 Symptoms of Pervasive Developmental Disorder Not Otherwise Specified (PDDNOS)

THE SYMPTOMS AND SIGNS OF PDDNOS

Generally, children are 3 to 4 years old before they exhibit enough symptoms for parents to seek a diagnosis. There is no set pattern of symptoms and signs in children with PDDNOS. It is important to realize that a very wide range of diversity is seen in children with PDDNOS. All the types of behavior described in this section are common in these children, but a single child seldom exhibits all of them at one time. In other words, all children with PDDNOS do not have the same degree or intensity of the disorder. PDDNOS can be mild, with the child exhibiting a few symptoms while in the school or neighborhood environment. Other children may have a more severe form of PDDNOS and have difficulties in all areas of their lives. Because of the possibility that PDDNOS and Autistic Disorder are on a continuum, many clinical features described in the following section are very similar to those being described in the literature for Autistic Disorder.

Deficits in Social Behavior

- Infants may tend to avoid eye contact and demonstrate little interest in the human voice.

- They do not usually put up their arms to be picked up in the way that most children typically do.

- They may seem indifferent to affection and seldom show facial responsiveness. As a result, parents often think the child is deaf.

- In children with fewer delays, lack of social responsiveness may not be obvious until well into the second or third year of life.

- In early childhood, children with PDDNOS may continue to show a lack of eye contact, but they may enjoy a tickle or may passively accept physical contact.

- They may not develop typical attachment behavior, and there may seem to be a failure to bond. Generally, they do not follow their parents about the house.

- The majority do not show normal separation; children may approach a stranger almost as readily as they do their parents.

- Many such children show a lack of interest in being with other children. They may even actively avoid other children.

- In middle childhood, such children may develop a greater awareness or attachment to parents and other familiar adults. However, social difficulties continue.

- They still have problems with group games and forming peer relations. Some of the children with less severe PDDNOS may become involved in other children's games.

- As these children grow older, they may become affectionate and friendly with their parents and siblings.

3.9 continued

- However, they still often have difficulty understanding the complexity of social relationships.
- Some individuals with less severe impairments may demonstrate a desire for friendships. But a lack of response to other people's interests and emotions, as well as a lack of understanding of humor, often results in these youngsters saying or doing things that can slow the development of friendships.

Impairment in Nonverbal Communication

- In early childhood, children with PDDNOS may develop the concrete gesture of pulling adults by the hand to the object that is wanted. They often do this without accompanying facial expressions.
- They seldom nod or shake their heads to substitute for or to accompany speech.
- They generally do not participate in games that involve imitation.
- They are less likely than typical children to copy their parents' activity.
- In middle and late childhood, such children may not frequently use gestures, even when they understand other people's gestures fairly well.
- Some children do develop imitative play, but this tends to be a repetitive type of interaction.
- Generally, children with PDDNOS are able to show joy, fear, or anger, but they may only show the extreme of emotions.
- They often do not use facial expressions that ordinarily show subtle emotion.

Impairment in Understanding Speech

- Comprehension of speech in children with PDDNOS is impaired to varying degrees, depending on where the child is within the wide spectrum of PDDNOS.
- Individuals with PDDNOS who also have mental retardation may never develop more than a limited understanding of speech.
- Children who have less severe impairments may follow simple instructions if given in an immediate context or with the aid of gestures (e.g., telling the child to "put your glass on the counter," while pointing to the counter).
- When impairment is mild, only the comprehension of subtle or abstract meanings may be affected. Humor, sarcasm, and common sayings (e.g., "it's raining cats and dogs") can be confusing for individuals with the mildest PDDNOS.

Impairment in Speech Development

- Many infants with PDDNOS do not babble, or may begin to babble in their first year but then stop. When the child develops speech, he or she often exhibits abnormalities.

- Echolalia (seemingly meaningless repetition of words or phrases) may be the only kind of speech some children acquire. Though echolalic speech might be produced quite accurately, the child may have limited comprehension of the meaning.

- Some children develop the appropriate use of phrases copied from others. This is often accompanied by pronoun reversal in the early stages of language development. For instance, when the child is asked, "How are you?" he or she may answer "You are fine."

- The actual production of speech may be impaired. The child's speech may be like that of a robot, characterized by a monotonous, flat delivery with little change in pitch, change of emphasis, or emotional expression.

- Problems of pronunciation are common in young children with PDDNOS, but these often diminish as the child gets older.

- There may be a striking contrast between clearly enunciated echolalic speech and poorly pronounced spontaneous speech.

- Some children have a chanting or singsong speech, with odd prolongation of sounds, syllables, and words.

- A question-like intonation may be used for statements.

- Odd breathing rhythms may produce staccato speech in some children.

Abnormal grammar is frequently present in the spontaneous speech of verbal children with PDDNOS. As a result:

- Phrases may be telegraphic (brief and monotone) and distorted.

- Words of similar sound or related meaning may be muddled.

- Some objects may be labeled by their use.

- New words may be coined.

- Prepositions, conjunctions, and pronouns may be dropped from phrases or used incorrectly.

3.10 Criteria Used to Diagnose Autistic Disorder

Kanner

- The child shows an inability to relate to people and extreme autistic aloneness.
- The child fails to assume an anticipatory posture in preparation to being picked up.
- The child exhibits speech problems such as delayed echolalia, repetition of personal pronouns, and just mute.
- The child shows an anxious obsessive desire for the maintenance of sameness.
- The child shows a limitation in the variety of spontaneous activity.
- The child reacts to external intrusions such as food, loud noises, and moving objects.
- The child seems interested in objects and reaches out to people as though they were objects.
- The child may show excellent rote memory.
- The child may appear to be physically normal.
- The child may come from a highly intelligent family.

Rutter

- The child exhibits profound and general failure to develop social relationships.
- The child exhibits language retardation with impaired comprehension, echolalia, and pronominal reversal.
- The child exhibits ritualistic or compulsive phenomena.
- The child may show repetitive movements.
- The child may exhibit a short attention span.
- The child may resort to frequent self-injury.
- The child may exhibit delayed bowel movements.

DSM-IV-R

- The child exhibits lack of awareness of the existence or feelings of others.
- The child exhibits no or abnormal seeking of comfort at times of distress.
- The child exhibits no or impaired imitation.
- The child exhibits no or abnormal social play.
- The child exhibits gross impairment in ability to make peer friendships.
- The child exhibits no mode of communication, such as communicative babbling, facial expression, gesture, mime, or spoken language.
- The child exhibits markedly abnormal nonverbal communication.
- The child exhibits absence of imaginative activity.

- The child exhibits marked abnormalities in the production of speech, including volume, pitch, stress, rate, rhythm, and intonation.
- The child exhibits marked abnormalities in the form or content of speech, including stereotyped and repetitive use of speech.
- The child exhibits marked impairment in the ability to initiate or sustain a conversation with others, despite adequate speech.
- The child exhibits stereotyped body movements.
- The child exhibits persistent preoccupation with parts of objects.
- The child exhibits marked distress over changes in trivial aspects of the environment.
- The child exhibits unreasonable insistence on following routines in precise detail.
- The child exhibits marked restricted range of interests and a preoccupation with one narrow interest.

3.11 Interdisciplinary Diagnosis of Autism

- *Audiologist*—The autistic child may be evaluated by an audiologist either as part of a multidisciplinary assessment or as a referral from a pediatrician who wants to rule out a hearing loss as a possible cause for the child's lack of responsiveness. Specialized procedures and equipment for eliciting responses to sounds have been developed for other groups of people who are difficult to test, and they can be applied to autistic children. Two such methods are:

  CORA (Conditioned Orienting Reflex Audiometry): a technique involving the pairing of an attractive visual object with a sound.

  TROCA (Tangible Reinforcement Operant Conditioning Audiometry): a technique that uses a machine that dispenses edible reinforcement (candy) when the child pushes a button in response to a sound.

- *Social Worker*—The social worker is able to contribute to the diagnostic treatment process provided to the family of an autistic child. The social worker provides the team with information on family dynamics, patterns of interaction among various family members, family member's perception of the autistic child, parenting responsibilities, and parent's use of behavior management techniques.

- *Pediatrician*—Different techniques are sometimes utilized by the physician when dealing with an autistic child. First, the medical history is obtained from records and the parents without the child present. Second, the pediatrician observes the child in the examination room with the parents present. The information gathered includes activity level, general state of physical health and development, and gross and fine motor coordination. Third, the general physical and neurological examinations are conducted with special attention directed toward looking for indicators of organic, not psychological dysfunction. The pediatrician does not make a diagnosis of autism, although it is possibly suggested by the conclusions.

- *Psychiatrist/Psychologist*—The psychiatrist and the psychologist are responsible for the diagnosis of autism and the psychological evaluations involved in this process. When first encountered by parents, psychiatrists and psychologists gather pertinent developmental history. This information—coupled with clinical interviews, evaluations, and parent intakes—assists in the diagnosis of autism.

- *Special Education Teacher*—The special education teacher may be involved on two separate levels. He or she may first be involved in the diagnostic evaluation of the child suspected of a disability. Second, the special education teacher will be responsible for carrying out the required services that will assist in the education of the child.

- *Speech and Language Therapist*—The parents of a potentially autistic child frequently begin their search for diagnostic answers at a speech and hearing clinic, because the child is unresponsive to speech and has either no language or unusual patterns of communication. The speech and language pathologist evaluates movement and behavior, cognitive skills, expressive language, deviant language patterns, and receptive language.

3.12 ADHD Fact Sheet

WHAT IS ADHD?

Attention Deficit Hyperactivity Disorder (ADHD) is a condition that can make it difficult for a person to sit still, control behavior, and pay attention. These difficulties usually begin before the person is 7 years old. However, these behaviors may not be noticed until the child is older.

Researchers who study the brain are coming closer to understanding what may cause ADHD. They believe that some people with ADHD do not have enough of certain chemicals (called neurotransmitters) in their brain. These chemicals help the brain control behavior. There are many things that both parents and teachers can do to help a child with ADHD. (See Lists 3.16 and 3.17.)

HOW COMMON IS ADHD?

As many as 5 out of every 100 children in school may have ADHD. Boys are three times more likely than girls to have ADHD.

WHAT ARE THE SIGNS OF ADHD?

There are three main signs, or symptoms, of ADHD. These are:

- Problems with paying attention
- Being very active (called hyperactivity)
- Acting before thinking (called impulsivity)

More information about these symptoms is listed in Diagnostic and Statistical Manual of Mental Disorders (DSM), which is published by the American Psychiatric Association (1994). Based on these symptoms, three types of ADHD have been found:

- *Inattentive type*, where the person cannot seem to get focused or stay focused on a task or activity
- *Hyperactive-impulsive type*, where the person is very active and often acts without thinking
- *Combined type*, where the person is inattentive, impulsive, and too active

Inattentive Type

Many children with ADHD have problems paying attention. Children with the inattentive type of ADHD often:

- Can't focus on details
- Can't stay focused on play or school work
- Don't follow through on instructions or finish school work or chores
- Can't seem to organize tasks and activities

3.12 continued

- Get distracted easily
- Lose things such as toys, schoolwork, and books (APA, 1994, pp. 83–84)

Hyperactive-Impulsive Type

Being too active is probably the most visible sign of ADHD. The hyperactive child is "always on the go." (As he or she gets older, the level of activity may decrease.) These children also act before thinking (impulsivity). For example, they may run across a road without looking or climb to the top of very tall trees. They may be surprised to find themselves in a dangerous situation. They may have no idea of how to get out of the situation.

Hyperactivity and impulsivity tend to go together. Children with the hyperactive-impulsive type of ADHD often may:

- fidget and squirm
- get out of their chairs when they're not supposed to
- run around or climb constantly
- have trouble playing quietly
- talk too much
- blurt out answers before questions have been completed
- have trouble waiting their turn
- interrupt others when they're talking
- butt in on the games others are playing (APA, 1994, p. 84)

Combined Type

Children with the combined type of ADHD have symptoms of both of the types described above. They have problems with paying attention, with hyperactivity, and with controlling their impulses.

Of course, from time to time, all children are inattentive, impulsive, and too active. With children who have ADHD, these behaviors are the rule, not the exception.

These behaviors can cause a child to have real problems at home, at school, and with friends. As a result, many children with ADHD will feel anxious, unsure of themselves, and depressed. These feelings are not symptoms of ADHD. They result from having problems again and again at home and in school.

3.13 Teacher's Checklist for ADHD

Accurate and early diagnosis is crucial for the child with Attention Deficit Disorder. This will facilitate a treatment plan and reduce the chances of secondary problems. Follow the checklist below if you think the child in your class may have Attention Deficit Disorder. Compare the child's behavior to the following list of symptoms:

INATTENTION—AT LEAST THREE OF THE FOLLOWING:
___The child often fails to finish things he or she starts.
___The child often doesn't seem to listen.
___The child is easily distracted.
___The child has difficulty concentrating on schoolwork or other tasks requiring sustained attention.
___The child has difficulty sticking to a play activity.

IMPULSIVITY—AT LEAST THREE OF THE FOLLOWING:
___The child often acts before thinking.
___The child shifts excessively from one activity to another.
___The child has difficulty organizing work.
___The child needs a lot of supervision.
___The child frequently calls out in class.
___The child has difficulty awaiting turn in games or group situations.

HYPERACTIVITY—AT LEAST TWO OF THE FOLLOWING:
___The child runs about or climbs on things excessively.
___The child has difficulty sitting still or fidgets excessively.
___The child has difficulty staying seated.
___The child moves about excessively during sleep.
___The child is always "on the go" or acts as if "driven by a motor."

- Onset before the age of 7
- Duration of at least 6 months
- Not due to schizophrenia, affective disorders (disturbance of mood) or profound retardation

See if the observed behaviors also appear in other school areas as well as in the classroom. If they do, ask the school psychologist to observe the child. If he or she agrees that such a possibility exists, have the psychologist notify the parents so that their doctor can examine the child. The doctor may suggest a neurological examination in order to determine the presence of the disorder. Medication may or may not be

(continued)

suggested. If the disorder is diagnosed, meet with the parent and psychologist in order to plan a management program at home and in school. If the disorder is serious and affects the child's ability to learn, he or she may need to be reviewed by your district's Eligibility Committee so that a suitable program can be determined. A full psychological and academic evaluation would also assist in determining a proper course of action. In conclusion, early diagnosis and active treatment will greatly enhance the child's opportunity for a meaningful and improved life both at home and in school.

3.14 Treatment Plans for Children with Attention Deficit Disorder

PSYCHOTHERAPY

- This process will help the child increase self-esteem, vent feelings and conflicts that may give rise to other symptoms, and gain some control over impulsive actions. It will also assist parents with their approach to behavior management.

- Some therapies may use a form of treatment called behavior modification. This is a process whereby children, assisted by parents and teachers, learn to modify unacceptable behavior through the use of a variety of management techniques including incentive systems, daily report cards, timeout, selective attention, and so on. Some treatment plans will include a combination of both medication and psychotherapy.

PHARMACOLOGICAL INTERVENTION (MEDICATION)

- The types of medication used may vary with age and severity.

- The most common psycho-stimulants used are Ritalin, Cylert, and Dexedrine.

- Such stimulants tend to heighten the child's awareness of the world around him or her and allow for greater selectiveness of behavior. Approximately 50 percent of children with this disorder (ADHD) will exhibit a decrease in inappropriate symptoms. Approximately 10 percent of these children respond so positively to this intervention that their behavior reaches the normative range.

- Reports may indicate improvements in attention span, classroom behavior, and ability to think more clearly during academic tasks.

- Keep in mind that such medication does not "cure" Attention Deficit Hyperactive Disorder; it merely alleviates the primary symptoms.

Other studies have indicated adverse side effects such as reduction of weight, nausea, and loss of appetite. Usually regulating the dosage can relieve such symptoms.

FAMILY THERAPY

This process assists parents in developing techniques that will reduce frustration at home in both the child and other family members.

SCHOOL/TEACHER CONSULTATION

Any treatment plan must include ongoing communication between the therapist/agency and the school and classroom teacher.

Weekly updates and suggestions involving classroom management can reduce frustration and feelings of helplessness on the part of the child and the teacher.

3.15 Behavior Management Techniques for Children with ADHD

Classroom teachers of children with ADHD can adjust certain factors to accommodate the individual needs of these children. Some examples include:

Social Interaction

- Identify appropriate social behavior for the child and reinforce it when exhibited.

- Sit with the child and set up a social contract, which clearly outlines what goals he/she would like to accomplish. Also include the behaviors that may be required to attain these goals.

- Use verbal and written praise whenever possible. This type of praise gives the child the feedback necessary to understand his/her own behavior.

- Expose the child to small-group interactions at first. Placing a child with ADHD in large groups may be detrimental. Allow the group to be goal-oriented and interdependent so that its members can accomplish some simple task and feel success.

- Use peer interaction and cooperative learning for certain academic tasks, which do not require sitting for long periods of time.

- Try to identify strengths in the child that can be publicly announced or praised. In this way, the other students will develop a more positive perception of the child.

- Role-play social situations with the child emphasizing the use of specific skills. In this way, the child can develop a "toolbox" of skills that can be applied at a later time.

Organizational Ability

- Prepare a copy of the homework assignments and hand it to the child at the end of the day. This will alleviate a great deal of stress on the part of the child especially if he or she is disorganized and frequently forgets to copy the assignment. The goal here is to create a comfortable and successful environment. In this case, having the child accomplish the homework is more important than the difficulty encountered in copying the assignment.

- Ask parents to organize the child at night. Have them develop a checklist so that the child's clothes, books, assignments, and so on are ready for the next morning. The stress and disorganization of the morning should be avoided at all costs. This will also make the child feel more secure when going to school.

- Avoid multiple directions or multiple assignments. Allow the child to finish one assignment or direction at a time before going on to the next.

- Reinforce word processing, typing, and spell checks on the computer, and the use of the computer in general. This device can be very motivating, and the end product (i.e., typed report) will make the child feel very good about himself or herself.

- Children with organizational problems will usually maintain disorganized notes, notebooks, desks, and lockers. Try to make it a weekly task to have them organize these areas. Making it part of their contract and routine will also make them feel better about themselves.

Inattentiveness

- If necessary, you may want to have the child finish all assignments in school. There are times when the child may be so inattentive that sending homework home to be accomplished may result in more stress, especially in parental interaction.

- Always allow extra time for completing assignments. Sometimes the time constraints set up by teachers are arbitrary and may not reflect the "real" time required by children with ADHD.

- Try to give shorter but more frequent assignments. Remember, confidence is repeated successful experiences, and the ADHD child will have a greater chance of success with shorter assignments.

- If the child has problems listening and taking notes, have a "buddy" take notes using carbon paper. A copy will then be available for the ADHD child, and the stress of listening and writing will be reduced.

- Stand in close proximity to the student while lecturing.

Impulsiveness

- Be realistic about your expectations concerning the child's behavior. Choose your guidelines wisely. Try to ignore minor incidents and focus on the more intrusive or inappropriate ones.

- Shape appropriate behavior by reinforcing positive responses or actions. Do not hesitate to set up specific consequences for inappropriate actions. In this way the child will have to work at being more consciously aware of his/her behavior.

- Build in periods of time when the child can leave the seat for some activity, e.g., collecting homework, getting some material for you from the closet, and so on.

- Try to offer immediate gratification for appropriate behavior. Waiting too long to reward may lose the desired effect.

- Assign a monitoring "buddy" to offer the child feedback and hints about appropriate and inappropriate behaviors. This may be especially helpful during recess and lunch.

- Try to preempt the child's behavior especially during changes in the schedule. Inform the child about 5 minutes before the change and offer him/her your expectations of what is appropriate behavior during this change.

Academic Skill Areas

- Allow the child to use graph paper while doing math. In this way the child will have a structured environment in which to place numbers. Use very large graph paper so that the child has little difficulty placing one number in each box. This will keep him/her organized and focused.

3.15 continued

- Allow child to use a calculator or basic math tables when doing his/her assignments. The goal here is for successful accomplishment of the assignment. If the child becomes frustrated because he/she can't recall the facts, the child may give up.

- Allow other forms of reporting information. A number of suggestions can be found in List 7.2.

- Do not use bubble sheets. Allow the child to answer directly in the booklet or on the paper. Reducing the amount of movement during academic tasks is more beneficial since ADHD children have difficulty refocusing.

- Use manipulative materials as often as possible

- Use books on tape as well as having the parent tape-record a chapter so that the child can read and listen at the same time.

- Window out single math problems so that the child only sees one at a time. This can be accomplished by cutting out a square on a piece of paper that the child can move from one problem to the next. When he/she does this, all the other problems will be covered.

- For older children, allow them to have a sheet with the formulas already printed. Asking them to memorize may reduce their ability to accomplish the task. The less they have to worry about, the more they may be able to finish.

- Determine what your goal is when presenting an assignment. Once you have done this, pave all the roads for the child up to that point. For example, if your goal is to see if the child can find the circumference of a circle, provide him/her with the formulas, definitions, and examples. These materials will reduce frustration and confusion and will increase chances of success.

- Have the child do 5 problems, 2 questions, and so on, at a time. Then have him/her come up for immediate feedback. Numerous successful tasks can only add to his/her confidence levels. This will also prevent the child from progressing too far and making the same error.

- Use unison reading when having the child read aloud. This means that both you and the child have the same book and read out loud together. The added sensory feedback and pacing will keep the child more focused.

- Try to use interactive CD reading programs if possible. The multisensory stimulation will keep the child focused. However, make sure the program does not require the child to do too many tasks at one time since this could overload him/her.

Emotional Expression

- Be aware of the child's frustration "aura." Knowing when an ADHD child is about to lose focus may prevent inappropriate behavior and feelings of failure. Do not be afraid to discuss this with the child so that both of you can identify the factors that lead to frustration.

- Offer children an emotional vocabulary. Tension and frustration come out either verbally or behaviorally. While ADHD children may not be able to control certain behaviors, the added tension resulting from stress should be reduced through venting. Having the proper labels enhances a child's ability to communicate feelings.

- Teach students the concept of healthy anger. Offer them the rules of healthy anger: Deal with the situation as close to when it happens as possible, deal directly with the person with whom the child is angry, and never use the word "you" when conveying feelings of anger. Using "I," "me," "we," and "us" is preferred.

- Try to empower ADHD children by focusing on all the parts of their lives over which they have control. Children with ADHD frequently feel out of control and helpless. This feeling can lead to depression and victimization. Empowering them with simple jobs, simple hobbies, choices of food, clothing, room arrangement, and so on will offer some control over the environment and may help to balance their feelings of powerlessness.

3.16 Tips for Parents of ADHD Children

- Learn about ADHD. The more you know, the more you can help yourself and your child. See the list of resources and organizations at the end of this book.

- Praise your child when he or she does well. Build your child's abilities. Talk about and encourage his or her strengths and talents.

- Be clear, be consistent, and be positive. Set clear rules for your child. Tell your child what he or she *should* do, not just what he or she shouldn't do. Be clear about what will happen if your child does not follow the rules. Have a reward program for good behavior. Praise your child when he or she exhibits appropriate behaviors.

- Learn about strategies for managing your child's behavior. These include valuable techniques such as: charting, having a reward program, ignoring behaviors, natural consequences, logical consequences, and timeout. Using these strategies will lead to more positive behaviors and cut down on problem behaviors. You can read about these techniques in many books. (See the resources at the end of this book.)

- Talk with your doctor about whether medication will help your child.

- Pay attention to your child's mental health (and your own!). Be open to counseling. It can help you deal with the challenges of raising a child with ADHD. It can help your child deal with frustration, feel better about himself or herself, and learn more about social skills.

- Talk to other parents whose children have ADHD. Parents can share practical advice and emotional support. Call NICHCY to find out how to find parent groups near you.

- Meet with the school and develop an educational plan to address your child's needs. Both you and your child's teachers should get a written copy of this plan.

- Keep in touch with your child's teacher. Tell the teacher how your child is doing at home. Ask how your child is doing in school. Offer support.

3.17 Tips for Teachers Working with Children with ADHD

- Learn more about ADHD. The resources and organizations at the end of this book will help you identify behavior support strategies and effective ways to support the student educationally.

- Figure out what specific things are difficult for the student. For example, one student with ADHD may have trouble starting a task, while another may have trouble ending one task and starting the next. Each student needs different help.

- Post rules, schedules, and assignments. Clear rules and routines will help a student with ADHD. Have set times for specific tasks. Call attention to changes in the schedule.

- Show the student how to use an assignment book and a daily schedule. Also teach study skills and learning strategies, and reinforce these regularly.

- Help the student channel his or her physical activity (e.g., let the student do some work standing up or at the board). Provide regularly scheduled breaks.

- Make sure directions are given step by step, and that the student is following the directions. Give directions both verbally and in writing. Many students with ADHD also benefit from doing the steps as separate tasks.

- Let the student do work on a computer.

- Work together with the student's parents to create and implement an educational plan tailored to meet the student's needs. Regularly share information about how the student is doing at home and at school.

- Have high expectations for the student, but be willing to try new ways of doing things. Be patient. Maximize the student's chances for success.

3.18 Evaluation Procedures that Can Be Used to Measure Giftedness

- Intelligence testing
    - Slosson Intelligence Test
    - Otis-Lennon Mental Ability Test
    - Stanford-Binet Intelligence Test
    - Lorge-Thorndike Intelligence Test
    - Wechsler Intelligence Scales
    - Short Form of Academic Aptitude
    - California Test of Mental Maturity
    - Peabody Picture Vocabulary Test
- Achievement testing
    - Gates-MacGinitie Reading Tests: Reading Skills
    - Metropolitan Readiness Test
    - Stanford Achievement Test
    - California Achievement Test
- Aptitude testing
    - Differential Aptitude Test
- Tests of creativity
    - Torrance Test of Creative Thinking
    - Creativity Assessment Packet (CAP)
- Screening assessment measures
    - Screening Assessment for Gifted Elementary Students-Primary (SAGES-P)
    - Screening Assessment for Gifted Elementary Students (SAGES)
    - Leadership Skills Inventory
    - Process Skills Rating Scales
- Parent recommendation
- Teacher checklist and recommendation
- Behavioral characteristics
    - Renzuili-Hartman Scale for Rating Behavioral Characteristics of Superior Students
- Motor development tests
- Rating scales
- Anecdotal records

- Personality tests
- Interest inventories
- Pupil products and work samples
- Observation of actual performance
- Parental interviews
- Peer nomination rating scales
- Autobiography

3.19   Classroom Activities to Enhance the Development of Thought Processes in the Gifted

Original thinking

- Think of new ways to use a shoe box.
- Write a new ending to a famous play.
- Design a new type of clothing.
- Design a mechanism to allow cars to park in narrow spaces.
- Create a school room of the future.

Fluent thinking

- How many ways can you prevent air pollution?
- What is the most useless expensive thing you can think of?
- Devise a list of household products that are the universal name for all products of that type (e.g., Brillo, Jell-O).
- List all the things you can fit through a hole the size of a dime.
- Name all the things that can be held up with Scotch tape.

Flexible thinking

- What different ways can you find to use a rubber band?
- How many items can you make from metal?
- List all the uses you can think of for a paper clip.
- Think of all the ways you can use items in your garbage can to reduce pollution.
- How would life be different if the wheel had not been discovered?

Elaborative thinking

- Decorate your jacket using an original idea.
- Draw a triangle and make as many objects as you can that include that shape.
- Expand on the safety items for cars that have already been developed.
- Add decorations to the outside of a house that will increase its beauty.
- Take a fictional character from a famous story and give him or her new qualities.

Curiosity

- Devise an experiment that will cause the cork in a bottle to shoot up and hit the ceiling.
- How do the five senses make us aware of the world around us?
- What would happen if all of a sudden you became taller?
- What do you think the world would be like without trees?
- Did you ever wonder how thermometers work?

Risk taking

- Predict how the world would look if we did nothing about pollution.
- Given an object in a box, determine how you would go about finding out what it is.
- Explain how you would defend Lee Harvey Oswald if you were his lawyer.
- Make a prediction about the laws governing abortion. Will they change?
- What would happen if you put a thermometer in hot water?

Imagination

- What do you think would happen if you could go to the center of the Earth?
- How do you think the street will look 10 years from now?
- Draw a picture of what you think the first alien to visit Earth, its family, and its spaceship would look like.
- Pretend you are a cloud.
- Suppose aliens landed on Earth and all they found was a penny. How many things can they tell about our society from the penny?

Complexity

- Make a city out of blocks and objects around you.
- Here are numerous pictures of all types of dogs. How would you classify them using your own system?
- What would you do if you were able to teach?
- What other ways of evaluation can be used in school besides numerical and letter grades?

3.20 Approaches to Educational Programming for Gifted Students

Enrichment Programs

- Pullout programs
- Special experiences within a regular classroom
- Tracking
- Special grouping within the regular classroom
- Resource rooms
- Mentor programs
- Guest speakers
- Internships
- Extracurricular activities
- Special clubs
- Summer camps and programs
- Special regular classes
- Seminars
- Mini-courses
- Team teaching
- Alternative schools
- Field trips and cultural programs

Acceleration Programs

- Honors classes
- Advanced placement classes for college credit
- Early admission to school
- Early admission to college
- Skipping a grade
- Seminars
- Programmed learning so that the student can accelerate at his/her own pace
- Ungraded classes
- Multi-aged classes
- Tutoring
- Correspondence courses
- Extra classes for extra credit
- Credit by examination
- Independent study
- Continuous progress curriculum
- Year-round school
- Flexible scheduling

3.21 Classroom Applications of Bloom's Taxonomy of the Cognitive Domain

Types of Learning	What Student Does	What Teacher Does
Mastery of subject matter	responds	directs
	absorbs	tells
	remembers	leads
	rehearses	shows
	covers	delineates
	recognizes	enlarges
	examines	
Comprehension (cognition)	explains	demonstrates
	extends	listens
	demonstrates	reflects
	translates	
	questions	
	interprets	
	compares	
	contrasts	
	examines	
Application (convergent and divergent production)	solves novel problems	shows
	demonstrates use of knowledge	
	facilitates	
	constructs	
	observes	
	criticizes	
Analysis	discusses	probes
	details	guides
	uncovers	
	observes	
	lists	acts as a resource
	dissects	
Synthesis	discusses	
	reflects	
	generalizes	
	evaluates	
	relates	extends
	compares	
	analyzes	
	contrasts	
	abstracts	
Evaluation	engages in commitment	accepts
	judges	
	disputes criteria	

3.22 Common Characteristics of Program Management for the Gifted

Pullout programs

- Gifted students are removed from the classroom and placed in an out-of-classroom location for a portion of the school day or week.
- Grouping in the pullout setting may be by grade or multi-aged.

Cluster grouping

- Identified gifted students from several classes are grouped or clustered into a regular class with other nongifted students.
- Cluster groups of gifted students within classroom receive differentiated instruction based on their special needs.

Acceleration

- Gifted students are moved more rapidly through the usual sequence of instruction.
- Acceleration above grade-level materials is used for instruction.
- May occur in one academic area, for example, mathematics, although in some cases it may occur by moving the gifted student into a higher grade.

Homogeneous grouping

- Identified gifted students are placed together in a single class exclusively for gifted students.

Gifted students in the regular classroom

- Identified gifted students remain in regular heterogeneous classes.
- Individualized instructional approaches are used to differentiate the program to meet the needs of gifted students.

Mentor program

- Gifted students are matched to mentors or guides who work with them in individually selected areas.
- Programs frequently involve out-of-school experiences for students.
- Mentors may assist gifted students in independent study projects, or acquaint gifted students with their particular area of expertise.
- Mentors are frequently community people in business and service areas or the arts.

3.23 Some Typical Characteristics of the Gifted and Talented

1. Keen power of observation
2. Sense of the significant
3. Willingness to examine the unusual
4. Power of abstraction
5. High-level conceptualization
6. Interest in inductive learning and problem solving
7. Interest in cause-and-effect relationships
8. Retentiveness
9. Verbal proficiency
10. Large vocabulary
11. Facility in expression
12. Interest in reading
13. Wide range of experiences and information
14. Questioning attitude
15. Intellectual curiosity
16. Inquisitive mind
17. Intrinsic motivation
18. Power of critical thinking
19. Creativeness and inventiveness
20. Power of concentration
21. Intense attention that excludes all else
22. Long attention span
23. Persistent
24. Goal directed
25. High energy levels
26. Alertness
27. Eagerness
28. Independence in work and study
29. Preference for individualized work
30. Self-reliance
31. Need for freedom of movement and action
32. Versatility
33. Diversity of interests and abilities
34. Varied hobbies

3.24 Teacher Checklist of Classroom Characteristics that May Indicate Giftedness

1. ___Reads earlier with greater comprehension of nuances in the language.

2. ___Learns basic skills faster than the other children.

3. ___Able to make abstractions when other children his or her age cannot.

4. ___Has a curiosity in interest areas beyond his or her age level.

5. ___Able to comprehend implications with almost nonverbal cues.

6. ___Takes independent direction earlier than peers.

7. ___Assumes responsibility more naturally than peers.

8. ___Can maintain longer periods of concentration when interested.

9. ___Able to express thoughts readily.

10. ___Wide range of reading.

11. ___Seems to expend limitless energy.

12. ___Manifests creative and original verbal responses.

13. ___Demonstrates a more complex processing of information than peers.

14. ___Responds and relates well to adult interaction in the higher-level thinking processes.

15. ___Enjoys working on many projects at a time.

16. ___Assumes leadership roles.

17. ___Has an innate sense of justice.

18. ___Displays a great curiosity about objects, situations, or events.

19. ___Pursues individual interests and seeks own direction.

20. ___Offers unusual, clever, or unique responses or ideas.

21. ___Has desire to express herself or himself in the arts (e.g., art, music, drama).

22. ___Generates many alternatives in problem-solving situations.

23. ___Seems to go at right angles to the mainstream of thought in the classroom.

24. ___Displays a willingness for complexity.

25. ___Thrives on problem-solving situations.

26. ___Seeks new associations among items of information.

27. ___Shows superior judgment in evaluating things.

28. ___Seeks logical answers.

29. ___Able to elaborate with ease.

30. ___Loves to embellish materials and ideas.

3.25 Residential Alternatives for Individuals with Developmental Disabilities

Institutions: These are large custodial institutions that offer severely and profoundly disabled persons 24-hour care and supervision. The concern with these institutions involves the level of humane treatment and the concept of normalization.

Regional facilities: These programs offer total-care, 24-hour residential programs similar to large state institutions, but on a much smaller basis, serving only those persons in a given geographical area within the state. The reduced distance between this type of facility and the individual's family allows for more normalized and individualized treatment programs.

Group homes: This type of facility consists of between 6 and 12 mentally disabled adolescents or adults living in a large family-type dwelling in a residential neighborhood. Professional staff is responsible for supervision and overall programming for the residents. The residents often work at sheltered workshops and participate in social and recreational activities in the community.

Board and care homes: Board and care homes are less structured than group homes. Residents sleep and eat in the home, but the family or staff is not generally responsible for supervision of the residents. The responsibility for scheduling daytime activities and services falls on the resident or on an outside case manager.

Apartment living: These types of alternatives include independent apartments with minimal supervision, apartment clusters, and co-residence arrangements (a disabled resident and a nondisabled roommate).

Sheltered workshops: These types of facilities provide supervised employment for many retarded teenagers and adults. Employees generally perform piecework labor and are paid on either an hourly or performance-output basis.

Special schools: These special schools offer an education and training curriculum especially designed for their students—usually children with moderate (trainable) mental disabilities. The children in these programs usually live at home with their families.

Regular public schools: Traditionally, the child with moderate disabilities was educated in a self-contained classroom. The regular public schools are now leaning toward the concept of inclusion for such students. Inclusion involves the education of these students within the normal classroom, supported by professionals and services that help them maintain such an educational setting.

3.26   Essential Services for the Developmentally Disabled

Category	Description

Developmental programs
  a. Day activity
  b. Education
  c. Training
	Include a variety of educational and care programs appropriate for an individual's age and severity of disability.

Residential services
  a. Domiciliary
  b. Special living arrangements
	Include living quarters away from the primary home; 24-hour lodging and supervision and less supervised living arrangements for less disabled persons.

Employment services
  a. Preparation
  b. Sheltered
  c. Competitive
	Include a continuum of vocational evaluation, training, and work opportunity in a supervised and independent environment.

Identification services
  a. Diagnosis
  b. Evaluation
	Include efforts to identify the presence of a disability and its etiology and to plan service needs of the individual.

Facilitating services	Include a variety of actions needed to ensure that disabled individuals are informed of current services that can assist them in their daily living.

Treatment services
  a. Medical
  b. Dental
	Include appropriate and available medical care, prosthetic devices needed for maintaining environmental involvement, and dental care.

Transportation	Transportation needs for training sites, work sites, and other daily activities.
Leisure and recreation	Structured and unstructured leisure opportunities need to be defined and offered and transportation made available if required.

3.27   Facts about Down Syndrome

DEFINITION

Down syndrome is the most common and readily identifiable chromosomal condition associated with mental retardation. It is caused by a chromosomal abnormality; for some unexplained reason, an accident in cell development results in 47 instead of the usual 46 chromosomes. This extra chromosome changes the orderly development of the body and brain. In most cases, the diagnosis is made according to results from a chromosome test administered shortly after birth.

INCIDENCE

Approximately 4,000 children with Down syndrome are born in the U.S. each year, or about 1 in every 800 to 1,000 live births. Although parents of any age may have a child with Down syndrome, the incidence is higher for women over 35. Most common forms of the syndrome do not usually occur more than once in a family.

CHARACTERISTICS

There are more than 50 clinical signs of Down syndrome, but it is rare to find all or even most of them in one person. Some common characteristics include:

- Poor muscle tone
- Slanting eyes with folds of skin at the inner corners (called epicanthal folds)
- Hyper flexibility (excessive ability to extend the joints)
- Short, broad hands with a single crease across the palm on one or both hands
- Broad feet with short toes
- Flat bridge of the nose
- Short, low-set ears
- Short neck
- Small head
- Small oral cavity
- Short, high-pitched cries in infancy

Individuals with Down syndrome are usually smaller than their nondisabled peers, and their physical as well as intellectual development is slower. Besides having a distinct physical appearance, children with Down syndrome frequently have specific health-related problems. A lowered resistance to infection makes these children more prone to respiratory problems. Visual problems such as crossed eyes and far- or nearsightedness are higher in those with Down syndrome, as are mild-to-moderate hearing loss and speech difficulty. Approximately one third of babies born with Down syndrome have heart defects, most of which are now successfully correctable. Some of these individuals are born with gastrointestinal tract problems that can also be surgically corrected.

3.27 continued

Some people with Down syndrome also may have a condition known as Atlantoaxial Instability, a misalignment of the top two vertebrae of the neck. This condition makes these individuals more prone to injury if they participate in activities, which overextend or flex the neck. Parents are urged to have their child examined by a physician to determine whether or not their child should be restricted from sports and activities, which place stress on the neck. Although this misalignment is a potentially serious condition, proper diagnosis can help prevent severe injury.

Children with Down syndrome may have a tendency to become obese as they grow older. Besides having negative social implications, this weight gain threatens these individuals' health and longevity. A supervised diet and exercise program may help reduce this problem.

EDUCATIONAL AND EMPLOYMENT IMPLICATIONS

Shortly after a diagnosis of Down syndrome is confirmed, parents should be encouraged to enroll their child in an infant development/early intervention program. These programs offer parents special instruction in teaching their child language, cognitive, self-help, and social skills, and specific exercises for gross and fine motor development. Research has shown that stimulation during early developmental stages improves the child's chances of developing to his or her fullest potential. Continuing education, positive public attitudes, and a stimulating home environment have also been determined to be effective for promoting the child's overall development.

Just as in the normal population, there is a wide variation in mental abilities, behavior, and developmental progress in individuals with Down syndrome. Their level of retardation may range from mild to severe, with the majority functioning in the mild-to-moderate range. Because of these individual differences, it is difficult to predict future achievements of children with Down syndrome.

Given the range of ability in children with Down syndrome, it is important that families and all members of the school's education team place few limitations on a child's potential capabilities. It may be effective to emphasize concrete concepts rather than abstract ideas. Teaching tasks in a step-by-step manner, with frequent reinforcement and consistent feedback, has proven successful. Improved public acceptance of persons with disabilities, along with increased opportunities for adults with disabilities to live and work independently in the community, have expanded goals for individuals with Down syndrome. Independent living centers, group shared and supervised apartments, and support services in the community have proven to be important resources for persons with disabilities.

3.28   Facts about Communication Disorders

DEFINITION OF SPEECH AND LANGUAGE DISORDERS

The term speech and language disorders refers to problems in communication and related areas such as oral motor function. These delays and disorders may range from simple sound substitutions to the inability to understand or use language or use the oral-motor mechanism for functional speech and feeding. Some causes of speech and language disorders include hearing loss, neurological disorders, brain injury, mental retardation, drug abuse, physical impairments such as cleft lip or palate, and vocal abuse or misuse. Frequently, however, the exact cause is unknown.

INCIDENCE

More than one million of the students served in the public schools' special education programs in the 1998–99 school year were categorized as having a speech or language impairment. This estimate does not include children who have speech/language problems secondary to other conditions such as deafness. Language disorders may be related to other disabilities such as mental retardation, autism, or cerebral palsy. It is estimated that communication disorders (including speech, language, and hearing disorders) affect one of every 10 people in the United States.

CHARACTERISTICS

A child's communication is considered delayed when the child is noticeably behind his or her peers in the acquisition of speech and/or language skills. Sometimes a child will have greater receptive (understanding) than expressive (speaking) language skills, but this is not always the case.

Speech disorders refer to difficulties producing speech sounds or problems with voice quality. They might be characterized by an interruption in the flow or rhythm of speech, such as stuttering, which is called dysfluency. Speech disorders may be problems with the way sounds are formed—called articulation or phonological disorders, or they may be difficulties with the pitch, volume, or quality of the voice. There may be a combination of several problems. People with speech disorders have trouble using some speech sounds, which can also be a symptom of a delay. They may say "see" when they mean "ski," or they may have trouble using other sounds such as /l/ or /r/. Listeners may have difficulty understanding what someone with a speech disorder is trying to say. People with voice disorders may be displeased with the way their voices sound.

A *language disorder* is impairment in the ability to understand and/or use words in context, both verbally and nonverbally. Some characteristics of language disorders include improper use of words and their meanings, inability to express ideas, inappropriate grammatical patterns, reduced vocabulary, and inability to follow directions. One or a combination of these characteristics may occur in children who are affected by language learning disabilities or developmental language delay. Children may hear or see a word but not be able to understand its meaning. They may have trouble getting others to understand what they are trying to communicate.

3.28 continued

EDUCATIONAL IMPLICATIONS

Because all communication disorders carry the potential to isolate individuals from their social and educational surroundings, it is essential to find appropriate timely intervention. While many speech and language patterns can be called "baby talk" and are part of a young child's normal development, they can become problems if they are not outgrown as expected. In this way an initial delay in speech and language or an initial speech pattern can become a disorder, which can cause difficulties in learning. Because of the way the brain develops, it is easier to learn language and communication skills before the age of 5. When children have muscular disorders, hearing problems, or developmental delays, their acquisition of speech, language, and related skills are often affected.

Speech-language pathologists assist children who have communication disorders in various ways. They provide individual therapy for the child; consult with the child's teacher about the most effective ways to facilitate the child's communication in the class setting; and work closely with the family to develop goals and techniques for effective therapy in class and at home. Technology can help children whose physical conditions make communication difficult. The use of electronic communication systems allows non-speaking people and people with severe physical disabilities to engage in the give and take of shared thought.

Vocabulary and concept growth continue during the years that children are in school. Reading and writing are taught and, as students get older, the understanding and use of language becomes more complex. Communication skills are at the heart of the education experience. Speech and/or language therapy may continue throughout a student's school year—either in the form of direct therapy or on a consultant basis. The speech-language pathologist may assist vocational teachers and counselors in establishing communication goals related to the work experiences of students and may suggest strategies that are effective for the important transition from school to employment and adult life.

Communication has many components. All serve to increase the way people learn about the world around them, utilize knowledge and skills, and interact with colleagues, family, and friends.

3.29   Causes of Communication Disorders

Articulation disorders

- Most prevalent among school-aged children.
- Children may omit certain sounds.
- Children may substitute one sound for another.
- Children may distort certain speech sounds, while attempting to produce them accurately.
- Children may add extra sounds, making comprehension difficult.
- These problems may disappear as the child matures.
- Severe articulation disorders are present when a child pronounces many sounds so poorly that his/her speech is unintelligible most of the time.

Voice disorders

- These occur when the quality, loudness, or pitch of the voice is inappropriate or abnormal.
- They are far less common in children than adults.
- Examples include hoarseness, breathiness, and nasality.
- Problems can have organic or functional causes.
- Problems include hyper-nasality (too many sounds come out through the air passages of the nose) and de-nasality (not enough resonance of the nasal passages).

Fluency disorders

- These disorders interrupt the natural, smooth flow of speech with inappropriate pauses, hesitations, or repetitions.
- One type of disorder is known as cluttering—a condition in which speech is very rapid and clipped to the point of unintelligibility.
- Another type is called stuttering, which is characterized by verbal blocks.
- Most children experience some dysfluency—repetitions and interruptions—at some time in their development.

Language disorders

- Receptive language disorder interferes with the understanding of language.
- The child may be unable to comprehend spoken sentences.
- The child may be unable to follow a sequence of directions.
- Expressive language disorder interferes with the production of language.
- The child may have a limited vocabulary.
- The child may use incorrect words and phrases.
- The child may communicate through gestures.
- Language disorders may be caused by environmental deprivation, emotional factors, structural abnormalities, or retardation.

3.30   Summary of Normal Language Development

Birth to 6 months

- Babies' first form of communication is crying.
- Babies also make sounds of comfort such as coos and gurgles.
- Babbling soon follows as a form of communication.
- Vowel sounds are produced.
- No meaning is attached to the words heard from others.

6 to 12 months

- Baby's voice begins to rise and fall while making sounds.
- Child begins to understand certain words.
- Child may respond appropriately to the word "no" or own name.
- Child may perform an action when asked.
- Child may repeat words said by others.

12 to 18 months

- Child has learned to say several words with appropriate meaning.
- Child is able to tell what she or he wants by pointing.
- Child responds to simple commands.

18 to 24 months

- Child exhibits a great spurt in the acquisition and use of speech at this stage.
- Child begins to combine words.
- Child begins to form words into short sentences.

2 to 3 years

- The child talks.
- The child asks questions.
- The child has vocabulary of about 900 words.
- The child participates in conversation.
- The child identifies colors.
- The child uses plurals.
- The child tells simple stories.
- The child begins to use some consonant sounds.

3 to 4 years

- Child begins to speak more rapidly.
- Child begins to ask questions to obtain information.
- Child's sentences are longer and more varied.
- Child can complete simple analogies.

4 to 5 years

- Child has an average vocabulary of more than 1500 words.
- Child forms sentences averaging 5 words in length.
- Child is able to modify speech.
- Child is able to define words.
- Child uses conjunctions.
- Child recites poems and sings songs from memory.

3.31   Treatment and Remediation of Communication Disorders

Articulation disorders

- Develop the child's ability to listen carefully and discriminate between similar sounds.
- Emphasize awareness and discrimination of sounds.
- Use a mirror so that the child can monitor her or his own speech production.
- Use tape recorder to record her or his own speech and listen carefully for errors.
- Provide good language models.
- Use positive reinforcement to encourage the child to talk.

Voice disorders

- Seek out a medical examination for possible organic causes.
- Recommend environmental modifications.
- Use vocal rehabilitation to help the child gradually learn to produce more acceptable and efficient speech.
- Use exercises and activities to increase breathing capacity.
- Use relaxation techniques to reduce tension.

Fluency disorders

- Emphasize counseling or behavior modification.
- Teach child to manage her or his stuttering by prolonging certain sounds.
- Teach child to manage her or his stuttering by speaking more slowly.
- Increase confidence by having child speak in groups.
- Teach children to monitor their own speech.
- Teach them to speak to a rhythmic beat.
- Use tape recorders for drills.

Language disorders

- Use pre-communication activities, which encourage the child to explore.
- Speak clearly to the child.
- Use correct inflections when speaking to the child.
- Provide a rich variety of words and sentences.
- Expose the child to group interaction.
- Emphasize the use of language through performing tasks.
- Use a variety of written and verbal labeling.

3.32   Facts about Learning Disabilities

DEFINITION OF LEARNING DISABILITIES

Public Law (P.L.) 101-476, the Individuals with Disabilities Education Act (IDEA), defines a learning disability as a "disorder in one or more of the basic psychological processes involved in understanding or in using spoken or written language, which may manifest itself in an imperfect ability to listen, think, speak, read, write, spell, or do mathematical calculations."

The Federal definition further states that learning disabilities include "such conditions as perceptual disabilities, brain injury, minimal brain dysfunction, dyslexia, and developmental aphasia." According to the law, learning disabilities do not include learning problems that are primarily the result of visual, hearing, or motor disabilities; mental retardation; or environmental, cultural, or economic disadvantage. Definitions of learning disabilities also vary among states.

Having a single term to describe this category of children with disabilities reduces some of the confusion, but there are many conflicting theories about what causes learning disabilities and how many there are. The label "learning disabilities" is all embracing; it describes a syndrome, not a specific child with specific problems. The definition assists in classifying children, not teaching them. Parents and teachers need to concentrate on the individual child. They need to observe both how and how well the child performs, to assess strengths and weaknesses, and develop ways to help each child learn. It is important to remember that there is a high degree of interrelationship and overlapping among the areas of learning. Therefore, children with learning disabilities may exhibit a combination of characteristics.

These problems may mildly, moderately, or severely impair the learning process.

INCIDENCE

Many different estimates of the number of children with learning disabilities have appeared in the literature (ranging from 1 percent to 30 percent of the general population). Differences in estimates perhaps reflect variations in the definition. In 1987, the Interagency Committee on Learning Disabilities concluded that 5 percent to 10 percent is a reasonable estimate of the percentage of persons affected by learning disabilities. The U.S. Department of Education (2000) reported that, in the 1998–99 school year, more than 2.8 million children with learning disabilities received special education and related services.

CHARACTERISTICS

Learning disabilities are characterized by a significant difference in the child's achievement in some areas, as compared to his or her overall intelligence.

Students who have learning disabilities may exhibit a wide range of traits, including problems with reading comprehension, spoken language, writing, or reasoning ability. Hyperactivity, inattention, and perceptual coordination problems may also be associated with learning disabilities.

3.32 continued

Other traits that may be present include a variety of symptoms such as uneven and unpredictable test performance, perceptual impairments, motor disorders, and behaviors such as impulsiveness, low tolerance for frustration, and problems in handling day-to-day social interactions and situations.

Learning disabilities may occur in the following academic areas:

- Spoken language: Delays and/or disorders with speaking
- Written language: Difficulty with reading, writing, and spelling
- Arithmetic: Difficulty in performing arithmetic functions or in comprehending basic concepts
- Reasoning: Difficulty in organizing and integrating thoughts
- Organization skills: Difficulty in organizing all facets of learning

EDUCATIONAL IMPLICATIONS

Because learning disabilities are manifested in a variety of behavior patterns, the Individualized Education Plan (IEP) must be designed carefully. A team approach is important for educating the child with a learning disability, beginning with the assessment process and continuing through the development of the IEP. Close collaboration among special class teachers, parents, resource room teachers, regular class teachers, and others will facilitate the overall development of a child with learning disabilities.

Some teachers report that the following strategies have been effective with some students who have learning disabilities:

- Capitalize on the student's strengths.
- Provide high structure and clear expectations.
- Use short sentences and a simple vocabulary.
- Provide opportunities for success in a supportive atmosphere to help build self-esteem.
- Allow flexibility in classroom procedures (e.g., allowing the use of tape recorders for note-taking and test-taking when students have trouble with written language).
- Make use of self-correcting materials, which provide immediate feedback without embarrassment.
- Use computers for drill and practice and teaching word processing.
- Provide positive reinforcement of appropriate social skills at school and home.
- Recognize that students with learning disabilities can greatly benefit from the gift of time to grow and mature.

3.33 Characteristics of Children with Dyslexia

Primary characteristics for early detection

1. The child has poor ability to associate sounds with corresponding symbols.

2. The child ignores details of words and has difficulty retaining the words in his or her mind.

3. The child exhibits frequent word guessing. The child won't look at the word but will seek pictorial clues.

4. The child has confused spatial orientation. He or she reverses words, letters, and numbers. Mirror reading and writing is frequently encountered.

5. The child has poor auditory discrimination.

6. The child exhibits confusion of left and right (referred to as mixed dominance).

7. The child frequently loses his or her place on a page and frequently skips lines.

8. The child has difficulty in working with jigsaw puzzles, holding his or her pencil, and/or walking a chalk line.

9. Newly learned words are forgotten from day to day. Reading rhythm is usually poor and labored.

Secondary characteristics for early detection

1. There is no mental disability, and intelligence is measured as average to superior.

2. The child exhibits general confusion in orientation and confuses days, time, distance, size, and right and left directions.

3. The child displays poor motor coordination, a swaying gait, and awkwardness when playing games.

4. There are speech delays, and the child has difficulty in pronunciation.

5. The child feels inadequate and exhibits low self-esteem.

6. Special tutoring with conventional reading methods does not work.

7. The child displays general irritability, aggressiveness, avoidance reactions, defensiveness, withdrawal, and other general behavioral problems.

3.34 Characteristics of Children with Learning Disabilities

A student with a learning disability is one who:

1. Is not succeeding in school in one or more of the following areas:

   ▪ Basic reading skill (decoding)

   ▪ Reading comprehension

   ▪ Mathematical calculations

   ▪ Mathematical reasoning

   ▪ Written expression

   ▪ Oral expression

   ▪ Listening comprehension

2. Has appropriate learning opportunities.

3. Has at least average intellectual potential.

4. Has a severe discrepancy between intellectual potential and achievement in one or several of the above areas of functioning.

A student with a learning disability may also:

1. Show performance variability across academic and nonacademic areas.

2. Exhibit attention and behavior problems that appear related to school failure and frustration.

A student with a learning disability is a student whose learning problems are not due primarily to:

1. Other disabling conditions such as:

   ▪ Mental disability

   ▪ Emotional disturbance

   ▪ Visual or hearing loss

   ▪ Motor handicaps

2. Limited learning opportunities because of:

   ▪ Prolonged absences from school

   ▪ Lack of consideration for language differences

   ▪ Inadequate instructional practices

3. Limited learning potential in all areas (i.e., slow learner whose achievement is commensurate with his or her potential).

4. Sociological causes, including environmental, cultural, or economic disadvantages; limited proficiency in English; or other conditions that may result in, but are not the result of, a learning problem.

3.35   Teaching Techniques Used to Compensate for Certain Learning Problems

High activity level (hyperactivity):

- Shorten length of tasks.
- Add more variety to tasks.
- Reduce seatwork expectations.

Forgetful (memory problems):

- Teach student to organize rather than memorize.
- Allow the child to use multiplication tables.
- Allow the child to use personal dictionaries.
- Use a peer assistant.

Poor handwriting:

- Encourage student to use graph paper for mathematical problems.
- Use paper with raised lines.
- Allow child to use pencil adaptations.
- Fold paper into sections.
- Decrease written work and increase response options.
- Encourage use of word processor.

Distractibility:

- Create a study section that is free from stimuli.

Focusing problems:

- Stand close to student during lectures.

Organizational problems:

- Allow extra time for responses.
- Give credit or attempted responses.

Test inconsistency:

- Allow student to take test in sections.
- Allow for untimed testing.
- Allow for flexible setting.
- Give typed, not handwritten tests.
- Underline key words in test directions.

133

3.36 Characteristics of Writing, Mathematical, and Reading Disorders

WRITING DISORDERS

Children who are phonetically accurate spellers:

- Make phonetically accurate errors.
- Spell words exactly as they sound—"lite" for "light."
- Spell words with only a general similarity to the actual word—"word" for "work."
- Have difficulty associating verbal labels with pictorial information.
- Have problems with advanced language expression, such as vocabulary definitions.

Children who are phonetically inaccurate spellers:

- Demonstrate significant weaknesses in basic auditory skills.
- Have difficulty breaking words into syllables.
- Have difficulty retaining auditory information.
- Do not process language effectively.

Children with mechanical writing disorders:

- Find writing a slow and labored process.
- Usually have poorly developed fine-motor coordination.
- Typically lack finger dexterity.
- May have had earlier problems with buttoning and tying.
- May have difficulty with the spatial aspects of writing.
- May form letters of varying sizes.
- May leave gaps between letters of a word.
- May run words together.
- May exhibit directional confusion by reversing letters.

MATHEMATICAL DISORDERS

Children with mathematical disorders:

- May not fully comprehend the rules of arithmetic because of problems in applying language.
- May not grasp language-based facts for arithmetic.
- May have difficulty remembering multiplication tables.

- May have trouble understanding teachers' verbal explanations.
- May have visual spatial problems.
- May have difficulty keeping track of numbers in the same column.
- May switch from one column to another as they add or subtract.
- May have trouble with the concepts of borrowing and carrying.

READING DISORDERS

Children with language-based disorders:

- Are slower at naming objects and pictures.
- Have auditory receptive areas of the brain that react more slowly to auditory stimuli.
- Have difficulty comprehending complicated verbal directions.
- Have difficulty separating words into phonetic segments.
- Have poor memory for sequential information.
- Have difficulty decoding words.

3.37 Facts about Emotional Disabilities

DEFINITION OF EMOTIONAL DISTURBANCE

Currently, students with emotional, behavioral, or mental disorders are categorized as having a *serious emotional disturbance*, which is defined under the Individuals with Disabilities Education Act, when there is . . .

"... a condition exhibiting one or more of the following characteristics over a long period of time and to a marked degree that adversely affects educational performance . . .

(A) An inability to learn that cannot be explained by intellectual, sensory, or health factors;

(B) An inability to build or maintain satisfactory interpersonal relationships with peers and teachers;

(C) Inappropriate types of behavior or feelings under normal circumstances;

(D) A general pervasive mood of unhappiness or depression; or

(E) A tendency to develop physical symptoms or fears associated with personal or school problems" [Code of Federal Regulations, Title 34, Section 300.7(b)(9)].

As defined by the IDEA, serious emotional disturbance includes schizophrenia but does not apply to children who are socially maladjusted, unless it is determined that they have a diagnosed emotional disturbance [Code of Federal Regulations, Title 34, Section 300.7(b)(9)].

It is important to know that the federal government is currently reviewing the way in which serious emotional disturbance is defined and that the definition may be revised.

INCIDENCE

For the 1998–1999 school year, 463,172 children and youth with a serious emotional disturbance were provided services in the public schools (Twenty-Second Annual Report to Congress, U.S. Department of Education, 2000).

CHARACTERISTICS

The causes of emotional disturbance have not been adequately determined. Although various factors such as heredity, brain disorder, diet, stress, and family functioning have been suggested as possible causes, research has not shown any of these factors to be the direct cause of behavior problems. Some of the characteristics and behaviors seen in children who have emotional disturbances include:

- Hyperactivity (short attention span, impulsiveness)
- Aggression/self-injurious behavior (acting out, fighting)
- Withdrawal (failure to initiate interaction with others, retreat from exchanges of social interaction, excessive fear or anxiety)

- Immaturity (inappropriate crying, temper tantrums, poor coping skills)
- Learning difficulties (academically performing below grade level)

Children with the most serious emotional disturbances may exhibit incoherence, excessive anxiety, bizarre motor acts, and abnormal mood swings. They are sometimes identified as children who have a severe psychosis or schizophrenia. Many children who do not have emotional disturbances may display some of these same behaviors at various times during their development. However, when children have serious emotional disturbances, these behaviors continue over long periods of time. Their behavior thus signals that they are not coping with their environment or peers.

EDUCATIONAL IMPLICATIONS

The educational programs for students with serious emotional disturbances need to include attention to mastering academics, developing social skills, and increasing self-awareness, self-esteem, and self-control. Career education (both academic and vocational programs) is also a major part of secondary education and should be a part of every adolescent's transition plan in his or her Individualized Education Plan (IEP).

Behavior modification is one of the most widely used approaches to helping a child with a serious emotional disturbance. However, there are many other techniques that are also successful and may be used in combination with behavior modification. Life Space Intervention and Conflict Resolution are two such techniques. Students eligible for special education services under the category of serious emotional disturbance may have IEPs that include psychological or counseling services as a related service. This is an important related service, which is available under the law and is to be provided by a qualified social worker, psychologist, guidance counselor, or other qualified professional.

There is growing recognition that parents, as well as their children, need support, respite care, intensive case management services, and multi-agency treatment plans. Many communities are working toward providing these wrap-around services, and there are a growing number of agencies and organizations actively involved in establishing support services in the community. Parent support groups are also important, and organizations such as the Federation of Families for Children's Mental Health and the National Alliance for the Mentally Ill (NAMI) have parent representatives and groups in every state. Both of these organizations are listed in the resource section of this book.

OTHER CONSIDERATIONS

Families of children with serious emotional disturbances may need help in understanding their children's condition and in learning how to work effectively with them. Help is available from psychiatrists, psychologists, or other mental health professionals in public or private mental health settings. Children should be provided services based on their individual needs, and all persons who are involved with these children should be aware of the care they are receiving. It is important to coordinate all services among home, school, and therapeutic community with open communication.

3.38   Common Developmental Disorders

DEVELOPMENTAL DISORDERS

Mental Disabilities

Description: A group of disorders characterized by severe delayed development in the acquisition of cognitive, language, motor, or social skills. The general characteristics of this diagnostic category are:

- consistent and significant subaverage intellectual performance
- significant deficits in the development of adaptive functioning
- onset prior to the age of 18

Types: There are several subtypes that are classified by educational or psychological terminology. They are:

Educational Category	DSM-IV-TR Classification	IQ Range	DSM-IV-TR Code
Mild Developmental Disability	Mild	55-77.5 approx.	317.00
Moderate Developmental Disability	Moderate	35-55 approx.	318.00
Severe Developmental Disability	Severe	25-35 approx.	318.10
Profound Developmental Disability	Profound	below 25	318.20

Educational Implications: The more severe the disability, the greater the possibility of associated symptoms such as seizures or visual, auditory, or cardiovascular problems being present. Other possible symptoms include poor social skills, severe academic deficits, and behavioral manifestations such as impulsivity, low frustration tolerance, aggressiveness, low self-esteem, and, in some cases, self-injurious behavior.

Least Restrictive Educational Setting: Least restrictive educational settings for this type of student usually range anywhere from self-contained in a regular school with mainstreaming options for educable students to institutionalization for profoundly retarded individuals.

PERVASIVE DEVELOPMENTAL DISORDERS

Autistic Disorder

Description: A very serious developmental disorder characterized by severe impairment in the development of verbal and nonverbal communication skills, marked impairment in reciprocal social interaction (a lack of responsiveness to, or interest in, people), and almost nonexistent imaginative activity. Also known as Infantile Autism or Kanner's syndrome.

Educational Implications: Poor social skills, impaired cognitive functioning and language. The onset of puberty may increase oppositional or aggressive behavior. Other complications may include seizures and low intellectual development.

Least Restrictive Educational Setting: Most children with this condition require the most restrictive educational setting possible. The student-teacher ratios are usually 6:1:2 or smaller because of the close supervision required. Those who cannot be maintained in this type of setting may have to be institutionalized. In rare cases, the individual may improve to the point of completing formal education or advanced degrees.

SPECIFIC DEVELOPMENTAL DISORDERS

Developmental Arithmetic Disorder

Description: A serious marked disability in the development of arithmetic skills. This condition, often called dyscalculia, cannot be explained by developmental disability, inadequate teaching, or primary visual or auditory defects, and may be consistent throughout school.

Educational Implications: Seriously impaired mathematical ability—which may require modifications such as extended time, use of a calculator, flexible settings for tests, and revised test formats—may lead to poor self-esteem, social self-consciousness, and avoidance, which may increase secondary problems.

Least Restrictive Educational Setting: Children with this disorder may receive assistance through special educational services such as a resource room or a consultant teacher, and are usually able to maintain placement within a normal class setting.

Developmental Expressive Writing Disorder

Description: A disorder characterized by a serious impairment in the ability to develop expressive writing skills that significantly interferes with the child's academic achievement. This condition is not the result of a developmental disability, inadequate educational experiences, visual or hearing defects, or neurological dysfunction.

Symptoms: The symptoms associated with this disorder include an inability to compose appropriate written text, coupled with serious and consistent spelling errors, grammatical or punctuation errors, and very poor organization of thought and text.

Educational Implications: Teachers should be aware that these children may exhibit a series of symptoms including avoidance, procrastination, denial, and possibly disruptive behaviors when written assignments are involved as a means of covering up the seriousness of the disorder.

Least Restrictive Educational Setting: Children with this disorder may receive assistance through special educational services such as a resource room or a consultant teacher, and are usually able to maintain placement within a normal class setting.

3.38 continued

Developmental Reading Disorder

Description: A disorder whose more common features include a marked impairment in the development of the child's decoding and comprehension skills, which significantly interfere with the child's academic performance. As with most developmental disorders, this condition is not the result of developmental disability, inadequate educational experiences, visual or hearing defects, or neurological dysfunction. Commonly referred to as "dyslexia."

Symptoms: Typical symptoms of this disorder include a slow, halting reading pace; frequent omissions; loss of place on a page; skipping lines while reading without awareness; distortions; substitutions of words; and a serious inability to recall what has been read.

Educational Implications: Teachers should be aware that early diagnosis of this disorder is crucial to avoid serious secondary symptoms of poor self-esteem, behavior disorders, and educational failure. Teachers should focus on the possible symptoms exhibited by children with this disorder so that they can assist in early identification of this high-risk child. Teachers should also be aware of the various reading techniques used to assist children with this disorder. (A more thorough description of this disorder appears in List 3.33.)

Least Restrictive Educational Setting: Children with this disorder may receive assistance through special educational services such as a resource room or a consultant teacher, and are usually able to maintain placement within a normal class setting.

Developmental Expressive Language Disorder

Description: A disorder characterized by a serious impairment in the child's ability to develop expressive language. This condition is not the result of developmental disability, inadequate educational experiences, visual or hearing defects, or neurological dysfunction.

Educational Implications: Teachers should be aware that from 3 to 10 percent of school-aged children suffer from this disorder, which may greatly hamper a child's social interaction skills as well as his or her academic performance.

Least Restrictive Educational Setting: Children with this disorder may receive assistance through special educational services such as a resource room, a consultant teacher, or services from a speech therapist, and are usually able to maintain placement within a normal class setting.

Developmental Articulation Disorder

Description: A disorder that causes children to experience consistent problems using developmentally expected speech sounds, including but not limited to misarticulations, substitutions, and omissions often sounding very similar to a more infantile form of speech. This condition is not the result of developmental disability; neurological, intellectual, or hearing disorders; or oral speech mechanism defects.

Educational Implications: The prognosis for complete recovery from this disorder is very positive, especially when speech therapy is part of the treatment plan. In some milder cases, the condition may run its course by age 8 without intervention.

Least Restrictive Educational Setting: Children with this disorder may receive assistance through special educational services such as a resource room, a consultant teacher, or services from a speech therapist, and are usually able to maintain placement within a normal class setting.

Developmental Receptive Language Disorder

Description: A disorder characterized by a serious impairment in the child's ability to develop language comprehension. This condition is not the result of developmental disability, inadequate educational experiences, visual or hearing defects, or neurological dysfunction.

Educational Implications: Teachers should be aware that children with this disorder may have a difficult time communicating with gestures and actively participating in activities that require imaginary play.

Least Restrictive Educational Setting: Children with this disorder may receive assistance through special educational services such as a resource room, a consultant teacher or services from a speech therapist, and are usually able to maintain placement within a normal class setting.

3.39 Common Disruptive Behavior Disorders

Conduct Disorder

Description: This condition is characterized by a persistent pattern of behavior in which the child intrudes on and violates the basic rights of others without concern or fear of implications. This pattern is not selective and is exhibited in the home, at school, with peers, and in the child's community. Other behaviors present with this condition may include vandalism, stealing, physical aggression, cruelty to animals, and fire setting.

Categories:		
Type	**Description**	**DSM-IV-TR Code**
Solitary Aggressive Type	aggressive behavior toward peers and adults	312.00
Group Type	conduct problems mainly with peers as a group	312.20
Undifferentiated Type	those not classified in either above group	312.90

Educational Implications: Children with this condition may be physically confrontational to teachers and peers, have poor attendance, have high levels of suspension (thereby missing a great deal of academic work), and exhibit other forms of antisocial behavior.

Least Restrictive Educational Setting: Children with this condition may be educated in a special class within a regular school if the condition is mild. However, the majority of students with this disorder are educated in a more restrictive program housed within a special school, a residential school, or an institution if the antisocial behavior is extreme.

Oppositional Defiant Disorder

Description: This disorder is usually characterized by patterns of negativistic, hostile, and defiant behaviors toward peers as well as adults. This disorder is considered less serious than a conduct disorder because of the absence of serious behaviors that violate the basic rights of others. Children with this disorder usually exhibit argumentative behaviors toward adults, which may include swearing and frequent episodes of intense anger and annoyance. These symptoms are usually considered to be more serious and intense than those exhibited by other children of the same age.

Educational Implications: Teachers who have children with this disorder in their classes may observe low frustration tolerance, frequent temper outbursts, low sense of confidence, an unwillingness to take responsibility for their actions, consistent blaming of others for their own mistakes or problems, and frequent behaviors associated with Attention Deficit Hyperactivity Disorder.

Least Restrictive Educational Setting: Children with this condition may be educated in a special class within a regular school if the condition is mild. However, the majority of students with this disorder are educated in a more restrictive program housed within a special school, residential school, or an institution if the antisocial behavior is extreme.

3.40 Common Anxiety Disorders of Childhood

Separation Anxiety Disorder

Description: This disorder is characterized by extreme anxiety associated with separation from someone whom the child views as a significant other. Although this reaction may be common among very young children on their first day of school, continuation of the anxiety for more than two weeks indicates a problem that needs to be addressed. This separation anxiety is frequently exhibited at school and at home. It should be noted that if symptoms of separation anxiety occur in an adolescent, other factors such as social or academic pressure may be contributing causes.

Educational Implications: Children with this disorder may require a great deal of the teacher's attention. The child may cling, be afraid to try new things, require a great deal of reassurance, and cry frequently. Panic attacks are common, and the teacher may find that reasoning with the child does not reduce the anxiety. Physical complaints are common and should never be ignored. However, in cases of separation anxiety, these physical symptoms are usually manifestations of the anxiety once medical causes are ruled out.

Least Restrictive Educational Setting: Children with this disorder can usually be maintained in the regular class setting through the help of the school psychologist working with the child and parents. If the condition persists and the diagnosis changes (e.g., major depression), then outside professional help may be required, and a more restrictive program, sometimes even homebound instruction if attendance at school is not possible, may have to be instituted.

Avoidant Disorder of Childhood or Adolescence

Description: This disorder results in the child's withdrawing from social contact or interaction with an unfamiliar peer or adult to the point of its becoming a significant factor in social development.

Educational Implications: Children with this disorder can maintain regular class placement as long as achievement levels do not present problems that possibly signify some other condition. Teachers with this type of student should watch for social isolation, withdrawal from activity-based assignments, and a complete unwillingness to try new situations involving social interaction with unfamiliar peers. Trying to force the child into new social interaction situations may only result in further withdrawal socially as well as verbally. Work alone with the child or have him or her work along with familiar peers for a while. Once a relationship is developed, your influence may be more rewarding. Referring the child to the school psychologist is also highly recommended. Individual outside counseling with a slow lead into small group counseling should be explored. However, this transition may cause a great deal of resistance on the part of the child.

Least Restrictive Educational Setting: Children with this disorder can usually be maintained in the regular class setting through the help of the school psychologist working with the child and his or her parents. However, children with other disabilities may also exhibit this disorder.

Overanxious Disorder

Description: The main feature of this disorder is an excessive level of anxiety or worry, extending over a six-month or longer period of time.

Educational Implications: Teachers who have students with this disorder should be aware of the possibility of poor academic performance because of the child's preoccupation with worry. The teacher should also try to reassure and compliment the child as much as possible when he or she is not drawing negative attention to himself or herself.

Least Restrictive Educational Setting: Most children with this disorder can be educated within a regular class placement unless the condition is coupled with more serious disabilities that require a more restrictive setting. Referral to the school psychologist is highly recommended.

3.41   Common Eating Disorders

Anorexia Nervosa

Description: People with this condition show a marked disturbance and unwillingness to maintain a minimal body weight for their age and height. An extremely distorted sense of body image exists and intense fears and worries about gaining weight become obsessive. It is not uncommon for bulimia nervosa (discussed later) to be an associated feature. Severe cases can be life-threatening.

Symptoms: People with this disorder may also exhibit self-induced vomiting, use of laxatives, increased reduction of food intake, preoccupation with becoming fat, and a noticeable increase in the frequency and intensity of exercise. In females, absence of menstrual cycles is common as their weight decreases and body chemistry changes.

Educational Implications: Teachers should be aware of frequent absences because of medical complications. These students are usually high-achieving individuals, but because of their medical conditions, academic consistency may be difficult.

Least Restrictive Educational Setting: Students with anorexia can be maintained in the regular school setting unless the condition becomes severe enough to warrant hospitalization. In some cases, where the student is at home and unable to attend school, homebound instruction is utilized.

Bulimia Nervosa

Description: A condition characterized by recurrent episodes of uncontrolled consumption of large quantities of food (binge eating) followed by self-induced vomiting (purging) and/or use of laxatives or diuretics over a period of at least two months.

Symptoms: The individual with bulimia nervosa exhibits obsessive preoccupation with body shape and weight and a feeling of lack of control over food consumption during binge episodes.

Educational Implications: Most teachers might not even know that a student is bulimic. Individuals hide this "secret" well and may not divulge the problem to anyone, not even a best friend. This is usually a private disorder until the person feels so out of control that he or she seeks help and support. Consequently, teachers should be aware of frequent trips to the bathroom especially in the morning after breakfast or after lunch. Changes in skin color and look may give some indications of problems. However, if you suspect anything, let the nurse investigate this further.

Least Restrictive Educational Setting: Unlike anorexia nervosa, people with bulimia nervosa seldom suffer incapacitating symptoms except in rare cases when the eating and purging episodes run throughout the day. Consequently, in most cases, these students can be maintained in the regular school setting unless the condition becomes severe enough to warrant hospitalization.

3.42 Other Disorders of Childhood and Adolescence

ELIMINATION DISORDERS

Functional Encopresis

Description: The major symptom of this disorder is repeated involuntary or intentional passage of feces into clothing or other places for which it is inappropriate. The condition is not related to any physical condition, must occur for a period of six months on a regular basis, and must be present in a child over the age of 4 for diagnosis to take place.

Educational Implications: Children with this disorder may experience social ridicule if the occurrences take place in school. The teacher needs to be sensitive to the condition and involve the school psychologist and parents. Try to intervene as quickly as possible if a pattern exists to avoid further embarrassment for the child and secondary complications (e.g., avoidance).

Least Restrictive Educational Setting: Children with this condition should have no problem maintaining a regular educational setting unless the condition is associated with other disabilities that require special education placement. However, this condition may create social pressures and isolation for the child.

Functional Enuresis

Description: This disorder is characterized by repeated involuntary or intentional elimination of urine during the day or night into the bed or the clothes at an age at which bladder control is expected. A frequency of at least two times per month must be present for the condition to be diagnosed between the ages of 5 and 6, and at least once a month for older children.

Educational Implications: Children with this condition may experience social ridicule if the occurrences take place in school. This condition may create social pressures and isolation for the child. The teacher needs to be sensitive to the condition and involve the school psychologist and the parents.

Least Restrictive Educational Setting: Children with this condition should have no problem in a regular educational setting unless the condition is associated with other disabilities that require special education placement.

3.42 continued

ANXIETY DISORDERS

Elective Mutism

Description: This disorder is characterized by persistent refusal to talk in one or more major social situations, including school, despite the ability to comprehend spoken language and to speak. The resistance to speak is not a symptom of any other major disorder.

Educational Implications: This condition may create a difficult situation for the classroom teacher. The teacher will not be able to measure certain language or social levels, will have to deal with social concerns and comments from classmates, and may have a difficult time encouraging the child to participate in class activities or group projects. If a teacher has such a child in the classroom, he or she should contact the school psychologist as soon as possible. Individual and family counseling is highly suggested for this disorder.

Least Restrictive Educational Setting: Children with this condition can usually be maintained in the regular educational setting as long as they maintain sufficient performance levels. However, if the child's academic performance becomes discrepant and/or social and intellectual factors interfere with performance, then a more restrictive placement may have to be explored.

Obsessive-Compulsive Disorder (OCD)

Description: The major characteristics associated with this disorder are persistent obsessions (persistent thoughts) or compulsions (repetitive acts) that significantly interfere with the individual's normal daily social, educational, occupational, or environmental routines.

Educational Implications: Children or adolescents with this disorder have difficulty concentrating and maintaining consistent academic performance. These individuals may also experience depression as a result of their difficulties, and medication may be prescribed to relieve the anxiety associated with this disorder.

Least Restrictive Educational Setting: Children with this condition can usually be maintained in the regular educational setting as long as they maintain sufficient performance levels. However, if the child's academic performance becomes discrepant, and/or social and intellectual factors interfere with performance, then a more restrictive placement may have to be explored.

MOOD DISORDERS

Dysthymia

Description: The essential feature of this disturbance is a chronic disturbance of the individual's moods involving chronic depression or irritable mood for a period of one year for children and adolescents.

Educational Implications: If the child is in treatment, his or her teachers should work closely with the school psychologist or private therapist. The teacher should also be aware that medication may be involved, and an understanding of the side effects should be investigated.

Least Restrictive Educational Setting: Students with this disorder can usually be maintained in a regular setting. However, if the symptoms become more intense, a more restrictive special education program will be required. The chronicity of this disorder rather than its severity usually accounts for a mild or moderate impairment. Consequently, hospitalization is rare unless suicide is attempted.

The above disorders represent only a cross section of the conditions that you may encounter in the classroom. An understanding and awareness of such disorders can only increase your effectiveness with those children who have them. A more elaborate explanation as well as further disorders associated with this developmental period can be found in the *Diagnostic and Statistical Manual of Mental Disorders* (DSM-IV-TR).

3.43 Specific Personality Disorders

Schizoid Personality Disorder

Description: The child with this disorder exhibits a restrictive range of emotional experiences and expression as well as indifference to social situations.

Educational Implications: In the classroom, a child with this type of disorder will be considered unapproachable. He or she will be resistant to group projects or group experiences; probably, he or she will remain on the outside and will not participate in discussions. Other children will eventually ostracize the child. The teacher will also have a very difficult time establishing any meaningful relationship. An outside professional or agency may suggest therapy and/or medication.

Least Restrictive Educational Setting: Usually, children with this disorder eventually are placed in a special education setting. However, some remain in the normal mainstream because their academic performance is sufficient, but they are viewed as "loners" by their classmates.

Antisocial Personality Disorder

Description: This disorder is characterized by a pattern of irresponsible and antisocial behavior. The condition is usually first seen in childhood or early adolescence and continues throughout the child's development. This diagnosis is usually made after the age of 18, and the individual must have had a history of symptoms indicative of a Conduct Disorder before the age of 15.

Educational Implications: The situation for the classroom teacher can be serious with this type of disorder. Since the individual has little or no regard for the personal rights of others, any antisocial act can occur, even ones that may place the teacher in danger. Medication may help reduce tension, and therapy may have limited success.

Least Restrictive Educational Setting: Individuals with this disorder may have aged out and may no longer be part of the educational system. However, if already classified as disabled, they would probably be placed in a very restrictive educational setting until the age of 21 if they had not been arrested by that time.

Borderline Personality Disorder

Description: The main features of this disorder include instability of self-image, inconsistent and unfulfilling interpersonal relationships, instability of mood, and persistent identity disturbance.

Educational Implications: In the classroom, this individual will have a hard time maintaining any consistent academic performance. Frequent outbursts, truancy, hospitalization, legal problems, or school disciplinary actions may provide an inconsistent pattern of attendance and involvement.

Least Restrictive Educational Setting: The individual with this condition will usually be placed in a more restrictive special education setting, a hospital program, or an institution.

Passive-Aggressive Personality Disorder

Description: Individuals with this disorder exhibit a pervasive pattern of passive resistance to the requests or requirements placed upon them in school and/or in social or occupational situations.

Educational Implications: Teachers will find that it can be very frustrating working with students with this disorder. Such students may become irritable, sulky, or argumentative, and they often blame external causes for their lack of production. Assignments may have to be readjusted so that some sense of accomplishment can be obtained. Counseling is strongly suggested.

Least Restrictive Educational Setting: Most students with this disorder can be educated within the normal setting. However, they may exhibit a pattern of constant underachievement. In some cases where the discrepancy becomes significant, a referral for a more restrictive setting may be indicated. A history of severe academic discrepancy resulting from this disorder may result in the child's being classified as emotionally disabled.

3.44   Description of Tics in Tourette's Syndrome

Tourette's syndrome (TS) is a neurological disorder that appears to be genetically transmitted in most cases. Tourette's is one of a number of disorders classified as tic disorders. Tics are involuntary movements, which present themselves through motor or sound.

The first tics or symptoms of Tourette's syndrome are usually simple motor tics of the head, face, and neck area.

Simple motor tics are usually rapid, apparently purposeless and repetitive movements of one muscle group. Examples of simple motor tics include the following:

- Eye-blinking
- Shoulder shrugs
- Mouth-opening
- Arm-extending
- Facial grimaces
- Lip-licking
- Rolling eyes
- Squinting

Simple phonic (sound) tics are repetitive sounds that are not linguistically meaningful. They may include the following:

- Throat-clearing
- Grunting
- Yelling or screaming
- Sniffing
- Barking
- Snorting
- Coughing
- Spitting
- Squeaking
- Humming
- Whistling

Complex motor tics are involuntary movements that involve the coordinated sequence or activation of two or more muscle groups. Examples include:

- Pulling at clothes
- Touching people
- Touching objects
- Smelling fingers
- Jumping or skipping
- Poking or jabbing

- Punching
- Kicking
- Hopping
- Kissing self or others
- Flapping arms
- Twirling around
- Thrusting movements of groin or torso
- Walking on toes
- Copropraxia: sexually touching self or others, obscene gestures
- Self-injurious behavior

Complex phonic tics represent involuntary linguistically meaningful utterances or expressions, such as repetitive use of phrases. Examples include:

- Making animal-like sounds
- Unusual changes in pitch or volume of voice
- Stuttering
- Coprolalia: socially taboo phrases or obscenities
- Echoing one's own words or those of others.

153

3.45 Diagnostic Criteria for Tic Disorders

Transient tic disorders

- Most common of the tic disorders.
- Onset during early school years.
- Affect 5–24 percent of all children.
- Single or multiple motor and/or vocal tics occur daily for at least two weeks but for no longer than one year.
- Three to four times more common in males than females.
- More common in the first-degree relatives of people who have transient tic disorders.

Chronic motor/vocal tic disorder

- Onset before age 21.
- Usually persist unchanged throughout a period of more than one year.
- Involves either motor or vocal tics.
- Generally related to Tourette's syndrome.

Tourette's syndrome (TS)

- Onset before age 21.
- Occurs for more than one year.
- Tics are highly variable, changing over time in anatomic location, number, complexity, and frequency.
- Associated problems may include obsessive-compulsive disorder.
- Associated behavioral difficulties may include problems in attention, hyperactivity, and emotional lability.
- Symptoms can be suppressed at school, only to emerge abruptly upon arriving in the safety of home.
- 50 to 60 percent of children with TS have Attention Deficit Hyperactivity Disorder.

3.46 Pharmacotherapy and Tourette's Syndrome

Pharmacotherapy has been reported to be the most widely used treatment for TS to date. The difficulty with this treatment is the attempt to balance the alleviation of symptoms with the side effects of the medication. The following is a brief overview of medications currently known to alleviate symptoms of Tourette's:

Neuroleptics

- Decrease symptoms of Tourette's in 70–80 percent of the patients.
- Side effects result in 50 percent of the patients discontinuing this medication.
- Side effects include Parkinsonian symptoms, sedation, weight gain, decreased concentration, impaired memory, depression, and personality changes.
- Usually used in patients whose symptoms cause significant impairment.
- Examples include Haldol, Orap, and Prolixin.

Clonodine

- Reported to be effective in 60 percent of Tourette's patients.
- Less disturbing side effects.
- May require up to a 12-week trial to evaluate efficacy.
- Common side effects are sedation and dry mouth.

Antidepressants

- Generally used to treat associated ADHD (Attention Deficit Hyperactivity Disorder) and/or OCD (Obsessive-Compulsive Disorder) symptoms.
- Some patients report a decrease in symptoms while others report an increase.
- Side effects include dry mouth, sedation, low blood pressure, dizziness, and constipation.
- Examples include Tofranil, Clomipramine, and Prozac.

3.47   Classroom Strategies for Children with Tourette's Syndrome

Many students with Tourette's have to face many pressures in school associated with tics, social concerns, reactions, and associated learning difficulties. The teacher's response to these conditions can make a critical difference. Following are some classroom suggestions when working with a child who has Tourette's:

- Keep in mind that motor or vocal tics are occurring involuntarily.
- Try not to react with anger or annoyance.
- Try to be a role model for the other students on how to react to the Tourette symptoms.
- Provide the child with opportunities for short breaks out of the classroom.
- Try to find a private place somewhere in the school where the child can "let out" the tics since some students try to suppress the tics for a period of time, causing a buildup of tension.
- Allow the student to take tests in a private room so that he or she does not waste energy suppressing the tics that may interfere with concentration.
- Work with the student's classmates to help them understand the tics and reduce ridicule and teasing.
- Secure materials (e.g., audio-visuals, pamphlets) that may provide information for your pupils and colleagues.
- If the student's tics are particularly disruptive, avoid recitation in front of the class.
- Have the student tape-record oral reports.
- Keep in mind that students with Tourette's often have visual-motor difficulties.
- Modify written assignments by reducing the number of problems presented.
- Allow parents to copy down work so that the pupil can dictate his or her ideas to facilitate concept formation.
- Allow the student to write the answers directly on a test paper or booklet rather than use computer scoring sheets.
- Allow the child untimed tests to reduce stress.
- Allow another child to take notes for the student so that he or she can listen to the lecture without the added stress of taking notes.
- Try not to penalize for spelling errors.
- Try to use a multisensory approach whenever possible.
- Avoid multiple directions.
- Use graph paper for math so that the student can place one number in each box.

3.48   Facts about Hearing Impairments

DEFINITION

The Individuals with Disabilities Education Act (IDEA), formerly the Education of the Handicapped Act (P.L. 94-142), includes "hearing impairment" and "deafness" as two of the categories under which children with disabilities may be eligible for special education and related service programming. Although the term "hearing impairment" is often used generically to describe a wide range of hearing losses, including deafness, the regulations for IDEA define hearing loss and deafness separately.

Hearing impairment is defined by IDEA as "an impairment in hearing, whether permanent or fluctuating, that adversely affects a child's educational performance."

Deafness is defined as "a hearing impairment that is so severe that the child is impaired in processing linguistic information through hearing, with or without amplification."

Thus, deafness may be viewed as a condition that prevents an individual from receiving sound in all or most of its forms. In contrast, a child with a hearing loss can generally respond to auditory stimuli, including speech.

INCIDENCE

Hearing loss and deafness affect individuals of all ages and may occur at any time from infancy through old age. The U.S. Department of Education (2000) reports that, during the 1998–99 school year, 70,813 students aged 6 to 21 (or 1.3 percent of all students with disabilities) received special education services under the category of "hearing impairment." However, the number of children with hearing loss and deafness is undoubtedly higher, as many of these students may have other disabilities as well and may be served under other categories.

CHARACTERISTICS

It is useful to know that sound is measured by its loudness or intensity (measured in units called decibels or dB) and its frequency or pitch (measured in units called hertz or Hz). Impairments in hearing can occur in either or both of these areas, and may exist in only one ear or in both ears. Hearing loss is generally described as slight, mild, moderate, severe, or profound, depending upon how well a person can hear the intensities or frequencies most greatly associated with speech. Generally, only children whose hearing loss is greater than 90 decibels (dB) are considered deaf for the purposes of educational placement.

EDUCATIONAL IMPLICATIONS

Hearing loss or deafness does not affect a person's intellectual capacity or ability to learn. However, children who are either hard of hearing or deaf generally require some form of special education services in order to receive an adequate education. Such services may include:

3.48 continued

- regular speech, language, and amplification systems
- services of an interpreter for those students who use manual communication
- favorable seating in the class to facilitate speech reading
- captioned films/videos
- assistance of a note taker who takes notes for the student with a hearing loss so that the student can fully attend to instruction
- instruction for the teacher and peers in alternate communication methods, such as sign language
- counseling

Children who are hard of hearing will find it much more difficult than children who have normal hearing to learn vocabulary, grammar, word order, idiomatic expressions, and other aspects of verbal communication. For children who are deaf or have severe hearing losses, early, consistent, and conscious use of visible communication modes (such as sign language, finger spelling, and cued speech) and/or amplification and aural/oral training can help reduce this language delay. By age 4 or 5, most children who are deaf are enrolled in school on a full-day basis and do special work on communication and language development. It is important for teachers and audiologists to work together to teach the child to use his or her residual hearing to the maximum extent possible, even if the preferred means of communication is manual. Because the great majority of deaf children (over 90 percent) are born to hearing parents, programs should provide instruction for parents on implications of deafness within the family.

People with hearing loss use oral or manual means of communication or a combination of the two. Oral communication includes speech, speech reading, and the use of residual hearing. Manual communication involves signs and finger spelling. Total communication, as a method of instruction, is a combination of the oral method plus signs and finger spelling.

Individuals with hearing loss, including those who are deaf, now have many helpful devices available to them. Text telephones (known as TTs, TTYs, or TDDs) enable persons to type phone messages over the telephone network. The Telecommunications Relay Service (TRS), now required by law, makes it possible for TT users to communicate with virtually anyone (and vice versa) via telephone. The National Institute on Deafness and Other Communication Disorders Information Clearinghouse (telephone: 1-800-241-1044, voice; 1-800-241-1055, TT) makes available lists of TRS numbers by state.

3.49   Causes of Hearing Impairments

Conductive Hearing Loss

Results from problems with the structures in the outer or middle ear, generally attributed to a blockage in the mechanical conduction of sound. In order to overcome this blockage, the sounds must be amplified. These conditions are usually temporary. The leading causes of this type of hearing loss are:

- Otitis Media (middle ear infection)
- Excessive earwax
- Otosclerosis—formation of a spongy-bony growth around the stapes which impedes its movement

Sensorineural Hearing Loss

Results from damage to the cochlea or the auditory nerve. This damage is caused by illness, disease, and other factors. Causes of this hearing loss include:

- Viral diseases (e.g., rubella—German measles, meningitis)
- Rh incompatibility
- Ototoxic medications (medicines that destroy or damage hair cells in the cochlea—e.g., streptomycin) taken by pregnant mothers or very young children
- Hereditary factors
- Exposure to noise
- Aging

Mixed Hearing Loss

A hearing loss caused by both sensorineural and conductive problems.

Functional Hearing Loss

Those problems that are not organic in origin. Examples include:

- Psychosomatic causes
- Hysterical conversion
- Malingering
- Emotional or psychological problems

Central Auditory Disorders

These disorders result in no measurable peripheral hearing loss. Children with this disorder have trouble learning and are often considered to have learning disabilities. Causes include:

- Auditory comprehension problems
- Auditory discrimination problems
- Auditory learning difficulties
- Language development delays

3.50   Audiometric Evaluation Measures

PURE TONE AUDIOMETRIC SCREENING

Pure tone screening is often referred to as sweep testing and is usually the child's first encounter with hearing testing. This type of testing, which is common in schools, presents the child with pure tones over a variety of frequency ranges. The child is then asked to respond if he or she hears a tone, usually by some gesture. If a child is unable to hear sounds at two or more frequencies, he or she is typically referred for further evaluation.

SPEECH AUDIOMETRY

This type of evaluation is used to determine a child's present ability to hear and understand speech through the presentation of words in a variety of loudness levels.

PURE TONE THRESHOLD AUDIOMETRY

In this procedure, the child is asked to make a gesture or push a button each time he or she hears a tone. The child is presented with a variety of frequencies through earphones. This type of air-conduction test reveals the presence of hearing loss.

SPECIAL AUDIOMETRIC TESTS

1. *Sound field audiometry:* This measure is used with very young children who cannot respond to manual responses or are unable or unwilling to wear headphones. The child is evaluated by observing the intensity levels at which he or she responds to different levels of sounds broadcast through speakers.

2. *Evoked response audiometry:* This measure, which incorporates an electroencephalograph and a computer, measures changes in brain-wave activity to a variety of sound levels. This measure can be used with infants who are suspected of being deaf.

3. *Impedance audiometry:* There are two major impedance audiometry tests. The first, tympanometry, measures the functioning level of the eardrum. The second, stapedial reflex testing, measures the reflex response of the stapedial muscle to pure tone signals. Because these tests do not require a response on the part of the child, they can be used with very young children.

4. *Behavioral play audiometry:* This technique involves placing the child in a series of activities that reward him or her for responding appropriately to tone or speech.

3.51   Modes of Communication for the Deaf

Oral-Aural Approach

Stresses the primary reception of language through the auditory channel via individually prescribed amplification. Examples include:

Auditory training: A process used to teach hearing-impaired individuals to use their residual hearing to the greatest extent possible. It is:

- usually provided by an audiologist or speech pathologist.
- usually provided in individual or group therapy sessions.
- reinforced in the classroom and at home.
- used to reinforce environmental cues in conversations.
- used to help sharpen the individual's ability to discriminate among sounds and words.

Cued speech: One method of supplementing oral communication. It is:

- considered a visual/oral method of communication since it carries no meaning without an accompanying speech signal.
- uses cues that consist of hand signals used near the lips.
- involves eight different hand shapes, used in four different positions.

Manual Communication

Sign systems used in the education of deaf children—American Sign Language, Pidgin Sign (Contact Sign), Signed English, Signing Exact English, and Cued Speech.

Finger spelling: A series of finger positions that represent the individual letters of the alphabet and are used to spell out words.

American Sign Language: A system of ideographic gestures representing words or concepts used by most deaf people. American Sign Language is the most common language of deaf Americans and Canadians. It is their native language, not merely a substitute for English words. In fact, many deaf people are not fluent in written English and cannot simply write notes to communicate. As with any language, people who want to become fluent must communicate with native speakers for many years. On the other hand, ASL is a unique language in that it is adapted to being learned quickly by people who are not children of native speakers.

Total Communication

This method combines the oral/aural and manual modes.

Technological Devices

Teletypewriter Assistance for the Deaf: Enables people to send and receive immediate written messages over telephone lines.

Caption Decoder: A device that allows deaf individuals to receive captions or subtitles on their television screen.

3.52   The Manual Alphabet

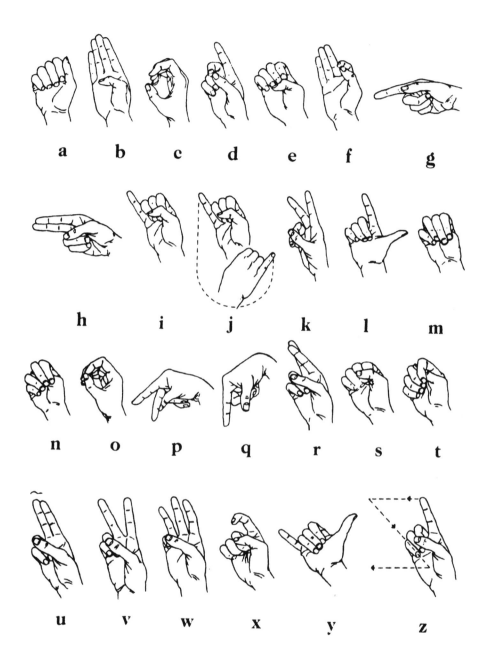

3.53   Degrees of Hearing Impairment

Degree of Hearing Loss	Decibel Loss	Resulting Impairment
Slight	27–40 dB	This individual has difficulty hearing faint noises or distant conversation. The individual with a slight hearing loss will usually not have difficulties in the regular school setting.
Mild	41–55 dB	This individual may miss as much as 50 percent of classroom conversations. The individual may also exhibit limited vocabulary and speech difficulties.
Moderate	56–70 dB	This individual will only be able to hear loud conversation; may exhibit defective speech, vocabulary, and language difficulties.
Severe	71–90 dB	This individual's hearing may be limited to a radius of one foot. The individual may be able to discriminate certain environmental sounds, shows defective speech and language ability, and has severe difficulty understanding consonant sounds.
Profound	91 dB or greater	This individual can sense sounds and tones but is unable to understand them. Vision becomes the primary sense of communication, and speech and language are likely to deteriorate.

3.54 Examples of Typical Sound Intensities

Intensity in Decibels (dB)	Examples
140	Jet plane taking off about 100 feet away
130	Industrial jackhammer
120	Dance club; rock and roll concert
110	Industrial punch press
105	Bulldozer and construction equipment
100	Chainsaw
90	Heavy street noises; factory noises
85	Person shouting from 5–10 feet away
80	The noise from cars on an expressway at 60 mph
75	Noise in a restaurant
70	Window air conditioner
40–65	Typical conversational level; typewriter; small office machines; washing machine
35	Typical house noise
30	Radio station studio
20	Whisper at 5 feet; windy day
10	Threshold of hearing
0	Weakest sounds

3.55   Cross Section of the Ear

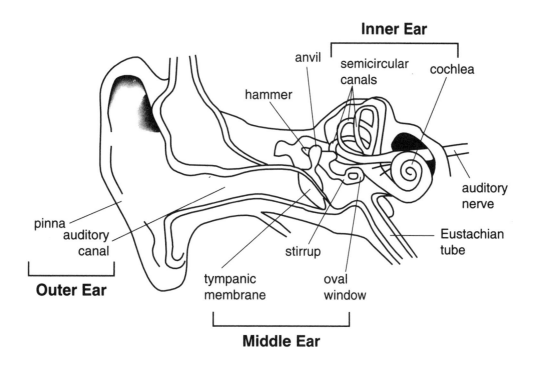

3.56   Facts about Visual Impairments

DEFINITIONS OF VISUAL IMPAIRMENTS

Visual impairment is the consequence of a functional loss of vision, rather than an eye disorder itself. Eye disorders, which can lead to visual impairments, can include retinal degeneration, albinism, cataracts, glaucoma, muscular problems that result in visual disturbances, corneal disorders, diabetic retinopathy, congenital disorders, and infection.

The terms "partially sighted," "low vision," "legally blind," and "totally blind" are used in the educational context to describe students with visual impairments. They are defined as follows:

1. "Partially sighted" indicates some type of visual problem has resulted in a need for special education.

2. "Low vision" generally refers to a severe visual impairment, not necessarily limited to distance vision. Low vision applies to all individuals with sight who are unable to read the newspaper at a normal viewing distance, even with the aid of eyeglasses or contact lenses. They use a combination of vision and other senses to learn, although they may require adaptations in lighting or the size of print, and, sometimes, Braille.

3. "Legally blind" indicates that a person has less than 20/200 vision in the better eye or a very limited field of vision (20 degrees at its widest point).

4. "Totally blind" indicates complete lack of vision and dependence on Braille or other nonvisual media.

INCIDENCE

The rate at which visual impairments occur in individuals under the age of 18 is 12.2 per 1,000. Severe visual impairments (legally or totally blind) occur at a rate of .06 per 1,000.

CHARACTERISTICS

The effect of visual problems on a child's development depends on the severity, type of loss, age at which the condition appears, and overall functioning level of the child. Many children who have multiple disabilities may also have visual impairments resulting in motor, cognitive, and/or social developmental delays.

A young child with visual impairments has little reason to explore interesting objects in the environment and, thus, may miss opportunities to have experiences and to learn. This lack of exploration may continue until learning becomes motivating or until intervention begins.

Because the child cannot see parents or peers, he or she may be unable to imitate social behavior or understand nonverbal cues. Visual handicaps can create obstacles to a growing child's independence.

EDUCATIONAL IMPLICATIONS

Children with visual impairments should be assessed early to benefit from early intervention programs, when applicable. Technology in the form of computers and low-vision optical and video aids enable many partially sighted, low-vision, and blind children to participate in regular class activities. Large-print materials, books on tape, and Braille books are available.

Students with visual impairments may need additional help with special equipment and modifications in the regular curriculum to emphasize listening skills, communication, orientation and mobility, vocation/career options, and daily living skills. Students with low vision or those who are legally blind may need help in using their residual vision more efficiently and in working with special aids and materials. Students who have visual impairments combined with other types of disabilities have a greater need for an interdisciplinary approach and may require greater emphasis on self-care and daily living skills.

3.57   Causes of Visual Impairments

- *Myopia*—Referred to as nearsightedness. This condition occurs when the rays of light from distant objects are not focused on the retina. The individual with this condition is able to see objects more clearly close up.

- *Hyperopia*—Referred to as farsightedness. This condition occurs when the eye is too short and the rays of light from near objects are not focused on the retina. The individual with this condition is able to see objects more clearly at a distance.

- *Astigmatism*—Referred to as "blurred vision." It is caused by uneven curvature of the cornea or lens. This curvature prevents light rays from focusing correctly on the retina. This condition can usually be corrected by corrective or contact lenses.

- *Cataracts*—A cloudiness in the lens of the eye, which blocks the light necessary for seeing clearly. Vision may be blurred, distorted, or incomplete.

- *Glaucoma*—A condition caused by the failure of the aqueous fluid to circulate properly. This results in an elevation of pressure in the eye, which may gradually destroy the optic nerve.

- *Diabetic retinopathy*—Found in children and adults with diabetes. These individuals frequently have impaired vision due to hemorrhages and the growth of new blood vessels in the area of the retina. This results in a condition known as diabetic retinopathy. May be helped with laser surgery.

- *Retinitis pigmentosa*—An inherited disease that causes a gradual degeneration of the retina. This condition is not treatable.

- *Usher's syndrome*—Results from a combination of congenital deafness and retinitis pigmentosa.

- *Macular degeneration*—A fairly common disorder in which the central area of the retina gradually deteriorates. The individual usually retains peripheral vision but loses the ability to see clearly in the center of the visual field.

- *Retrolental fibroplasia*—A condition that results from the use of too much oxygen in the incubation of premature babies.

3.58   The Braille Alphabet

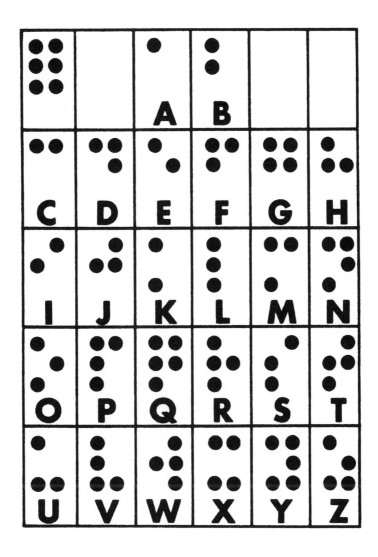

3.59 Typical Characteristics of Children with Visual Impairments

1. The lack of vision or reduced vision may result in delays or limitations in motor, cognitive, and social development.

2. Without visual input, an infant may not be motivated to reach and move toward interesting objects in the environment.

3. As soon as the infant with a visual impairment finds it exciting to hear sounds, he or she will begin to reach and move toward the objects in the environment that make sound.

4. Cognitively, the child who has a visual impairment cannot perceive objects in the environment beyond his or her grasp, including those that are too large or too small or are moving.

5. Although use of other senses enables the child to obtain information about the environment, a cognitive limitation does exist in the range and variety of experiences.

6. Socially, a child with a visual impairment is limited in interaction with the environment. The child cannot see the facial expressions of parents, teachers, and peers; cannot model social behaviors through imitation; and sometimes is unaware of the presence of others unless a sound is made.

7. Although touch provides direct information, it is often socially unacceptable. When older, the child is limited in the ability to orient to environmental cues and cannot travel freely.

8. The unique curriculum for students who are blind includes reading and writing through the use of Braille, listening skills, personal–social and daily living skills, orientation and mobility skills, career education, and instruction in the use of special aids and equipment.

9. Students with low vision and visual limitations may need instruction in the efficient use of vision and in the use of optical aids and alternative learning materials.

10. Many students with visual impairments have additional disabilities and may require a curriculum that emphasizes functional living skills and communication skills.

11. Appropriate educational settings and services for children with visual impairments vary according to individual needs. Self-contained classrooms, residential schools, or regular classrooms with or without special assistance may be appropriate options for individual students.

3.60 Cross Section of the Eye

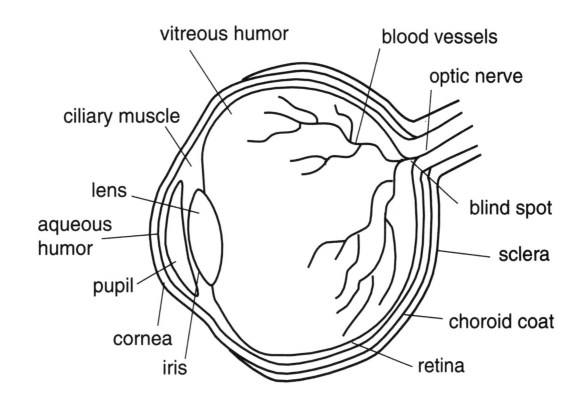

vitreous humor

blood vessels

optic nerve

ciliary muscle

lens

aqueous humor

pupil

cornea

iris

blind spot

sclera

choroid coat

retina

3.61 Variables that May Influence Placement Decisions for Bilingual Children with Disabilities

Placement decisions for the bilingual student with disabilities should include the type and nature of instruction to be provided, the language of instruction, the conveyor of instruction, the duration of instruction, and the student's learning needs and style. The following special education variables and bilingual factors should be addressed in determining placements:

1. Student's age

2. Type and degree of impairment or disability

3. Age at which disability occurred

4. Level of language involvement because of the disability

5. Level of academic achievement

6. Entry-level language skills (upon entering school)

7. Measured intellectual ability

8. Method and language used in measuring academic achievement and intellectual ability

9. Level of adaptive behavior

10. Time spent in United States

11. Current cultural home setting

12. Social maturity

13. Level of language proficiency in English and other language

14. Amount and type of language input received in the home environment

15. Speech and language capabilities in both languages

16. Presence of multiple handicaps

17. Ambulation or mobility

18. Success in past and present placements

19. Wishes of students and parents

3.62 Basic Elements of an Individualized Education Plan (IEP) for Bilingual Children with Disabilities

IEPs for bilingual students with disabilities should include the following elements:

1. The child's current educational status, including all service programs the child is receiving.

2. Goals, including adaptation to acculturation and growth in both the first and second languages. The goals must be realistic in regard to the time necessary; years could be involved.

3. The sequence of short-term instructional objectives leading up to each goal.

4. A list of instructional and service requirements including a balance between the first and second languages, as well as delineation of who will assist with acculturation needs.

5. An indication of how much and what aspects of the program will be in the mainstream.

6. The program's duration.

7. Realistic criteria for the IEP and a schedule for evaluation of the IEP's effectiveness.

8. A statement of the role of the parents.

9. Specification of changes to be made in the physical, social, and instructional realms, including the first and second languages and cross-cultural adaptation (Collier, pp. 272–273).

3.63   Selecting and Adapting Materials for Bilingual Children with Disabilities

SELECTING MATERIALS

The following guidelines represent some of the many considerations teachers should bear in mind when evaluating, selecting, adapting, or developing materials. The teacher should:

1. Know the specific language abilities of each student.

2. Include appropriate cultural experiences in material adapted or developed.

3. Ensure that material is presented at a rate commensurate with student needs and abilities.

4. Document the success of selected materials.

5. Adapt only specific materials requiring modifications, and do not attempt to change too much at one time.

6. Try out different materials and adaptations until an appropriate education for each student is achieved.

7. Strategically implement adaptations to ensure smooth transitions into the new materials.

8. Follow some consistent format or guide when evaluating materials.

9. Be knowledgeable about particular cultures and heritages and their compatibility with selected materials.

10. Follow a well-developed process for evaluating the success of adapted or developed materials as the individual language and cultural needs of students are addressed.

ADAPTING MATERIALS

The following list is not designed to be all-inclusive; variations may be required in order to meet individual needs.

1. Adjust the method of presentation or content.

2. Develop supplemental material.

3. Tape-record directions for the material.

4. Provide alternatives for responding to questions.

5. Rewrite brief sections to lower the reading level.

6. Outline the material for the student before reading a selection.

7. Reduce the number of pages or items on a page to be completed by the student.

8. Break tasks into smaller subtasks.

9. Provide additional practice to ensure mastery.

10. Substitute a similar, less complex task for a particular assignment.

11. Develop simple study guides to complement required materials.

3.64 Suggested Identification Procedures for Students with Limited English Proficiency (LEP)

The procedures for the identification of students with Limited English Proficiency (LEP) who are experiencing difficulty in the general educational setting may be divided into two areas:

LEP STUDENTS WITH FORMAL SCHOOL EXPERIENCES

Before you consider referring an LEP student with previous academic experiences for special education services, the following should be implemented and documented:

- Provide instruction in the native language for content area development plus extensive instruction in English as a second language (ESL).

- Try to provide educationally-related support services, i.e., speech and language services, as well as psychological, social work, and non-career counseling services by qualified bilingual/bicultural professional personnel, as appropriate.

- Document the extent to which these services have been provided in the regular education setting.

LEP STUDENTS WITH LITTLE OR NO FORMAL SCHOOL EXPERIENCE

This area includes students who:

- Speak a language other than English.
- Have had limited schooling.
- Have nonequivalent academic instruction.
- Have no formal schooling in their native country.
- Perform poorly on standardized tests whose norms and content are based on experience and acculturation patterns of children raised in the United States.
- Experience some level of difficulty when enrolled, for perhaps the first time, in a formal educational setting.

SUGGESTED STRATEGIES/ACTIVITIES

As a result, the following strategies and activities are suggested prior to a referral for special education services:

- School and community orientation by staff members.
- Native language development and enrichment.
- Reinforcement of self-identity.
- Reinforcement of self-concept.

3.64 continued

- Reinforcement of interpersonal skill development across contexts.
- Use of specialized ESL methodology and strategies across all curriculum areas.
- Experientially-based educational methodology and techniques.
- Hands-on enrichment activities and community/school participation.
- Instruction in literacy skills in the native language along with English.
- Strategies designed to develop proficiency in behaviors necessary in academic settings (e.g., sitting in chair, raising hand).
- Planned parent orientation and involvement.
- Intensive English as a Second Language instruction.
- Educationally-related support services.
- Speech and language improvement services in the native language of the student.
- Documented statements indicating the extent of provisions provided.

3.65 Causes of Physical Disabilities

Cerebral Palsy

A disorder of movement and posture due to damage to areas of the brain that control motor function. Important information about this condition includes:

- The condition becomes evident in infancy or early childhood.
- The incidence is around 3 per every 1,000 live births.
- The impairment may involve different parts of the body including:

  Hemiplegia—involves the arm, leg, and trunk on the same side;

  Paraplegia—legs only;

  Quadriplegia—both arms and both legs as well as the trunk and neck;

  Diplegia—legs more involved than the arms;

  Double hemiplegia—arms more involved than the legs, and one side more involved.

Arthogyposis Multiplex Congenita

A condition of fixed stiffness and deformity of the limbs in any joint prior to birth, sometimes referred to as "fixed joint" disorder. Important facts include:

- Limb muscles are absent or much smaller and weaker than usual.
- Child has little or no joint motion.
- Curvature of the spine may also be present.

Hypertonia

A condition, found in 60 percent of cerebral palsy victims, involving increased stiffness.

Athetosis

A condition affecting the extra pyramidal tract of the central nervous system, resulting in involuntary movements. Facts about this condition include:

- The arms, hands, and facial muscles are typically more involved than the legs.
- The condition is exhibited by about 20 percent of individuals with cerebral palsy.
- The individual has little or no control over his/her movements.
- Attention deficit is exacerbated by a lack of head control.
- The condition results in severe dependence in activities of daily living and locomotion.

Ataxia

A rare condition of cerebral palsy characterized by an inability to achieve coordination in balancing and hand use.

3.65 continued

Hemophilia

Often called the "bleeder's disease," this condition is characterized by poor blood-clotting ability due to the absence of the clotting factor in the blood.

Juvenile Rheumatoid Arthritis

This is a metabolic disorder caused by the body's inability to burn sugars and starches to create energy. The pancreas does not produce adequate insulin.

Limb Deficiency

This condition, which is characterized by the absence of a limb, may be congenital or acquired after birth. The acquisition of an artificial limb (prosthesis) can be important to the physical and psychological well-being of the individual.

Muscular Dystrophy

This condition is characterized by increasing weakness of skeletal muscles. Progressive muscle weakness, awkwardness, and slowness in movement eventually force the child to become confined to a wheelchair. Further characteristics include:

- Progression is usually rapid with death typically occurring in the teen years.
- Students fatigue more easily as the disease progresses.
- Initial symptoms may hamper a child while running or climbing stairs.

Osteogenesis Imperfecta

This condition is characterized by brittle bones. It results from the defective development of both quality and quantity of bone tissue. The condition is further characterized by:

- Abnormal growth of bones in length and thickness.
- Bone development results in brittle composition.

Spina Bifida

This congenital disease is caused by a defect in development of the vertebral column, which results in spinal cord and nerve root damage. As a result, related neurological problems develop. Important facts about this disease include the following:

- Myelomeningocele is the most severe form.
- Deficits in spina bifida range from minor sensory and ambulatory problems to paraplegia and lack of sensation.

- Orthopedic deformities may exist.
- Incontinence may occur in the severe form.
- Urinary tract infections are common.
- Individuals are more susceptible to the development of hydrocephalus, which is an abnormal buildup of cerebrospinal fluids in the cranial cavity.

Spinal Cord Injury

This condition can result from automobile, bicycle, skiing, and other accidents causing traumatic injury to the spinal cord. The extent of the injury varies according to the level and type of lesion or injury to the spinal cord.

Traumatic Brain Injury

This condition results from an insult to the brain caused by an external physical force, resulting in an impairment of cognitive abilities or physical functioning.

Cystic Fibrosis

This is a hereditary disorder characterized by chronic pulmonary involvement and pancreatic deficiency.

3.66 Potential Classroom Modifications and Teacher Skills Required for Certain Physical Disabilities

Chronic Condition	Modification	Skill Required
Asthma	avoidance of allergens participation in physical activity administration of medication as needed	—CPR —recognition of signs of respiratory stress —recognition of medication side effects
Congenital heart disease	participation in physical activity administration of medication as needed diet or fluids	—CPR —recognition of signs and symptoms of heart failure —recognition of medication side effects
Cystic fibrosis	physical activity administration of medication as needed diet	—recognition of signs and symptoms of respiratory stress —recognition of medication side effects
Diabetes	diet, bathroom frequency, snacks, balance of exercise and food	—recognition of signs and symptoms of hypoglycemia (rapid onset)
Hemophilia	physical activity	—recognition of signs and symptoms of bleeding —management of bleeding (cuts and scrapes)
Juvenile rheumatoid arthritis	participation in physical activity environment (stairs) administration of medication as needed	—recognition of signs and symptoms of increased inflammation —recognition of infrequency of movement —recognition of broken bones

(continued)

Chronic Condition	Modification	Skill Required
Kidney disease	physical activity diet and fluids bathroom privileges medication administration	—recognition of signs and symptoms of fluid retention
Leukemia	participation in physical activity exposure to communicative diseases	—recognition of signs and symptoms of infection —recognition of signs and symptoms of bleeding
Seizure disorder	participation in physical activity environment administration of medication as needed	—seizure management —recognition of signs and symptoms of distress during and after seizures —recognition of medication side effects
Spina bifida	participation in physical activity environment to accommodate mobility	—recognition of signs and symptoms of shunt blockage

Note: This chart contains general information only. Health care plans on an individualized basis with a qualified physician are recommended.

3.67 Physical and Occupational Therapy Measurement Areas

Evaluation by respective therapists may include but is not limited to the measurement of the following areas:

Areas of Assessment Common to Both Services:

- Developmental assessment levels
- Range of motion
- Muscle-testing functions
- Sensory integration
- Activities of daily living
- Needs and uses of adaptive equipment

Physical Therapy:

- Endurance
- Balance and equilibrium
- Postural and joint deviation
- Gait analysis
- Personal independence
- Wheelchair management
- Checking of prosthetic and orthotic equipment/devices
- Architectural barriers and transportation needs

Occupational Therapy:

- Oral-motor dysfunction and feeding problems
- Sensory processing
- Visual-perceptual-motor status
- Neuromuscular function
- Manual dexterity
- Psychosocial behaviors
- Play and leisure-time abilities
- Self-help skills
- Effect of physical facilities and environment on the child's performance
- Pre-vocational skills

3.68   Guidelines for a Physical Therapy Evaluation

REQUIRED EVALUATION

A formal physical therapy evaluation is required only in the following situations:

New to program—When a student is new to a program, whether it be a homebound, a preschool program, or a school program where the Eligibility Committee mandates therapy for the student. If a formal physical therapy evaluation is available from the referring agency, school district, or private physical therapist, it may be used.

Preschooler advancing to kindergarten—When a preschool student is advancing to an elementary program and the child has been receiving physical therapy in a preschool program, a formal evaluation should be forwarded to the Eligibility Committee upon the request of the appropriate building administrator or local school district. This can be done only with parental consent.

CONTENT OF EVALUATION

Depending upon the program to which the therapist is assigned, the following general areas may be addressed during the physical therapy evaluation. Guidelines for these areas have been prepared for a diverse student population. The therapist is expected to evaluate only those areas appropriate to the assigned population.

- *Background information*—Report any pertinent medical or social history.
- *Behavior*—Report behaviors that interfere with program implementation and/or affect the student's compliance, e.g., level of alertness, concentration, personality disorder, etc.
- *Vision*—Significant findings would include field deficits and tracking, focusing, or visual acuity problems.
- *Communication*—Significant findings would include receptive or expressive language deficits, augmentative devices (e.g., communication board, handivoice, etc.).
- *Neuromuscular*—Significant findings would include alterations in muscle tone (hypertoncity, hypotonicity, rigidity), sensation, coordination, motor planning, and muscle strength.

  Muscle strength should be reported using standardized grades for consistency. Muscle strength grades are reported as follows: Normal, Good, Fair, Poor, Trace, (plus/minus) Zero.

  Note progression through a developmental sequence noting any deviations.
- *Range of motion and muscle length*—Significant findings would include any deviation from normal standardized joint range of motion and muscle length. Document this finding in standardized goniometric measurements.

3.68 continued

- *Skeletal and joint condition*—Report should include any skeletal or joint condition that limits function. Significant findings would include absence or asymmetry of extremity, joint disease or deformity, x-ray report of skeletal deviation (scoliosis, lordosis, kyphosis, subluxation, or dislocation of hip), surgical intervention (date and procedure).

- *Skin and soft tissue*—Review the integrity of the skin and soft tissue. Significant findings would include decubiti, lesions, edema, discoloration, rash, scars, skin temperature, and measurement of circumferential abnormality.

- *Pain and tenderness*—Note complaints of pain or tenderness, onset, location, and frequency.

- *Developmental test*—When utilizing a standardized developmental test for the birth-to-3 population, report pertinent achievement of developmental milestones including gross motor, perceptual-fine motor, cognitive, social/emotional and language. If an occupational therapist and/or speech and language pathologist are following a child, defer reporting on the developmental areas that they would be addressing.

- *Balance and equilibrium*—Significant findings would include the inability to maintain independent static and dynamic balance in sitting, standing, walking, unilateral stance, or tandem walking. Note the degree of assistance/guarding required. Note presence or absence of protective reactions.

- *Posture*—Note deviations from normal segmental alignment—supine, sitting, or standing.

- *Gait pattern*—Note all deviations from normal gait patterns, weight-bearing status, assistive devices, and guarding required.

- *Functional mobility*—Note the student's functional ability in the school environment including wheelchair mobility, level of independence during transfers, ability to negotiate stairs and curbs, and getting on/off school bus and ramps.

- *Endurance*—Significant findings would include easy fatigue ability and limited distance, time, and speed.

- *Equipment*—Note assistive devices, orthosis, prosthesis, and wheelchairs as well as need for, condition of, and fit of appliance.

3.69 Areas of Dysfunction Requiring Occupational Therapy and Their Impact on School Performance

APRAXIA

School performance:

- Difficulty learning any unfamiliar skilled activity (e.g., writing, crafts, sports)
- Poor tool usage
- Clumsiness, falling, especially when ascending or descending from equipment (gym, playground)
- Poor dressing skills, especially gloves, belt, shoe laces, etc.
- Poor self-esteem
- Disorganized behavior
- Inordinate fear of failure

DEFICIENT BILATERAL INTEGRATION

School performance:

- Poor development of hand dominance
- Inefficient use of hands
- Poor gross coordination (e.g., in sports such as baseball)
- Poor skilled manipulation
- Difficulty with arts and crafts, playing an instrument
- Difficulty cutting, pasting, and writing

DEFICIENT BALANCE

School performance:

- Poor gym and playground skills
- Difficulty negotiating obstacles
- Clumsiness
- Fear of movement in space

3.69 continued

DEFICIENT BILATERAL COORDINATION

School performance:

- Poor gym and playground skills
- Difficulty with skilled manipulation
- Difficulty with arts and crafts, home activities, wood shop, playing a musical instrument
- Difficulty pasting, cutting
- Difficulty with clothing closures, opening containers, wrapping and unwrapping objects (packages)

DIFFICULTY CROSSING

School performance:

- Poor development of hand dominance
- Inefficient use of preferred hand for skilled manipulation

DEFICIENT RESPONSE SPEED

School performance:

- Delayed reaction time—poor timed-test performance, gym performance, and activities (e.g., baseball)

DEFICIENT RUNNING SPEED AND AGILITY

School performance:

- Poor gym and playground skills
- Clumsiness
- Difficulty climbing stairs
- Difficulty getting on and off bus

DEFICIENT UPPER LIMB COORDINATION

School performance:

- Poor gym skills, especially with equipment such as bat and ball
- Difficulty doffing and donning garments

DEFICIENT UPPER LIMB SPEED AND DEXTERITY

School performance:

- Difficulty copying, writing, cutting, pasting
- Poor gym performance
- Poor skilled manipulation
- Difficulty manipulating classroom computer
- Poor performance in art and crafts at home, work
- Difficulty playing musical instruments

DEFICIENT STRENGTH

School performance:

- Easily fatigues
- Difficulty opening heavy doors or lifting heavy objects

IMMATURE, BIZARRE, OR DEFICIT DRAWING

School performance:

- Poor body image
- Poor spatial relations
- Poor motor planning
- Poor dressing skills
- Poor skilled manipulation
- Poor self-esteem
- Clumsiness

IMPAIRED FIGURE-GROUND PERCEPTION

School performance:

- Difficulty unwrapping packages
- Difficulty reading—cannot attack a word phonetically
- Poor organization
- Difficulty negotiating around crowded classroom and hallways
- Poor attention
- Difficulty reading maps

3.69 continued

- Difficulty locating objects in room
- Scanning problems
- Careless in his or her work

IMPAIRED FORM CONSTANCY

School performance:

- Poor letter formation
- Difficulty learning basic number skills
- Difficulty doing puzzles
- Difficulty reading maps
- Difficulty reading music

GENERAL SENSORY-MOTOR IMPAIRMENT

School performance:

- Antisocial behaviors
- Poor self-esteem
- Poor peer relationships

IMPAIRED SPATIAL RELATIONS

School performance:

- Difficulty reading and writing letters (reversals, etc.), and/or in spelling and arithmetic
- Difficulty copying letters or shapes from sample or from chalkboard
- Poor arts and crafts skills (difficulty drawing and making three-dimensional crafts)
- Difficulty deciphering musical notes
- Difficulty reading maps
- Difficulty understanding graphs

POOR FINE-MOTOR COORDINATION

School performance:

- Difficulty writing, cutting
- Difficulty with skilled manipulation

- Poor written-test performance
- Sloppy manipulation
- Difficulty opening containers
- Difficulty with clothing closures

IMPAIRED POSITION IN SPACE

School performance:

- Clumsy, hesitant movement
- Inability to understand words designating spatial position
- Reversals of numbers, letters, or words (e.g., 42-24, b-d, saw-was)

TACTILE DEFICIENCY

School performance:

- Poor attention span, distractibility, hyperactivity
- Antisocial or acting-out behaviors
- Dislike of "messy" activities (arts and crafts)
- Sloppy eaters, food fetishes
- Self-stimulatory behaviors
- Decreased awareness of pain

VISUAL CLOSURE DEFICITS

School performance:

- Difficulty with geometry
- Poor prewriting skills
- Poor craft performance
- Difficulty reading maps
- Difficulty completing puzzles

VISUAL DISCRIMINATION DEFICITS

School performance:

- Poor reading and writing
- Difficulty doing puzzles

3.69 continued

- Difficulty reading maps
- Difficulty using alternative communication system

VESTIBULAR DYSFUNCTION

School performance:

- Fear of movement, especially on equipment or in playground
- Clumsiness, frequent falling
- Poor gym performance, especially on equipment
- Possible hyperactivity

VISUAL FORM AND SPACE PERCEPTION DEFICITS

School performance:

- Difficulty with reading, writing, math
- Difficulty negotiating obstacles (in hallway, around classroom)
- Poor visual attention
- Difficulty using classroom computers and visual screen equipment
- Difficulty wrapping/unwrapping packages, opening containers

VISUAL MEMORY DEFICITS

School performance:

- Difficulty with math and reading
- Poor test performance
- Poor arts and crafts skills

3.70   Facts about Traumatic Brain Injury (TBI)

WHAT IS TBI?

A traumatic brain injury (TBI) is an injury to the brain caused by the head being hit by something or being shaken violently. (The exact definition of TBI, according to special education law, is given below.) This injury can change how the person acts, moves, and thinks. A traumatic brain injury can also change how a student learns and functions in school.

The term *TBI* is used for head injuries that can cause changes in one or more of these areas:

Thinking and reasoning	Talking
Understanding words	Behaving
Remembering things	Walking and other physical activities
Paying attention	Seeing and/or hearing
Solving problems	Learning
Thinking abstractly	

The term *TBI* is not used for a person who was born with a brain injury. It also is not used for brain injuries that happen during birth.

The definition of TBI below comes from the Individuals with Disabilities Education Act (IDEA). The IDEA is the federal law that guides how schools provide special education and related services to children and youth with disabilities.

IDEA'S DEFINITION OF TBI

Our nation's special education law, the Individuals with Disabilities Education Act (IDEA) defines traumatic brain injury as . . .

". . . an acquired injury to the brain caused by an external physical force, resulting in total or partial functional disability or psychosocial impairment, or both, that adversely affects a child's educational performance. The term applies to open or closed head injuries resulting in impairments in one or more areas, such as cognition; language; memory; attention; reasoning; abstract thinking; judgment; problem-solving; sensory, perceptual, and motor abilities; psycho-social behavior; physical functions; information processing; and speech. The term does not apply to brain injuries that are congenital or degenerative, or to brain injuries induced by birth trauma." [34 Code of Federal Regulations §300.7(c)(12)].

HOW COMMON IS TBI?

More than one million children receive brain injuries each year. More than 30,000 of these children have lifelong disabilities as a result of the brain injury.

3.70 continued

WHAT ARE THE SIGNS OF TBI?

The signs of brain injury can be very different, depending upon where the brain is injured and how severely. Children with TBI may have one or more difficulties, including:

- *Physical disabilities:* Individuals with TBI may have problems speaking, seeing, hearing, and using their other senses. They may have headaches and feel tired often. They may also have trouble with skills, such as writing and drawing. Their muscles may suddenly contract or tighten (this is called spasticity). They may also have seizures. Their balance and walking may also be affected. They may be partly or completely paralyzed on one side of the body, or both sides.

- *Difficulties with thinking:* Because the brain has been injured, it is common that the person's ability to use the brain changes. For example, children with TBI may have trouble with short-term memory (being able to remember something from one minute to the next, such as what the teacher just said). They may also have trouble with their long-term memory (being able to remember information from the past, such as facts learned last month). People with TBI may have trouble concentrating and only be able to focus their attention for a short time. They may think slowly. They may have trouble talking and listening to others. They may also have difficulty with reading and writing, planning, understanding the order in which events happen (called sequencing), and judgment.

- *Social, behavioral, or emotional problems:* These difficulties may include sudden changes in mood, anxiety, and depression. Children with TBI may have trouble relating to others. They may be restless and may laugh or cry a lot. They may not have much motivation or much control over their emotions.

A child with TBI may not have all of the above difficulties. Brain injuries can range from mild to severe, and so can the changes that result from the injury. This means that it's difficult to predict how an individual will recover from the injury. Early and ongoing help can make a big difference in how the child recovers. This help can include physical or occupational therapy, counseling, and special education.

It's also important to know that, as the child grows and develops, parents and teachers may notice new problems. This is because, as students grow, they are expected to use their brain in new and different ways. The damage to the brain from the earlier injury can make it difficult for the student to learn new skills that come with getting older. Sometimes, parents and educators may not even realize that the student's difficulty comes from the earlier injury.

3.71 Tips for Parents of Children with TBI

- Learn about TBI. The more you know, the more you can help yourself and your child. See the list of resources and organizations at the back of this book.

- Work with the medical team to understand your child's injury and treatment plan. Don't be shy about asking questions. Tell them what you know or think. Make suggestions.

- Keep track of your child's treatment. A 3-ring binder or a box can help you store this history. As your child recovers, you may meet with many doctors, nurses, and others. Write down what they say. Put any paperwork they give you in the notebook or throw it in the box. You can't remember all of this! Also, if you need to share any of this paperwork with someone else, make a copy. Don't give away your original!

- Talk to other parents whose children have TBI. There are parent groups all over the U.S. Parents can share practical advice and emotional support. Call NICHCY (1-800-695-0285) to find out how to find parent groups near you.

- If your child was in school before the injury, plan for his or her return to school. Get in touch with the school. Ask the principal about special education services. Have the medical team share information with the school.

- When your child returns to school, ask the school to test your child as soon as possible to identify his or her special education needs. Meet with the school and help develop a plan for your child called an Individualized Education Plan (IEP).

- Keep in touch with your child's teacher. Tell the teacher about how your child is doing at home. Ask how your child is doing in school.

RECORDS

3.72   Tips for Teachers of Children with TBI

- Find out as much as you can about the child's injury and his or her present needs. Find out more about TBI. See the list of resources and organizations at the back of this book.

- Give the student extra time to finish schoolwork and tests.

- Give directions one step at a time. For tasks with many steps, it helps to give the student written directions.

- Show the student how to perform new tasks. Give examples to go with new ideas and concepts.

- Have consistent routines. This helps the student know what to expect. If the routine is going to change, let the student know ahead of time.

- Check to make sure that the student has actually learned the new skill. Give the student lots of opportunities to practice the new skill.

- Show the student how to use an assignment book and a daily schedule. This helps the student get organized.

- Realize that the student may get tired easily. Let the student rest as needed.

- Reduce distractions.

- Keep in touch with the student's parents. Share information about how the student is doing at home and at school.

- Be flexible about expectations. Be patient. Maximize the student's chances for success.

ASSIGNMENTS

3.73   Asperger's Syndrome

WHAT IS ASPERGER'S SYNDROME?

Asperger's syndrome (AS) is a pervasive developmental disorder characterized by an inability to understand how to interact socially. Other features include clumsy and uncoordinated motor movements, social impairment with extreme obtuseness, limited interests and/or unusual preoccupations, repetitive routines or rituals, speech and language peculiarities, and nonverbal communication problems. Generally, children with AS have few facial expressions apart from anger or misery. Most have excellent rote memory and musical ability, and become intensely interested in one or two subjects (sometimes to the exclusion of other topics). They may talk at length about a favorite subject or repeat a word or phrase many times. Children with AS tend to be "in their own world" and preoccupied with their own agenda. AS is commonly recognized after the age of 3. Some individuals who exhibit features of autism (a developmental brain disorder characterized by impaired social interaction and communication skills) but who have well-developed language skills may be diagnosed with AS, although high-functioning autism differs from AS in early language delay.

IS THERE ANY TREATMENT?

There is no specific course of treatment or cure for AS. Treatment, which is symptomatic and rehabilitational, may include both psychosocial and psychopharmacological interventions such as psychotherapy, parent education and training, behavioral modification, social skills training, educational interventions, and/or medications including psychostimulants, mood stabilizers, beta blockers, neuroleptics, and tricyclic antidepressants.

WHAT IS THE PROGNOSIS?

Children with AS have a better prognosis than those with other forms of pervasive developmental disorders, and they are much more likely to grow up to be independently functioning adults. Nonetheless, in most cases, these individuals will continue to demonstrate, to some extent, subtle disturbances in social interactions. There is also an increased risk for development of psychosis (a mental disorder) and/or mood problems such as depression and anxiety in the later years.

WHAT RESEARCH IS BEING DONE?

The NINDS (National Institute of Neurological Disorders and Stroke) conducts and supports a broad range of research on developmental disorders including AS. The goals of these studies are to increase understanding of these disorders and to find ways to treat, prevent, and ultimately cure them.

Information is provided by the National Institute of Neurological Disorders and Stroke.

3.74 Fragile X Syndrome

WHAT IS FRAGILE X?

Fragile X is similar to Down syndrome, yet it affects people differently. Most symptoms are not noticeable to the human eye, and some are extremely difficult to point out. Some of the symptoms of Fragile X include:

- Mental impairment ranging from learning disabilities to mental retardation.
- Attention deficit, hyperactivity, anxiety, and an unstable mood.
- Autistic-like behaviors.
- Large ears, long face, flat feet.
- Hyperextensive joints (especially fingers).

Boys are typically more severely affected than girls. Although most boys with the disease have mental retardation, only one third to one half of the girls have significant intellectual impairment; the rest have either normal IQ or small learning disabilities. Emotional and behavioral problems are common in both sexes. Fragile X syndrome is the single most common inherited cause of mental impairment. Current estimates of its prevalence vary, but some experts believe that Fragile X affects at least 1 in 1,000 males and females of all races and ethnic groups. More appropriate estimates put the frequency at 1 in 1,500 males and 1 in 2,500 females. In either case, Fragile X is one of the most common genetic diseases in humans. It is estimated that 80 to 90 percent of people with Fragile X are not yet diagnosed.

Recent studies suggest that 1 in 290–400 women of all races are Fragile X carriers. The number of men who are carriers of this disease is thought to be 1 in 800. These extremely high rates make Fragile X syndrome one of the most commonly inherited diseases in humans.

GENETIC CAUSE

Fragile X is inherited from a direct family member. Carrier men (transmitting males) pass the permutation to all of their daughters but none of their sons. Each child of a carrier woman has a 50 percent chance of inheriting the gene. The Fragile X permutation can be passed down silently through generations in a family before the syndrome affects a child or until they are aware of it. Under normal circumstances, each cell in the body contains 46 chromosomes (23 pairs). These chromosomes are made up of genetic material (DNA) necessary for the production of proteins that lead to growth, development, and physical and intellectual characteristics. The first 22 pairs of chromosomes are the same in both males and females. The remaining two chromosomes are called sex chromosomes (X and Y), which determine whether a person is male or female.

Males have only one X chromosome that is inherited from the mother at conception. They get a Y chromosome from the father. Females inherit two X chromosomes, one from each parent.

CURES

There currently is no cure for Fragile X, although appropriate education and medications can help maximize the potential of each child. Recent progress has been made in understanding mechanisms and potential treatments for inherited diseases that are caused by a single gene, such as Fragile X.

CURRENT MEDICAL RESEARCH FOCUS

■ *Gene therapy:* Studying the gene that causes Fragile X in order to determine whether a healthy gene may be inserted into the DNA of affected individuals, thereby replacing the mutated, ineffective gene.

■ *Protein replacement therapy:* Studying the protein product that is lacking due to the mutation, in hopes that the protein may be supplemented from an external source.

■ *Psychopharmacology:* Treating symptoms of the disorder with medications.

Many researchers believe that when medical treatment becomes available, it will help Fragile X individuals of all ages.

3.75   Prader-Willi Syndrome

Prader-Willi syndrome (PWS) is a genetic developmental disorder with a unique set of medical, cognitive, and behavioral characteristics. First recognized as a "syndrome" in 1956 by Prader, Labhart, and Willi, PWS is now recognized as one of the most common micro deletion syndromes and genetic causes of obesity. Over the last 25 years, many children and adults have been diagnosed with this complex, genetic developmental disorder.

Symptoms of Prader-Willi syndrome include many, but not necessarily all, of the following:

- Central nervous system malfunction, including impaired body control and mental retardation with an average IQ around 70. Dysfunction of the hypothalamus affects physical growth, sexual development, appetite, temperature control, and emotional stability.

- Hypotonia during infancy with poor motor control, weak crying, and poor sucking ability. Although children get stronger as they grow older, muscle tone usually remains lower than normal.

- Short stature, with adults reaching about five feet, and having small hands and feet, plus a narrow forehead.

- Insatiable appetite begins somewhere between ages 2 and 5 years. Because individuals with PWS have low metabolism, which is only 60 percent of normal, they require fewer calories to maintain weight. An uncontrollable preoccupation with food usually leads to obesity, serious health problems, and early death unless access to food is strictly controlled. With adequate supervision and careful control of food intake, persons with PWS can maintain healthy weight.

- Scratching and skin picking due to increased pain tolerance and decreased sensory input.

- Behavior difficulties beginning in early childhood and persisting throughout adult life include temper tantrums, stubbornness, noncompliance, and resistance to transitions. Most persons with PWS show signs of obsessive-compulsive disorder (OCD), apart from their obsessions with food. OCD symptoms in PWS include ordering and arranging, concerns with symmetry, rewriting, and a compulsion to tell or ask the same thing over and over.

Prader-Willi syndrome is caused by a very small deletion in chromosome 16. Approximately 1 in 10,000 to 15,000 individuals are affected by Prader-Willi syndrome.

Individuals with PWS may experience other health problems:

- The most common physical abnormality associated with PWS is obesity. Hyperphagia, i.e., overeating characterized by obsessive-compulsive food-seeking behavior (including hoarding, foraging, and eating unappealing substances), is the cause of obesity in most cases. Because obesity is the source of other medical problems, it is important to treat and control hyperphagia.

- Thick, viscous saliva is often a problem. A toothpaste called Biotine can moderate this.

- Osteoporosis is common.

- Hypotonia is almost always present at birth and is associated with failure to thrive and with poor sucking, resulting in the need for specialized feeding techniques.

- Hypogonadism or genital hypoplasia is also identifiable from birth.

- A characteristic set of physical features, including narrow bifrontal diameter, almond-shaped eyes, narrow nasal bridge, a downturned mouth with a thin upper lip, and short stature, is common. Growth hormone therapies have greatly improved the growth rate of many children with PWS.

- Other characteristics are a high pain threshold, skin picking, and a high threshold for vomiting.

Individuals with PWS experience a range of cognitive deficits and behavioral problems:

- Individuals with PWS experience a gross motor delay as well as a delay in language development.

- People with PWS experience social difficulties in relating to peers and other people in their environment.

- They tend to be hypo-aroused and often experience daytime sleepiness.

- Behaviors indicative of PWS include temper tantrums, stubbornness, controlling and manipulative behavior, obsessive-compulsive characteristics, and rigidity with regards to daily routines. Lying, stealing, and aggression are also common, especially when dealing with food-seeking behaviors.

- Most people with PWS have mild cognitive deficits but show strengths in reading, visual-spatial skills, and long-term memory.

- Jigsaw puzzles and word searches are often keen interests of individuals with PWS.

3.76 Turner's Syndrome

Turner's syndrome is a disorder of the chromosomes that affect females, and in which the two X chromosomes are partially or completely absent. Women with Turner's syndrome lack all or part of one of the so-called X chromosomes (i.e., sex chromosomes) that carry genes for conditions relating to the development of ovaries, sex-hormone production, and physical development in general. This relationship leads to faulty development of the ovaries and sex-hormone production; because of this, these women usually cannot become pregnant. Menstruation usually also fails to occur, and usually they do not have normal development of breasts and pubic hair. Estrogen treatment should be given from about the age of 12, starting with very small doses.

- As there are height determination genes in the X chromosomes, the lacking X chromosome leads to decreased growth and final height. The average height of women with Turner's syndrome is 4.82 feet, varying between 4.43 feet and 5.35 feet. This is 0.65 feet below the height of women with normal chromosomes. The reduced height is a handicap, but growth velocity and final height can be increased with growth hormone treatment from the age of 7.

- Approximately 40 percent of girls with Turner's syndrome have a so-called "bed-neck," and in a number of cases, it may be necessary to perform surgery for this. Ten percent have a stricture of the main artery, and approximately 12 percent have other less serious heart anomalies. Surgery is often necessary for strictures of the main artery, but this is done with good results.

- The mental development of girls with Turner's syndrome is within the normal range, but due to their delayed mental maturation process, it is important that they be stimulated in childhood, especially by parents. It is also very important that they be treated according to their age and not according to their reduced height.

3.77 William's Syndrome

WHAT IS WILLIAM'S SYNDROME?

William's syndrome is a rare, congenital (present at birth) disorder characterized by physical and developmental problems including an impulsive and outgoing (excessively social) personality, limited spatial skills and motor control, and intellectual disability (i.e., developmental delay, learning disabilities, mental retardation, or attention deficit disorder). Other features include characteristic "elfin-like" facial features, heart and blood vessel problems, hypercalcemia (elevated blood calcium levels), low birth weight, slow weight gain, feeding problems, irritability during infancy, dental and kidney abnormalities, hyperacusis (sensitive hearing), and musculoskeletal problems. Symptoms vary among patients. Although individuals with William's syndrome may show competence in areas such as language, music, and interpersonal relations, their IQs are usually below average, and they are considered moderately to mildly retarded. Scientists have learned that most individuals with William's syndrome have a deletion of genetic material on chromosome 7. This probably causes the physical and developmental problems experienced by patients.

IS THERE ANY TREATMENT?

There is neither a cure for William's syndrome nor a standard course of treatment. Treatment is symptomatic and supportive. Individuals with William's syndrome need regular monitoring for potential medical problems by a physician familiar with the disorder, as well as specialized services to maximize their potential.

WHAT IS THE PROGNOSIS?

The prognosis for individuals with William's syndrome varies. Some may be able to master self-help skills, complete academic or vocational school, and live in supervised homes or on their own, while others may not progress to this level.

WHAT RESEARCH IS BEING DONE?

The NINDS (National Institute of Neurological Disorders and Stroke) supports research on the neurological, behavioral, and genetic components of William's syndrome.

Information is provided by the National Institute of Neurological Disorders and Stroke.

3.78 Psychostimulants and Sedatives*

PSYCHOSTIMULANTS

Medication

1. Amphedroxyn
2. Benzedrine
3. Biphetamine
4. Cylert
5. Deaner
6. Desoxyn
7. Dexedrine
8. Pondimin
9. Ritalin

Generic Name

methamphetamine
amphetamine
amphetamine+dextroamphetamine
pemoline
deanol
methamphetamine
dextroamphetame
fenfluramine
methylphenidate

SEDATIVES/HYPNOTICS

Medication

1. Alurate
2. Amytal
3. Dalmane
4. Doral
5. Doriden
6. Halcion
7. Mebaral
8. Nembutal
9. Noludar
10. Nortec
11. Paral
12. Placidyl
13. ProSom
14. Quaalude
15. Restoril
16. Seconal
17. Solfoton
18. Tuinal

Generic Name

aprobarbital
amobarbital
flurazepam
quazepam
gluthimide
triazolam
mephobarbital
pentobarbital
methyprylon
chloralhydrate
paraldehyde
ethchlorvynol
estazolam
methaqualone
temazepam
secobarbital
phenobarbital
secobarbital+amobarbital

*In no way is the author recommending specific medications. These lists are for information purposes only.

3.79   Anti-Psychotic Medications*

These medications work by blocking one of the chemical messengers of the central nervous system: dopamine. These drugs are sometimes referred to as neuroleptic drugs because they block the dopamine receptors in the brain and restore the imbalance of nerve transmissions associated with psychotic behaviors.

Neuroleptic drugs should be considered very powerful. As a result, they pose potential risks. Careful monitoring is required and withdrawal symptoms such as headaches, nausea, dizziness, and increased heart rate may occur if medication is abruptly stopped. It should also be noted that alcohol consumption during the time the individual is on these medications may increase the effects of the drug and increase the risk of depression.

Medication	Generic Name
1. Clozaril	clozapine
2. Compazine	prochlorperazine
3. Daxoline	loxapine
4. Etrafon	perphenazine+amitriptyline
5. Haldol	haloperidol
6. Inapsine	droperidol
7. Loxitane	loxapine
8. Mellaril	thioridazine
9. Moban	molindone
10. Navane	thiothixene
11. Orap	pimozide
12. Orazine	chlorpromazine
13. Permitil	fluphenazine
14. Prolixin	fluphenazine
15. Serentil	mesoridazine
16. Serpasil	reserpine
17. Sparine	promazine
18. Stelazine	trifluoperazine
19. Thorazine	chlorpromazine
20. Tindal	acetophenazine
21. Triavil	perphenazine+amitriptyline
22. Trilafon	perphenazine
23. Vesprin	triflupromazine

*In no way is the author recommending specific medications. These lists are for information purposes only.

3.80   Anti-Depressant Medications*

Sometimes referred to as tricyclic drugs, these drugs affect the symptoms associated with depression by adjusting the levels of neurotransmitters in the brain such as dopamine, serotonin, and epinephrine. These medications are usually prescribed when the treatment of the condition is considered long-term. Doctors do not usually like to use such powerful tricyclic anti-depressants for short-term or transitory depression.

These medications tend to elevate the individual's mood, improve sleep patterns, increase energy levels and physical activity, and restore perception to a more positive level.

In the case of some anti-depressants, once the doctor feels comfortable with the levels of medication attained, he or she may prescribe a single dose at night, a practice called night-loading.

Medication	*Generic Name*
1. Adapin	doxepin
2. Anafranil	clomipramine
3. Asendin	amoxapine
4. Aventyl	nortriptyine
5. Desyrel	trazadone
6. Elavil	amitriptyline+hydrochloride
7. Endep	amitriptyline
8. Etrafon	perphenazine+amitriptyline
9. Janimine	imipramine
10. Limbitrol	chlordiazepoxide+amitriptyline
11. Ludiomil	maprotiline
12. Marplan	isocarboxazid
13. Nardil	phenelzine
14. Norpramin	desipramine
15. Pamelor	nortriptyline
16. Pertofrane	desipramine
17. Parnate	tranylcypromine
18. Prozac	fluoxetine
19. Sinequan	doxepin
20. Surmontil	trimipramine
21. Tofranil	imipramine
22. Vivactil	protriptyline
23. Wellbutrin	buproprion
24. Zoloft	sertraline

*In no way is the author recommending specific medications. These lists are for information purposes only.

3.81   Anti-Anxiety Medications*

These medications work by diminishing the activity of certain parts of the brain, called the limbic system. The symptoms associated with anxiety may include tension, agitation, irritability, panic attacks, or feelings of dying or going crazy. Physical symptoms include excessive sweating, heart palpitations, chills, fainting, racing pulse, and flushes. Anxiety may be a disorder by itself or a component of other psychiatric disorders.

Medication	*Generic Name*
1. Atarax	hydroxyzine
2. Ativan	lozazepam
3. BuSpar	buspirone
4. Catapres	clonidine
5. Centrax	prazepam
6. Corgard	nadolol
7. Dalmane	flurazepam
8. Deprol	meprobamate+benactyzine
9. Doral	quezepam
10. Equanil	meprobamate
11. Halcion	triazolam
12. Klonopin	clonazepam
13. Inderal	propranolol
14. Librium	chlordiazepoxide
15. Libritabs	chlordiazepoxide
16. Lopressor	metoprolol
17. Miltown	meprobamate
18. Paxipam	halazepam
19. Restoril	temazepam
20. Serax	oxazepam
21. Tenormin	atenolol
22. Tranxene	chlorazepate
23. Transcopal	chlormezanone
24. Valium	diazepam
25. Valrelease	diazepam
26. Vistaril	hydroxyzine
27. Xanax	alprazolam

*In no way is the author recommending specific medications. These lists are for information purposes only.

205

PART 4

Special Education Assessment

4.1 Scoring Terminology Used in Assessment

■ *Raw scores:* The first step in scoring any test will almost always be to calculate the number of correct items the student obtained. For example, if a student took a 20-question spelling test in your class, the first thing you would do is determine how many words the student spelled correctly. This score is known as the raw score. The **raw score** normally indicates the number of items correctly answered on a given test.

■ *Percentile ranks (percentiles):* A **percentile rank** (often referred to as a percentile) is a score indicating the percentage of people or scores that occur at or below a given score. For example, if you have a percentile rank of 75 in a class, this means that you did as well as or better than 75 percent of the students in the class. A percentile rank of 16 means that you scored as well as or better than only 16 percent of the population. Percentile ranks range from the lowest (1st percentile) to the highest (99th percentile).

■ *Quartiles:* Divide scores into 4 units: 1–25, 26–50, 51–75, and 76–99. The first **quartile** (1–25) marks the lower quarter (bottom 25 percent) or bottom fourth of all scores; the fourth quartile represents the upper quarter (top 25 percent).

■ *Deciles:* Divide scores into tenths or 10 equal units. For example, the sixth **decile** is the point at which 60 percent of the scores fall below; the ninth decile is the point at which 90 percent of the scores fall below.

■ *Standard scores:* A **standard score** is a score that has been transformed to fit a normal curve, with a mean and standard deviation that remain the same across ages. Normally, standard scores have a mean of 100 and a standard deviation of 15. Perhaps the most well-known version of the standard score with a mean of 100 and a standard deviation of 15 is the Wechsler Intelligence Scales.

■ *z scores:* A **z score** indicates how many standard deviations a score is above or below the mean. A z score is a standard score distribution with a mean of zero and a standard deviation of one. For example, if a student has a z score of +1.0, this means that she or he scored 1 standard deviation above the mean on the test. If a student has a z score of −1.7, this means that she or he scored 1.7 standard deviations below the mean.

■ *T scores:* **T scores** are another way to express test performance. T scores have a mean of 50 with a standard deviation of 10. Therefore, if you have a T score of 40, you are 1 standard deviation below the mean, and a T score of 60 would be 1 standard deviation above the mean.

■ *Stanines:* A **stanine**, an abbreviation for standard nines, is a type of standard score that has a mean of 5 and a standard deviation of 2. Stanine scores can range from 1 to 9. A stanine of 7 is 1 standard deviation above the mean (5+2). A stanine of 9 is 2 standard deviations above the mean (5+2+2). Conversely, a stanine of 3 is 1 standard deviation below the mean (5−2) and a stanine of 1 is two standard deviations below the mean (5−2−2).

- *Age equivalent scores:* An **age equivalent** is a very general score that is used to compare the performance of children at the same age with one another. It is the estimated age level that corresponds to a given score. Age equivalent scores are almost always given in years and months. For example, a child who gets an age equivalent score of 11.5 is performing as well as the average 11-year 5-month-old child.

- *Grade equivalent scores:* A **grade equivalent** is a very general score that is used to compare the performance of children in the same grade with one another. It is the estimated grade level that corresponds to a given score. Grade equivalent scores are almost always given in years and months in school. For example, a child who gets a grade equivalent score of 3.5 is performing as well as the average student in the 3rd grade-5th month.

4.2 Objectives of Intellectual, Educational, and Perceptual Evaluations

Intellectual Evaluation Objectives

- To determine the child's present overall level of intellectual ability.

- To determine the child's present verbal intellectual ability.

- To determine the child's non-language intellectual ability.

- To explore indications of greater potential.

- To find possible patterns involving learning style, e.g., verbal comprehension, concentration.

- To ascertain possible influences of tension and anxiety on testing results.

- To determine the child's intellectual ability to deal with present grade-level academic demands.

- To explore the influence of intellectual ability as a contributing factor to a child's past and present school difficulties, e.g., limited intellectual ability found in retardation.

Educational Evaluation Objectives

- To help determine the child's stronger and weaker academic skill areas. The evaluation may give us this information, which is very useful when making practical recommendations to teachers about academic expectations, areas in need of remediation, and how to best input information to assist the child's ability to learn.

- To help the teacher gear the materials to the learning capacity of the individual child. A child reading two years below grade level may require modified textbooks or greater explanations prior to a lesson.

- To develop a learning profile that can help the classroom teacher understand the best way to present information to the child and therefore increase his or her chances of success.

- Along with other information and test results, to help determine if the child's academic skills are suitable for a regular class or so limited that he or she may require a more restrictive educational setting (an educational setting or situation best suited to the present needs of the student other than a full-time regular class placement, e.g., a resource room, self-contained class, special school, etc.).

Whatever achievement battery the special educator chooses, it should be one that covers enough skill areas to make an adequate diagnosis of academic strengths and weaknesses.

Perceptual Evaluation Objectives

▦ To help determine the child's stronger and weaker modality for learning. Some children are visual learners, some are auditory, and some learn best through any form of input. However, if a child is a strong visual learner in a class where the teacher relies on auditory lectures, then it is possible that his or her ability to process information may be hampered. The evaluation may give us this information, which is very useful when making practical recommendations to teachers about how to best input information to assist the child's ability to learn.

▦ To help determine a child's stronger and weaker process areas. A child having problems in memory and expression will fall behind the rest of her or his class very quickly. The longer these processing difficulties continue, the greater the chance for secondary emotional problems (emotional problems resulting from continued frustration about the ability to learn) to develop.

▦ To develop a learning profile that can help the classroom teacher understand the best way to present information to the child and therefore increase his or her chances of success.

▦ Along with other information and test results, to help determine if the child's learning process deficits are suitable for a regular class or so severe that he or she may require a more restrictive educational setting (an educational setting or situation best suited to the present needs of the student other than a full-time regular class placement, e.g., a resource room, self-contained class, special school, etc.).

4.3   Understanding a Student's Behavior During Testing

There are many behaviors that should be observed when administering tests. Recording these observations will greatly facilitate report writing. Some suggestions of behaviors to be observed follow.

ADJUSTMENT TO THE TESTING SITUATION

- What was the child's initial reaction?
- How did the child react to the examination?
- Were there any initial signs of overt tension?

Several factors need to be considered when the child first encounters the testing situation. These include:

1. Children's **initial adjustment** to the testing situation can vary greatly. The key to any adjustment period is not necessarily the initial reactions but the duration of the period of maladjustment. Children are usually initially nervous and uptight but relax as time goes on with the reassurance of the examiner. However, children who maintain a high level of discomfort throughout the sessions may be harboring more serious problems that need to be explored.

2. Examiner variables (conditions that may affect test outcome that are directly related to the examiner—e.g., examiner style, gender, examiner tension, examiner expectations, etc.) may need to be considered, especially if test results vary greatly from examiner to examiner.

3. Be aware of overt signs of tension (observable behaviors indicative of underlying tension) that may affect the outcome of the test result. Some overt signs of behavior often manifested by children include constant leg motion, little or no eye contact with the examiner, consistent finger or pencil tapping, oppositional behaviors (behaviors that test the limits and guidelines of the examiner), singing or making noises while being tested, keeping jacket on or a hat almost covering his or her face, etc. If this type of tension is extreme you may want to explore the possibility that the results may be minimal indications of ability.

REACTION TIME

- Were responses delayed, blocked, irregular?
- Was there any indication of negativism?
- Were responses impulsive or well thought out?

The speed in which a child answers questions on a test can indicate several things:

1. The child who impulsively answers incorrectly without thinking may be a child with high levels of anxiety that interfere with his or her ability to delay and concentrate.

2. The child who is negative or self defeating—e.g., "I'm so stupid, I'll never get any of these right"—may be exhibiting a very low level of self-confidence or hiding a learning problem.

3. The child who blocks or delays may be a child who is afraid of reaction or criticism and uses these techniques to ward off what he or she perceives as an ego-deflating situation.

NATURE OF RESPONSES

- Are some nonsensical, immature, childlike?
- Are they inconsistent?
- Does subject ask to have responses repeated?
- Is the subject critical of responses?

The types of response a child gives during an evaluation may indicate the following:

1. A child who continuously asks to have questions repeated may have hearing difficulties. This should always be ruled out first along with lack of visual acuity prior to a testing situation.

2. The child who asks to have questions repeated may be having problems processing information and may need more time to understand what is being asked.

VERBALIZATIONS

- Is the student verbose?
- Is she or he spontaneous in responding?
- Does she or he have peculiarities of speech?

The verbal interaction with the examiner during an evaluation can be very telling. This factor may indicate the following:

1. Some children with high levels of anxiety may tend to vent them through constant verbalizations. This may be a factor if these verbalizations begin to interfere and the child has to be constantly reminded to focus on the task at hand.

2. Verbal hesitations may be due to immature speech patterns, expressive language problems, poor self-esteem, or lack of understanding of the question due to limited intellectual capacity.

ORGANIZATIONAL APPROACH USED DURING TESTING

- Does subject plan and work systematically?
- Does she or he make false starts?
- Does she or he use trial and error?

4.3 continued

The manner in which a child handles individual tasks and organizes his/her approach may indicate the following:

1. A child who sizes up a situation and systematically approaches a task using trial and error may be a child with excellent internal organization, the ability to delay, and low levels of tension and anxiety. However, some children with emotional problems may also perform well on short-term tasks because they see them as challenges and can organize themselves to perform over a relatively short period of time. Their particular problems in organization and consistency may come when they are asked to perform this way over an extended period.

2. Children with chaotic internal organization may appear as if they know what they are doing, but the overall outcome of a task indicates a great deal of energy input with very low production. It's almost as if they are "spinning wheels" and the energy output is a cover for not knowing what to do.

3. Some children may become less organized under the stress of a time constraint. The factor of style under time restrictions is one aspect to consider in determining the child's overall learning style.

4. Children with attention deficit hyperactivity disorder may also exhibit a confused sense of organization. However, there are other factors as well as attention that go into the diagnosis of this disorder.

ADAPTABILITY DURING TESTING

- Does student make a smooth transition from one test to the next?
- Is interest sustained in all types of test items?

The ability of a child (or adult, for that matter) to adapt or shift from one task to another without difficulty is a very important factor in determining learning style and may be one predictor for successful outcome of a task. Other factors include the following:

1. Adaptability in life is one crucial aspect to well adjustment. The ability to shift without expending a great deal of energy offers the person more available resources for the next task. A child who is rigid or does not adapt well is using up much of his or her available energy, thus reducing the chances of success on the subsequent task.

2. Sustaining interest may also be a direct result of available energy. A child who loses interest quickly may be immature, overwhelmed, or preoccupied. Some of these reactions may be normal for the early ages. However, as the child gets older, such reactions may be symptomatic of other factors, e.g., learning problems, emotional issues, and limited intellectual capacity.

EFFORT DURING TESTING

- Is student cooperative?
- Does he/she give evidence of trying hard?
- Does child become frustrated easily?

The effort that a child puts into a testing situation may be reflective of the effort exhibited within the classroom and may indicate the following:

1. A child who is oppositional or uncooperative may be a child who needs to control. Always keep in mind that the more controlling a child is, the more out of control she or he feels. Control on the part of a child is aimed at securing predictability so that she or he can deal with a situation even though energy levels may be lowered by conflict and tension. If children can control a situation or person, they know what to expect. Because of their tension levels, they do not adapt well and are easily thrown by new situations or people.

2. A child who tries hard to succeed may do so for several reasons. He or she may enjoy success and find the tasks normally challenging. This type of child is normally not thrown by a mistake and can easily move to the next task without difficulty.

In conclusion, always keep in mind that all behavior is a message and the way a child interacts with the examiner may be clues to learning style or problem areas. If you can "hear" a child's behavior by being aware of significant signs, you may come to a better understanding of the child's needs.

4.4 How to Report Test Results to Parents

An important skill for special education teachers is their ability to report test results to other professionals or to parents in such a way that these people walk away with an understanding of the causes, specific areas of strength and weakness, and practical recommendations to alleviate the situation. Many times parents will leave a conference having been "bombarded" with jargon and statistics and understand nothing. Reporting results so that they are understood may be accomplished in the following ways:

1. When setting up the appointment with a parent, never allow yourself to begin the explanation of the results over the phone, even if the parent requests a "quick" rundown of how the child performed. If the parent does request this, gently say that the type of information that you have is better explained and understood in person. If you sense further anxiety, try to reassure the parent that you will meet as soon as possible. It is important to visually encounter the parent(s) so that you can further explain areas in which they seem confused or uncomfortable. The face-to-face contact also makes the conference a more human approach. Hearing results from our doctor over the phone may not be as comforting as in person.

2. Again, as with an intake (see List 2.27), make the parent(s) feel comfortable and at ease by setting up a receptive environment. If possible, hold the meeting in a pleasant setting, use a round table—or any table instead of a desk—and offer some type of refreshment to ease possible tension of the situation.

3. It may be helpful to refresh the parent's memory about the reasons for the evaluation and the symptoms that brought the child to the attention of the team. Explain the tests that comprised your test battery, why they were used, and what specific types of information you hoped to arrive at by using these measures.

4. Go over strength areas first no matter how few there may be. You can also report positive classroom comments and any other information that may help set the tone for acceptance of problem areas.

5. Provide a typed outline of the tests and scores for the parents to take with them if the report is not ready. If possible, always try to have the report typed and ready to hand them. It looks more professional and may help alleviate problems that may occur when reports are sent home and the parents read it without a professional present.

6. Explain in simple language any statistical terms you may be using, e.g., percentiles, stanines, mental ages, etc. In fact, it may be a good idea to define these on the same sheet with the scores so that parents have a key to refer to when they go back and review the scores.

7. Again, as with the intake, you should offer them a pad and pen so that they can write down information, terms, or notes on the meeting. Further indicate that they should feel free to call you with any questions or concerns they may have.

8. Put aside a sufficient amount of time for difficult conferences. This is not the type of situation in which you want to run out of time. The parents should leave in a natural manner and not feel rushed.

9. Take time to explain the differences between symptoms and problems. This explanation can go a long way in alleviating parents' frustration.

10. It is helpful for parents to hear how the problems or deficiencies you found were contributing to the symptoms in the classroom and at home. It is reassuring for parents to know that what they were seeing were only symptoms—even though they may have been quite intense—and that the problems have been identified and recommendations are available. Offer them as much realistic hope as possible.

11. Be as practical and specific as you can when offering suggestions on how parents can help at home. Offer them printed sheets with step-by-step procedures for any recommendation that you make. Parents should not be teachers and should never be given general recommendations that require their interpretation. This may aggravate an already tense situation at home. Offer them supportive materials that they can use with the child. Although having a parent working with a child can be positive, in some cases, e.g., low parental frustration levels, you may want to shy away from this type of interaction.

12. If the case is going to be reviewed by the Committee on Special Education, take some time to alleviate their fears by explaining the process and what they can expect. Indicate that your report is part of the packet that will be presented and that they are entitled to a copy of all materials. Some school districts may charge for copies, so indicate that fact if it is a policy.

13. Again, reassure the parents about the confidentiality of the information gathered. Indicate the individuals on the team who will be seeing the information and the purpose for their review of the facts. Also indicate that in order to send out this information, you must always obtain permission from parents in the form of a signed release.

4.5   The Purpose of Intelligence Testing

Intelligence tests are most helpful (and probably most appropriate) when they are used to determine specific skills, abilities, and knowledge that a child either has or does not have. When such information is combined with other evaluation data, it can be directly applied to school programming. There are a number of skills that intelligence tests attempt to measure. These include:

1. Social judgment
2. Level of thinking
3. Language skills
4. Perceptual organization
5. Processing speed
6. Spatial abilities
7. Common sense
8. Long- and short-term memory
9. Abstract thinking
10. Motor speed
11. Word knowledge

Many of the above skills are very dependent on experience, training, and the intact verbal abilities of the child being tested. However, responses to items concerning perceptual organization, processing speed, and spatial abilities are less dependent on experience and verbal skill and more on hand–eye coordination and reasoning abilities.

Intelligence tests can yield valuable information about a student's ability to process information. In order to learn, every person must take in, make sense of, store, and retrieve information from memory in an efficient and accurate way. Each of us can process certain kinds of information more easily than others. In school, children need certain skills to function effectively, such as listening attentively so that other movements, sounds, or sights do not distract them. They must be able to understand the words spoken to them. This often requires children to hold multiple pieces of information in memory (e.g., page number, questions to answer) in order to act upon them. For example, they must be able to find the words they need to express themselves and, ultimately, commit these words to paper. This involves another whole series of processing skills such as holding a writing implement; coordinating visual and motor actions; holding information in memory until it can be transferred to paper; transforming sounds into written symbols; and understanding syntax, punctuation, and capitalization rules. They also must be able to interpret the nonverbal messages of others, such as a frown, a smile, a shake of the head. Moreover, they must do all of these things quickly and accurately and often in a setting with many distractions.

A thorough interpretation of an intelligence test can yield information about how effectively a child processes and retrieves information. Most individually administered intelligence tests can determine—at least to some degree—a child's ability to attend, process information quickly, distinguish relevant from less relevant details, put events in sequence, and retrieve words from memory.

4.6   IQ Range and Classification

IQ Range	Classification	Percent Included
130 and over	Very superior	2.2
120–129	Superior	6.7
110–119	High average	16.1
90–109	Average	50.0
80–89	Low average	16.1
70–79	Borderline	6.7
69 and below	Intellectually deficient Mentally retarded Developmentally delayed	2.2

Kamphaus (1993) summarizes a number of research findings related to IQ scores:

- IQ scores are more stable for school-aged children than for preschoolers and more stable among individuals with disabilities than among those without disabilities.

- IQ scores can change from childhood to adulthood.

- It is likely that environmental factors, socioeconomic status, values, family structure, and genetic factors all play a role in determining IQ scores.

- Factors such as low birth weight, malnutrition, anoxia (lack of oxygen), and fetal alcohol exposure have a negative impact on IQ scores.

- Intelligence and academic achievement appear to be highly related.

Once an IQ score is calculated, the psychologist can make several determinations. The psychologist can then report back to parents, teachers, and all members of the assessment process the following information:

- The child's present overall levels of intellectual ability.

- The child's present verbal intellectual ability.

- The child's non-language intellectual ability.

- Indications of greater intellectual potential.

- Possible patterns involving learning style, e.g., verbal comprehension, concentration.

- Possible influence of tension and anxiety on testing results.

- Intellectual ability to deal with present grade-level academic demands.

- The influence of intellectual ability as a contributing factor to a child's past and present school difficulties, e.g., limited intellectual ability found in retardation.

4.7 The Wechsler Scales of Intelligence

Author: David Wechsler

Publisher: The Psychological Corporation

Description of Test: Test comprises two areas of assessment: Verbal and Performance. The verbal areas are considered auditory/vocal tasks (auditory input and vocal output) while the performance areas are visual/vocal and visual/motor tasks (visual input and vocal or motoric output). The three tests include:

> Wechsler Preschool and Primary Scale of Intelligence-III (WPPSI-III)
>
> Wechsler Intelligence Scale for Children-III (WISC-III)
>
> Wechsler Adult Intelligence Scale-III (WAIS-III)

Administration Time: 60–75 minutes; individually administered

Age/Grade Levels: The three tests are designed for children and adults ages 4½ to adult. The age ranges for the three Wechsler tests are:

> The Wechsler Preschool and Primary Scale of Intelligence-III (WPPSI-III)—ages 2.6 to 3.11 and 4.0 to 7.3
>
> Wechsler Intelligence Scale for Children-III (WISC-III)—ages 6½ to 16½
>
> Wechsler Adult Intelligence Scale-III (WAIS-III)—ages 16½ and over

Subtest Information: The three Wechsler Scales consist of a total of 17 possible subtests. Unless otherwise noted, all subtests are contained in each scale. The specific subtests for each Wechsler Scale are shown in List 4.49.

Strengths of the Wechsler Scales

▪ There is strong evidence of the test's reliability and validity.

▪ A thorough interpretation in the manual of information regarding interpretation of scaled score differences is provided.

▪ Scores on the test correlate highly with academic achievement.

▪ The test provides valuable information as one of the measures in the diagnosis of learning disabilities.

▪ The test is well organized and easy to use.

▪ The test provides strong objective and projective potential.

Weaknesses of the Wechsler Scales

▪ Some of the test's questions may be culturally biased.

▪ The test does not allow for the distinction of full scale IQs below 40, making it less useful than other instruments in distinguishing among levels of retardation.

▪ The test cannot be used alone in the diagnosis of learning disabilities.

The Wechsler Scales are one of the individual evaluation measures of intelligence most widely used in today's schools. Although the Wechsler Scales are usually administered by psychologists, there is a great deal of useful information that can be obtained by all special educators from this test. Because it is inevitable that special education teachers will more than likely come in contact with this test, it is critical that they understand the nature of the scores and the implications of the results. Strengths and weaknesses of a child's learning style, indications of greater potential, organizational skills, processing abilities, reasoning abilities, and adjustment to timed tasks are examples of useful information that can be obtained from this test.

There are three different versions of the Wechsler Tests.

1. Wechsler Preschool and Primary Scale of Intelligence-III (WPPSI-III)—ages 2.6 to 3.11 and 4.0 to 7.3.

2. Wechsler Intelligence Scale for Children-III (WISC-III)—ages 6½ to 16½.

3. Wechsler Adult Intelligence Scale-III (WAIS-III)—ages 16 and up.

The following subtests are part of all three Wechsler Scales of Intelligence; however, not all the subtests appear on each scale.

Wechsler Verbal Subtests

- *Information*—Measures general information acquired from experience and education, remote verbal memory, understanding, and associative thinking. The socioeconomic background and reading ability of the student may influence the subtest score.

- *Similarities*—Measures abstract and concrete reasoning, logical thought processes, associative thinking, and remote memory.

- *Arithmetic*—Measures mental alertness, concentration, attention, arithmetic reasoning, reaction to time pressure, and practical knowledge of computational facts. This is the only subtest directly related to the school curriculum, and it is affected greatly by anxiety.

- *Vocabulary*—Measures a child's understanding of spoken words, learning ability, general range of ideas, verbal information acquired from experience and education, and kind and quality of expressive language. This subtest is relatively unaffected by emotional disturbance, but it is highly susceptible to cultural background and level of education. It is also considered by many to be the best single measure of intelligence in the entire battery.

- *Comprehension*—Measures social judgment, common-sense reasoning based on past experience, and practical intelligence.

- *Digit span*—Measures attention, concentration, immediate auditory memory, auditory attention, and behavior in a learning situation. This subtest correlates poorly with general intelligence.

- *Sentences*—Measures attention, concentration, immediate auditory memory, auditory attention, and behavior in a learning situation.

4.7 continued

- *Letter–number sequencing*—Assesses short-term auditory memory by presenting a mixed series of numbers and letters that the student must repeat back to the examiner, with the numbers in ascending order and the letters in alphabetical order. This subtest is optional.

- *Word context*—Presents an increasingly specific series of one to three clues, which the child uses to identify the common object or concept being described.

- *Receptive vocabulary*—Allows the practitioner to examine differences between a child's receptive and expressive vocabulary abilities.

Performance Subtests

- *Picture completion*—Measures visual alertness to surroundings, remote visual memory, attention to detail, and ability to isolate essential from nonessential detail.

- *Picture arrangement*—Measures visual perception, logical sequencing of events, attention to detail, and ability to see cause–effect relationships.

- *Block design*—Measures ability to perceive, analyze, synthesize, and reproduce abstract forms; visual motor coordination; spatial relationships; and general ability to plan and organize.

- *Object assembly*—Measures immediate perception of a total configuration, part–whole relationships, and visual-motor spatial coordination.

- *Coding*—Measures ability to associate meaning with symbol, visual-motor dexterity (pencil manipulation), flexibility, and speed in learning tasks.

- *Digit symbol*—Measures ability to associate meaning with symbol, visual-motor dexterity (pencil manipulation), flexibility, and speed in learning tasks.

- *Symbol search*—Measures visual discrimination.

- *Mazes*—Measures ability to formulate and execute a visual-motor plan, pencil control and visual-motor coordination, speed and accuracy, and planning capability.

- *Animal house*—Measures ability to associate meaning with symbol, visual-motor dexterity, flexibility, and speed in learning tasks.

- *Geometric design*—Measures a child's pencil control and visual-motor coordination, speed and accuracy, and planning capability.

- *Matrix reasoning*—Presents visual stimuli that the student must evaluate to determine which of the visual stimuli will complete the visual pattern. In the WPPSI-III, the Matrix Reasoning subtest has been adapted for young children and includes several types of nonverbal reasoning tasks, including analogy reasoning, classification, pattern completion, and serial completion.

For each subtest, a student receives a raw score. This raw score is then transformed into a scaled score. Scaled scores are very specific subtest scores on the Wechsler Scales of Intelligence. Scaled scores can range from 1 to 19 with a mean of 10. They follow the following classification format:

222

Scaled score	Classification
1–3	Developmentally delayed
4–5	Borderline
6–8	Low average
9–12	Average
13–14	High average
15–16	Superior
17–19	Very superior

For example, if a student only gets a scaled score of 7 on the Vocabulary subtest but a 13 on the Comprehension subtest, this indicates a much greater strength with respect to comprehension than with vocabulary as compared to the norms of his age group. Also, when detecting learning disabilities in psychoeducational assessment for a given child, there will often be great variance in the distribution of scaled scores when a learning disability is present.

The scaled scores are calculated to get three separate IQ scores: Verbal IQ, Performance IQ, and a Full Scale IQ (the student's overall IQ score). When there is a discrepancy between the Verbal and Performance sections on the Wechsler tests, this is often an indication of a learning disability.

4.8   The Stanford-Binet Intelligence Scale—Fourth Edition

Authors: R. L. Thorndike, E. P. Hagen, and J. M. Sattler

Publisher: The Riverside Publishing Company

Description of Test: This test is an individual intelligence test and is a measure of global or general intelligence; it offers results in terms of a mental age and IQ. This test is generally used with younger children and with intellectually limited youngsters.

Administration Time: 45–90 minutes

Age/Grade Levels: Ages 2 to adult

Subtest Information: The Stanford-Binet comprises 15 tests divided according to four areas:

Verbal Reasoning (four subtests)

- *Vocabulary*—The respondent is required to name pictures of common objects.

- *Comprehension*—The respondent is required to point to body parts on a picture of a child.

- *Absurdities*—The respondent is required to point to which of three pictures shows something that is wrong or is silly.

- *Verbal Relations*—The respondent reads four words and is required to tell how three of the four words are alike and which of the four is different.

Quantitative Reasoning (three subtests)

- *Quantitative*—The respondent is required to use dice to match, count, add, subtract, or form logical series of numbers.

- *Number Series*—The respondent is required to find the next two numbers that would be consistent according to a certain rule.

- *Equation Building*—The respondent is required to build mathematical statements from a list containing several numbers and operational symbols.

Abstract/Visual Reasoning (four subtests)

- *Pattern Analysis*—The respondent is required to complete a three-hole form board with a circle, square, and triangle and then with combinations of pieces that together fit into the holes.

- *Copying*—The respondent is required to arrange blocks or draw copies of designs.

- *Matrices*—The respondent is required to choose from four or five options the symbol or picture that completes a pattern.

- *Paper Folding and Cutting*—The respondent is required to choose which of five drawings would look like a paper design if it were unfolded.

Short-Term Memory (four subtests)

- *Bead Memory*—The respondent is required to identify beads or patterns of beads from memory.
- *Memory for Sentences*—The respondent is required to correctly repeat a sentence spoken by the examiner.
- *Memory for Digits*—The respondent is required to repeat a series of digits spoken by the examiner.
- *Memory for Objects*—The respondent is required to identify the correct order of pictures presented in a series.

Strengths of the Stanford-Binet

- A rating scale is included on the cover of the test booklet.
- The Examiner's Manual includes many informative case studies.
- The test employs adaptive testing format (whereby tests are administered only to children at certain entry levels), which prevents excessive frustration or boredom for the very dull or very bright child.

Weaknesses of the Stanford-Binet

- This is not a particularly valuable test for children in the 2½-to-4-year age ranges, especially if there are developmental delays.
- Some of the subtests have a ceiling that is much too low for older and some very bright individuals.
- Several subtests contain two types of items that seem quite dissimilar, e.g., easy items requiring pointing, harder items involving enhanced language responses.
- Time limits are suggested, but the examiner may have to rely on clinical judgment regarding enforcement of the limits.
- To keep testing time to 60–90 minutes, the test developers suggest several abbreviated batteries, thereby reducing test reliability.
- The norming samples for some tests at some age levels are inadequate.

4.9 Kaufman Assessment Battery for Children (K-ABC): Mental Processing Scales

Authors: Alan S. Kaufman and Nadeen L. Kaufman

Publisher: American Guidance Service

Description of Test: This individually administered intelligence test was developed in 1983 in an attempt to minimize the influence of language and acquired facts and skills on the measurement of a child's intellectual ability.

Administration Time: 35–85 minutes, depending upon age group

Age/Grade Levels: Ages 2½ to 12½

Subtest Information: The intelligence test contains 10 subtests:

- *Hand Movements*—The child (ages 2½ to 12½) is required to perform a series of hand movements presented by the examiner.

- *Number Recall*—The child (ages 2½ to 12½) is required to repeat a series of digits in the same sequence as presented by the examiner.

- *Word Order*—The child (ages 4 to 12½) is required to touch a series of silhouettes of objects in the same order as presented verbally by the examiner.

- *Magic Windows*—The child (ages 2½ to 5) is required to identify a picture that the examiner exposes slowly through a window; only a small part is shown.

- *Face Recognition*—The child (ages 2½ to 5) is required to choose from a group photo the one or two faces that were exposed briefly.

- *Gestalt Closure*—The child (ages 2½ to 12½) is required to name an object or scene from a partially constructed inkblot.

- *Triangles*—The child (ages 4 to 12½) is required to assemble several identical triangles into an abstract pattern.

- *Matrix Analogies*—The child (ages 5 to 12½) is required to choose a meaningful picture or abstract design that best completes a visual analogy.

- *Spatial Memory*—The child (ages 5 to 12½) is required to recall the placement of a picture on a page that was briefly exposed.

- *Photo Series*—The child (ages 6 to 12½) is required to place photographs of an event in the proper order.

Strengths of the K-ABC

- This test has excellent norming samples.

- This test has excellent reliability and validity data.

- This test provides substantial data profiles of various groups of exceptional children.

- This test provides the examiner with clues regarding what strengths and weaknesses children with various types of special needs may demonstrate.

- This test provides profile differences related to sex, socioeconomic status, and ethnic group membership.

- This test provides suggestions for educational programming.

- This test can be used with children under the age of 2½.

Weaknesses of the K-ABC

- The use of the term "mental processing" for some subtests and the term "achievement" for others may be misleading.

- The K-ABC should not be used in the intellectual diagnosis of the mentally disabled in the preschool years because low scores at this age are very difficult to obtain.

- The test's heavy reliance on short-term memory may affect children with attention and short-term-recall difficulties.

4.10 Kaufman Brief Intelligence Test (KBIT)

Authors: Alan S. Kaufman and Nadeen L. Kaufman

Publisher: American Guidance Service

Description of Test: This test is an assessment device for developing and evaluating students for placement in remedial programs for the mentally disabled. It may also be used for normal children aged birth to 10 years.

Administration Time: 15–30 minutes

Age/Grade Levels: Ages 4 to 90

Subtest Information: The test consists of two subtests:

- *Vocabulary*—This subtest measures verbal knowledge through pictures.
- *Matrices*—This subtest measures the ability to perceive relationships and complete analogies through pictures or abstract designs.

Strengths of the KBIT

- Instructions are given for motor items and the scoring sheet is clear and easy to complete.
- This test is a good quick screening measure of intelligence.
- This test is a psychometrically sound measure of verbal, nonverbal, and composite intelligence.

Weaknesses of the KBIT

- The manual lacks clarity and organization.
- Caution should be exercised in interpreting standard scores for older subjects, i.e., ages 20 to 90, because of the small number of subjects used in the norming sample.
- Further validation studies are needed.

4.11   Columbia Mental Maturity Scale (CMMS)

Authors: Bessie B. Burgemeister, Lucille Hollander Blurn, and Irving Lorge

Publisher: The Psychological Corporation

Description of Test: The Columbia is an individual type scale that requires perceptual discrimination involving color, shape, size, use, number, kind, missing parts, and symbolic material. Items are printed on 95 6-inch by 19-inch cards, arranged in a series of eight overlapping levels. The subject responds by selecting the picture in each series that is different from, or unrelated to, the others.

Administration Time: 15–30 minutes

Age/Grade Levels: Ages 3½ to 10

Subtest Information: There are no formal subtests on this scale; rather, it is a 95-item test of general reasoning abilities.

Strengths of the CMMS

- Most children enjoy taking this test.
- The test can be administered in a relatively short period of time.
- A trained examiner can get quality judgments of the child and his or her method of attacking problems.

Weaknesses of the CMMS

- The test manuals need to be updated.
- The test has been standardized on a nondisabled population only.
- Little has been determined about the test's possible educational or clinical value.

4.12 McCarthy Scales of Children's Abilities

Author: Dorothea McCarthy

Publisher: The Psychological Corporation

Description of Test: The test consists of 18 separate tests that are grouped into six scales: Verbal, Perceptual Performance, Quantitative, Composite (General Cognitive), Memory, and Motor.

Administration Time: 45–60 minutes

Age/Grade Levels: Ages 2 years 4 months to 8 years 7 months

Subtest Information: The test consists of 6 scales comprising a variety of 20 subtests. Some subtests fall into more than one scale. Listed below are each scale and the corresponding subtests measuring that skill:

Verbal Scale (five subtests)

- *Pictorial Memory*—The child is required to recall names of objects pictured on cards.

- *Word Knowledge*—In Part 1, the child is required to point to pictures of common objects named by the examiner. In Part 2, the child is required to give oral definitions of words.

- *Verbal Memory*—In Part 1, the child is required to repeat word series and sentences. In Part 2, the child is required to retell a story read by the examiner.

- *Verbal Fluency*—The child is required to name as many articles as possible in a given category within 20 seconds.

- *Opposite Analogies*—The child is required to complete sentences by providing opposites.

Perceptual Performance Scale (seven subtests)

- *Block Building*—The child is required to copy block structures built by the examiner.

- *Puzzle Solving*—The child is required to assemble picture puzzles of common animals or foods.

- *Tapping Sequence*—The child is required to imitate sequences of notes on a xylophone, as demonstrated by the examiner.

- *Right–Left Orientation*—The child is required to demonstrate knowledge of right and left.

- *Draw-A-Design*—The child is required to draw geometrical designs as presented in a model.

- *Draw-A-Child*—The child is required to draw a picture of a child of the same sex.
- *Conceptual Grouping*—The child is required to classify blocks on the basis of size, color, and shape.

Quantitative Scale (three subtests)

- *Number Questions*—The child is required to answer orally presented questions involving number information or basic arithmetical computation.
- *Numerical Memory*—In Part 1, the child is required to repeat a series of digits exactly as presented by the examiner. In Part 2, the child is required to repeat a digit series in exact reverse order.
- *Counting and Sorting*—The child is required to count blocks and sort them into equal groups.

Motor Scale (five subtests)

- *Leg Coordination*—The child is required to perform motor tasks that involve lower extremities, such as walking backwards or standing on one foot.
- *Arm Coordination*—In Part 1, the child is required to bounce a ball; in Part 2, the child is required to catch a beanbag; and in Part 3, the child is required to throw a beanbag at a target.
- *Imitative Action*—The child is required to copy simple movements, such as folding hands or looking through a tube.
- *Draw-A-Child**
- *Draw-A-Design**

General Cognitive

This scale consists of 15 subtests from many of the measures shown above. Please refer to the four prior scales for a complete explanation of the subtests.

- *Pictorial Memory*
- *Word Knowledge*
- *Verbal Memory*
- *Verbal Fluency*
- *Opposite Analogies*
- *Block Building*
- *Puzzle Solving*
- *Right–Left Orientation*

- *Draw-A-Design*
- *Draw-A-Child*
- *Conceptual Grouping*
- *Number Questions*
- *Numerical Memory*
- *Counting and Sorting*
- *Tapping Sequence*

*These subtests are explained under the Perceptual Performance Scale.

4.12 continued

Memory

This scale consists of four subtests. Please refer to the first four scales for a complete explanation of these subtests.

- *Pictorial Memory*
- *Tapping Sequence*
- *Verbal Memory*
- *Numerical Memory*

Strengths of the McCarthy Scales

- The test's Technical Manual contains elaborate information about the standardization process, norm tables, and guidelines for administration and interpretation.
- The test creates a framework within which the child being tested can function comfortably.
- The test is game-like, without any threatening material.
- Reliability and validity are good determinants of achievement for children in school.

Weaknesses of the McCarthy Scales

- The test excludes exceptional children from the standardization sample.
- The test lacks social comprehension and judgment tasks.
- This test may not be appropriate for older or gifted children because of a low ceiling level.
- The test may take a long time to administer and interpret. Furthermore, there is a lengthy scoring procedure, which may be problematic for new users.

4.13   Slosson Intelligence Test–Revised (SIT-R)

Authors: Richard L. Slosson; Revised by Charles L. Nicholson and Terry L. Hibpschman

Publisher: Slosson Educational Publications

Description of Test: This IQ test measures six different categories with 187 oral questions. Tasks are arranged in order of difficulty. This is a question-and-answer test with no reading or writing required.

Administration Time: 15–30 minutes

Age/Grade Levels: Ages 4 to 65 years

Subtest Information: This test measures six cognitive areas:

- *Vocabulary*—33 items measuring word knowledge.
- *General Information*—29 items measuring general knowledge and long-term memory.
- *Similarities and Differences*—30 items measuring abstract reasoning.
- *Comprehension*—33 items measuring social judgment and common sense.
- *Quantitative*—34 items measuring arithmetic abilities.
- *Auditory Memory*—28 items measuring short-term and sequential memory.

Strengths of the SIT-R

- The test has excellent reliability.
- The test can be administered and scored quickly.
- The test can provide useful information about probable level of mental ability.

Weaknesses of the SIT-R

- The test is of limited use for young children with language difficulties.
- The test does not contain any performance tasks.
- Visual spatial difficulties may be difficult to assess on this test.

4.14 Comprehensive Test of Nonverbal Intelligence (CTONI)

Authors: Donald D. Hammill, Nils A. Pearson, and Lee Wiederholt

Publisher: PRO-ED, Inc.

Description of Test: The CTONI is an unbiased test that measures six different types of nonverbal reasoning ability. No oral responses, reading, writing, or object manipulation are involved.

Administration Time: 60 minutes

Age/Grade Levels: Ages 6 to 18

Subtest Information: There are six subtests arranged according to three abilities. The three ability areas are:

- *Analogical Reasoning*—The two subtests on Analogical Reasoning are Pictorial Analogies and Geometric Analogies. This section identifies the ability to recognize a fourth object that bears the same relation to the third as the second does to the first.

- *Categorical Classification*—The two subtests in this section are Pictorial Categories and Geometric Categories. Categorical Classification assesses the ability to understand the common attributes by which objects are grouped.

- *Sequential Reasoning*—The two subtests in this section are Pictorial and Geometric Sequences. Sequential Reasoning assesses the ability to understand the successive relationship of objects.

Strengths of the CTONI

- This test is designed and documented to be unbiased with regard to gender, race, and disability.

- The test directions can be administered orally or through simple pantomime.

- The test can be individually administered in less than 60 minutes.

Weakness of the CTONI

- As this test is new, further study is required to determine the limitations, if any, of its validity and reliability.

4.15 Woodcock-Johnson Tests of Cognitive Abilities—III® (WJ-III)

Author: Richard W. Woodcock and Mary Bonner Johnson

Publisher: The Riverside Publishing Company

Description of Test: This test provides a comprehensive set of tests for measuring general intellectual ability and specific cognitive abilities.

Administration Time: Varies, about 5 minutes per test; 7 tests (35–40 minutes)

Age/Grade Levels: Ages 2.0 to 90+; Grades K.0 to graduate school

Subtest Information: The Cognitive Battery comprises the following subtests:

The descriptions below are not the "official" descriptions provided by the WJ-III® manual.

Comprehension-Knowledge (Gc)

1. *Verbal Comprehension.* The student completes four subsidiary tests: Picture Vocabulary, Synonyms, Antonyms, and Verbal Analogies.

11. *General Information.* The student completes two subsidiary tests: Where and What (e.g., Where would you find [an object]? What would you do with [an object]?)

Long-Term Retrieval (Glr)
[Note: "Long-term" can be as short as several minutes.]

2. *Visual-Auditory Learning.* The student is asked to learn and recall a series of rebuses (pictographic representations of words) that eventually are combined into phrases, then sentences, of increasing length and complexity.

12. *Retrieval Fluency.* The student names as many examples as possible from a given category (e.g., things to drink) in 60 seconds.

Visual-Spatial Thinking (Gv)

3. *Spatial Relations.* The student identifies two or three pieces that form a complete shape.

13. *Picture Recognition.* The student is asked to recognize a subset of previously presented pictures within a field of distracting pictures. Varieties of the same object (e.g., different types of leaves or lamps) are used both as stimuli and distraction to avoid verbal mediation.

4.15 continued

Auditory Processing (Ga)

4. *Sound Blending.* The student listens to a series of syllables or phonemes and is asked to blend them into a word.

14. *Auditory Attention.* The student listens to a word while looking at four pictures and is asked to point to the correct picture for the word. Difficulty increases as background noise becomes louder and sound discrimination becomes more difficult.

Fluid Reasoning (Gf)

5. *Concept Formation.* The student examines a stimulus set, then formulates a rule that applies to the item.

15. *Analysis-Synthesis.* The student is given instructions that help him or her examine and solve a series of puzzles.

Processing Speed (Gs)

6. *Visual Matching.* This subtest measures the speed at which the student can make visual symbol discriminations. There are two versions, one for preschool children and those with developmental delays and the other for those who function at or above the level of an average five-year-old.

16. *Decision Speed.* The student is presented with a row of objects and must quickly locate the two that are most similar conceptually.

Short-Term Memory (Gsm)

7. *Numbers Reversed.* The student listens to a group of numbers, then repeats them backwards.

17. *Memory for Words.* The student repeats lists of unrelated words in correct sequence.

Additional Tests

8. *Incomplete Words.* The student listens to a word from an audio recording that is missing one or more phonemes and must identify the complete word. This subtest provides information about auditory processing *(Ga)*.

9. *Auditory Working Memory.* The student listens to a series containing both digits and words (e.g., dog, 1, shoe, 5, 2, apple), then tries to reorder the information, repeating first the objects in sequential order and then the digits in sequential order. This subtest also measures short-term memory *(Gsm)* and working memory or divided attention.

10. *Visual-Auditory Learning—Delayed*. This subtest is presented 30 minutes to eight days after Subtest 2 and is a memory exercise requiring the student to recall the symbol/word relationships from that test. It also provides information about long-term retrieval abilities *(Glr)*—specifically, aspects of associative and meaningful memory.

18. *Rapid Picture Naming*. The student must quickly name a series of stimulus pictures. This test of cognitive fluency provides information about processing speed *(Gs)*.

19. *Planning*. The student traces a pattern without removing the pencil from the paper or retracing lines. This test of executive processing measures the mental control process involved in determining, selecting, and applying solutions to problems using forethought. It also draws on fluid reasoning *(Gf)* and visual-spatial thinking abilities *(Gv)*.

20. *Pair Cancellation*. The student must find and mark a repeated pattern of objects throughout a page full of objects within 3 minutes. This subtest provides information about executive processing, attention/concentration, and processing speed abilities *(Gs)*.

Subtest explanations adapted from *Essentials of WJ III® Cognitive Abilities Assessment* by Fredrick A. Schrank, Dawn P. Flanagan, Richard W. Woodcock, and Jennifer T. Mascolo (Wiley, 2002, pp. 27–54). Used by permission.

Strength of the WJ-III

▪ Due to the newness of the test, there was no analysis of strengths at press time.

Weakness of the WJ-III

▪ Due to the newness of the test, there was no analysis of weaknesses at press time.

4.16   Relationship of IQ Scores to Percentiles

IQ	Range	Scaled Score	Percentile
145	Very superior	19	99.9
140	Very superior	18	99.6
135	Very superior	17	99
130	Very superior	16	98
125	Superior	15	95
120	Superior	14	91
115	Above average	13	84
110	Above average	12	75
105	Average	11	63
100	Average	10	50
95	Average	9	37
90	Average	8	25
85	Low average	7	16
80	Low average	6	9
75	Borderline	5	5
70	Borderline	4	2
65	Mentally deficient	3	1
60	Mentally deficient	2	0.4
55	Mentally deficient	1	0.1

4.17 Overview of Academic Skill Areas

Reading

■ Decoding
Phonic skills
Sight word recognition
Oral paragraph reading
■ Comprehension
Oral reading comprehension
Silent reading comprehension
Listening comprehension
Comprehension in specific content areas

Writing

■ Penmanship
Manuscript
Cursive
■ Written expression
Fluency
Syntax
Mechanics
Content

Spelling

■ Written
Phonics words
Irregular words
■ Recognition of sight words
■ Oral

Arithmetic

■ Concepts
■ Computation
Addition
Subtraction
Multiplication
Division

4.17 continued

- Applications
- Operations
- Word problems
  - Oral
  - Written
- Mathematical reasoning

Oral Language

- Receptive
  - Vocabulary
  - Listening comprehension
- Expressive
  - Articulation
  - Morphology
    - Syntax
    - Semantics

4.18   Reading Comprehension Skills

There are several general areas relating to the area of reading comprehension. They are:

The Literal Level: Occurs when the student understands the primary or direct meaning of words, sentences, or passages. Examples of this include:

- Recognizing main ideas
- Recognizing details
- Recognizing a sequence
- Recognizing comparisons
- Recognizing cause-and-effect relationships
- Recognizing character traits
- Recalling details
- Recalling main idea
- Recalling a sequence
- Recalling comparisons
- Recalling cause-and-effect relationships
- Recalling character traits

The Inferential Level: Occurs when the student understands the deeper meanings that are not literally stated in the passage. Examples of this area include:

- Inferring the main idea
- Inferring comparisons
- Inferring character traits
- Inferring cause-and-effect relationships
- Inferring supporting details
- Inferring sequence
- Predicting outcomes
- Drawing conclusions
- Using picture clues and captions to add comprehension

The Reorganization Level: Occurs when the student is able to analyze, synthesize, and/or organize ideas or information gleamed from a passage or selection. Examples of this include:

- Classifying
- Outlining
- Summarizing
- Synthesizing

4.18 continued

The Evaluation Level: Occurs when the student is able to make an evaluative judgment by comparing and contrasting ideas presented in the selection while drawing upon outside criteria provided by the teacher or other sources or with internal criteria provided by the student himself or herself. Examples of this include:

- Judging reality or fantasy
- Judging fact or opinion
- Judging adequacy and validity
- Judging appropriateness
- Judging worth, desirability, and acceptability
- Identifying author bias

The Appreciation Level: Occurs when the student senses a reaction or internal response to a selection. Examples of this include:

- Emotionally responding to the content
- Identifying with characters or incidents
- Reacting to the author's use of language
- Creating mental pictures, or imagery

4.19   Analysis for Interpreting Oral Reading

Reading provides a fundamental way for individuals to exchange information. It is also a means by which much of the information presented in school is learned. As a result, reading is the academic area most associated with academic failure. Reading is a complex process that requires numerous skills for its mastery. Consequently, identifying the skills that lead to success in reading is extremely important.

There are numerous reading tests available for assessing a student's ability to read. Choosing which test to use depends upon what area needs to be assessed. Different reading tests measure different reading subskills:

- Oral reading

- Reading comprehension

- Word attack skills

- Word recognition

Oral Reading

A number of tests or parts of tests are designed to assess the accuracy and fluency of a student's ability to read aloud. According to Salvia and Ysseldyke (1998), different oral reading tests record different behaviors as errors or miscues in oral reading. Common errors seen on oral reading tests include, but are not limited to, the following:

- *Omission of a word or groups of words*—The student will skip individual words or groups of words.

- *Insertion of a word or groups of words*—The student inserts one or more words into the sentence being read.

- *Substitution of one meaningful word for another*—The student replaces one or more words in the passage by one or more meaningful words.

- *Gross mispronunciation of a word*—The student's pronunciation of a word bears little resemblance to the proper pronunciation.

- *Hesitation*—The student hesitates for two or more seconds before pronouncing a word.

- *Inversion or changing of word order*—The student changes the order of words appearing in a sentence.

- *Disregard of punctuation*—The student fails to observe punctuation, e.g., may not pause for a comma; stop for a period; or indicate a vocal inflection, a question mark, or exclamation point.

4.20 Analyzing Oral Reading Miscues

An oral reading error is often referred to as a miscue. By definition, a *miscue* is the difference between what a reader states is on a page and what is actually on the page. According to Vacca et al. (1986), differences between what the reader says and what is printed on the page are not the result of random errors. Instead, these differences are "cued" by the thought and language of the reader, who is attempting to construct what the author is saying. Analysis of miscues can be of two types. These are:

1. *Quantitative miscues*—With this type of miscue, the evaluator counts the number of reading errors made by the student.

2. *Qualitative miscues*—With this type of miscue, the focus is on the quality of the error rather than the number of different mistakes. It is not based on the problems related to word identification, but rather, on the differences between the miscues and the words on the pages. Consequently, some miscues are more significant than others (Vacca et al., 1991).

According to John (1985), a miscue is significant if it affects meaning. Miscues are generally **significant** when:

- The meaning of the sentence or passage is significantly changed or altered and the student does not correct the miscue.
- A nonword is used in place of the word in the passage.
- Only a partial word is substituted for the word or phrase in the passage.
- A word is pronounced for the student.

Miscues are generally **not significant** when:

- The meaning of the sentence or passage undergoes no change or only minimal change.
- They are self-corrected by the student.
- They are acceptable in the student's dialect.
- They are later read correctly in the same passage.

Through miscue analysis, teachers can determine the extent to which the reader uses and coordinates graphic sound, syntactic and semantic information from the text. According to Goodman and Burke (1972), to analyze miscues you should ask at least four crucial questions:

1. **Does the miscue change meaning?** If it doesn't, then it's semantically acceptable within the context of the sentence or passage.

2. **Does the miscue sound like language?** If it does, then it's grammatically acceptable within the context. Miscues are grammatically acceptable if they sound like language and serve as the same parts of speech as the text words.

3. **Do the miscue and the text word look and sound alike?** Substitution and mispronunciation miscues should be analyzed to determine how similar they are in approximating the graphic and pronunciation features of the text words.

4. **Was an attempt made to self-correct the miscue?** Self-corrections are revealing because they demonstrate that the reader is attending to meaning and is aware that the initial miscuing did not make sense.

4.21 Analyzing Reading Comprehension

Reading comprehension assesses a student's ability to understand what he or she is reading. Many children can read, yet do not understand what it is that they have read. Therefore, when doing a reading assessment, it is always necessary to assess not just decoding but also the ability to understand what is being decoded. Diagnostic reading tests often assess six kinds of reading comprehension skills. According to Salvia and Ysseldyke (1998), these are:

1. *Literal comprehension*—The student reads the paragraph or story and is then asked questions based on it.

2. *Inferential comprehension*—The student reads a paragraph or story and must interpret what has been read.

3. *Listening comprehension*—The student is read a paragraph or story by the examiner and is then asked questions about what he or she has read.

4. *Critical comprehension*—The student reads a paragraph or story and then analyzes, evaluates, or makes judgments on what he or she has read.

5. *Affective comprehension*—The student reads a paragraph or story and his or her emotional responses to the text are evaluated by the examiner.

6. *Lexical comprehension*—The student reads a paragraph or story and his or her knowledge of vocabulary words is assessed by the examiner.

When evaluating the reading behavior of a child on reading comprehension subtests, it is important for the evaluator to ask the following questions:

- Does the student guess at answers to the questions presented?
- Does the student show an unwillingness to read or to attempt reading?
- Does the student skip unknown words?
- Does the student disregard punctuation?
- Does the student exhibit inattention to the story line?
- Does the student drop the tone of his or her voice at the end of sentences?
- Does the student display problems with sounding out word parts and blends?
- Does the student exhibit a negative attitude toward reading?
- Does the student express difficulty attacking unknown words?

4.22 Analyzing Word Recognition Skills

The purposes of word recognition tests are to explore the student's ability with respect to sight vocabulary. According to Salvia and Ysseldyke (1998, p. 464), "A student learns the correct pronunciation of letters and words through a variety of experiences. The more exposure a student has to specific words and the more familiar those words become, the more readily he or she recognizes those words and is able to pronounce them correctly." Word recognition subtests form a major part of most diagnostic reading tests. Students who recognize many words are said to have good sight vocabularies or good word recognition skills.

Word Attack Skills

When assessing the reading abilities of the student, evaluators will often examine the word attack/word analysis skills of the child. Word attack skills are those used to derive meaning and/or pronunciation of a word through context clues, structural analysis, or phonics. In order to assess the word attack skills of the student, the examiner will normally read a word to the student who must then identify the consonant, vowel, consonant cluster, or digraph that has the same sound as the beginning, middle, or ending letters of the word.

According to Salvia and Ysseldyke (1998, p. 463), "Students must be able to decode words before they can gain meaning from the printed page. Since word-analysis difficulties are among the principle reasons students have trouble reading, a variety of subtests of commonly used diagnostic reading tests specifically assess word-analysis skills."

4.23 Questions to Consider When Doing a Reading Assessment

Although most reading tests cover many areas of assessment, each has its own unique style, method of scoring, and interpretative value. However, when looking at a student's reading behavior, there are certain questions that one must address regardless of the test administered:

- Does the student have excessive body movements while reading?
- Does the student prefer to read alone or in a group?
- How does the student react to being tested?
- Does the student avoid reading?
- When the student reads, what types of materials will he or she read?
- Does the student read at home?
- Does the student understand more after reading silently than after listening to someone else read the material orally?
- Does the student value reading?
- Is the student's failure mechanical or is he or she deficient in comprehension?

4.24　Gates-MacGinitie Silent Reading Test—Fourth Edition (GMRT)

Authors: Walter MacGinitie and Ruth MacGinitie

Publisher: The Riverside Publishing Company

Description of Test: The test comprises a series of multiple-choice pencil-and-paper subtests designed to measure silent reading skills

Administration Time: About 1 hour

Age/Grade Levels: Grades 1 to 12

Subtest Information: The test provides a comprehensive assessment of reading skills in two domains:

■ *Vocabulary*—This subtest domain assesses reading vocabulary. The difficulty of the task varies with the grade level.

■ *Comprehension*—This subtest domain assesses the ability to read and understand whole sentences and paragraphs.

Strengths of the Gates-MacGinitie

■ The student and teacher test booklets are written in easy-to-understand language that facilitates the administration of the test for first-time users.

■ The test covers a wide age range.

■ The test has alternate forms that are very useful for test-retest purposes.

■ The test is excellent for screening purposes because of the various areas measured.

Weaknesses of the Gates-MacGinitie

■ The silent reading format makes analysis of certain error types difficult. These include but are not limited to:

Omission

Repetition

Mispronunciation

Decoding skills

Substitution

4.25 Gray Oral Reading Test—3 (GORT-3)

Authors: J. Lee Wiederholt and Brian R. Byrant

Publisher: PRO-ED, Inc.

Description of Test: The GORT-3 comprises two alternate equivalent forms, each of which contains 13 developmentally sequenced passages with five comprehension questions. The GORT-3 provides a means of assessing the accuracy and rate of a student's oral reading skill. A system for analyzing the student's oral reading errors is built into the test format.

Administration Time: The time required to administer each form of the GORT-3 will vary from 15 to 30 minutes. Although the test is best administered in one session, examiners may use two sessions if the reader becomes fatigued or uncooperative.

Age/Grade Levels: Grade 1 to College

Subtest Information: The GORT-3 yields clinically useful information about the following:

- Oral Reading Rate and Accuracy
- Oral Reading Comprehension
- Total Oral Reading Ability
- Oral Reading Miscues

Strengths of the GORT-3

- There are convenient charts in the examiner's booklet that make scoring easier than it was in prior editions.
- The authors provide guidance in interpreting scores, seeking further assessment, and/or planning interventions.
- Test administration instructions are clear.
- The test results have high validity and reliability.

Weaknesses of the GORT-3

- The necessity of keeping track of separate basal and ceiling criteria may confuse some examiners who are trying to determine when to discontinue the test.
- The test manual omits normative data stratified along race, ethnic, and socioeconomic lines.
- Some slow readers with high accuracy levels may be penalized on this test because time is a variable in scoring.

4.26   Durrell Analysis of Reading Difficulty (DARD)

Authors: Donald O. Durrell and Jane H. Catterson

Publisher: The Psychological Corporation

Description of Test: This test has long served a population of experienced teachers whose primary purpose was to discover and describe weaknesses and faulty habits in children's reading. The kit includes an examiner's manual, student record booklets, tachistoscope, and a subtest presentation booklet containing reading passages.

Administration Time: 30–90 minutes

Age/Grade Levels: Grades 1 to 6

Subtest Information: The Durrell Analysis consists of a series of subtests designed to assess a student's reading and listening performance. They are included in the following sections:

- *Oral Reading*—The student reads orally and answers questions that require the recall of explicit information.

- *Silent Reading*—The student reads silently and answers questions that require the recall of explicit information.

- *Listening Comprehension*—The examiner is directed to read one or two paragraphs aloud to determine the student's ability to comprehend information presented orally.

- *Word Recognition*—The examiner reads lists of words at increasing difficulty levels and the score is based on the total number of words that the child recognizes correctly.

- *Word Analysis*—The examiner reads lists of words at increasing difficulty levels and the score is based on the total number of words that the child analyzes correctly.

- *Listening Vocabulary*—This test requires the child to listen to a series of words and indicate the category to which it belongs.

- *A Sound in Isolation*—This test assesses the student's mastery of sound/symbol relationships—including letters, blends, digraphs, phonograms, and affixes.

- *Spelling of Words*—The examiner reads lists of words at increasing difficulty levels and the student's score is based on the total number of words he or she spells correctly.

- *Phonic Spelling of Words*—The examiner reads lists of words at increasing difficulty levels, and the student's score is based on the total number of words he or she spells phonetically correctly.

- *Visual Memory of Words*—The examiner reads visually presented lists of words at increasing difficulty levels, and the student's score is based on the total number of words the student can recall correctly when the word list is presented again.

■ *Identifying Sounds in Words*—The examiner reads lists of words at increasing difficulty levels, and the student's score is based on the total number of identifying sounds in words that the student can correctly recall.

■ *Prereading Phonics Abilities Inventory*—This is an optional subtest that includes syntax matching, naming letters in spoken words, naming phonemes in spoken words, naming lowercase letters, and writing letters from dictation.

Strengths of the DARD

■ The manual for the Third Edition is improved, providing clearer procedures for testing.

■ A continuing strength of the test is its set of behavioral checklists, urging close observation of individual reader characteristics.

■ The addition of several new subtests makes for a more complete battery for assessment; however, the major focus of the test continues to be on specific skills.

Weaknesses of the DARD

■ The test only provides grade levels, which may not be accurate especially in cases of children who have been retained.

■ There is still a need for establishing the test's validity.

■ The standardization sample is not well described in the manual.

4.27   Gates-McKillop-Horowitz Diagnostic Reading Tests—Fourth Edition

Authors: Arthur I. Gates, Anne S. McKillop, and Elizabeth Horowitz

Publisher: Teachers College Press

Description of Test: This test is a verbal paper–pencil test. Not all parts need to be given to all students. Subtests are selected based on the student's reading levels and reading difficulties.

Administration Time: 40–60 minutes

Age/Grade Levels: Grades 1 to 6

Subtest Information: The subtests are listed and described below:

- *Oral Reading*—The student is required to read seven paragraphs orally. No comprehension is required.

- *Reading Sentences*—The student is required to read four sentences with phonetically regular words.

- *Words/Flash Presentation*—The student is required to identify words presented by a tachistoscope in ½-second intervals.

- *Words—Untimed*—The student is required to read the same word list as presented in Words/Flash Presentation; however, the student is given the opportunity to use word attack skills in an untimed setting.

- *Syllabication*—The student is required to read a list of nonsense words.

- *Recognizing and Blending Common Word Parts*—The student is required to read a list of nonsense words made up of common word parts.

- *Reading Words*—The student is required to read 15 one-syllable nonsense words.

- *Letter Sounds*—The student is required to give the sound of a printed letter.

- *Naming Capital Letters*—The student is required to name uppercase letters.

- *Naming Lowercase Letters*—The student is required to name lowercase letters.

- *Vowels*—The student is required to determine which vowel is associated with a nonsense word presented by the examiner.

- *Auditory Blending*—The student is required to blend sounds to form a whole word.

- *Auditory Discrimination*—The student is required to listen to a pair of words and to determine whether the words are the same or different.

- *Spelling*—The student is required to take an oral spelling test.

- *Informal Writing*—The student is required to write an original paragraph on a topic of his or her choice.

Strengths of the Gates-McKillop-Horowitz

- It tests many critical reading skills.
- A careful selection of subtests allows every student some successful reading experiences during the testing procedure.
- Students can maintain a high level of interest throughout the test because of its varied format and the informal tone of the procedures.

Weaknesses of the Gates-McKillop-Horowitz

- Manner of reporting results does not include percentiles.
- The test offers no measure of reading comprehension.

4.28 Gilmore Oral Reading Test

Authors: John V. Gilmore and Eunice C. Gilmore

Publisher: The Psychological Corporation

Description of Test: This test measures three aspects of oral reading competency: pronunciation, comprehension, and reading rate. It is used for diagnosing the reading needs of students identified as having reading problems.

Administration Time: 15–20 minutes

Age/Grade Levels: Grades 1 to 8

Subtest Information: The test is made up of 10 paragraphs in increasing order of difficulty that form a continuous story about episodes in a family group. There are five comprehension questions on each paragraph and a picture that portrays the characters in the story.

Strengths of the Gilmore

- The updated Gilmore is among the best standardized tests of accuracy in oral reading of meaningful material.

- The test directions are clear and concise.

- No special training is required to administer this test satisfactorily.

Weaknesses of the Gilmore

- The test seeks to measure comprehension ability with an oral test. This may be a problem because certain oral reading skills may interfere in a child's ability to recall what he or she is reading.

- The test is time-consuming.

4.29   Slosson Oral Reading Test—Revised (SORT-R)

Authors: Richard L. Slosson; Revised by Charles L. Nicholson

Publisher: Slosson Educational Publications

Description of Test: The Slosson Oral Reading Test-Revised (SORT-R) contains 200 words arranged in ascending order of difficulty in groups of 20 words. These word groups approximate reading grade levels. For example, group 1 is at the 1st-grade level, group 5 is at the 5th-grade level, etc. The last group is listed as grades 9–12. This list contains the most difficult words and words frequently encountered at the adult level.

Administration Time: Untimed (approx. 3–5 minutes)

Age/Grade Levels: Preschool to Adult

Subtest Information: The test has no subtests.

Strengths of the SORT-R

- The test is easy to administer.
- The test is easy to score.
- The test is quick.

Weaknesses of the SORT-R

- The test has limited relevance to school-based instruction because of the nature of the questions presented.
- Given the newness of the revision, further research is necessary to assess the test's validity and reliability.

4.30   Spache Diagnostic Reading Scales

Author: George D. Spache

Publisher: CTB Macmillan/McGraw-Hill

Description of Test: The Diagnostic Reading Scales (*DRS*) consists of a battery of individually administered tests that are used to estimate the instructional, independent, and potential reading levels of a student.

Administration Time: 60 minutes

Age/Grade Levels: Grades 1 to 7 and poor readers in grades 8 to 12

Subtest Information: The subtests are listed and described below:
- *Word Recognition List*—This test contains graded word lists that are used to determine a student's reading ability.
- *Oral Reading*—The student is required to read paragraphs aloud and answer questions orally.
- *Silent Reading*—The student is required to read a passage silently and to respond orally to questions asked by the examiner.
- *Auditory Comprehension*—The student is required to respond to questions orally about paragraphs read aloud by the examiner.
- *Supplementary Phonics Test*—This subtest measures the student's word attack skills and phonics knowledge.

Strengths of the Spache

- The latest version of the DRS represents a substantial improvement over the previous version.
- The revised examiner's manual, the training tape cassette, and the guidelines given for testing students who speak nonstandard dialects are all positive features.

Weaknesses of the Spache

- The definitions of instructional and independent reading levels in the DRS differ substantially from those in ordinary use. Therefore, results from the DRS are of limited value to practitioners who wish to place a student at appropriate levels for reading instructions.
- The comprehension score can be misleading for students with short-term memory problems.

4.31   Woodcock Reading Mastery Test—
Revised (WRMT-R)

Author: Richard W. Woodcock

Publisher: American Guidance Service

Description of Test: The Woodcock Reading Mastery Test-Revised (WMRT-R) is composed of six individually administered tests. There are two forms of the test, G and H. Form G includes all six tests while Form H includes only four reading achievement tests.

Administration Time: 40–45 minutes

Age/Grade Levels: Grades K to 12

Subtest Information: The six subtests found on Form G include the following:

- *Visual Auditory Learning*—Here, the student is required to associate unfamiliar visual stimuli (rebuses) with familiar oral words and to translate sequences of rebuses into sentences.

- *Letter Identification*—This test measures a student's skill in naming or pronouncing letters of the alphabet. Uppercase and lowercase letters are used.

- *Word Identification*—This tests measures skill in pronouncing words in isolation.

- *Word Attack*—This test assesses skill in using phonic and structural analysis to read nonsense words.

- *Word Comprehension*—There are three parts to this section: Antonyms, Synonyms, and Analogies. In the Antonyms section, the student must read a word and then provide a word that means the opposite. In the Synonyms section, the student must provide a word with similar meanings to the stimulus words provided. In the Analogies section, the student must read a pair of words, ascertain the relationship between the two words, read a third word, and then supply a word that has the same relationship to the third word as exists between the initial pair of words read.

- *Passage Comprehension*—In this subtest, the student must read silently a passage that has a word missing and then tell the examiner a word that could appropriately fill in the blank space. The passages are drawn from actual newspaper articles and textbooks.

4.31 continued

Strengths of the WRMT-R

- The test is administered in a short period of time.
- The test is relatively inexpensive.
- There is good reliability and validity data on the test.
- A computer scoring program is available for both IBM and Apple formats.
- Alternate forms of the test allow for test/retest administration.

Weaknesses of the WRMT-R

- It may require numerous administrations for the examiner to make a valid interpretation of a child's results.
- Reliability data for many of the grade levels measured by the test are not reported in the manual.
- There is no explanation in the manual as to whether or not special education students were used in the norming population.

4.32 Test of Reading Comprehension— Third Edition (TORC-3)

Authors: Virginia L. Brown, Donald D. Hammill, and J. Lee Wiederholt

Publisher: PRO-ED, Inc.

Description of Test: The materials in the test kit include an examiner's manual, student booklets, answer sheets, individual and student profile sheets, and separate response forms for several subtests. This current revision of the TORC offers new normative data based on a sample of 1,962 students from 19 states stratified by age, keyed to the 1990 census data, and presented by geographic region, gender, residence, race, ethnicity, and disabling condition.

Administration Time: 30 minutes

Age/Grade Levels: Ages 7 to 18

Subtest Information: There are four general reading comprehension core subtests:

- *General Vocabulary*—This subtest measures the reader's understanding of sets of vocabulary items that are all related to the same general concept.

- *Syntactic Similarities*—This subtest measures the reader's understanding of sentence structures that are similar in meaning but syntactically different.

- *Paragraph Reading*—This subtest measures the reader's ability to answer questions related to story-like paragraphs.

- *Sentence Sequencing*—This subtest measures the reader's ability to build relationships among sentences.

There are also three supplemental tests that measure content area vocabulary in mathematics, social studies, and science and a fourth that measures the student's ability to read directions in schoolwork.

Strengths of the TORC-3

- The test is useful in comparing reading comprehension with other conceptual and linguistic abilities.

- The test is useful for planning remediation and IEPs.

- The test demonstrates an absence of gender and racial bias.

Weaknesses of the TORC-3

- Several of the TORC-3 subtests measure abilities seldom taught in classrooms, e.g., Syntactic Similarities.

- TORC-3 is best used along with other measures of reading skills to arrive at a total evaluation of a child's reading abilities.

4.33   Nelson-Denny Reading Test (NDRT)

Authors: James T. Brown, Vivian Vick Fishco, and Gerald Hanna

Publisher: The Riverside Publishing Company

Description of Test: This test is a 136-item paper-and-pencil reading measure comprising two parts.

Administration Time: 35–45 minutes

Age/Grade Levels: Grades 9 to College

Subtest Information: The test contains two parts as follows:

- *Vocabulary*—This section contains 80 multiple-choice items and assesses a student's vocabulary development.

- *Comprehension*—This section contains seven reading passages and 38 multiple-choice questions and assesses a student's comprehension and reading rate.

Strengths of the Nelson-Denny

- The Nelson-Denny is a very good screening assessment measure of potential reading difficulties for secondary-level students.

- The measure of reading rate allows this test to be used by evaluators in assessing a student's need for extended time.

- The norms allow for assessing the reading potential of college-level students.

Weakness of the Nelson-Denny

- The manual is limited in terms of information regarding reliability and validity, which is provided in another manual at extra cost.

4.34   Interpreting Handwriting and Written Composition

Handwriting

Handwriting refers to the actual motor activity that is involved in writing. Most students are taught *manuscript* (printing) initially and then move to *cursive* writing in later grades. There are those who advocate that only manuscript or only cursive should be taught. In truth, problems may appear among students in either system.

Handwriting skills are usually measured through the use of informal assessment measures, such as rating scales, observation measures, error analysis—rather than norm-referenced measures. Given the fact that most measures are informal, handwriting is not normally part of a psychoeducational battery. However, handwriting should always be evaluated and examples gathered and informally assessed if it appears to warrant concern.

Written Composition

Writing is a highly complex method of expression involving the integration of eye–hand, linguistic, and conceptual abilities. As a result, it is usually the last skill to be mastered by children. Reading is usually considered the receptive form of a graphic symbol system, and writing is considered the expressive form of that system. The primary concern in the assessment of composition skills is the content of the student's writing, not its form.

The term *writing* refers to a variety of interrelated graphic skills, including:

- *Composition*—The ability to generate ideas and to express them in an acceptable grammar, while adhering to certain stylistic conventions.

- *Spelling*—The ability to use letters to construct words in accordance with accepted usage.

- *Handwriting*—The ability to physically execute the graphic marks necessary to produce legible compositions or messages.

4.35   Picture Story Language Test (PSLT)

Author: Helmer R. Myklebust

Publisher: The Psychological Corporation

Description of Test: The test is a multiple-item pencil-and-paper test in which the examiner asks the student to write the best story he/she can about a picture on an easel.

Administration Time: 20–30 minutes

Age/Grade Levels: Ages 7 to 17

Subtest Information: The writing sample is scored in terms of three aspects of written language: productivity, correctness, and meaning. The three scales of the PSLT correspond to these dimensions:

- *Productivity scale*—The length of writing sample is used to evaluate the child's productivity. The words in the sample are counted along with the sentences.

- *Syntax scale*—The purpose of this scale is the evaluation of the child's accuracy in the mechanical aspects of writing.

- *Abstract-Concrete scale*—This scale attempts to assess the content of the child's writing.

Strengths of the PSLT

- The test is easy to administer.
- The wide age range makes it a good instrument for measuring the child's progress in writing skills in relation to age.

Weaknesses of the PSLT

- The test's norms are dated.
- The test is no longer widely used, as people are more likely to use the newest version of the TOWL (see List 4.37) in place of this test because of its updated norms.
- Scoring of the writing sample is subjective and lengthy.
- Serious questions have been raised about its technical adequacy.

4.36   Test of Early Written Language—2 (TEWL-2)

Author: Wayne P. Hresko

Publisher: PRO-ED, Inc.

Description of Test: The test was developed to assess early writing abilities and covers five areas of writing transcription, conventions of print, communication, creative expression, and record keeping. The TEWL has a total of 42 items. The starting items vary by age level. An item is graded as 1 if correct and 0 if incorrect. Each item counts equally, although some require more responses or information than others. It is individually administered.

Administration Time: 10–30 minutes

Age/Grade Levels: Ages 3 to 7

Subtest Information: The test consists of two subtests:

- *Basic Writing*
- *Contextual Writing*

Strengths of the TEWL-2

- The TEWL is one of several recent efforts to provide assessments for the developmental skills and academic abilities of young children.
- The test is useful in assessing and planning educational activities.
- The test is useful for evaluating educational programs designed to promote the writing skills of young children.

Weaknesses of the TEWL-2

- In reporting the results, the manual's scoring definition and scales look similar to those for IQ, which could lead to misinterpretation of results.
- Additional validity is needed on the test especially for younger age groups.

4.37   Test of Written Language—3 (TOWL-3)

Authors: Donald D. Hammill and Stephen C. Larsen

Publisher: PRO-ED, Inc.

Description of Test: This test is organized into three composites: Overall Written Language, Contrived Writing, and Spontaneous Writing.

Administration Time: Untimed

Age/Grade Levels: Grades 2 to 12

Subtest Information: The TOWL-3 contains eight subtests. The skills measured by each subtest are as follows:

- *Vocabulary*—This subtest measures the student's knowledge of word meanings and classes through the writing of meaningful sentences.

- *Spelling*—This subtest measures the student's ability to spell dictated words.

- *Style*—This subtest measures the student's ability to punctuate sentences and capitalize properly.

- *Logical Sentences*—This subtest measures the student's ability to recognize—and correct through rewriting—illogicalities existing in stimulus sentences.

- *Sentence Combining*—This subtest measures the student's ability to incorporate the meaning of several sentences into a comprehensive single sentence containing phrases and clauses.

- *Contextual Conventions*—This subtest measures the student's skills in capitalization, punctuation, and spelling.

- *Contextual Language*—This subtest measures the student's vocabulary, syntax, and grammar.

- *Story Construction*—This subtest measures the student's plot development, character development, and general composition.

Strengths of the TOWL-3

- Easy items have been added to make the test more friendly to poor writers.

- Results are shown to be unbiased relative to gender and race.

- All aspects of reliability and validity have been strengthened.

Weakness of the TOWL-3

- Both reading and writing skills are required and students cannot be given reading assistance.

4.38 Analysis for Interpreting Mathematics Tests

Mathematical thinking is a process that begins early in most children. Even before formal education begins, children are exposed to various situations that involve the application of mathematical concepts. As they enter formal schooling, they take the knowledge of what they had previously learned and begin to apply it in a more formal manner.

It is necessary to understand that mathematics and arithmetic are actually two different terms. Although most people use them interchangeably, they each have distinct meanings. *Mathematics* refers to the study of numbers and their relationships to time, space, volume, and geometry; *arithmetic* refers to the operations or computations performed. Arithmetic is a category of mathematical skill.

Mathematics involves many different skills. These include:

■ The ability to solve problems.

■ The ability to interpret results.

■ The ability to apply mathematics in practical situations.

■ The ability to use mathematics for prediction.

■ The ability to estimate.

■ The ability to do computational skills.

■ The ability to understand measurement.

■ The ability to create and read graphs and charts.

All schools, whether regular education or special education, use some form of mathematical assessment. Schools begin the process of teaching math skills in kindergarten and continue throughout the child's formal education. Even at the college level, mathematics is often a core requirement in many liberal arts schools. In general, next to reading, mathematics is probably the area most frequently assessed in school systems.

Mathematics can be assessed at the individual or group level. Consequently, it is a skill that is stressed and measured by various tests in schools. Mathematics tests often cover a great many areas. However, according to Salvia and Ysseldyke (1998), there are three types of classifications involved in diagnostic math tests. Each classification measures certain mathematical abilities:

1. *Content*—This consists of Numeration, Fractions, Geometry, and Algebra.

2. *Operations*—This consists of Counting, Computation, and Reasoning.

3. *Applications*—This consists of Measurement, Reading Graphs and Tables, Money and Budgeting Time, and Problem Solving.

Furthermore, according to the National Council of Supervisors of Mathematics, basic mathematical skills include:

■ Arithmetic computation

■ Problem solving

■ Applying mathematics in everyday situations

■ Alertness to the reasonableness of results

4.38 continued

- Estimation and approximation
- Geometry
- Measurement
- Reading charts and graphs
- Using mathematics to predict
- Computer literacy

There are fewer diagnostic math tests than there are diagnostic reading tests. However, math assessment is more clear-cut. Most diagnostic math tests generally sample similar behaviors.

According to McLoughlin and Lewis (1994), mathematics is one of the school subjects best suited for error analysis because students respond in writing on most tasks, thereby producing a permanent record of their work. Also, there is usually only one correct answer to mathematics questions and problems, so scoring is unambiguous. Today, the most common use of error analysis in mathematics is assessment of computation skills.

McLoughlin and Lewis (1990, p. 354) identified four error types in computational analysis:

1. *Incorrect operation*—The student selects the incorrect operation. For example, the problem requires subtraction and the student adds.

2. *Incorrect number fact*—The number fact recalled by the student is inaccurate. For example, the student recalls the product of 9×6 as 52.

3. *Incorrect algorithm*—The procedures used by the student to solve the problem are inappropriate. The student may skip a step, apply the correct steps in the wrong sequence, or use another inaccurate method.

4. *Random error*—The student's response is incorrect and apparently random. For example, the student writes 100 as the answer to 42×6.

There are other types of errors that can occur in the mathematics process in addition to the four mentioned above. For example, a student may make a mistake or error in applying the appropriate arithmetical operations. An example would be $50 - 12 = 62$. Here, the student used the operation of addition rather than subtraction. The student may understand how to do both operations, but consistently gets these types of questions wrong on the tests he or she takes due to the improper interpretation of the sign involved.

Another problem that the student may encounter is a *slip*. When a slip occurs, it is more likely the result of a simple mistake rather than a pattern of problems. For example, if a child subtracts $20 - 5$ in eight problems, but for some reason not in the ninth problem, his or her error is probably due to a simple slip rather than a serious operational or processing problem. One error on one problem is not an error pattern. Error patterns can be assessed by analyzing all correct and incorrect answers. When designing a program plan for a particular child in mathematics, it is critical to establish not only what the nature of the problem is, but also the patterns of problems that occur in the child's responses.

Handwriting can play an important role in mathematics. Scoring a math test often involves reading numbers written down on an answer sheet by the student. If a student's handwriting is difficult to interpret or impossible to read, this can create serious problems for the evaluator with respect to obtaining valid scores. When a student's handwriting is not clear on a math test, it is important that the evaluator ask the student to help him or her read the answers. By doing so, the evaluator is analyzing the math skills that need to be assessed rather than spending his or her time trying to decode the student's responses.

4.39 Key Math Diagnostic Arithmetic Test— Revised (KEY MATH-R)

Authors: Austin J. Connolly, William Nachtman, and E. Milo Pritchett

Publisher: American Guidance Service

Description of Test: The KEY MATH-R is a point-to and paper-and-pencil test measuring math skills in 14 areas. Two forms of the KEY MATH-R are available to use: Forms A and B. Each form contains 258 items. The materials include a test manual, two easel kits for presentation of test items, and individual record forms for recording responses.

Administration Time: Approximately 30–45 minutes

Age/Grade Levels: Preschool to Grade 6

Subtests: The test is broken down into three major areas consisting of 14 subtests:

1. *Basic Concepts*—This part has 3 subsets that investigate basic mathematical concepts and knowledge:
   - Numeration
   - Rational numbers
   - Geometry

2. *Operations*—This part consists of basic computation processes:
   - Addition
   - Subtraction
   - Multiplication
   - Division
   - Mental computation

3. *Applications*—This section focuses on the functional applications use of mathematics necessary to daily life:
   - Measurement
   - Time
   - Money
   - Estimation
   - Interpretation of data
   - Problem solving

Strengths of the KEY MATH-R

- The test manual guides teachers as to appropriate remediation procedures for students who have mathematics deficiencies.
- The test has a broad range of item content.
- The test has a diversity of item content.
- The test is useful with exceptional children because of the range of norms provided and skills tested.

Weaknesses of the KEY MATH-R

- Further information is needed about the test's concurrent validity.
- Scoring of the test can be particularly time consuming.
- The test takes a long time to administer and as a result may have to be completed in multiple sessions.

4.40   Test of Early Mathematics Ability—2 (TEMA-2)

Authors: Herbert P. Ginsberg and Arthur J. Baroody

Publisher: PRO-ED, Inc.

Description of Test: Designed to reflect the mathematical thinking that begins prior to school experiences, the informal components include concepts of relative magnitude, counting skills, and calculation skills.

Administration Time: With a few exceptions, the TEMA-2 is not a timed test; therefore, no precise time limits are imposed on the children being tested.

Age/Grade Levels: Ages 3 to 9

Subtest Information: The test is administered either as a 50-item oral-response or as a paper–pencil test assessing mathematical abilities in the following domains:

- *Informal Mathematics*—This test domain measures a student's knowledge of concepts of relative magnitude, counting, and calculation.

- *Formal Mathematics*—This test domain measures a student's knowledge of conventional facts, calculation, and base-10 concepts.

Strength of the TEMA-2

- The new manual, Assessment Probes and Instructional Activities, can be of great benefit to elementary teachers who want further insights into how their students think mathematically.

Weaknesses of the TEMA-2

- The test does not sufficiently identify the strengths of the student's mathematical thinking.

- The test does not sufficiently identify the weaknesses of the student's mathematical thinking.

4.41   Test of Mathematical Abilities—2 (TOMA-2)

Authors: Virginia L. Brown, Mary E. Cronin, and Elizabeth McEntire

Publisher: PRO-ED, Inc.

Description of Test: The test comprises five paper–pencil subtests that assess various areas of mathematical ability.

Administration Time: Varies

Age/Grade Levels: Ages 8.0 to 18.11

Subtest Information: The test consists of four core subtests and one supplemental subtest:

- *Vocabulary*—In this subtest, students are presented with mathematical terms, which they are asked to define briefly as they are used in a mathematical sense.

- *Computation*—In this subtest, students are presented with computational problems consisting of basic operations and involving manipulation of fractions, decimals, money, percentages, etc.

- *General Information*—In this subtest, the student is read questions by the examiner involving basic general knowledge and must reply orally. This subtest is usually administered individually.

- *Story Problems*—In this subtest, the student reads brief story problems that contain extraneous information and must extract the pertinent information required to solve the problem. Work space is provided for calculation.

- *Attitude Toward Math* (supplemental subtest)—Here the child is presented with various statements about math attitudes and must respond with "agree," "disagree," or "don't know."

Strengths of the TOMA-2

- The new manual can be of great benefit to elementary teachers who want further insight into how their students think mathematically.

- The TOMA-2 can help educators answer the following questions:
  - Where should a student be placed in a curriculum?
  - What are the student's expressed attitudes toward mathematics?
  - Do the student's attitudes, vocabulary, and level of general math information differ markedly from those of a group of age peers?

Weaknesses of the TOMA-2

- Students need both reading and writing skills to complete the TOMA-2.
- Further information about the test's validity is necessary.

4.42   Interpreting Spelling Tests

Spelling is one of the academic skills often included in the evaluator's test battery of individual achievement tests used in special education assessment. Spelling is the ability to use letters to construct words in accordance with accepted usage. Spelling ability is viewed by some teachers and school administrators equally with other academic skills. Being a poor speller does not necessarily mean that a child has a learning disorder. However, when poor spelling occurs with poor reading and/or arithmetic, there is reason for concern. It appears that many of the learning skills required for good spelling are also the ones that enable students to become good readers.

Spelling, like all written language skills, is well suited to work-sample analysis because a permanent product is produced. Learning to spell is a developmental process, and young children go through a number of stages as they begin to acquire written language skills. Writing begins in the preschool years as young children observe and begin to imitate the act of writing.

There are several questions that should be addressed before one begins to analyze the results of the spelling subtest. These questions include:

1. **Does the child have sufficient mental ability to learn to spell?** This information can be obtained from the school psychologist if an intellectual evaluation was administered. However, if no such test was administered, then a group school abilities index may be present in the child's permanent folder.

2. **Are the child's hearing, speech, and vision adequate?** This information can be obtained through the permanent record folder, information in the nurse's office, or informal screening procedures.

3. **What is the child's general level of spelling ability according to teachers' comments and past evaluations or standardized tests?** Teacher comments and observations about the child's spelling history are very important to show patterns of disability. Also, look at standardized tests to see if patterns exist through the years on such tests.

Other information should be obtained from the classroom teacher as well. The teacher can offer you some foundational information on the child's patterns. You may want to ask for the following information from the teacher:

- The child's attitude toward spelling in the classroom.
- The extent to which the child relies on a dictionary in the classroom.
- The extent of spelling errors in classroom written work.
- Any patterns of procrastination or avoidance of written work.
- The student's study habits and methods of work in the classroom.
- The history of scores on classroom spelling tests.
- Any observable handwriting difficulties.
- Any evidence of fatigue as a factor in the child's spelling performance.

4.43   Spelling Errors Primarily Due to Auditory or Visual Channel Deficits

Certain spelling errors may be evident in students with certain auditory channel deficits:

- *Auditory discrimination problems or dialect differences in pronunciation*—The child substitutes *t* for *d* or *sh* for *ch*.

- *Auditory discrimination problems*—The child confuses vowels—for example, spells *bit* as *bet*.

- *Auditory acuity or discrimination problems*—The child does not hear subtle differences in, or discriminates between, sounds and often leaves vowels out of two-syllable words.

- *Auditory–visual association*—The child uses a synonym (such as *house* for *home*) in spelling.

- *Auditory–visual associative memory*—The child takes wild guesses with little or no relationship between the letters or words used and the spelling words dictated, such as spelling *dog* for *home* or writing *phe* for *home*.

Certain spelling errors may be evident in students with certain visual channel deficits:

- *Visual memory problems*—The child visualizes the beginning or the ending of words but omits the middle of the words—for example, spells *hpy* for *happy*.

- *Visual memory sequence*—The child gives the correct letters but in the wrong sequence—for example, writes the word as *teh* or *hte*.

- *Visual discrimination problems*—The child inverts letters—for example, writing *u* for *n*, *m* for *w*.

- *Visual memory*—The child spells words phonetically that are nonphonetic in configuration—for example, *tuff* for *tough*.

4.44 Diagnostic Word Patterns

Author: Evelyn Buckley

Publisher: Educators Publishing Service Inc.

Description of Test: This standardized diagnostic word pattern test consists of three lists of 100 words each to be administered to a group as a spelling test. It measures basic phonic and word analysis skills of each student in the class. Each list contains 10 different spelling patterns, with each set of 10 more difficult than the previous set.

Administration Time: 20–45 minutes

Age/Grade Level: Grades 2 and up

Subtest Information: There are no formal subtests.

Strengths of the Diagnostic Word Patterns

- The test is easy to administer.
- Student answers can be recorded on answer sheets which facilitates scoring.

Weaknesses of the Diagnostic Word Patterns

- There are many words on the test that could be misspelled as a result of dialect or sound language mismatches.
- Many of the words included in the sample—especially those having short vowels—do not really exemplify the true sound of the vowel.

4.45   Test of Written Spelling—3 (TWS-3)

Authors: Stephen C. Larsen and Donald D. Hammill

Publisher: PRO-ED, Inc.

Description of Test: The test divides spelling of English words into two categories: those that follow orthographic rules (predictable words) and those that do not (unpredictable words).

Administration Time: 15 to 25 minutes

Age/Grade Levels: Ages 6.0 to 18.11.

Subtest Information: The test consists of two subtests:

- *Predictable Words*—This test contains words that follow the general spelling rules, e.g., *spend*.

- *Unpredictable Words*—This test contains words that do not conform to general spelling rules, e.g., *campaign*.

Strengths of the TWS-3

- The manual is clear and concise.

- The administration and scoring section of the manual details how to determine the basal and ceiling ages, as well as the scoring procedures.

- Reliability estimates indicate that the test can be accepted as a consistent measure of written spelling ability.

- The test is easily administered.

Weaknesses of the TWS-3

- Sample sizes of the studies were limited to 20 students per grade which may be problematic in generalizing results to the entire population.

- The TWS-3 does not assess all aspects of the spelling process.

The following tests are comprehensive in their assessment of academic areas. These tests normally offer a thorough approach to the assessment of a child's strengths and weaknesses in reading, math, spelling, and writing.

4.46   Brigance Diagnostic Inventory of Basic Skills

Author: Albert Brigance

Publisher: Curriculum Associates, Inc.

Description of Test: The test is presented in a plastic ring binder that is designed to be laid open and placed between the examiner and the student. A separate student booklet provided for the student's answers is designed so that the skills range from easy to difficult; thus, the teacher can quickly ascertain the skills level the student has achieved.

Administration Time: Specific time limits are listed on many tests; others are untimed.

Age/Grade Levels: Grades K through 6. It is also used for academic assessment of older students functioning below sixth-grade academic levels.

Subtest Information: There are four subtest areas including 143 pencil-and-paper or oral response tests:

- *Readiness*—The skills assessed include color naming; visual discrimination of shapes, letters, and short words; copying designs; drawing shapes from memory; drawing a person; gross motor coordination; recognition of body parts; following directional and verbal instructions; fine-motor self-help skills; verbal fluency; sound articulation; personal knowledge; memory for sentences; counting; alphabet recitation; number naming and comprehension; letter naming; and writing name, numbers, and letters.

- *Reading*—This test evaluates word recognition, oral reading and comprehension, oral reading rate, structure analysis, syllabication, and vocabulary.

- *Language Arts*—This test assesses cursive handwriting, grammar and mechanics, spelling, and reference skills.

- *Mathematics*—This test assesses rote counting; writing numerals in sequence; reading number words; ordinal concepts; numeral recognition; writing to dictation; counting in sets; Roman numerals; fractions; decimals; measurement (money, time, calendar, linear/liquid/weight measurement, temperature); and two- and three-dimensional geometric concepts.

Strengths of the Brigance

- It helps determine what a student has or has not learned.
- The test contains suggestions for specific instructional objectives.
- It requires no testing expertise.
- It can help with referral decisions.
- This test is considered to be one of the most comprehensive elementary grade-level, criterion-referenced instruments.
- The Brigance is also viewed as being well suited to determining mastery of very specific teaching objectives.
- The test manual states that results of the Brigance should be considered in conjunction with evaluation of the student's classroom performance, classroom observation, and scrutiny of actual curricular goals.

Weaknesses of the Brigance

- Guidelines on where to begin testing are imprecise.
- No data are offered on reliability.
- There is no description of norms for 10 of the subtests.
- There are no suggested standards of mastery for 65 percent of the tests.
- The test is not appropriate for making decisions that compare children against one another or for class or reading group placement.
- This test has no norm to validate the sequence, difficulty level, or percent-correct criteria for items within tests. Hence, the Brigance inventory is stated to be on shaky grounds in determining a student's grade-level performance on the tested skill.

4.47   Kaufman Tests of Educational Achievement (KTEA)

Authors: Alan S. Kaufman and Nadeen L. Kaufman

Publisher: American Guidance Service

Description of Test: The test includes a brief achievement battery, two parallel forms of an educational achievement battery, and a design that facilitates diagnostic interpretation in addition to standard score data.

Administration Time: 60–75 minutes

Age/Grade Levels: Grades 1 to 12

Subtest Information: The test contains five subtests:

- *Reading/Decoding*—This subtest presents words visually for the student to read aloud to the examiner.

- *Mathematics Applications—This subtest presents story-type problems printed* on easel pages. The student can use a pencil and paper to figure out his or her answer but must answer orally.

- *Spelling*—This subtest is presented as a typical spelling test.

- *Reading Comprehension*—This subtest presents sentences and passages for the student to read silently and respond to orally.

- *Mathematics Computation*—This subtest includes 60 math problems presented in the student's answer booklet.

Strengths of the KTEA

- The KTEA appears to be a well-standardized, reliable measure with some innovative features that could make it the measure of choice for analyzing academic strengths and weaknesses.

- The KTEA provides valid scores for the basic achievement areas covered in school.

Weaknesses of the KTEA

- Final assessment of the validity of the measure must await a more complete study by independent investigators.

- The test lacks a breakdown of scores for the ethnic groups included in the standardization sample.

4.48 Peabody Individual Achievement Test— Revised (PIAT-R)

Author: Frederick C. Markwardt, Jr.

Description of Test: The PIAT-R is used in special education for identifying academic deficiencies. It is made up of six subtests. The most typical response format on the PIAT-R is multiple choice. The student is shown a test plate with four possible answers and asked to select the correct response.

Administration Time: 50–70 minutes

Age/Grade Levels: Level 1, grades K to 1; Level 2, grades 2 to 12

Subtest Information: The test's six subtests are as follows:

- *General Information*—This subtest has 100 questions that are open-ended and presented orally. They measure the student's factual knowledge related to science, social studies, humanities, fine art, and recreation.
- *Reading Recognition*—There are 100 items. Items 1–16 are multiple choice and measure prereading skills. Items 17–100 measure decoding skills and require the student to read orally individually presented words.
- *Reading Comprehension*—This subtest consists of 82 items and measures the student's ability to draw meaning from printed sentences.
- *Spelling*—Items 1–15 are multiple-choice tasks that assess reading skills. Items 16–100 require the student to select from four possible choices the correct spelling of a word read orally by the examiner.
- *Written Expression*—This subtest has two levels. Level 1 consists of 19 copying and dictation items that are arranged in order of ascending difficulty. In Level 2, the student is presented with one or two picture plates and given 20 minutes to write a story about the picture(s).
- *Mathematics*—In this subtest, the student is asked the question orally and must select the correct response from four choices. Questions cover topics ranging from numerical recognition to trigonometry.

Strengths of the PIAT-R

- The revision is broader in scope and contains more items than the original test.
- The test manual presents evidence to support content, concurrent, and construct validity.
- The test is useful for the assessment of school performance across a range of academic subjects.

Weaknesses of the PIAT-R

- The test does not produce results specific enough to provide direction for instructional planning.
- The test assesses some skills with tasks that are dissimilar to typical classroom activities.

4.49 Wechsler Individual Achievement Test—II (WIAT-II)

Author: David Wechsler

Publisher: The Psychological Corporation

Description of Test: The WIAT-II is made up of eight subtests. The test format includes easels and paper-and-pencil tasks.

Administration Time: 30–75 minutes

Age/Grade Levels: Ages 5 to 19

Subtest Information: The test consists of eight individually administered subtests:

- *Basic Reading*—This subtest measures decoding and sight-reading ability.

- *Mathematics Reasoning*—This subtest encompasses major curriculum objectives in problem solving, geometry, measurement, and statistics.

- *Spelling*—This subtest assesses the student's encoding and spelling ability.

- *Reading Comprehension*—This subtest taps skills that include comprehension of detail, sequence, cause-and-effect relationships, and inference.

- *Numerical Operations*—This subtest tests the student's ability to write dictated numerals; to solve basic addition, subtraction, multiplication, and division problems; to solve problems with whole numbers, fractions, and decimals; and to solve algebraic equations.

- *Listening Comprehension*—This subtest measures the student's levels of comprehension, ranging from understanding of details to making inferential conclusions.

- *Oral Expression*—This subtest assesses the student's ability to name targeted words, describe scenes, give directions, and explain steps in sequential tasks.

- *Written Expression*—This subtest consists of a free writing task. It affords the assessment of idea development and organization as well as capitalization and punctuation.

Strengths of the WIAT-II

- The WIAT-II is the only achievement battery standardized with the Wechsler Intelligence Scale for Children–Third Edition (WISC-III).

- The test meets regulatory requirements for assessing or reevaluating children and adolescents.

- The manual includes the scope and sequence of objectives and how they relate to curricula.

- The manual provides guidelines for creating curriculum-related IEPs.

Weaknesses of WIAT-II

- Cultural bias may be present on some subtests.

- The test provides limited assessment of kindergarten and first-grade students because it covers a wide range. Therefore, as with any achievement test, the scores are more valid in the middle of the age range than at the extremes.

- The three subtests involved in Oral Expression measure very different skills. As a result, the total oral expression score may not be as useful with certain students.

4.50   Wide Range Achievement Test—3 (WRAT-3)

Author: Gary S. Wilkinson

Publisher: Jastak Associates/Wide Range Inc.

Description of Test: This new edition of the Wide Range Achievement Test has returned to a single-level format. The test contains a Blue and a Tan form that can be used in a pretest/posttest format, test/retest format, or administered together in a combined test format.

Administration Time: Each form of the WRAT-3 takes approximately 15–30 minutes to administer. However, age, ability, and behavioral style of the student will vary the length of the test administration.

Age/Grade Levels: Ages 5 to 75

Subtest Information: The three subtests contained on both the Blue and Tan forms are:

- *Reading*—This is a subtest involving decoding where the subject is asked to recognize and rename letters and pronounce words in isolation.

- *Spelling*—This is a subtest of written spelling where the subject is asked to write his or her name and letters and words from dictation.

- *Arithmetic*—This is a subtest of mathematical computation where the subject is asked to count, read numbers, identify number symbols, solve oral problems, and perform written computation within a defined time limit.

Strengths of the WRAT-3

- This test makes for a very useful screening instrument because of the short administration time and specific areas measured.

- The test is quick and reliable.

- The test is reasonably valid in measuring achievement in its subtest areas.

- The written spelling subtest is an excellent test and one of the few available in this area.

Weaknesses of the WRAT-3

- This test is often referred to as tedious.

- The test only provides a few items at each level, which can make interpreting diagnostic patterns of strengths and weaknesses less reliable.

- The reading subtest measures word recognition only, so additional achievement testing is often needed to test other reading skills, such as comprehension.

- The mathematics subtest measures computational math only, so additional testing is often needed to test other mathematics skills, such as applications and word problems.

4.51 Woodcock-Johnson Tests of Achievement—III® (WJ-III)

Author: Richard W. Woodcock and Mary Bonner Johnson

Publisher: The Riverside Publishing Company

Description of Test: This test provides a comprehensive set of tests for measuring general intellectual ability, specific cognitive abilities, scholastic aptitude, oral language, and academic achievement.

Administration Time: Varies; about 5 minutes per test; Achievement Standard 11 tests (55–65 minutes)

Age/Grade Levels: Ages 2.0 to 90+; Grades K.0 to Graduate School

Subtest Information: The test consists of the Standard Battery and the Extended Battery, which comprise the following subtests:

The descriptions below are not the "official" ones provided by the WJ-III® manual.

1. *Letter-Word Identification*	Identifying and pronouncing isolated letters and words
2. *Reading Fluency*	Rapidly reading and comprehending simple sentences
9. *Passage Comprehension*	Reading a short passage silently, then supplying a key missing word
13. *Word Attack*	Pronouncing nonsense words (e.g., plurp) that conform to English spelling rules
17. *Reading Vocabulary*	Reading stimulus words for three different tasks: providing synonyms, providing antonyms, and completing analogies
7. *Spelling*	Writing words presented orally
8. *Writing Fluency*	Formulating and writing simple sentences quickly when given three words and a picture
11. *Writing Samples*	In response to a variety of demands, writing sentences that are then evaluated based on the quality of expression
16. *Editing*	Identifying and correcting mistakes in spelling, punctuation, capitalization, or word usage in written passages
20. *Spelling of Sounds*	Spelling nonsense words that conform to English spelling rules

4.51 continued

22. *Punctuation and Capitalization*	Using correct punctuation and capitalization in dictated words and phrases
5. *Calculation*	Mathematical computations ranging from simple addition to complex equations
6. *Math Fluency*	Rapid calculation (simple single-digit addition, subtraction, and multiplication)
10. *Applied Problems*	Analyzing and solving practical mathematical problems
18. *Quantitative Concepts*	Applying mathematical concepts and analyzing numerical relationships
3. *Story Recall*	Listening to passages of gradually increasing length and complexity, then recalling the story elements
4. *Understanding Directions*	Pointing to objects in a picture after listening to instructions that increase in linguistic complexity
12. *Story Recall—Delayed*	Recalling, after a 30-minute to eight-day delay, the story elements presented in the Story Recall test.
14. *Picture Vocabulary*	Naming pictured objects that range from common to less familiar
15. *Oral Comprehension*	Listening to short passages, then supplying the missing final word
19. *Academic Knowledge*	Answering questions about curricular knowledge in the biological and physical sciences, social sciences, and humanities
21. *Sound Awareness*	Rhyming, deletion, substitution, and reversal of spoken sounds

Unofficial subtest explanations are adapted from Figure 1, "WJ III ACH-Like Sample Items," in *Essentials of WJ III™ Tests of Achievement Assessment,* by Nancy Mather, Barbara J. Wendling, and Richard W. Woodcock (Wiley, 2001). Used with permission.

Strengths of the WJ-III

■ Due to the newness of the test, there was no analysis of strengths at the time of this printing.

Weaknesses of the WJ-III

■ Due to the newness of the test, there was no analysis of weaknesses at the time of this printing.

4.52   Observation Methods Used for the Assessment of Problem Behavior

The purpose of *observation* is to gain an awareness of what factors, if any, are influencing the behavior that the child is exhibiting. In order to do a complete and thorough observation, it is critical that the following situations are included:

- *Observation of a specific situation*—An observation of the child is done during a specified time (lunch time, at recess, during show and tell, etc.)

- *Observation in various settings*—An observation of the child is done in the classroom, the playground, during band, etc.

- *Observation at different times during the day*—An observation of the child is done in the morning, afternoon, and by parents in the evening.

There are many different ways to record a child's behavior for assessment purposes. Regardless, the first goal of observation is to determine the target behaviors. Target behaviors are those that the person seeks to observe when doing the observation. Once the target behavior is established, recording of behaviors can begin. In assessment, there are various types of recording that are often used when doing an observation:

- *Anecdotal recording*—The observer records all behaviors and interactions within a given time frame (e.g., recording a child's behavior from 9:00 A.M. until 10:00 A.M.).

- *Event recording*—The observer is looking specifically for one target behavior and records the frequency with which it occurs. Event recording is also referred to as frequency counting because the observer is simply "counting" the number of times a behavior occurs (e.g., recording the number of times a child gets out of his chair in a given period of time).

- *Latency recording*—The observer determines the amount of time between a given stimulus for the child and the response (e.g., the time it takes a student to get out his pencil after the teacher says "Take out your pencil").

- *Duration recording*—The observer notes the amount of time a target behavior occurs (e.g., watching a child for one hour who is supposed to be reading; the child reads only 12 minutes of that time).

When doing the above observations, information about the child becomes much more comprehensive. Collectively, the observations should provide the following:

- Information about the nature of the most frequently seen behaviors.

- Information that can be related to the types of services the child may need.

- Information to help with intervention plans and instructional goals for the child.

- Baseline information against which progress can be measured once intervention begins.

4.53 Interview Methods Used for the Assessment of Problem Behavior

In addition to observations, *interviews* play a very important part in the behavioral assessment. An interview is a research method conducted face to face between two people (the interviewer and the interviewee) where recorded responses to questions are obtained. Interviews can be very effective because they are personal, emotional, and flexible. Interviews can be of two types:

- *Structured Interview*—Individuals are asked a specific set of predetermined questions in a controlled manner.

- *Unstructured Interview*—The questions are not predetermined, thereby allowing for substantial discussion and interaction between the interviewer and interviewee.

Parents, teachers, and the child should be interviewed in order to gain insight into the nature and history of the child's difficulties. It is important to interview the child because the evaluator needs to know whether or not the child has any awareness that there is a concern about his or her behaviors and the degree to which the child may be willing to change.

4.54 Types of Psychological Tests Used in Assessment of Problem Behavior

There are numerous psychological tests used in the assessment of problem behavior in children. The school psychologist almost always administers psychological tests. Tests include:

- *Projective drawing tests*—Projective drawing tests simply ask the child to draw a picture. The tests are used to get the child to "project" his feelings about himself onto paper. The examiner looks for certain patterns in the drawings and in the way in which the child handles what is being asked of him. (For example, a child who draws himself away from everyone else may have low self-esteem; a child who takes the pencil and writes very hard on the paper may be exhibiting anger.)

- *Apperception tests*—Apperception tests require the child to view various picture cards and "tell a story" about what it is he is seeing. He would normally tell a story of what happened before, during, and after the scene shows. Apperception tests try to elicit central themes from the child. For example, a child may consistently tell stories of loneliness, sadness, or perhaps anger. The examiner writes down every word the child says in narrative form and then tries to decipher general patterns of thoughts that the child may be projecting about himself.

- *Sentence completion tests*—Sentence completion tests provide the student with a beginning of a sentence that the student needs to finish. The "fill ins" are supposed to give indications to the emotions and feelings that the student is experiencing. Sentence completion tests can be extremely useful because one response can elicit many questions to ask the child in future interviews. For example, if a child completes the sentence "I could do better if _____" with a response of "I tried harder," you can ask many questions about why her or his effort is poor or not up to a certain level.

- *Rating scales*—Rating scales are often given not only to the student, but to the parents and teachers as well. A rating scale gives a statement about a behavior of a child whereupon the individual has to rate the frequency, intensity, and/or duration of that behavior. By rating various situations, the examiner gets an idea of where the child's strengths and weaknesses lie. Raters are normally asked to evaluate whether a given behavior is present or absent. The tremendous value of a rating scale is that it allows the examiner to get differing viewpoints from other people who interact with the child. A teacher may have a different perception of a child's behavior than a parent. By getting various viewpoints, a more comprehensive evaluation of the child's daily functioning can be established.

4.55 Goodenough-Harris Drawing Test (GHDT)

Authors: Florence L. Goodenough and Dale B. Harris

Publisher: The Psychological Corporation

Description of Test: The test comprises a formal system of administering and scoring human figure drawings to screen children for intellectual maturity as well as emotional problems. Practitioners can detect children who are at risk of having an emotional disturbance by comparing the scores obtained on their figure drawings with the scores from a normative sample.

Administration Time: 15–20 minutes

Age/Grade Levels: Ages 3 to 15.11, but the preferred ages are 3 to 10

Subtest Information: The test has no subtests.

Strengths of the GHDT

- The test's reliability is relatively high.

- The test manual provides a clear description of the scoring system. The record form is clear and efficient.

- The test is psychometrically sound as well as easily and objectively quantified.

Weakness of the GHDT

- Because of the subjective nature of the test and the drawings involved, there are issues concerning the validity of this test.

4.56   Draw-A-Person: Screening Procedure for Emotional Disturbance (DAP:SPED)

Authors: Jack A. Naglieri, Timothy J. McNeish, and Achilles N. Bardos

Publisher: The Psychological Corporation

Description of Test: The test comprises a formal system of administering and scoring human figure drawings to screen children for emotional problems. Practitioners can detect children who are at risk of having an emotional disturbance by comparing the scores obtained on their figure drawings with the scores from a normative sample.

Administration Time: 15 minutes

Age/Grade Levels: Ages 6 to 17, but the preferred ages are 3 to 10

Subtest Information: The test has no subtests.

Strengths of the DAP:SPED

- The test reliability is relatively high.
- The test manual provides a clear description of the scoring system. The record form is clear and efficient.
- The test is psychometrically sound as well as easily and objectively quantified.

Weaknesses of the DAP:SPED

- Because of the subjective nature of the test and the drawings involved, there are issues concerning the validity of this test.
- This test should never be used alone for decision-making processes.

4.57   Kinetic-House-Tree-Person Drawings (K-H-T-P)

Author: Robert C. Burns

Publisher: Western Psychological Services

Description of Test: The student is asked to draw a house, a tree, and a person in action using one page of paper for each.

Administration Time: Untimed

Age/Grade Levels: Children and adolescents

Subtest Information: The test has no subtests.

Strengths of the K-H-T-P

- The test is easy to administer.
- The test is nonthreatening because the objects being drawn by the child are familiar.

Weaknesses of the K-H-T-P

- Because of the subjective nature of the test and the drawings involved, there are issues concerning the validity of this test.
- This test should never be used alone for decision-making processes.

4.58   Children's Apperception Test (CAT)

Authors: Leopold Bellack and Sonya Sorel Bellack

Publisher: C.P.S. Incorporated

Description of Test: This test uses a storytelling technique for personality evaluation. It employs pictures of animal figures in a variety of situations because it is assumed that children will be more comfortable expressing their feelings with pictures of animals than humans.

Administration Time: Untimed

Age/Grade Levels: Ages 5 to 10

Subtest Information: There are no subtests.

Strengths of the CAT

- This test is a good indicator of the presence of psychological needs.
- This test is easy to administer.
- This is a very popular test within school systems as part of a psychological battery.

Weaknesses of the CAT

- There are issues of validity and reliability.
- The test is prone to a very subjective interpretation by examiner.
- Nonverbal students will have difficulty with this test because of its verbal nature.

4.59 Thematic Apperception Test (TAT)

Author: Henry A. Murray

Publisher: Harvard University Press

Description of Test: The test comprises a series of 20 pictures about which the individual being tested is instructed to tell stories, usually with a beginning, middle, and end. During this process, the story is coded to evaluate certain emotional and behavioral characteristics.

Administration Time: Untimed

Age/Grade Levels: Ages 14 and up

Subtest Information: The test has no subtests.

Strengths of the TAT

- The test is a good indicator of the presence of psychological needs.
- The test is easy to administer.
- The test is very popular within school systems as part of a psychological battery because of the easy administration and the quality of information that can be obtained.

Weaknesses of the TAT

- Because of the subjective nature of the test and the drawings involved, there are issues concerning the validity of this test.
- This test should never be used alone for decision-making processes.
- Nonverbal students will have difficulty with this test because of the test's verbal nature.

4.60   Rorschach Psychodiagnostic Test

Author: Hermann Rorschach

Publisher: The Psychological Corporation

Description of Test: The test is a 10-card oral response projective personality test in which the subject is asked to interpret what he or she sees in 10 inkblots. Although not an "apperception test," the Rorschach requires students to look at inkblots and explain what they see. Again, as with other projective tests, patterns are examined for central themes.

Administration Time: Untimed

Age/Grade Levels: Ages 3 and up

Subtest Information: The test has no subtests.

Strengths of the Rorschach

- With proper scoring, the test can yield valuable information about the emotional state of a person.

- The test is easy to administer.

- Directions are simple and easily understood by test administrators and those taking the test.

Weaknesses of the Rorschach

- The test is very difficult to score because of the many variables involved in the scoring procedure.

- Because of the subjective nature of the test and the drawings involved, there are issues concerning the validity of this test.

4.61   Politte Sentence Completion Test (PSCT)

Author: Alan Politte

Publisher: Psychologists and Educators Incorporated

Description of Test: The test is a 35-item paper-and-pencil test measuring personality. Items are sentence stems that the subject completes.

Administration Time: 15 minutes

Age/Grade Levels: Grades 1 to 12

Subtest Information: The test has no subtests.

Strengths of the PSCT

- The test is easy to administer.
- The test is useful for clinical interpretation of personality.
- The test has a relatively short administration time.

Weaknesses of the PSCT

- Because of the subjective nature of the test and the drawings involved, there are issues concerning the validity of this test.
- This test should never be used alone for decision-making processes.

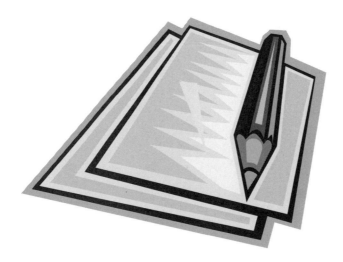

4.62 Conners' Parent and Teacher Rating Scales (CPRS/CTRS)

Author: C. Keith Conners

Publisher: Multi-Health Systems Incorporated

Description of Test: This test is a paper–pencil or computer administered instrument used to evaluate problem behaviors of children as reported by the child's teacher, parents, or alternate caregiver.

Administration Time: Untimed

Age/Grade Levels: The Conners' Parent Rating Scale can help identify behavior problems in children 3 to 17 years of age. The Conners' Teacher Rating Scale provides measures for identifying a variety of behavioral problems in children 4 to 12 years old.

Subtest Information: There are four forms available:

- *Conners' Teacher Rating Scale* (CTRS)—The person providing the information about the child is the teacher. This scale is utilized for children ages 3 to 17.
- *Conners' Teacher's Rating Scale*, 39—The person providing the information about the child is the teacher. This scale is utilized for children ages 4 to 12.
- *Conners' Parent Rating Scales*, 93—The person providing the information about the child is the parent. This scale is utilized for children ages 6 to 14.
- *Conners' Parent Rating Scale*, 48—The person providing the information about the child is the parent. This scale is utilized for children ages 3 to 17.

These forms measure a variety of behavioral characteristics grouped into several scales:

- Conduct problems
- Hyperactivity
- Inattentive–passive behavior
- Anxious–passive behavior
- Asocial behavior
- Daydream attention problems
- Emotional overindulgent behavior
- Anxious–shy behavior
- Conduct disorders
- Hyperactive–immature behavior
- Learning problems
- Obsessive–compulsive behavior
- Psychosomatic behavior
- Restless–disorganized behavior
- Anxiety
- Impulsive–hyperactive behavior

4.62 continued

Strengths of the Conners'

- Professionals have used the instrument for more than 20 years.
- This test is a thorough measure of a student's behavioral characteristics because of the number of questions rated.

Weaknesses of the Conners'

- The test standardization sample is not well described, which may be problematic for generalizability.
- The test has not been updated to measure more current definitions of ADD and ADHD.

4.63   Attention Deficit Disorders Evaluation Scale— Revised (ADDES-R)

Author: Stephen B. McCarney

Publisher: Hawthorne Educational Services

Description of Test: There are two versions of this test. The Home Version, completed by parents, has 46 items that assess certain behaviors in the home. The School Version has 60 items that teachers must rate.

Administration Time: 15 minutes

Age/Grade Levels: Ages 4 to 18

Subtest Information: The two forms of this test measure the following:

- Inattention
- Impulsivity
- Hyperactivity

Strengths of the ADDES-R

- The test's Computerized Quick Scoring Program makes scoring of both versions efficient and convenient.
- The test proves very helpful to evaluators in planning IEP development because of the amount of information obtained.
- This test has the largest normative sample of any ADD rating scale.

Weakness of the ADDES-R

- Given the newness of the test, further studies are needed to determine reliability and validity.

4.64   Assessment of Adaptive Behavior

The assessment of **adaptive behavior** is a very important part of the overall assessment process. Adaptive behavior refers to the effectiveness or degree with which individuals meet the standards of personal independence and social responsibility expected for age and cultural groups. When doing an evaluation of adaptive behavior, there are a number of areas in which the examiner should focus. These areas include:

- Communication
- Community use
- Self-direction
- Health and safety
- Functional academics
- Self-care
- Home living
- Social skills
- Leisure
- Work

Understanding adaptive behavior is very important when working with or assessing the mentally retarded population. Adaptive behavior is a required area of assessment when a classification of mental retardation is being considered for a student. IDEA specifies "deficits in adaptive behavior" as one of the two characteristics necessary for a student to be classified as mentally retarded (the other being "significantly sub-average general intellectual functioning").

There are many different ways in which an evaluator can measure adaptive behavior. Because it is often used to assess those with lower levels of intellectual functioning, the student being evaluated may not have to take part directly in the evaluation. The way many of these diagnostic assessment instruments work is that the examiner records information collected from a third person who is familiar with the student (e.g., parent, teacher, direct service provider). Perhaps the greatest problem with doing an assessment on adaptive behavior is the fact that many of the scales and tests do not have high validity and reliability. Also, there are serious concerns about the cultural bias of the tests. Consequently, great care must be taken when selecting the most appropriate measure for an individual student. With respect to minority students, it should also be noted that it is imperative to develop an understanding of what types of behavior are considered adaptive (and thus appropriate) in the minority culture before making diagnostic judgments about the functioning of a particular student.

4.65   AAMR Adaptive Behavior Scale—Residential and Community—2 (ABS-RC-2)

Authors: Kazuo Nihira, Henry Leland, and Nadine Lambert

Publisher: PRO-ED, Inc.

Description of Test: The test is intended for persons with disabilities in residential and community settings. It measures various domain areas and is available as a kit or on software for administration and scoring.

Administration Time: 15–30 minutes

Age/Grade Levels: Ages 18 to 80

Subtest Information: The test has no subtests.

Strengths of the ABS-RC-2

- It is one of the few tests available as a measure for persons with disabilities in the area of adaptive behaviors and factors.
- Many different factors are considered, which is helpful for evaluation.

Weaknesses of the ABS-RC-2

- The test is difficult to evaluate.
- Scoring the test is time consuming.

4.66   AAMR Adaptive Behavior Scale— School (ABS-S-2)

Authors: Nadine Lambert, Kazuo Nihira, and Henry Leland

Publisher: PRO-ED, Inc.

Description of Test: There are 16 subscores that are measured from this test. The test includes an examiner's manual, examiner booklets, computer scoring systems, and profile summary forms.

Administration Time: 15–30 minutes

Age/Grade Levels: Ages 3 to 18.11

Subtest Information: The scale is divided into two parts. Part I focuses on personal independence and is designed to evaluate coping skills considered to be important to independence and responsibility in daily living. The skills within Part I are grouped into nine behavior domains:

- Independent Functioning
- Physical Development
- Economic Activity
- Language Development
- Numbers and Time
- Prevocational/Vocational Activity
- Self Direction
- Responsibility
- Socialization

Part II of the scale contains content related to social adaptation. The behaviors in Part II are assigned to seven domains:

- Social Behavior
- Conformity
- Trustworthiness
- Stereotyped and Hyperactive Behavior
- Self-Abusive Behavior
- Social Engagement
- Disturbing Interpersonal Behavior

Strengths of the ABS-S-2

- The scale has an excellent standardization sample and is appropriate for use with a wide variety of individuals.
- The scale's psychometric qualities are good.
- It has been and remains one of the best available scales for assessment of adaptive behavior.

Weakness of the ABS-S-2

- The test requires further validity research, especially regarding construct validity.

4.67   Adaptive Behavior Evaluation Scale—Revised (ABES-R)

Author: Stephen B. McCarney

Publisher: Hawthorne Educational Services

Description of Test: The ABES-R consists of 105 items assessing adaptive behaviors that are not measured by academic skill testing, but is necessary for success in an educational setting.

Administration Time: 20–25 minutes

Age/Grade Levels: Norms are for students in grades K–12

Subtest Information: The test comprises 10 adaptive skill areas:

- Communication Skills
- Self Care
- Home Living
- Social Skills
- Community Use
- Self Direction
- Health and Safety
- Functional Academics
- Leisure
- Work Skills

Strengths of the ABES-R

- This test is a good measure of adaptive behavior for the identification of students with intellectual disabilities.
- The test comes with an Adaptive Behavior Intervention Manual that may be useful in developing a student's IEP.

Weaknesses of the ABES-R

- The test's interpretive materials only address students with mental retardation.
- The test's literature offers no profiles to show how the mentally retarded may differ from those with behavioral or learning handicaps.

4.68   Vineland Adaptive Behavior Scale (VABS)

Authors: Sara S. Sparrow, David A. Balla, and Domenie V. Cicchetti

Publisher: American Guidance Service

Description of Test: The VABS assesses the social competence of handicapped and non-handicapped individuals. It requires that a respondent familiar with the behavior of the individual in question answer behavior-orientation questions posed by a trained examiner. There are three versions of this test: the Interview Edition–Survey Form, Interview Edition–Expanded Form, and the Classroom Edition.

Administration Time: 20–60 minutes

Age/Grade Levels: Birth to 18.11 and low-functioning adults; Classroom Edition, ages 3 through 12.11

Subtest Information: All versions measure the following domains:

   ▧ *Communication*, which contains the subdomains of receptive, expressive, and written communication.

   ▧ *Daily Living Skills*, which contains the subdomains of personal, domestic, and community daily living skills.

   ▧ *Socialization*, which contains the subdomain of interpersonal relationships, play and leisure time, and coping skills.

   ▧ *Motor Skills*, which contains the subdomains of gross and fine motor skills.

Strengths of the VABS

   ▧ The test is a useful tool for the assessment of adaptive behavior.

   ▧ The test has adequate validity and reliability.

Weakness of the VABS

   ▧ At the present time, no significant criticisms of the VABS have been reported.

4.69 IDEA and Functional Behavioral Assessments

■ Functional behavioral assessments should be implemented as an integrated set of practices throughout the IEP decision-making process.

■ Functional behavioral assessments identify and measure specific problem behaviors (as opposed to "diagnosing"). Describing and analyzing the student's interactions within his or her environment can only determine the function of a behavior.

■ All functional behavioral assessments need not be conducted with the same set of resources and procedures. The nature of the assessment provided must match the level of need demonstrated by the student.

■ Functional behavioral assessments provide data for the design of behavioral strategies and supports (e.g., intervention programs).

REQUIREMENTS OF THE INDIVIDUALS WITH DISABILITIES EDUCATION ACT (IDEA)

References to consideration of a student's behavior that impedes learning can be found in several sections of IDEA '97 including those on evaluation, considerations in the development of the IEP, and the role of the general education teacher in the development of the IEP and discipline. (See List 1.3.)

Evaluation

In conducting the evaluation, the local educational agency shall . . . use technically sound instruments that may assess the relative contribution of cognitive and behavioral factors, in addition to physical or developmental factors. [Section 614(b)(2)(C)]

Each local educational agency shall ensure that . . . the child is assessed in all areas of suspected disability; and assessment tools and strategies that provide relevant information that directly assists persons in determining the educational needs of the child are provided. [Section 614(b)(3)(C)-(D)]

IEP Team (Eligibility Committee)

The regular education teacher of the child as a member of the IEP Team, shall, to the extent appropriate, participate in the development of the IEP of the child, including the determination of appropriate positive behavioral interventions and strategies and the determination of supplementary aids and services, program modifications, and support for school personnel consistent with paragraph (1)(A)(iii). [Section 614(d)(3)(C)]

IEP Contents and Considerations

In developing each child's IEP, the IEP Team, subject to subparagraph (C), shall consider . . . in the case of a child whose behavior impedes his or her learning or that of others, when appropriate, strategies, including positive behavioral interventions, strategies and supports to address that behavior. [Section 614(d)(3)(B)(i)]

Discipline

Either before or not later than 10 days after taking a disciplinary action described in subparagraph (A)—

(i) if the local educational agency did not conduct a functional behavioral assessment and implement a behavioral intervention plan for such child before the behavior that resulted in suspension described in subparagraph (A), the agency shall convene an IEP meeting to develop an assessment plan to address that behavior; or

(ii) if the child already has a behavioral intervention plan, the IEP Team shall review the plan and modify it, as necessary, to address the behavior. [Section 615(k)(1)(B)]

4.70 Overview of Functional Behavioral Assessment (FBA)

Functional behavioral assessment is the process of determining why a student engages in challenging behavior and how the student's behavior relates to the environment. Functional assessments describe the relationship between a skill or performance problem and variables that contribute to its occurrence. The purpose of functional behavioral assessment is to gather broad and specific information in order to better understand the specific reasons for the student's problem behavior. Functional behavioral assessments can provide the district's Eligibility Committee with information to develop a hypothesis as to:

- Why the student engages in the behavior,
- When the student is most likely to demonstrate the behavior, and
- Situations in which the behavior is least likely to occur.

This type of assessment often involves reviewing:

- Curriculum
- Instructional and motivational variables in relation to the student's behavior
- Classroom arrangements
- Individuals present in the classroom
- Present health issues
- Instructional subject and work demands

WRITING FUNCTIONAL BEHAVIORAL ASSESSMENTS AND INTERVENTION PLANS

A variety of techniques are available to conduct a functional behavioral assessment including, but not limited to:

- Indirect assessment (e.g., structured interviews, review of existing evaluation information).
- Direct assessment (e.g., standardized assessments or checklists or observing and recording situational factors surrounding the behavior).
- Data analysis (e.g., a comparison and analysis of data to determine whether or not there are patterns associated with the behavior).

A functional behavioral assessment should minimally include the following components:

- Identification of the problem area.
- Definition of the behavior in concrete terms.
- Identification of the contextual factors that contribute to the behavior (including affective and cognitive factors).
- Formulation of the hypothesis regarding the general conditions under which a behavior usually occurs and probable consequences that serve to maintain it.

When writing the FBA, you may need to consider the various requirements for each stage in the plan.

Stage I—Identify and define the target behavior. These behaviors should be observable, descriptive, and defined in such a way that everyone is in agreement with what the behavior(s) actually means (operational definition). In order to collect this information, one can:

- Interview the student and determine her or his perception of the problem behavior.

- Interview the student's parents.

- Interview all the child's past and present teachers for their analysis and history concerning the targeted behavior(s).

- Use direct observation.

- Use behavioral checklists or rating scales and ask parents and teachers to fill them out.

- Speak with the principal or dean of students to determine if there is a history of this target behavior in the records.

Stage II—Gather broad information about the student's skills, abilities, interests, preferences, general health, and well-being. You can:

- Speak with the school nurse.

- Ask the parents for recent medical records.

- Have the child fill out an interest inventory checklist.

- Speak with the physical education teacher to determine physical strengths and weaknesses and any areas of exception.

- Ask the parents for a list of activities, clubs, organizations, lessons, etc., that the child may have been involved with over the years.

- Identify the student's strengths.

Stage III—The IEP Team gathers contextual information that pinpoints the circumstances/situations that are regularly associated with the occurrence of problem behavior and the function of the student's problem behavior. Six basic questions may be asked during this stage:

1. When is the student most likely to engage in the problem behavior?

2. What specific events or factors appear to be contributing to the student's problem behavior?

3. What function(s) does the problem behavior serve the student?

4. What might the student be communicating through the problem behavior?

5. When is the student most successful, and therefore less likely to engage in the problem behavior?

6. What other factors might be contributing to the student's problem behavior?

Stage IV—Define the function or reason why the behavior continues. This is usually the result of getting something, avoidance, or control.

4.70 continued

Stage V—Develop a hypothesis about the target behavior in which statements are formed that describes the relationship of the behavior to the event and circumstances. Further, in this stage, the person writing the FBA attempts to identify specific variables to be manipulated and observed.

Stage VI—Develop an intervention plan based on the results from Stage V. In this intervention plan, the teacher shaping his/her behavior and manipulating variables within the classroom and school teaches the student acceptable alternatives.

4.71 Role of the Eligibility Committee in the Functional Behavioral Assessment

IDEA requires that, in the case of a child whose behavior impedes the learning of the child or others, the district's Eligibility Committee (i.e., CST, IEP Team, etc., as appropriate) must consider strategies, including positive behavioral interventions and supports, to address that behavior. The results of a student's individual evaluation information, including the functional behavioral assessment, are reviewed at an eligibility meeting. IDEA requires that one of the members of the Eligibility Committee be an individual who can interpret the instructional implications of evaluation results. Therefore, for students with behaviors that impede learning, it is recommended that an individual knowledgeable about behavioral assessments and intervention planning participate in these meetings. This individual could be the school psychologist or the special or regular education teacher. In addition, the regular education teacher of the child, as a member of the Eligibility Committee, participates in the development of the IEP of the student, including the determination of appropriate positive behavioral interventions and strategies.

It may be the responsibility of the Eligibility Committee to ensure that functional behavioral assessments, where appropriate, are conducted and reviewed to:

  ▪ Identify supplementary aids and services, modifications, and/or related services appropriate to address the identified behaviors to promote a student's involvement and progress in the general curriculum.

  ▪ Determine a student's eligibility for special education services.

  ▪ Develop the IEP, which includes behavioral goals and objectives and positive behavioral supports and strategies.

4.72   Overview of Perception

The perceptual evaluation is theoretically based upon the concept of the learning process (Pierangelo & Giuliani, 2000). When we evaluate a child's perceptual abilities, we are looking to see if there is a deficit in some area of the learning process that may be slowing down the processing of information, thereby interfering in the child's ability to receive, organize, memorize, or express information. Severe deficits in the learning process can have adverse effects upon a child's ability to function in the classroom.

In order to understand how learning takes place, we must first understand the process by which information is received and the manner in which it is processed and expressed. In very simple terms, the learning process can be described in the following way:

Step 1—Input information.

Step 2—Organize information.

Step 3—Express information.

Information is received in some manner and is filtered through a series of internal psychological processes. As information progresses along this "assembly line," it is given meaning and organized in some fashion and then expressed through a variety of responses. In order to understand how learning takes place, we must first understand the specific parts that make up the learning process. There are six modalities or channels (avenues through which information is received):

1. *Auditory Modality*—The delivery of information through sound.

2. *Visual Modality*—The delivery of information through sight.

3. *Tactile Modality*—The delivery of information through touching.

4. *Kinesthetic Modality*—The delivery of information through movement.

5. *Gustatory Modality*—The delivery of information through taste.

6. *Olfactory Modality*—The delivery of information through smell.

Skills are usually taught using all six modalities in the primary grades—nursery school to grade 1. By grade 2, most teachers teach through approximately four of the modalities with a greater emphasis on visual and auditory input. By the upper elementary grades, this can shift to skill development through the use of only two modalities, visual and auditory. This generally remains the source of informational input in most classrooms until possibly college, where information in many cases is presented through only one modality, auditory (lectures). Children should be taught using multisensory approaches (the input of information through a variety of receptive mechanisms, e.g., seeing, hearing, touching, etc.) whenever possible as retention of information is enhanced by increased sensory input.

Information is delivered to the senses through one or several of the previously mentioned modalities. Once delivered, the information goes through a series of processes that attempt to give meaning to the material received. There are several subprocesses that comprise the learning process:

- *Reception*—The initial receiving of information.

- *Perception*—The initial organization of information.

- *Association or Organization*—Relating new information to other information and giving meaning to the information received.

- *Memory*—The storage or retrieval process that facilitates the associational process to give meaning to information or help in relating new concepts to other information that might have already been learned. This process involves short-term, long-term, and sequential memory.

- *Expression*—The output of information through vocal, motoric, or written responses.

4.73 Purpose of Perceptual Evaluations

The objectives of the perceptual evaluation are as follows:

- **It is important to help determine the child's stronger and weaker modality for learning.** Some children are visual learners, some are auditory, and some learn best through any form of input. However, if a child is a strong visual learner in a class where the teacher relies on auditory lectures, then it is possible that his/her ability to process information may be hampered. An evaluation may provide information, which is very useful when making practical recommendations to teachers about how to best present information to assist the child's ability to learn.

- **It is important to determine a child's stronger and weaker processing modes.** For instance, a child having problems in memory and expression will fall behind the rest of his or her class very quickly. The longer these processing difficulties continue, the greater the chance for secondary emotional problems to develop (emotional problems resulting from continued frustration with the ability to learn).

- **It is important to develop a learning profile.** This can help the classroom teacher understand the best way to present information to the child and therefore increase his/her chances of success.

- **It is important to help determine if the child's learning processing deficits are adaptive to a regular class.** Along with other information and test results, the child may require a more restrictive educational setting (an educational setting or situation best suited to the present needs of the student other than a full-time regular class placement, e.g., a resource room, self-contained class, special school, etc.).

4.74 Visual Perception Skills

The following are assessment area skills most often associated with visual perception:

- *Visual coordination*—The ability to follow and track objects with coordinated eye movements.

- *Visual discrimination*—The ability to differentiate visually the forms and symbols in one's environment.

- *Visual association*—The ability to organize and associate visually presented material in a meaningful way.

- *Visual long-term memory*—The ability to retain and recall general and specific short-term visual information.

- *Visual short-term memory*—The ability to retain and recall general and specific short-term visual information.

- *Visual sequential memory*—The ability to recall in correct sequence and detail prior visual information.

- *Visual vocal expression*—The ability to reproduce vocally prior visually presented material or experiences.

- *Visual motoric expression* (visual motor integration)—The ability to reproduce motorically prior visually presented material or experiences.

- *Visual figure-ground discrimination*—The ability to differentiate relevant stimuli (the figure) from irrelevant stimuli (the background).

- *Visual spatial relationships*—The ability to perceive the relative positions of objects in space.

- *Visual form perception* (visual constancy)—The ability to discern the size, shape, and positions of visual stimuli.

4.75 Diagnostic Symptoms for Visual-Motor Perceptual Disabilities

There are many symptoms that may indicate problems in a certain perceptual area. Some of these are observable; others are discovered through intakes and testing. What follows is a list of symptoms that may reflect perceptual disabilities in a variety of visual areas.

General Visual-Perceptual Problems

The student:

- Exhibits poor motor coordination.
- Is awkward motorically—frequent tripping, stumbling, bumps into things, has trouble skipping, jumping.
- Demonstrates restlessness, short attention span, perseveration.
- Exhibits poor handwriting, artwork, drawing.
- Exhibits reversals of b, d, p, q, u, n when writing beyond a chronological age of 7 or 8.
- Inverts numbers (17 for 71), reverses as well.
- Gives correct answers when teacher reads test, but can't put answers down on paper.
- Exhibits poor performance in group achievement tests.
- Appears brighter than test scores indicate.
- Exhibits poor perception of time and space.

Visual-Receptive Process Disability

The student:

- Does not enjoy books, pictures.
- Fails to understand what is read.
- Is unable to give a simple explanation of contents of a picture.
- Is unable to categorize pictures.

Visual-Association Disability

The student:

- Is unable to tell a story from pictures; can only label objects in the pictures.
- Is unable to understand what he or she reads.
- Fails to handle primary workbook tasks.
- Needs auditory cues and clues.

Manual-Expressive Disability

The student:

- Has poor handwriting and drawing.
- Communicates infrequently with gestures.
- Is poor at "acting out" ideas, feelings.
- Is clumsy, uncoordinated.
- Can't imitate other children in games.

Visual-Memory Disability

The student:

- Exhibits frequent misspellings, even after extensive practice.
- Misspells his own name frequently.
- Can't write alphabet, numbers, computation facts.
- Identifies words one day and fails to do so the next day.

4.76 Developmental Test of Visual-Motor Integration—Fourth Edition (VMI-4)

Author: Keith E. Beery

Publisher: PRO-ED, Inc.

Description of Test: This test is intended for use primarily with pre-kindergarten children and those enrolled in the early grades. The short form of the VMI-4 uses 18 items to assess visual-motor integration in children 3 to 8 years of age. The long form uses 27 items to assess functioning in examinees 3 to 18 years of age.

Administration Time: 10–15 minutes

Age/Grade Levels: Ages 3 to 18; Grades preschool to 12

Subtest Information: The 27 items that make up this test are weighted in terms of their developmental difficulty.

Strengths of the VMI-4

- The VMI can be used to provide assessors with information on how well students copy geometric shapes.
- The test provides a larger behavior sample than tests like the Bender Visual-Motor Gestalt Test and the Memory-for-Designs Test.
- The test has high reliability.
- The test is very easy to administer.
- The test is a good screening device.

Weaknesses of the VMI-4

- Objectivity on the part of the scorer can be somewhat problematic.
- The test should never be used alone to make any determinations about a child's potential.
- Due to the newness of the Fourth Edition test, further studies are necessary to assess its validity and reliability.

4.77   Test of Gross-Motor Development— Second Edition (TGMD-2)

Authors: Dale Ulrich

Publisher: PRO-ED, Inc.

Description of Test: The TGMD-2 assesses common motor skills. The primary uses of this test are:

- To identify children who are significantly behind their peers in gross motor skill development.
- To assist in the planning of an instructional program in gross motor skill development.
- To evaluate the gross motor program.

The test is a multiple-item, task-performance test consisting of two subtests. The examiner records observations in a student record book. The TGMD-2 allows examiners to administer one test in a relatively brief time and gather data for making important educational decisions.

Administration Time: 15 minutes

Age/Grade Levels: Ages 3 to 10

Subtest Information: The test is divided into two subtests:

- *Locomotion*—This subtest measures the run, gallop, hop, leap, horizontal jump, and slide skills that move a child's center of gravity from one point to another.
- *Object Control*—This subtest measures the ability to strike a stationary ball, stationary dribble, catch, kick, underhand roll, and overhand throw skills that include projecting and receiving objects.

Strength of the TGMD-2

- Given the newness of this revised edition of the TGMD, no strengths have been reported as of this printing.

Weakness of the TGMD-2

- Given the newness of this revised edition of the TGMD, no weaknesses have been reported as of this printing.

4.78   Bender Visual-Motor Gestalt Test (BVMGT)

Author: Lauretta Bender

Publisher: The American Orthopsychiatric Association, Inc.

Description of Test: The test consists of a set of nine stimulus cards, which the student is asked to reproduce on a blank piece of paper one figure at a time.

Administration Time: 10 minutes for an individual; 15–25 minutes for group administration

Age/Grade Levels: Ages 4 to 50

Subtest Information: There are no subtests.

Strengths of the BVMGT

- The test is quick to administer.
- The test is easy to administer.
- The test is one of the oldest (1938) and most popular tests used to assess visual-motor abilities.
- The test provides developmental data on a child's perceptual maturity.
- Group administration is a time saver.
- The test is effective as a screening instrument when combined with other tests.

Weaknesses of the BVMGT

- The norms provided cannot be used to gauge the performance of individuals because of the extremely small sample size, ambiguity of the samples, and overall lack of information about the nature of the groups.
- The test scoring systems still require some subjectivity.
- Projective interpretations of the test results are questionable because of the absence of objective scoring criteria.
- There are serious concerns about the test's reliability and validity.

4.79   Developmental Test of Visual Perception—2 (DTVP-2)

Authors: Donald Hammill, N. Pearson, and J. Voress

Publisher: PRO-ED, Inc.

Description of Test: The test is designed to measure specific visual perceptual abilities and to screen for visual perceptual difficulties at early ages. The DTVP-2 is a revision of the Developmental Test of Visual Perception (Frostig et al., 1964, 1966). The DTVP-2 is a comprehensive diagnostic instrument for assessing the visual-processing skills of children from ages 4 to 10.

Administration Time: Varies based on individual ability levels

Age/Grade Levels: Ages 4 to 10

Subtest Information: The tasks are arranged in increasing order of difficulty in eight areas:

- *Eye Motor Coordination*—This task requires the child to draw lines between increasingly narrow boundaries. These may include straight, curved, or angled lines.
- *Figure Ground*—This task requires the child to distinguish and then outline embedded figures between intersecting shapes.
- *Form Constancy*—This task requires the child to discriminate common geometric shapes presented in different shapes, sizes, positions, and textures from other, similar shapes.
- *Position in Space*—This test requires the child to distinguish between figures in an identical position and those in a reversed rotated position.
- *Spatial Relations*—This task requires the child to copy simple forms and patterns by joining dots.
- *Copying*—The child is asked to copy increasingly complex figures from model drawings.
- *Visual Closure*—The child is required to view a geometric figure and then select the matching figure from a series of figures that all have missing parts.
- *Visual-Motor Speed*—On this test, the child is required to draw special marks in selected geometric designs on a page filled with various designs.

Strengths of the DTVP-2

- The norms are adequate.
- Reliability appears to be strong.
- This test is useful as a screening instrument for evaluating individual subjects or groups of children.
- The manual is well written and easy to understand.

Weakness of the DTVP-2

- More research is necessary on the test to be comfortable with its use.

4.80 Motor-Free Visual Perceptual Test— Revised (MVPT-R)

Authors: Ronald Colarusso and Donald D. Hammill

Publisher: Academic Therapy Publications

Description of Test: The test consists of a test-item book with design plates, a manual, and a scoring protocol. The child is required to point to the correct answer among four alternatives for 40 items arranged into five subtests.

Administration Time: 10–15 minutes

Age/Grade Levels: Ages 4.0 to 11.11

Subtest Information: The test is arranged into five tasks used to assess visual perception:

- *Spatial Relationships*—The student must select the drawing in which the stimulus figure is reproduced. The choices may be smaller, bigger, darker, or turned to the side.
- *Visual Discrimination*—The student must select the drawing that is different from the other three.
- *Figure Ground*—The student must select the correct response by locating the drawing in which the stimulus figure is embedded.
- *Visual Closure*—The student must select the drawing that, if completed, would be identical to the stimulus drawing.
- *Visual Memory*—After viewing a picture for five seconds, having it removed, and being shown samples from which to choose, the student must select the response similar to the stimulus.

Strengths of the MVPT-R

- The test is easy to administer.
- The test is not excessively time-consuming.
- The test is a useful diagnostic tool that helps to determine which area of visual perception may be a problem for a particular student.
- The test employs a useful method of reporting scores.
- The test's directions are clear and simple.

Weaknesses of the MVPT-R

- There is still some question surrounding the perceptual categories presented by the authors. They tend to be loosely defined and confusing.
- Due to the newness of the revision, further reliability and validity studies are necessary.

4.81   Overview of Auditory Perception

Auditory perception has long been a concern for special educators because of its relationship to speech and language development. The areas that compromise auditory perception are listed below:

- *Auditory discrimination*—The ability to differentiate auditorily the sounds in one's environment.

- *Auditory association*—The ability to organize and associate auditorily presented material in a meaningful way.

- *Auditory long-term memory*—The ability to retain and recall general and specific long-term auditory information.

- *Auditory short-term memory*—The ability to retain and recall general and specific short-term auditory information.

- *Auditory sequential memory*—The ability to recall in correct sequence and detail prior auditory information.

- *Auditory vocal expression*—The vocal ability to reproduce prior auditorily presented material or experiences.

- *Auditory motoric expression*—The motor ability to reproduce prior auditorily presented material or experiences.

4.82 Diagnostic Symptoms for Auditory Perceptual Disabilities

As previously indicated, a major objective of a perceptual evaluation is to identify those areas that may have a direct impact on a child's ability to adequately process information and that may possibly interfere in his/her academic achievement. What follows is a list of symptoms that may reflect perceptual disabilities in a variety of auditory areas.

General Auditory Perceptual Indicators

The student:

- Appears less intelligent than IQ tests indicate.
- Does many more things than one would expect: puts puzzles together, fixes broken objects, and so on.
- Appears to have a speech problem.
- May emphasize wrong syllables in words.
- May sequence sounds oddly.
- May use "small words" incorrectly.
- Appears not to listen or comprehend.
- Watches teacher's or adult's face intently, trying to grasp words.

Auditory Receptive Process Disability

The student:

- Fails to comprehend what he or she hears.
- Exhibits poor receptive vocabulary.
- Fails to identify sounds correctly.
- Fails to carry out directions.

Auditory Association Disability

The student:

- Does not enjoy being read to by someone else.
- Has difficulty comprehending questions.
- Raises hand to answer question but gives foolish response.
- Is slow to respond; takes a long time to answer.
- Has difficulty with abstract concepts presented auditorily.

Verbal Expressive Disability

The student:

- Mispronounces common words.
- Uses incorrect word endings and plurals.
- Omits correct verbal endings.
- Makes grammatical or syntactical errors.
- Has difficulty blending sounds.

Auditory Memory Disability

The student:

- Does not know address or phone number.
- Fails to remember instructions.
- Has difficulty memorizing nursery rhymes or poems.
- Has difficulty reciting the alphabet.

4.83   Goldman-Fristoe-Woodcock Test of Auditory Discrimination

Authors: Ronald Goldman, Macalyne Fristoe, and Richard W. Woodcock

Publisher: American Guidance Service

Description of Test: This is a two-part test in which the examiner presents a test plate containing four drawings. The test-taker responds to a stimulus word (presented via audio cassette to ensure standardized presentation) by pointing to one of the drawings on the plate.

Administration Time: 20–30 minutes

Age/Grade Levels: Ages 4 to 70

Subtest Information: The test has three parts:

   * *Training Procedure*—During this time, the examinee is familiarized with the pictures and the names that are used on the two subtests.

   * *Quiet Subtest*—In this subtest, the examinee is presented with individual words in the absence of any noise. This subtest provides a measure of auditory discrimination under ideal conditions.

   * *Noise Subtest*—In this subtest, the examinee is presented with individual words in the presence of distracting background noise on the tape. This subtest provides a measure of auditory discrimination under conditions similar to those encountered in everyday life.

Strengths of the Goldman-Fristoe-Woodcock

   * More reliability and validity data are given for this test than for most other discrimination tests.

   * The test is applicable to a wide age range.

   * The test is easy to administer.

   * The test manual provides clear instruction.

Weaknesses of the Goldman-Fristoe-Woodcock

   * For some students, the pace of the auditory presentation may be too rapid.

   * The test lacks adequate validity and reliability.

4.84 Tests of Auditory Perceptual Skills— Revised (TAPS-R)

Author: Morrison F. Gardner

Publisher: Psychological and Educational Publications

Description of Test: This is a multiple-item response test consisting of six subtests.

Administration Time: Approximately 5–10 minutes

Age/Grade Levels: Ages 4 to 13

Subtest Information: The test is divided into six subtests:

- *Auditory Number Memory, Digits Forward*—This subtest measures a student's rote memory of nonsensical auditory matter.

- *Auditory Number Memory, Digits Reversed*—This subtest requires the child's ability to hear the sounds of digits forward and to repeat them in reverse.

- *Auditory Sentence Memory*—This subtest measures a child's ability to remember for immediate recall not only rote auditory matter but also auditory matter in sequence, thus measuring two processes.

- *Auditory Word Memory*—This subtest measures a child's ability to understand and interpret what he or she perceives by ear.

- *Auditory Word Discrimination*—This subtest measures a child's ability to discriminate paired one- and two-syllable words with phonemically similar consonants, cognates, or vowel differences.

- *Auditory Processing* (Thinking and Reasoning)—This subtest measures a student's ability to use common sense and ingenuity in solving common thought problems.

Strengths of the TAPS-R

- This test is useful in the diagnosing of students who have auditory difficulties.
- The test is useful in diagnosing language problems that could be the basis for learning problems.

Weakness of the TAPS-R

- Given the newness of the test, more research is necessary to assess its validity and reliability.

4.85 Wepman Test of Auditory Discrimination— Second Edition (ADT-2)

Authors: Joseph M. Wepman and William M. Reynolds

Publisher: Western Psychological Services

Description of Test: The mode of presentation is the same for all editions of the test. The test consists of 40 word pairs of similar sounding words or contrasts of similar words. The child has to say if the word pairs read aloud are the same or different.

Administration Time: 10 minutes

Age/Grade Levels: Ages 4 to 8

Subtest Information: There are no subtests on this instrument.

Strengths of the ADT-2

- The test has a simple administration procedure.
- The test is useful for preschool and kindergarten screening.
- The test-retest reliability is high.
- The test is easy to score and interpret.

Weaknesses of the ADT-2

- Children with attentional problems may have difficulty attending to task.
- Very young children may not understand the concept of same or different.
- There are concerns about the sample used for the norm standardization.
- Not enough research has been presented to feel confident of the test's validity.

In addition to the assessment measures already discussed under visual and auditory perception, there are many comprehensive measures of perceptual ability. These tests are sometimes referred to as multiprocess tests (tests that contain a variety of subtests used to measure many perceptual areas). Following is a review of some available comprehensive perceptual tests.

4.86   Detroit Tests of Learning Aptitudes— Fourth Edition (DTLA-4)

Author: Donald D. Hammill

Publisher: PRO-ED, Inc.

Description of Test: The DTLA-4 is a multiple-item oral-response paper–pencil battery of 11 subtests. The test provides the examiner with a profile of the student's perceptual abilities and deficiencies.

Administration Time: 50–120 minutes

Age/Grade Levels: Ages 6.0 to 17.11

Subtest Information: The latest edition of this test contains 11 subtests that are grouped into three domains. Within each domain are two sub-areas called composites. Listed below are the subtests included in each domain:

Linguistic Domain

1. *Verbal Composite*—This composite tests the student's knowledge of words and their use. The subtests making up this composite are:

   Basic Information   Picture Fragments

   Reversed Letters   Sentence Imitation

   Story Construction   Word Opposites

   Word Sequences

2. *Nonverbal Composite*—This composite does not involve reading, writing, or speech. The subtests making up this composite are:

   Design Reproduction   Story Sequences

   Design Sequences   Symbolic Relations

4.86 continued

Attentional Domain

1. *Attention-Enhanced Composite*—This composite emphasizes concentration, attending, and short-term memory. The tests that make up this composite are:

Design Reproduction	Sentence Imitation
Design Sequences	Story Sequences
Reversed Letters	Word Sequences

2. *Attention-Reduced Composite*—This composite emphasizes long-term memory. The subtests that make up this composite are listed below:

Basic Information	Symbolic Relations
Picture Fragments	Word Opposites
Story Construction	

Motoric Domain

1. *Motor-Enhanced Composite*—This is emphasizes complex manual dexterity. The subtests that make up this composite are:

Design Reproduction	Reversed Letters
Design Sequences	Story Sequences

2. *Motor-Reduced Composite*—This subtest requires very little motor involvement. The subtests that make up this composite are:

Basic Information	Story Construction
Picture Fragments	Story Sequences
Sentence Imitation	Word Opposites
Word Sequences	

Strengths of the DTLA-4

- The test offers the examiner some worthwhile scales for examining various abilities in learning disabled or neurologically impaired subjects.
- The test provides some potentially valuable information about diverse abilities.
- Internal-consistency reliability is good.
- The manual is clear and easy to read.

Weaknesses of the DTLA-4

- The test should not be regarded as a substitute for some of the better-developed measures of intelligence.
- The demographics of the normative sample are not satisfactorily presented and the published qualifications for examiners are difficult to interpret.

4.87 Slingerland Screening Tests for Identifying Children with Specific Language Disability

Author: Beth H. Slingerland

Publisher: Educators Publishing Service, Inc.

Description of Test: This is not a test of language but rather a test of various auditory, visual, and motor skills related to specific academic areas. It is a multiple-item verbally presented paper-and-pencil examination containing eight subtests.

Administration Time: 60–80 minutes for Forms A, B, and C; 110–130 minutes for Form D

Age/Grade Levels: Grades 1 to 6

Subtest Information: Each subtest focuses on curriculum-related skills. They are as follows:

- *Far Point Copying*—This subtest requires the student to copy a printed paragraph from far points to probe visual perception and graphomotor responses. The subtest assesses visual-motor skills related to handwriting.

- *Near Point Copying*—This subtest requires the student to copy a printed paragraph from near points in order to probe visual perception and graphomotor responses. The subtest assesses visual-motor skills related to handwriting.

- *Visual Perception Memory*—This subtest requires the student to recall and match printed words, letters, and numbers presented in brief exposure with a delay before responding. This subtest assesses visual memory skills related to reading and spelling.

- *Visual Discrimination*—This subtest requires the student's immediate matching of printed words and eliminates the memory component of Visual Perception Memory. The subtest assesses basic visual discrimination without memory or written response.

- *Visual Kinesthetic Memory*—This subtest requires the student's delayed copying of words, phrases, letters, designs, and number groups presented with brief exposure. The subtest assesses the combination of visual memory and written response that is necessary for written spelling.

- *Auditory Kinesthetic Memory*—This subtest requires the student to write groups of letters, numbers, and words to dictation after a brief delay with distraction. This subtest combines auditory perception and memory with written response.

- *Initial and Final Sounds*—This subtest requires the student to write the initial phoneme and later to write the final phoneme of groups of spoken words. This subtest assesses auditory discrimination and sequencing related to basic phonics with a written response.

4.87 continued

■ *Auditory / Visual Integration*—This subtest requires the student's delayed matching of spoken words, letters, or number groups. This subtest assesses visual discrimination related to word recognition.

There are four different forms of this test (Forms A, B, C, and D). Some of the forms contain subtests other than those already mentioned:

■ *Following Directions*—This subtest requires the student to give a written response from a series of directions given by the examiner. This subtest assesses auditory memory and attention with a written response.

■ *Echolalia*—This subtest requires the student to listen to a word or phrase given by the examiner and to repeat it four or five times. This is an individual auditory test. This subtest assesses auditory kinesthetic confusion related to pronunciation.

■ *Word Finding*—This subtest requires the student to fill in a missing word from a sentence read by the examiner. This is an individual auditory test; it assesses comprehension and the ability to produce a specific word on demand.

■ *Story Telling*—This subtest requires the student to retell a story previously read by the examiner. This is an individual auditory test; it assesses auditory memory and verbal expression of content material.

Strengths of the Slingerland

■ This is very useful for those who need a test to screen for academic problems.

■ The test uses skills related to classroom tasks.

■ This is one of the few group tests designed for disability screening for treatment purposes.

■ This test has the power to predict reading problems.

Weaknesses of the Slingerland

■ There is a lack of information concerning the test's reliability and validity.

■ The author states that standardized national norms would destroy the usefulness of the tests. As a result, it is a diagnostic test with subjective scoring criteria.

■ Because of its lack of normative data, this test may be a problem for more inexperienced evaluators because of the general scoring rules and the generalization of the results to classroom recommendations.

4.88 Assessment and Evaluation Process for Early Intervention

This process normally consists of five stages. These are:

1. *Casefinding / Child Find*—To alert parents, professionals, and the general public to children who may have special needs and to illicit their help in recruiting candidates for screening.

2. *Screening*—To identify children who are not within normal ranges of development and need further evaluation and who may be candidates for early intervention programs.

3. *Assessment for Diagnosis and Determination of Eligibility*—To conduct an in-depth evaluation to verify if a problem exists; to determine the nature and severity of the problem and prescribe the treatment or type of intervention services needed.

4. *Program Planning*—Refers to those procedures used by the assessment team to develop the Individualized Family Service Plan (IFSP, List 4.89) and to revise those plans as necessary. The outcome of assessment for program planning is the identification of special services needed by the child and the family, the service delivery format that will be used (including location of services), and the delineation of intervention objectives as specified in the IFSP.

5. *Program Evaluation*—To evaluate the quality of the overall intervention program and to document its impact upon the children or parents it serves. Information collected on an ongoing basis allows the team to determine to what extent progress is being made toward goals and objectives and, as a result, to identify changes that should be made in intervention strategies or objectives. When such data are collected across all of the children in a given program, it may be possible to measure overall program impact.

According to Hanson and Lynch (1995, p. 179), the following questions can be used to review and evaluate procedures used to assess young children and identify family concerns, priorities, and resources:

- Are diagnostic or eligibility assessment procedures clearly identified?

- Are child assessment and family procedures linked to programming?

- Are the staff members who are conducting the child assessments trained in measurement, the particular strategies being used, and assessment of young children and infants?

- Are the assessment instruments being used valid and reliable?

- Is the assessment being conducted by an interdisciplinary team that includes the parents or primary caregivers as equal partners?

- Is adequate time allocated for the team to jointly plan assessments with the family?

- Are assessments conducted in a setting that is familiar to the child, with the parents or primary caregivers present and assisting?

4.88 continued

■ Are assessment data collected in a variety of ways (observation, interview, etc.)?

■ Are assessments of the child's strengths and needs and the family's concerns, priorities, and resources culturally and linguistically appropriate?

■ Is there a standard procedure for writing reports and sharing the findings with all team members, including the parents?

■ Are written and verbal reports free of judgment, stereotyping, and negative labeling?

■ Is ample time allocated for discussing and sharing findings and making programming decisions?

■ Is follow-up done soon after placement to determine the appropriateness of the program, the child's performance, and the family and staff's satisfaction with the program?

■ Is the identification of family concerns, priorities, and resources nonintrusive, nonjudgmental, and conducted with sensitivity?

■ Does the information collected about the family's concerns, priorities, and resources assist in finding resources or developing programs?

4.89   Individualized Family Service Plan (IFSP)

After a child has been evaluated, it is mandated under P.L. 99-457 that an Individualized Family Service Plan (IFSP) be written. This plan sets forth critical information pertaining to both the child and the family's services. IFSP stands for:

- *Individualized*—The plan will be specially designed for the child and the family.

- *Family*—The plan will focus on the family and the outcomes they hope for the child and the family through early intervention.

- *Service*—The plan will include all the details about the services provided for both the child and the family.

- *Plan*—The plan is a written blueprint for services.

The IFSP is based on the premise that a child's home environment strongly influences that child's overall experiences and successes; therefore, it includes goals and objectives for the family as a unit, as well as goals and objectives for the individual child (Bigge & Stump, 1999, p. 15).

Under the IDEA Amendments of 1997, Section 636(d), the components of an IFSP must include the following:

1. A statement of the infant's or toddler's present levels of physical development, cognitive development, communication development, social or emotional development, and adaptive development, based on objective criteria.

2. A statement of the family's resources, priorities, and concerns relating to enhancing the development of the family's infant or toddler with a disability.

3. A statement of the major outcomes expected to be achieved for the infant or toddler and the family, and the criteria, procedures, and timelines used to determine the degree to which progress toward achieving the outcomes is being made and whether modifications or revisions of the outcomes or services are necessary.

4. A statement of specific early intervention services necessary to meet the unique needs of the infant or toddler and the family, including the frequency, intensity, and method of delivering services.

5. A statement of the natural environments in which early intervention services shall appropriately be provided, including a justification of the extent, if any, to which the services will not be provided in the natural environment.

6. The projected dates for initiation of services and the anticipated duration of the services.

7. The identification of the service coordinator from the profession most immediately relevant to the infant's or toddler's family's needs (or who is otherwise qualified to carry out all applicable responsibilities under this part) who will be responsible for the implementation of the plan and coordination with other agencies and persons.

8. The steps to be taken to support the transition of the toddler with a disability to preschool or other appropriate services.

4.89 continued

The IFSP must be reviewed at six-month intervals or more frequently as needed. Every 12 months, the child must be reevaluated. After assessment is completed, a program must be established for each child.

Under Part C of IDEA, the following services can be given to infants and toddlers in the IFSP:

- Family training, counseling, and home visits
- Special instruction
- Speech and language instruction
- Occupational and physical therapy
- Psychological testing and counseling
- Service coordination
- Medical services necessary for diagnostic and evaluation purposes
- Social work services
- Assistive technology
- Early identification, screening, and assessment services
- Health services, when necessary
- Transportation and related costs as necessary

Only qualified professionals—individuals who are licensed, certified, or registered in their discipline and approved by their state—can deliver early intervention services. All early intervention services can be given using any of the following service models (NYS Department of Health, 2000):

1. *Home- and community-based visits*—In this model, services are given to a child and/or parent or other family member or caregiver at home or in the community.

2. *Facility or center-based visits*—In this model, services are given to a child and/or parent or other family member or caregiver where the service provider works (such as an office, hospital, clinic, etc.).

3. *Parent–child groups*—In this model, parents and children get services together in a group led by a service provider. A parent–child group can happen anywhere in the community.

4. *Family support groups*—In this model, parents, grandparents, or other relatives of the child get together in a group led by a service provider for help and support and to share concerns and information.

5. *Group development intervention*—In this model, children receive services in a group setting led by a service provider or providers without parents or caregivers. A group means two or more children who are eligible for early intervention services. The group can include children without disabilities and can happen anywhere in the community.

4.90 Working with the Family in Early Childhood Assessment

Listed below are some practical suggestions for special educators when conducting parent interviews in early intervention (cited in Hanson and Lynch's *Survival Guide for Interviewers*, 1995, p. 161):

1. Write down the address, directions, and a phone number where you can reach or leave a message for the family that you are interviewing. It's easy to get lost when you are busy or nervous.

2. There are different cultural rules related to being in someone's house. Do not be surprised if the father or elder does all of the talking in some situations or if a male interventionist cannot visit the home unless the husband is present.

3. If you are conducting the interview through an interpreter, allow time to discuss the interview questions with the interpreter first. Give the family and interpreter time to get acquainted and comfortable with one another, and be sure that you address your questions and comments to the family, *not* to the interpreter.

4. Dress professionally yet in keeping with the norms of the family and community.

5. If you are taking toys or materials to the home, take something that can remain (picture books, crayons, animal crackers, etc.), remembering that there may be several brothers and sisters who will be very interested in what you are doing and what you have brought.

6. Don't be afraid to admit if you are nervous. Parents always recognize bluffing.

7. It is not okay to tell your own stories or say you know just how they feel, but it is okay to laugh and cry with someone who is sharing joy or pain.

8. Do not feel that you have to answer all of the family's concerns or questions. For some, you may be able to find answers; for others, you may be able to help them find answers; and for still others there never will be an answer.

9. If you do not feel safe in a neighborhood, take someone with you for the interview or arrange to conduct it outside the home.

10. Remember the Golden Rule as you embark on any interview: Interview others as you would like to be interviewed.

Parents often share feelings about experiences that they have had with professionals. The following comments are excerpted from "Notes to the Experts from the Parent of a Handicapped Child" (Alexander, 1987):

- The most important suggestion I can offer you is to put yourself in my place.

- See my child in more than one dimension. Remember that my child is a person whom I love.

- Judge my child in terms of his or her own progress.

4.90 continued

- ▧ Value my comments about my child. In general, the parent is the real expert. Listen to me. Give me time to speak.

- ▧ Create an environment where I feel comfortable enough to speak.

- ▧ Speak plainly.

- ▧ Consider my child as part of a family.

- ▧ Distinguish between fact and opinion.

- ▧ Steer me toward solutions and resources. Do not just give me a diagnosis and send me on my way.

- ▧ Tell me about other families in similar situations.

- ▧ Provide me with some ray of hope.

4.91 Bayley Scales of Infant Development—Second Edition (BSID-II)

Author: Nancy Bayley

Publisher: The Psychological Corporation

Description of Test: This individually administered test has three subscales: the Mental Scale, the Motor Scale, and the Behavior Rating Scale. The items on the Mental and Motor scales are mixed together; thus, examiners are required to identify which items go on each scale and tally them separately. The Behavior Rating Scale is completed after the Mental and Motor scales have been administered. This second edition has more than 100 new items created to apply to the expanded age range. The test includes the examiner's manual, stimulus booklet, Mental Scale record forms, Motor Scale record forms (with tracing design sheet), Behavior Rating Scale record forms, visual stimulus cards, map, and all necessary manipulatives.

Administration Time: Under 15 months of age, 25–30 minutes; over 15 months of age, up to 60 minutes

Age/Grade Levels: Ages 1–42 months

Subtest Information: The test comprises three subtests:

- The Mental Developmental Index (MDI) assesses a variety of abilities including:

    Sensory/perceptual acuity, discriminations, and responses

    Acquisition of object constancy

    Memory, learning, and problem solving

    Vocalization, beginning of verbal communication

    Basis of abstract thinking

    Habituation

    Mental mapping

    Mathematical concept formation

- The Psychomotor Developmental Index (PDI) assesses a variety of abilities including:

    Degree of body control

    Large muscle coordination

    Finer manipulatory skills of the hands and fingers

    Dynamic movement

    Postural imitation

    Stereognosis

4.91 continued

- The Behavior Developmental Index (BDI) is a separate scale made up of its own items. It assesses qualitative aspects of the child's test-taking behavior and allows an examiner to rate:

  Arousal

  Attention

  Orientation

  Engagement

  Emotional regulation

  Motor quality

Strengths of the BSID-II

- The scales' norms are representative in terms of race, ethnicity, geographic region, parental education, and sex.

- The BSID-II is a well-standardized and very comprehensive test of infant development.

- The BSID-II is a very popular test used by early intervention clinicians.

- Data are provided in the manual for the following groups: children who were born prematurely, have the HIV antibody, were prenatally drug exposed, were asphyxiated at birth, are developmentally delayed or have frequent otitis media, are autistic, or have Down syndrome.

- There is evidence of strong construct validity.

- It is a good screening instrument for children with disabilities.

Weakness of the BSID-II

- The test demands a great deal on the part of the examiner with respect to administration and interpretation.

4.92   Preschool Language Scale—3 (PLS-3)

Authors: Irla Lee Zimmerman, Violette G. Steiner, and Roberta L. Evatt

Publisher: The Psychological Corporation

Description of Test: This test is divided into three sections: Auditory Comprehension, Verbal Ability, and Articulation. The test consists of pictures and items that each child must point to or explain. Ranking depends upon the child's developmental level at the time of testing. This test may be used as a criterion-referenced test for older children functioning within the range of behaviors assessed by PLS-3 and, with suggested modifications, for children with physical or hearing impairments. The test includes an examiner's manual, picture book, and record forms.

Administration Time: 30 minutes

Age/Grade Levels: Ages birth to 6.11

Subtest Information: The test includes two separate scales:

- *Auditory Comprehension Scale*—The scale requires nonverbal responses such as pointing to a picture that the examiner has named.

- *Expressive Communication Scale*—In this section, items are presented that require the child to name or explain the items. The difficulty varies depending on the child's developmental level during the time of testing.

The items on the test assess the following areas in both the receptive and expressive modes:

> Vocabulary
>
> Concepts of quality
>
> Concepts of quantity
>
> Space and time
>
> Morphology
>
> Syntax
>
> Integrative thinking skills

Strengths of the PLS-3

- This test may be useful to a preschool teacher who wishes to identify a pattern of strengths and weaknesses in a child's conceptual and auditory abilities.

- The test offers a comprehensive assessment of receptive and expressive language in young children.

4.92 continued

- The test meets general federal and state guidelines—including IDEA legislation—for evaluating preschoolers for special services.

- The test is a good screening measure for qualification in early intervention programs like Head Start, Even Start, or Title I programs.

Weaknesses of the PLS-3

- The areas assessed in some subtests are headed with ambiguous terms such as "differentiation of self," "temporal ordering," and many others, which are not operationally defined.

- The PLS-3 Total Test Score is simply an average of both scales. This presents a problem if there is wide variability between the scales.

4.93   Metropolitan Readiness Tests— Fifth Edition (MRT-5)

Authors: Joanne R. Nurss and Mary E. McGauvran (1986)

Publisher: The Psychological Corporation

Description of Test: The MRT-5 is the primary assessment tool of the Metropolitan Readiness Assessment Program (MRAP). The MRAP is intended for use in evaluating the general development and prereading skill of students at the prekindergarten, kindergarten, and grade 1 levels of schooling.

Administration Time: Approximately 90 minutes per actual test level and 5 minutes for practice booklet for each level

Age/Grade Levels: Prekindergarten through Grade 1

> *Level 1*—intended for administration at the beginning and middle of kindergarten.
>
> *Level 2*—intended for administration at the middle and end of kindergarten and beginning of grade 1.

Subtest Information: The test is offered at two levels. Each level is made up of several subtests:

- Level 1 consists of six subtests:

  Auditory Memory

  Beginning Consonants

  Letter Recognition

  Visual Matching

  School Language and Listening

  Quantitative Language

- Level 2 consists of eight subtests:

  Beginning Consonants

  Sound-Letter Correspondence

  Visual Matching

  Finding Patterns

  School Language

  Listening

  Quantitative Concepts

  Quantitative Operations

4.93 continued

Strengths of the MRT-5

- The directions are clear and well written.
- The directions and forms for scoring, summarizing, and interpreting completed tests are well written, clear, and user-friendly.
- There is strong evidence of the test's reliability.
- The test provides evidence of the internal consistency of the subtests.
- The test's norms are representative of the United States' population.
- The test is one of the most popularly used tests for assessing infant development.
- Having both norm-referenced and criterion-referenced scoring options makes the test a valuable assessment instrument.

Weakness of the MRT-5

- Due to the newness of the Fifth Edition, no weaknesses have yet to be reported in *Buros Mental Measurement Yearbook* as of this printing.

4.94   Boehm Test of Basic Concepts— Revised (BTBC-R)

Author: Ann F. Boehm

Publisher: The Psychological Corporation

Description of Test: The test consists of 50 concept items, placed in two test booklets to facilitate administration in two sessions to children in grades K, 1, 2, and 3. The test has two alternate forms, C and D. The examiner reads the test questions, and the students are required to mark the correct response directly in the individual test booklet. The test materials include individual student test booklets and the examiner's manual.

Administration Time: Up to 40 minutes for Form C or D; 15–20 minutes for the Applications form

Age/Grade Levels: Grades K to 3

Subtest Information: The test has no subtests.

Strengths of the BTBC-R

- A section in the manual devoted to score interpretation and to the use of the results instruction is very practical.

- Most young children find this test interesting.

- The test has two equivalent forms that allow for the determination of progress with pre- and post-testing.

Weaknesses of the BTBC-R

- The norms of the test are based on a national school population, but only 15 states are reported, which might have implications for generalizability.

- Although this is a good screening test for language development, better tests are available if the examiner is interested in cognitive development.

4.95 Bracken Basic Concept Scale (BBCS)

Author: Bruce A. Bracken

Publisher: The Psychological Corporation

Description of Test: This test measures 10 diagnostic subtest areas. Items are multiple-choice. The child is shown four monochrome pictures and asked to identify the picture that depicts a particular concept. The test includes an examiner's manual, diagnostic stimulus manual, diagnostic record forms, one Screening Test Form A, and one Screening Test Form B.

Administration Time: 20–40 minutes

Age/Grade Levels: Ages 2.6 to 7.11

Subtest Information: The following lists the subtests and corresponding concepts:

- *Color/Letter Identification*—Children are tested on their knowledge of colors and letters.

- *Numbers/Counting*—Children are required to tell how many items and recognize numbers.

- *Comparisons*—Children are required to compare things.

- *Shapes*—Children are tested regarding their ability to recognize different shapes.

- *Direction/Position*—Children are tested on their ability to distinguish between different directions and positions.

- *Social/Emotional*—Children are tested to determine their social and emotional development.

- *Size*—Children are tested on their ability to differentiate between sizes.

- *Texture/Material*—Children are given objects of different textures and must identify the objects.

- *Quantity*—Children are tested on their ability to distinguish amounts.

- *Time/Sequence*—Children are given numbers and asked to tell the missing number or the number that comes next.

Strengths of the BBCS

- One of the major strengths of the BBCS is the detailed and well-organized Examiner's Manual.

- The test administration procedures for the BBCS are fairly well planned and coordinated.

- The test is a very comprehensive test of basic concept identification for young children.

- The test can be used for norm-referenced, criterion-referenced, or curriculum-based purposes.
- A criterion-referenced record form is available in Spanish.

Weaknesses of the BBCS

- The explanation of the standardization sample does not fully elaborate on the minority sample.
- Color-blind children will not perform as well on the color subtests as other children.

4.96   Preschool Evaluation Scales (PES)

Author: Stephen B. McCarney

Publisher: Hawthorne Educational Services

Description of Test: This test is designed as a rating scale completed by the child's parents or childcare provider. It consists of a technical manual, rating forms, and a computerized scoring system.

Administration Time: 20–25 minutes

Age/Grade Levels: Ages birth to 72 months

Subtest Information: The subscale areas assessed by this instrument are:

- Large muscle skill
- Small muscle skill
- Cognitive thinking
- Expressive language
- Social/emotional behavior
- Self-help skills

Strengths of the PES

- This test is a good screening device for developmental delays for preschool-aged children.
- The test has strong validity.

Weaknesses of the PES

- As is true of all rating-type scales, the test is subject to interpretation of the individual completing the scale.
- There are concerns about the test's reliability.

4.97 Kindergarten Readiness Test (KRT)

Authors: Sue L. Larson and Gary Vitali

Publisher: Slosson Educational Publications

Description of Test: The test assesses five general areas of readiness: awareness of one's environment, reasoning, numerical awareness, fine-motor coordination, and auditory attention span.

Administration Time: 15–20 minutes

Age/Grade Level: Ages 4 to 6

Subtest Information: The test has no subtests.

Strengths of the KRT

- Specialists, teachers, or paraprofessionals can readily administer the test.
- The test assesses various key areas shown to be critical for school readiness and consolidates information on one form.
- The test is easy to administer.
- The test is appropriate for school, preschool, and clinical settings.

Weakness of the KRT

- At the time of printing, no review regarding weaknesses of the KRT was done in *Buros Mental Measurement Yearbook.*

4.98 Battelle Developmental Inventory (BDI)

Author: J. Newborg, J. R. Stock, and J. Wnek

Publisher: The Riverside Publishing Company

Description of Test: The BDI is a multiple-item test assessing key developmental skills. Information is obtained through structured interactions with the child in a controlled setting, observation of the child, and interviews with the child's parents, teachers, and caregivers. The test consists of five test-item books, an examiner's manual, scoring booklets, and VHS overview videotape.

Administration Time: 10 minutes to 2 hours depending on the age and cognitive ability of the child

Age/Grade Levels: Ages birth to 8

Subtest Information: The test consists of five subtests:

- *Personal-Social Domain*—This subtest measures coping skills, self-concept, expressions of feelings, and adult interaction.
- *Adaptive Domain*—This subtest measures attention, eating skills, dressing skills, personal responsibility, and toileting.
- *Motor Domain*—This subtest measures muscle control, body coordination, locomotion, fine muscle skills, and perceptual-motor skills.
- *Communication Domain*—This subtest measures receptive and expressive communication.
- *Cognitive Domain*—This subtest measures memory, reasoning skills, perceptual discrimination, academic skills, and conceptual development.

Strengths of the BDI

- The BDI is a multifactor assessment measure.
- The BDI can be administered in the home setting, which may be important when dealing with very young children.
- The test is very comprehensive.
- Standardization procedures appear to be adequate.

Weaknesses of the BDI

- The scoring procedure may be time consuming.
- Learning how to administer this test may require more time due to the five test-item books, screening test, and examiner's manual.
- Many of the answers to test items for very young children are obtained through parent interviews, which may be problematic with respect to objectivity.
- Children with severe disabilities may not be able to handle the inventory.

4.99 Assessment Measures Used in the Identification of a Hearing Loss

When symptoms are observed, the first step is usually a referral to an audiologist for a screening. There are several assessment measures that are utilized in the possible identification of a hearing loss.

Audiometric Evaluation Measures

Qualified audiologists who measure the level of hearing loss through the use of several techniques use these assessment measures. These may include:

- *Pure Tone Audiometric Screening*—Pure tone screening is often referred to as sweep testing, and is usually the child's first encounter with hearing testing. This type of testing, which is common in schools, presents pure tones over a variety of frequency ranges. The child is then asked to respond, usually by some gesture, if he or she hears a tone. A child who is unable to hear sounds at two or more frequencies is usually referred for further evaluation.

- *Speech Audiometry*—This type of evaluation is used to determine a child's present ability to hear and understand speech through the presentation of words in a variety of loudness levels.

- *Pure Tone Threshold Audiometry*—In this procedure, the child is asked to make a gesture or push a button each time he or she hears a tone. The child is presented with a variety of frequencies through earphones. This type of ear conduction test reveals the presence of hearing loss.

Special Audiometric Tests

- *Sound Field Audiometry*—This measure is used with very young children who cannot respond to manual responses or are unable or unwilling to wear headphones. The child is evaluated by observing the intensity levels at which he or she responds to different levels of sounds broadcast through speakers.

- *Evoked Response Audiometry*—This test uses an electroencephalograph and a computer to measure changes in brain-wave activity at a variety of sound levels. This measure can be used with infants who are suspected of being deaf.

- *Impedance Audiometry*—There are two major impedance audiometry tests. The first, tympanometry, measures the functioning level of the eardrum. The second, stapedial reflex testing, measures the reflex response of the stapedial muscle to pure tone signals. As these tests do not require a response on the part of the child, they can be used with very young children.

- *Behavioral Play Audiometry*—This technique involves placing the child in a series of activities that reward him or her for responding appropriately to tone or speech.

4.100 Auditory Perception Test for the Hearing Impaired (APT/HI)

Authors: Susan G. Allen and Thomas S. Serwatka

Publisher: Slosson Educational Publications

Description of Test: The test is designed to assess the building-block processes used to decode speech. It allows for specific analysis of the individual's ability to decode phonemes in isolation and in the context of words and sentences. The test allows for specific analysis of the student's ability to decode phonemes in isolation and in the context of words and sentences. It consists of a manual, plates, and record forms.

Type of Test: Criterion-referenced

Administration Time: 30 minutes

Type of Administration: Individual

Who Administers This Test: Special education teacher, psychologist, speech/language therapist

Age/Grade Levels: Ages 5 and up

Subtest Information: The test has no subtests.

Scoring Information: The test results are given in a performance profile that enables comparison of an individual's pre- and post-treatment performance to determine the efficacy of treatment and the need for further therapy.

Strengths of the APT/HI

- Although designed specifically for the hearing impaired, the test can also be used with children who have other auditory processing deficits.
- The test analyzes auditory decoding skills at the most basic level.

Weakness of the APT/HI

- To date, no review regarding weaknesses of this test was done in *Buros Mental Measurement Yearbook*.

4.101 Carolina Picture Vocabulary Test for Deaf and Hearing Impaired (CPVT)

Authors: Thomas L. Layton and David W. Holmes

Publisher: PRO-ED, Inc.

Description of Test: The test is designed to measure the receptive sign vocabulary in individuals for whom manual signing is the primary mode of communication. The CPVT consists of a manual, record forms, and a picture book.

Type of Test: Norm-referenced

Administration Time: 10–30 minutes

Type of Administration: Individual

Who Administers This Test: Special education teacher, psychologist, speech/language therapist

Age/Grade Levels: Ages 4 to 11.5

Subtest Information: The test contains no subtests.

Scoring Information: The test provides the following:

Scaled scores

Percentile ranks

Age equivalents

Strengths and Weaknesses of the CPVT

- At the time of printing, no review of this test's strengths or weaknesses had been done in *Buros Mental Measurement Yearbook*.

4.102   Hiskey-Nebraska Test of Learning Aptitude

Author: Marshall S. Hiskey

Publisher: Marshall S. Hiskey

Description of Test: The test is designed as a nonverbal measure of mental ability that has been found helpful in the intellectual assessment of a variety of language handicapped children and youth. The test is a performance scale that can be administered entirely via pantomimed instructions and requires no verbal response from the subject. The scale consists of a series of performance tasks that are organized in ascending order of difficulty within subscales.

Type of Test: Norm-referenced

Administration Time: Approximately 60 minutes

Type of Administration: Individual

Who Administers This Test: Special education teacher, psychologist, speech/language therapist

Age/Grade Levels: Ages 2 to 18

Subtest Information: The test comprises the following subtests:

- *Memory Colored Objects*—The child is required to perform memory tasks using colored objects.
- *Bead Stringing*—The child is required to put beads on a string.
- *Pictorial Associations*—The child has to decide what various pictures look like.
- *Block Building*—The child is required to build things with blocks.
- *Memory for Digits*—The child is given groups of numbers and asked to repeat them.
- *Completion of Drawings*—The child is required to finish a picture that is not completed.
- *Pictorial Identification*—The child has to say what the picture is that is being shown.
- *Visual Attention Span*—The child must focus on an object for a set period of time.
- *Puzzle Blocks*—The child is required to arrange the blocks into a picture that is shown.
- *Pictorial Analogies*—The child is required to compare two pictures and pick a picture that goes with the third picture.

Strengths of the Hiskey-Nebraska

- The test is easy to administer.
- The test results are reported as a learning quotient rather than pure IQ; that may be easier for parents to understand.

Weaknesses of the Hiskey-Nebraska

- The test is a poor tool for children aged 7 and up.
- It is too time consuming, and children often show very little interest.

4.103   Leiter-R International Performance Scale

Authors: Russel Graydon Leiter and Grace Arthur

Publisher: C. H. Stoelting Co.

Description of Test: The test is designed as a totally nonverbal intelligence and cognitive abilities test. The Leiter-R does not require the child to read or write any materials. The test does not require a spoken word from the examiner or the child. It is presented in a game-like administration. The test is administered by having the child match the full-color response cards with corresponding illustrations on the easel display.

Type of Test: Standardized

Administration Time: 30–60 minutes

Type of Administration: Individual

Who Administers This Test: Special education teacher, psychologist, speech/language therapist

Age/Grade Levels: Ages 2 to 17

Subtest Information: The Leiter-R includes 20 subtests, listed below, that are combined to create numerous composites that measure both general intelligence and discrete ability areas. The test consists of two batteries measuring a variety of skills.

1. Visualization and Reasoning Battery

Visualization skills measured in this battery include:

- Matching
- Form Completion
- Paper Folding
- Figure Ground
- Picture Context
- Figure Rotation

Reasoning skills measured in this battery include:

- Classification
- Sequential Order
- Repeated Patterns
- Design Analogies

2. Attention and Memory Battery

Attention skills measured in this battery include:

- Attention Sustained
- Attention Divided

Memory skills measured in this battery include:

- Memory Span (Forward)
- Spatial Memory
- Associative Memory
- Immediate Recognition

- Memory Span (Reversed)
- Visual Coding
- Associative Delayed Memory
- Delayed Recognition

Scoring Information: The test provides the following:

IQ scores

Percentiles

Grade equivalents

Age equivalents

Strengths of the Leiter-R

- The scale is a useful instrument. Because of its nonverbal approach, it has made possible the testing of many children who could not be properly evaluated by the Stanford-Binet or WISC.
- The test has a high correlation (.84) with the WISC-III Full-Scale IQ.
- The extensive age range measured by the test allows for the use of one test throughout a child's school career that enhances comparisons of performance over time.
- Because the test is nonverbal, there is no dominant language bias as found on other IQ tests.

Weaknesses of the Leiter-R

- Work needs to be done to establish more comprehensive norms.
- A better scoring system may need to be investigated.

4.104   Rhode Island Test of Language Structure (RITLS)

Authors: Elizabeth Engen and Trygg Engen

Publisher: Slosson Educational Publications

Description of Test: This test is designed to provide a measure of English language development and a profile of the child's understanding of language structure. It is primarily designed for use with hearing-impaired children. The test measures syntax-response errors for 20 sentence types, both simple and complex.

Type of Test: Criterion-referenced and norm-referenced

Administration Time: 25–35 minutes

Type of Administration: Individual

Who Administers This Test: Special education teacher, psychologist, speech/language therapist

Age/Grade Levels: Hearing-impaired children ages 3 to 20; hearing children ages 3 to 6

Subtest Information: This test measures syntax response errors for 20 sentence types, both simple and complex. The sentence elements are:

- Relative and Adverbial Clauses
- Subject and other Complements
- Reversible and Nonreversible Passives
- Datives
- Deletions
- Negations
- Conjunctivas
- Embedded Imperatives

Scoring Information: The test provides the following:

Percentiles

Age equivalents

Strengths of the RITLS

- The test includes hearing-impaired individuals as part of the standardized group, which adds to the effectiveness of generalizability.
- The test is useful in areas where level of language development is of concern, e.g., mental retardation, learning disability, and bilingual programs.
- The RITLS is easy to administer, score, and interpret.
- A variety of syntactic structures are included in the test.

Weaknesses of the RITLS

- There is an absence of reliability and validity information.
- There is an overreliance on syntax without consideration of the pragmatic aspects of comprehension.
- Omission of morphemes may fail to pick up mildly hearing-impaired children.
- It lacks a complete test-subject description.
- There is a limited number of minority individuals in the sample.
- The absence of a method of error analysis misses valuable data interpretation.

357

4.105   Test of Early Reading Ability—2: Deaf or Hard of Hearing (TERA-2, D/HH)

Authors: D. Kim Reid, Wayne P. Jiresko, Donald D. Hammill, and Susan Wiltshire

Publisher: PRO-ED, Inc.

Description of Test: The test is designed to measure the ability of children with moderate to profound hearing loss to attribute meaning to printed symbols, their knowledge of the alphabet and its functions, and their knowledge of the conventions of print. It isolates key components of early print experiences and assesses children's relative competence in deriving meaning from these print symbols. The test includes a sheet that allows the examiner to picture the student's "Instructional Target Zone." By examining the student's item performance in the three components of early reading, the examiner can identify the types of concepts that might be profitably taught.

Type of Test: Norm-referenced

Administration Time: 15–30 minutes

Type of Administration: Individual

Who Administers This Test: Special education teacher, psychologist, speech/language therapist

Age/Grade Levels: Ages 3 to 10

Subtest Information: Three aspects of early reading behavior are specifically addressed:

- *Constructing meaning from print*—The construction of meaning encompasses a child's ability to read frequently encountered signs, logos, and words; relate words to one another; and understand the contextual nature of written discourse.

- *Knowledge of the alphabet*—This aspect is defined as letter and word decoding (either orally or through sign).

- *Understanding print conventions*—This aspect evaluates the child's awareness of text orientation and organization (e.g., book handling, the spatial orientation of print on a page, and ability to uncover textual or print errors).

Scoring Information: The test provides the following:

Standard scores

Percentiles

Normal curve equivalents

Strengths of the TERA-2, D/HH

- The authors provide a comprehensive and informative manual.
- The student record form is complete and easy to follow.

Weaknesses of the TERA-2, D/HH

- Some of the test materials may be dull and uninteresting for younger children.
- There is little reliability information on preschool-aged groups. Standard deviations were not offered in the manual on the standardization sample's mean raw score performance on the test. This is most damaging to its use as a measure of early reading skill because of its effect on generalizability.
- The lack of reliability and validity information raises serious questions regarding the measure's capacity to provide more than a gross and limited overview of deaf and hard-of-hearing children's recognition of print.

4.106 Overview of Occupational Therapy

Physical and occupational therapies are important components of the special education process. Many school districts now have occupational and physical therapists as part of their staff. These therapists may help students individually, in small groups, or as consultants. These two services are related therapies but specific in their function. Occupational therapy focuses mainly on fine motor/upper body functions, whereas physical therapy concentrates on lower body/gross motor difficulties. The services are provided for students with disabilities who exhibit a range of difficulties, such as learning disabilities (e.g., fine and gross motor problems or perceptual problems), developmental delays (e.g., mental retardation, vision or hearing impairment), respiratory problems (e.g., cystic fibrous or asthma), neuromuscular problems (e.g., muscular dystrophy, cerebral palsy), muscle skeletal problems (e.g., arthritis, orthopedic problems, postural deviations), or traumatic accidents (e.g., amputations, brain injuries, burns). In addition to providing therapy for such students, physical and occupational therapists provide many other services including evaluations, screenings, consultations, education, and training.

4.107   The Role of the Occupational Therapist

Therapists should meet with all of the professionals involved with a particular child as well as the child's parents to fully explain the nature of the disability, to train them to work with the child in the areas of dysfunction, and to provide assistive devices or environmental aids that will help the child function in the least restrictive environment. The therapists should also model remedial techniques that can be duplicated by the parents and by other teaching professionals. Parents should be reminded that many of the school activities suggested by occupational and physical therapists can be duplicated in the home. Many of the exercises are really activities for daily living, such as hopping, jumping, buttoning, etc.

Occupational and physical therapists serve important roles as consultants. Some examples of their services follow:

- Refer families to appropriate sources for assistance.
- Help families order adaptive or prosthetic equipment.
- Coordinate with physical education programs.
- Instruct families regarding methods used in physical therapy.
- Formulate long-range developmental plans for children's education.
- Train school professionals with special equipment.
- Help families and children learn how to deal with architectural barriers.

Occupational and physical therapists should act as liaisons between the Eligibility Committee, the teaching staff, medical professionals, outside agencies, and parents. Many pupils in need of physical and occupational therapy have severe medical conditions, which often require supervision by a family doctor. The therapist should help with the coordination between the school physician and the family doctor. The therapists play an important role in severe cases.

The following is a list of problems requiring occupational therapy:

- Perceptual problems (eye–hand coordination).
- Sensory problems (sensitive to sound, sensitive to visual changes, sensitive to odors, overly sensitive to touch).
- Gross motor difficulties (trouble with balance, coordination, moving).
- Fine motor problems (difficulty with coordination, handwriting, using scissors).
- Hardship with daily living activities (cannot dress, feed, or care for self).
- Organizational problems (difficulties with memory, time, spatial concepts).
- Attention span difficulties (difficulties focusing on task, short attention span).
- Interpersonal problems (difficulty with environmental and school-related social situations).

4.108   Milani-Comparetti Motor Development Test

Authors: Wayne Stuberg, Pam Dehne, Jim Miedaner, and Penni White

Publisher: Meyer Rehabilitation Institute

Description of Test: The test consists of 27 motor behaviors that are evaluated in two categories: evoked responses and spontaneous behaviors. The test is designed to provide the clinician with a synopsis of the child's motor development by systematically examining the integration of primitive reflexes and the emergence of volitional movement against gravity.

Administration Time: 10–15 minutes

Type of Administration: Individual

Who Administers This Test: Special education teacher, psychologist, occupational therapist

Age/Grade Levels: 1 to 16 months

Subtest Information: There are a total of 27 motor behaviors involved with two subtests.

■ *Evoked Responses*—These include equilibrium reactions (tilting), protective extension reaction (parachute), righting reaction, and primitive reflexes.

■ *Spontaneous Behaviors*—These include postural control and active movements such as sitting, crawling, and walking. The scores here involve: Body Lying Supine, Hand Grasp, Foot Grasp, Supine Equilibrium, Body Pulled Up from Supine, Sitting Posture, Sitting Equilibrium, Sideways Parachute, Backward Parachute, Body Held Vertical, Head Righting, Downward Parachute, Standing, Standing Equilibrium, Locomotion, Landau Response, Forward Parachute, Body Lying Prone, Prone Equilibrium, All Fours, All Fours Equilibrium, Symmetric Tonic Neck Reflex, Body Denotative, Standing Up from Supine, Body Rotative, Asymmetrical Tonic Neck Reflex, Moro Reflex.

Strengths of the Milani-Comparetti

■ One of the major strengths of this instrument is that it incorporates both quantitative and qualitative judgments about motor performance.

■ The test manual provides good interrater and test reliability.

■ The test is quick to administer.

Weaknesses of the Milani-Comparetti

■ There are norming sample limitations in the population used for standardization.

■ There is a lack of validity data.

4.109 Miller Assessment for Preschoolers (MAP)

Author: Lucy Jane Miller

Publisher: The Psychological Corporation

Description of Test: This test is designed to identify children who exhibit moderate pre-academic problems. The MAP is a short but comprehensive preschool assessment instrument that evaluates children for mild to moderate developmental delays. The test includes an examiner's manual, item score sheets, and all materials needed for administration.

Type of Test: Standardized and norm-referenced

Administration Time: 20–30 minutes

Type of Administration: Individual

Who Administers This Test: Special education teacher, psychologist, occupational therapist

Age/Grade Levels: Ages 2.9 to 5.8

Subtest Information: The test consists of five performance areas:

- *Foundations Index*—Assesses abilities involving basic motor tasks and the awareness of sensations, both of which are fundamental for the development of complex skills.
- *Coordination Index*—Assesses complex gross, fine, and oral motor abilities.
- *Verbal Index*—Assesses memory, sequencing, comprehension, association, and expression in a verbal context.
- *Nonverbal Index*—Assesses memory, sequencing, visualization, and the performance of mental manipulations not requiring spoken language.
- *Complex Tasks Index*—Measures sensorimotor abilities in conjunction with cognitive abilities.

Scoring Information: The test provides:

Percentile ranks
Standard scores

4.109 continued

Strengths of the MAP

- A strong feature of the MAP is the detailed information presented in the manual for the administration of each of the five indexes.
- It is a short, carefully developed, and well-standardized test.
- The test is quick to score.

Weaknesses of the MAP

- The cost of the MAP is moderately high.
- It is unable to do predictive validity studies because children in the standardization sample have not reached school age.

4.110 Quick Neurological Screening Test (QNST)

Authors: Margaret Motti, Harold M. Steling, Norma V. Spalding, and C. Slade Crawfold

Publisher: Academic Therapy Publications

Description of Test: The test is designed to assess neurological integration as it relates to learning. It is used for the early screening of learning disabilities. The QNST is a screening test that assesses 15 areas of neurological integration. It requires the examinee to perform a series of motor tasks adapted from neurological pediatric examinations and from neuropsychological and developmental scales. Each of the 15 areas tested involves a motor task similar to those observed in neurological pediatric examinations. The test includes recording forms, examiner's manual, reproduction sheets, remedial guidelines, and an administration and scoring flip card.

Type of Test: Criterion-referenced

Administration Time: Untimed

Type of Administration: Individual

Who Administers This Test: Special education teacher, psychologist, occupational therapist

Age/Grade Levels: Ages 5–18

Subtest Information: The areas of neurological integration measured by the QNST include:

- Motor development
- Fine/gross motor control
- Motor planning and sequencing and rhythm
- Visual/spatial perception
- Spatial organization
- Balance/vestibular function
- Attentional disorders

Scoring Information: Because this test is subjectively scored, scoring patterns are used to suggest possible avenues of further diagnostic assessment.

4.110 continued

Strengths of the QNST

- The test is useful as a supplement for the pediatric neurological examination.
- The test is exceptionally good in identifying children with abnormal neurological patterns.

Weaknesses of the QNST

- The authors never define the term "learning disabilities" even though they propose the test as an LD screener.
- The test is scored subjectively.
- No direct measure of scorer reliability exists for the test.

4.111   Sensory Integration and Praxis Test (SIPT)

Author: Jean Ayres

Publisher: Western Psychological Services

Description of Test: The test is designed to measure the sensory integration processes that underlie learning and behavior. By showing how children organize and respond to sensory input, the SIPT helps pinpoint specific organic problems associated with learning disabilities, emotional disorders, and minimal brain dysfunction. The test measures visual, tactile, and kinesthetic perception as well as motor performance.

Type of Test: Norm-referenced

Administration Time: The entire battery can be administered in two hours.

Type of Administration: Individual

Who Administers This Test: Special education teacher, psychologist, occupational therapist

Age/Grade Levels: Ages 4 to 9

Subtest Information: The SIPT measures visual, tactile, and kinesthetic perception as well as motor performance. It is composed of 17 brief tests:

- Space Visualization
- Figure-Ground Perception
- Standing and Walking Balance
- Design Copying
- Postural Praxis
- Bilateral Motor Coordination
- Praxis on Verbal Command
- Constructional Praxis
- Postrotary Nystagmus
- Motor Accuracy
- Sequencing Praxis
- Oral Praxis
- Manual-Form Perception
- Kinesthesia
- Finger Identification
- Graphesthesia
- Localization of Tactile Stimuli

4.111 continued

Scoring Information: All SIPT tests are computer scored, using WPS Test Report. Any combination of the 17 tests can be scored; the entire battery need not be administered.

Strengths of the SIPT

- This test is a helpful clinical tool.
- Any of the individual tests can be administered separately. Therefore, one does not need to administer the entire battery.
- The computerized scoring provides a detailed report explaining the SIPT results.

Weaknesses of the SIPT

- SIPT administration and interpretation requires professional training.
- A training program may be necessary to administer and score the test and interpret the results.

4.112 Purdue Perceptual Motor Survey (PPM)

Authors: Eugene G. Roach and Newell C. Kephart

Publisher: The Psychological Corporation

Description of Test: The test is designed to identify those children lacking perceptual motor abilities necessary for acquiring academic success. This is not a test but a series of tasks designed to provide the examiner with a structure for observing a student's motor skills. In order for the examiner to ensure the child's optimum performance levels, each subtest allows the examiner four possible levels of administration: unstructured instruction (general verbal directions), verbal directions (more explicit verbal directions), demonstration (task demonstrated by evaluator), or guided movements (child is physically guided through task).

Type of Test: Criterion-referenced

Administration Time: 30–40 minutes

Type of Administration: Individual

Who Administers This Test: Special education teacher, psychologist, occupational therapist

Age/Grade Levels: Preschool to Grade 8

Subtest Information: There are five skill areas measured, composing a total of 11 subtests:

- Balance and Posture—This skill area includes:

    Walking Board—This subtest measures the child's ability to walk and balance him- or herself on a narrow walking board, forward, backward, and sideways.

    Jumping—This subtest measures the child's ability to jump and hop on each foot and both feet.

- Body Image and Differentiation—This skill area includes:

    Identification of Body Parts—This subtest measures the child's ability to recognize and point to different body parts.

    Imitation of Movement—This subtest measures the child's ability to transfer visually presented information by the examiner into motor acts.

    Obstacle Course—This subtest measures the child's spatial orientation through a series of obstacle course maneuvers, e.g., duck under a broom handle.

    Kraus-Weber Test of Physical Fitness—This subtest is a measure of the child's physical strength and muscular fitness.

4.112 continued

Angels in the Snow—This subtest measures the child's ability to perform a series of tasks involving specific limbs individually and in pairs.

■ Perceptual Motor Match—This skill area includes:

Chalkboard—This subtest measures the child's ability with visual-motor coordination tasks and directionality.

Rhythmic Writing—This subtest measures the child's ability to reproduce a series of continuous writing themes on a chalkboard.

■ Ocular Control—This skill area includes:

Ocular Pursuits—This subtest measures a child's visual tracking skills.

■ Form Perception—This skill area includes:

Developmental Drawings—This subtest measures a child's ability to copy geometric forms to assess his or her visual-motor coordination.

Scoring Information: No objective scores are obtained but a profile is determined. The examiner notes the level of structure that the child requires for each task and other observations on the record form. Each task item is then rated on a four-point scale following the guidelines in the examiner's manual.

Strengths of the PPM

■ The PPM is explicitly based on a well-developed, if unique, perceptual-motor theory described by Kephart (1960) in his book *The Slow Learner in the Classroom*.

■ The test provides a good basis for assessing gross and fine motor tasks.

■ The manual is clearly written.

■ The test is easy to score.

Weaknesses of the PPM

■ On several subtests, the equipment must be gathered from around the school, e.g., walking board, small pillow. That may hinder the administration of certain subtests.

■ The abilities tested sometimes overlap, resulting in redundancy.

■ The test requires a skilled examiner.

■ Many abilities tested are unrelated to academic success and are not well assessed by the survey.

4.113 Overview of Bilingual Assessment

It is a well-known fact that the demographics of American schools are changing. Many students come from ethnic, racial, or linguistic backgrounds that are different from the dominant culture, and this number is steadily increasing (National Center for Education Statistics, 1992). Much concern has been expressed in recent years about the overrepresentation of minority students in special education programs, particularly in programs for students with mild disabilities, and a great deal of research has been conducted to identify the reasons why. Many factors appear to contribute, including considerable bias against children from different cultural and linguistic backgrounds, particularly those who are poor (Harry, 1992). The style and emphasis of the school may also be very different from those found in the cultures of students who are racially or linguistically diverse. Because culture and language affect learning and behavior (Franklin, 1992), the school system may misinterpret what students know, how they behave, or how they learn. Students may appear less competent than they are, leading educators to mistakenly refer them for assessment. Once referred, inappropriate methods may then be used to assess the students, leading to false conclusions and placement into special education.

4.114 Referral of Culturally and Linguistically Diverse Students

The materials and procedures required for a referral of culturally and linguistically diverse children to the Committee on Special Education might involve more than the normal packet of materials. The evaluation team needs to:

- Identify the reason for the referral and include any test results in both languages as appropriate.

- Include any records or reports upon which the referral is based.

- Attach a home language survey indicating the home language(s).

- Specify the level of language proficiency.

- Describe the extent to which the LEP (Limited English Proficiency) student has received native language instruction and/or ESL (English as a Second Language) services prior to the referral.

- Describe experiential and/or enrichment services for students from diverse cultural and experiential backgrounds.

- Describe the school's efforts to involve parents prior to referral.

- Describe the amount of time and extent of services in an academic program for students who have had little or no formal schooling.

- Identify length of residency of the referred student in the United States and prior school experience in the native country and in an English-language school system.

- Describe all attempts to remediate the pupil's performance prior to referral, including any supplemental aids or support services provided for this purpose.

In conclusion, it is necessary for those entering into or currently involved in the field of special education to be aware of the growing number of students designated as limited English proficient. Federal law mandates that minority students have rights for protection when being assessed. Consequently, knowledge of various tests, their limitations, and controversies surrounding the biases of bilingual assessment is imperative.

4.115   ESL Literacy Scale (ELS)

Author: Michael Roddy

Publisher: Academic Therapy Publications

Description of Test: The test is designed to identify the appropriate starting level for ESL (English as a Second Language) and literacy instruction with adult learners.

Type of Test: Informal assessment

Administration Time: 15–20 minutes

Type of Administration: Individual or group

Age/Grade Levels: Ages 16–Adult

Subtest Information: Subtests include:

- Listening Comprehension
- Grammar
- Life Skills
- Reading Comprehension
- Composition

Scoring Information: The test results are charted on a profile showing which level of ESL class (Beginning, Intermediate, or Advanced) will best suit each student.

Strengths of the ELS

- It is easy to administer.
- It is easy to score.
- It is normed on many different ethnic backgrounds including Hispanic, Asian, Middle Eastern, and European.

Weaknesses of the ELS

- The ELS should only be used as a screening device.
- Group administration may limit direct student observation of behaviors that may affect results.

4.116   Language Proficiency Test (LPT)

Authors: Joan Gerard and Gloria Weinstock

Publisher: Academic Therapy Publications

Description of Test: The test is designed to assess oral/aural, reading, and writing skills. The LPT is designed to be used with students whose English speaking, reading, or writing skills are preventing them from succeeding in the academic or vocational environment.

Type of Test: Criterion-referenced

Administration Time: 90 minutes

Type of Administration: Individual or group

Age/Grade Levels: Grades 9 and up

Subtest Information: Subtests include:

- *Aural/Oral Commands Test*—Consists of commands, short answers, and comprehension questions.
- *Reading Test*—Consists of vocabulary and comprehension.
- *Writing Test*—Consists of grammar, sentence response, paragraph response, and translation.

Scoring Information: The test provides:

Percentile ranks

Levels of English competency

Strengths of the LPT

- It is very appropriate for the identification of competency levels of ESL students.
- It is very appropriate for the detection of specific language deficiencies of ESL students.
- The LPT assesses a wide range of English language abilities.
- The test uses materials that are not insulting to older students.

Weaknesses of the LPT

- It should only be used as a screening device.
- Group administration may limit direct student observation of behaviors that may affect results.

4.117   Matrix Analogies Test (MAT)

Author: Jack A. Naglieri

Publisher: The Psychological Corporation

Description of Test: The test is designed to measure nonverbal reasoning ability. The items present a visual stimulus with a missing element or sequence. The student selects the option best completing the stimulus. Variables include size, shape, color, and direction.

Type of Test: Norm-referenced

Administration Time: Short Form 25–30 minutes; Expanded Form 48 minutes

Type of Administration: Individual

Age/Grade Levels: Ages 5.0 to 17.11

Subtest Information: Subtests include:
- *Group 1: Pattern Completion*—Student accurately completes the pattern shown.
- *Group 2: Reasoning by Analogy*—Student determines how changes in two or more variables converge to result in a new figure.
- *Group 3: Serial Reasoning*—Student discovers the order in which items appear throughout a matrix.
- *Group 4: Spatial Visualization*—Student imagines how a figure would look when two or more components are combined.

Scoring Information: The test provides:

Standard scores

Percentile ranks

Age equivalents

Strengths of the MAT

- The MAT offers national norms.
- There are nonexistent or minimal signs of bias for women and blacks.
- There are reduced color-blindness effects.
- It has high internal consistency reliability.

Weaknesses of the MAT

- The test does not distinguish well in the upper age ranges among students of superior ability or in the lower age ranges among students of low average ability.
- No information is given concerning distracter development.

4.118   Screening Test of Spanish Grammar

Author: Allen S. Toronto

Publisher: Northwestern University Press

Description of Test: The test is broken into two parts, receptive and expressive. In the expressive section, an examiner utters two sentences, each of which relates to one of the pictures on a page, pointing first to one, and then to the other. The subject then has to repeat the sentence that better corresponds to the picture indicated. In the receptive section, the subject has to point to one of the four pictures that best corresponds to the sentence uttered by the examiner. There are two test sentences for each page of four pictures.

Administration Time: 15–25 minutes

Type of Administration: Individual

Age/Grade Levels: Spanish-speaking children, ages 3–6

Subtest Information: This test has no subtests.

Strengths of the Test

- This test helps to meet the needs of an educational community lacking in faculty and material resources in the Spanish language.
- It helps to point out children with comprehension and identification problems.

Weaknesses of the Test

- There is too much reliance on an English model.
- Some visual stimuli are ambiguous or misleading.
- Reliability and validity have not yet been adequately established.

4.119   Nonstandardized Forms of Assessment

Ecological assessment basically involves directly observing and assessing the child in the many environments in which he or she routinely operates. The purpose of conducting such an assessment is to probe how the different environments influence the student and his or her school performance. Where does the student manifest difficulties? Are there places where he or she appears to function appropriately? What is expected of the student academically and behaviorally in each type of environment? What differences exist in the environments where the student manifests the greatest and the least difficulty? What implications do these differences have for instructional planning?

Direct assessment of academic skills is one alternative that has recently gained in popularity. Although there are a number of direct assessment models that exist (Shapiro, 1989), they are similar in that they all suggest that assessment needs to be directly tied to instructional curriculum.

Curriculum-based assessment (CBA) is one type of direct evaluation. "Tests" of performance in this case come directly from the curriculum. For example, a child may be asked to read from his or her reading book for one minute. Information about the accuracy and the speed of reading can then be obtained and compared with other students in the class, building, or district. CBA is quick and offers specific information about how a student may differ from peers.

Because the assessment is tied to curriculum content, it allows the teacher to match instruction to a student's current abilities and pinpoints areas where curriculum adaptations or modifications are needed. Unlike many other types of educational assessment, such as intelligence tests, CBA provides information that is immediately relevant to instructional programming (Berdine & Meyer, 1987, p. 33). CBA also offers information about the accuracy and efficiency (speed) of performance. The latter is often overlooked when assessing a child's performance but is an important piece of information when designing intervention strategies. CBA is also useful in evaluating short-term academic progress.

Dynamic assessment refers to several different, but similar approaches to evaluating student learning. The goal of this type of assessment "is to explore the nature of learning, with the objective of collecting information to bring about cognitive change and to enhance instruction" (Sewell, 1987, p. 436).

One of the chief characteristics of dynamic assessment is that it includes a dialogue or interaction between the examiner and the student. Depending on the specific dynamic assessment approach used, this interaction may include modeling the task for the student, giving the student prompts or cues as he or she tries to solve a given problem, asking what the student is thinking while working on the problem, sharing on the part of the examiner to establish the task's relevance to experience and concepts beyond the test situation, and giving praise or encouragement (Hoy & Gregg, 1994). The interaction allows the examiner to draw conclusions about the student's thinking processes (i.e., why he or she answers a question in a particular way) and his or her response to a learning

4.119 continued

situation (i.e., whether, with prompting, feedback, or modeling, the student can produce a correct response, and what specific means of instruction produce and maintain positive change in the student's cognitive functioning).

Typically, dynamic assessment involves a test-train-retest approach. The examiner begins by testing the student's ability to perform a task or solve a problem without help. Then, a similar task or problem is given the student, and the examiner models how the task or problem is solved or gives the student cues to assist his or her performance. In Feuerstein's (1979) model of dynamic assessment, the examiner is encouraged to interact constantly with the student, an interaction that is called *mediation*, which is felt to maximize the probability that the student will solve the problem. Other approaches to dynamic assessment use what is called *graduated prompting* (Campione & Brown, 1987) where "a series of behavioral hints are used to teach the rules needed for task completion" (Hoy & Gregg, 1994, p. 151). These hints do not evolve from the student's responses, as in Feuerstein's model, but rather are scripted and preset, a standardization that allows comparison across students. The prompts are given only if the student needs help in order to solve the problem. In both these approaches, the "teaching" phase is followed by a retesting of the student with a similar task but with no assistance from the examiner. The results indicate the student's "gains" or responsiveness to instruction—whether he or she learned and could apply the earlier instructions of the examiner and the prior experience of solving the problem.

An approach known as "testing the limits" incorporates the classic training and interactional components of dynamic assessment but can be used with many traditional tests, particularly tests of personality or cognitive ability (Carlson & Wiedl, 1978, 1979, as cited in Jitendra & Kameenui, 1993). Modifications are simply included in the testing situation. While taking a particular standardized test, for example, the student may be encouraged to verbalize before and after solving a problem. Feedback, either simple or elaborated, may be provided by the examiner as well.

Portfolio assessment is perhaps the most important type of assessment for the classroom teacher. According to Paulson, Paulson, & Meyer (1991, p. 60), a portfolio is "a purposeful collection of student works that exhibits the student's efforts, progress, and achievement in one or more areas. The collection must include student participation in selecting contents, the criteria for selection, the criteria for judging merit, and evidence of student self-reflection." A portfolio collection contains work samples, permanent products, and test results from a variety of instruments and measures. For example, a portfolio of reading might include a student's test scores on teacher-made tests, including curriculum-based assessments; work samples from daily work and homework assignments; error analyses on work and test samples; and the results of an informal reading inventory with miscues noted and analyzed (Overton, 1996, p. 250).

Authentic assessment is a performance-based assessment technique that involves the application of knowledge to real-life activities, real-world settings, or a simulation of such a setting using real-life, real-world activities (Taylor, 1997). For example, when an individual is being assessed in the area of artistic ability, typically he or she presents art work and is evaluated according to various criteria, not simply by the person's knowledge of art, materials, artists, or history.

Outcome-based assessment has been developed, at least in part, to respond to concerns that education, to be meaningful, must be directly related to what educators and parents want the child to have gained in the end. Outcome-based assessment involves considering, teaching, and evaluating the skills that are important in real-life situations. Learning such skills will result in the student becoming an effective adult. Assessment, from this point of view, starts by identifying what outcomes are desired for the student (e.g., being able to use public transportation). In steps similar to what is used with task analysis, the team then determines what competencies are necessary for the outcomes to take place (i.e., the steps or subskills the student needs to have mastered in order to achieve the outcome desired) and identifies which subskills the student has mastered and which he or she still needs to learn. The instruction that is needed can then be pinpointed and undertaken.

Task analysis is very detailed; it involves breaking down a particular task into the basic sequential steps, component parts, or skills necessary to accomplish the task. The degree to which a task is broken down into steps depends upon the student in question. "It is only necessary to break the task down finely enough so that the student can succeed at each step" (Wallace, Larsen, & Elksnin, 1992, p. 14).

Taking this approach to assessment offers several advantages to the teacher. For one, the process identifies what is necessary for accomplishing a particular task. It also tells the teacher whether or not the student can do the task, which part or skill causes the student to falter, and the order in which skills must be taught to help the student learn to perform the task. According to Bigge (1990), task analysis is a process that can be used to guide the decisions made regarding:

- What to teach next.
- Where students encounter problems when they are attempting but are not able to complete a task.
- What steps are necessary to complete an entire task.
- What adaptations can be made to help the student accomplish a task.
- What are the options for those students for whom learning a task is not a possible goal.

Task analysis is an approach to assessment that goes far beyond the need to make an eligibility or program placement decision regarding a student. It can become an integral part of classroom planning and instructional decision-making.

Learning styles assessment suggests that students may learn and problem-solve in different ways and that some ways are more natural for them than others. When they are taught or asked to perform in ways that deviate from their natural style, they are thought to learn or perform less well. A learning style assessment, then, would attempt to determine those elements that impact on a child's learning and "ought to be an integral part of the individualized prescriptive process all special education teachers use for instructing pupils" (Berdine & Meyer, 1987, p. 27).

4.119 continued

Some of the common elements that may be included here would be the way in which material is typically presented (e.g., visually, auditorily, tactilely) in the classroom, the environmental conditions of the classroom (e.g., hot, cold, noisy, light, dark), the child's personality characteristics, the expectations for success that are held by the child and others, the response the child receives while engaging in the learning process (e.g., praise or criticism), and the type of thinking the child generally utilizes in solving problems (e.g., trial and error, analyzing). Identifying the factors that positively impact the child's learning may be very valuable in developing effective intervention strategies.

4.120   Overview of Report Writing

Writing a report is not a simple task. It takes knowledge and skill because it is being written for parents, teachers, and administrators. After reading the following lists, you should be able to understand why reports need to be written, general guidelines to follow when writing a report, and all sections needed in a comprehensive report. These sections include:

- Identifying Data
- Reason for Referral
- Background History
- Observations
- Tests Administered
- Test Results

- Test-by-Test Analysis
- Content Area-by-Content Area Analysis
- Conclusions
- Recommendations
- Summary Table

Many different professionals may provide input in the assessment of a child with a suspected disability. When this occurs, a comprehensive report based on the findings must be written. The purpose of this report is to communicate results in such a way that the reader will understand the rationale behind the recommendations and will be able to use the recommendations as practical guidelines for intervention. This report may be presented to the parent, sent to an outside doctor or agency, or presented to the Committee on Special Education. In any case, the report needs to be as professional, comprehensive, and practical as possible.

Writing a good report is a real skill. The fact is that all the wonderful data collection becomes useless if it cannot be interpreted and explained in a clear and concise manner. For example, being too general or explaining results poorly creates many problems and confusion for readers. Also, citing numerous general recommendations will not be practical for the school, teacher, or parents. Writing a report that contains loads of jargon that no one other than you understands is also useless. Completing an extremely lengthy report in an attempt to be too comprehensive will only result in losing your reader.

4.121   Practical Guidelines for Report Writing

When writing a report, the key is to be as comprehensive as possible while being clear and concise. To do this effectively, it is important to understand some very practical guidelines.

- **Write the report in the third person.** Use phrases such as:

    According to the examiner . . .

    It was felt that . . .

    There seems to be . . .

    It is the professional opinion of this evaluator that . . .

    Never write "I think . . ." or "If it were up to me. . . ." This is not a term paper; it is a legal document. As such, the professional approach is to remain in the third person.

- **Single space your report to condense the length.** A report of 3 to 5 pages is not overwhelming. Break up the report so that the format is very easy on the reader. (See the model report in List 4.123.)

- **In general, try to separate your recommendation section into three parts—one for the school, one for the teacher, and one for the parents.** This approach will make it easy to follow the recommendations and allow those interested parties to see their responsibilities.

- **Try to write the report in the past tense as often as possible.** Because the data was already collected and you have already done the assessment, the use of the past tense is most appropriate. For example:

    Billy scored in the 95th percentile on the Reading subtest.

    Sally exhibited shyness during testing.

    Throughout the interview, Tommy showed no signs of hyperactivity.

    Karen appeared to lack confidence when doing tasks that required hand-eye coordination.

- **Separate sections (e.g., Reason for Referral and Background History) by skipping two lines.** This is done simply for purposes of clarity.

- **Underline paragraph headings so that they stand out and are easy to locate.** Any time you create a new section in your report, underline it so that the reader knows that this starts a different area of the report.

- **Write reports using complete sentences.** A report should never read like a telegram. Be sure that all sentences make sense. Always check spelling and grammar to make sure there are no errors. Nothing looks more unprofessional than a report that is sloppy and contains mistakes.

4.122 Criteria for Writing a Comprehensive Report

Reports can be written in many ways. The format is decided by the personal choice of the examiner, the supervisor, or the district. However, it is important that certain information not be overlooked. What follows is one suggested outline that would meet all the criteria for a professional and comprehensive report.

IDENTIFYING DATA

The first section is called Identifying Data and contains all the necessary basic information about the child. This section is important to the reader, especially if further contact is required. It allows the reader to have all the basic information in one place. The parts of this section include those shown in this sample.

Name: _____	Parents' Names: _____
Address: _____	Teachers: _____
_____	_____
Phone: _____	Referred by: _____
Date of Birth: _____	Date/s of Testing: _____
Grade: _____	Date of Report: _____
School: _____	Examiner: _____
Chronological Age at time of testing (CA): _____	

Name: _Sally Jones_	Parents' Names: _Paul and Mary Jones_
Address: _123 ABC Street_	Teachers: _Mrs. Smith_
ABC City, New York 10007	
Phone: _(516) 555-5555_	Referred by: _Mother_
Date of Birth: _8-17-90_	Date/s of Testing: _9-17-99, 9-18-99_
Grade: _4_	Date of Report: _10-12-99_
School: _XYZ Elementary School_	Examiner: _Ms. Jane Doe, M.S._
Chronological Age at time of testing (CA): _9.1_	

Although most of this information is usually found in the school records, having it all in one place saves time. Make sure that the date(s) of testing and the date of the report are always included for comparisons. Some evaluations are finished several months before the report is typed and the scores can be misleading if the reader assumes that they represent the child's present levels on the date of the report when they may really be reflective of ability levels in prior months. It is always more acceptable when the two dates are within one month of each other. Also keep in mind that the chronological age (CA) is at the time of initial testing and is presented in years and months, e.g., 12.6.

4.122 continued

REASON FOR REFERRAL

The second section is called Reason for Referral and explains to the reader the specific reasons why this evaluation is taking place. It should not be more than two to three sentences, but should be comprehensive enough to clarify the purpose. The following are some examples of this section:

> Brian was referred by his teacher for evaluation as a result of inconsistent academic performance and poor social skills.
>
> Mary was referred by her parents for evaluation in order to determine if a learning disability was interfering in her ability to learn.
>
> Benjamin is being tested as part of the triennial evaluation.
>
> Matthew is being screened for a suspected disability.
>
> Bruce was referred by the pupil personnel team in order to determine his present intellectual, academic, and perceptual levels.

This section should not contain a great deal of parent or teacher information. There may be a tendency here to bring in other information to substantiate the reason for the evaluation. Avoid this and keep comments short and to the point. Substantiation for this referral is part of another section, which offers a more detailed explanation of the child.

BACKGROUND HISTORY

The next section is called Background History and contains a very thorough description of the child's Family History, Developmental History, Academic History, and Social History.

This general section is very comprehensive and establishes a foundation for what will follow. If you suspect a disability that may have historical features, then you need to present the development of this disability and its interfering factors in depth. The reader should come away from the section seeing the substantiation for a suspected disability. There are certain areas that should always be covered in the Background History section. These include:

Family History: This information provides the reader with a general understanding of the family structure, siblings, parental perceptions, and so on. Examples of sentences that would appear in this section include the following:

> Billy lives at home with his mother and a younger brother, Tommy. His parents are divorced and Billy has no contact with his father.
>
> Sally lives at home with her father, mother, and two older sisters.
>
> Karen is an only child who was adopted at the age of 6 months by her parents, Ted and Jane. She knows that she is adopted and has never had any contact with her biological parents.

Developmental History: The purpose of this information is to give the reader any relevant background history pertaining to developmental milestones. This section need not read like a hospital report but should contain the basic developmental history. Examples of sentences that would appear in this section include the following:

> All of Billy's developmental milestones were reached in the normal limits.
>
> Sally started to talk at the age of 2 years and received early intervention to help her with language ability.
>
> Teddy had many ear infections during the first year of life and needed tubes put in when he was 13 months of age.
>
> Bruce started to walk at 21 months of age, which is later than the norm.

Academic History: This section provides the reader with relevant academic performance during the child's school years. If you suspect a learning disability, then the Academic History section must be extensive. Trace the child's educational performance as far back as possible and establish the consistency of the pattern to the reader. Include all pertinent academic information, such as past teacher comments, grades, attendance, group scores, etc., and lead the reader grade-by-grade in establishing a pattern of concern or a pattern that may rule out a specific type of suspected disability. Example sentences used in this section might read as follows:

> Billy has always done poorly in math and has never received a grade of higher than C throughout his educational career.
>
> Sally's first-grade teacher reported that she had great difficulty in the area of spelling.
>
> Fred's Reading scores on the ABC National Standardized Test were well below the norm (8th percentile) when he took it two years ago in the fourth grade.

Social History: This section should provide the reader with an understanding of the child in his social world. Group participation, organizations, hobbies, interests, interaction with peers, social style, etc., should all be discussed. Examples of sentences that would appear in this section include the following:

> According to Billy, he enjoys playing baseball and hanging out with his friends at the mall.
>
> Sally reported that she has no friends and does not participate in any extracurricular activities.
>
> Teddy is the 11th-Grade Class President of his school and plays on the junior varsity basketball and varsity baseball teams.

When the Background History section is complete, it should provide the reader with a clear understanding of the child and his or her world at the present time.

BEHAVIORAL OBSERVATIONS

The fourth section is called Behavioral Observations and includes a description of the child's behavior during the testing sessions. This can be a very important section, as it

4.122 continued

may either reinforce what is seen in the class or may be very different, in which case the structure of the testing environment should be explored for clues to learning style. Here, for the first time, you are providing the reader with your professional and firsthand observation of this child in a controlled setting. This type of structure provides a great deal of valuable information that may be later transferred to recommendations about the way in which the child learns best. Examples of sentences that would appear in this section include the following:

> Sally approached the testing situation in a reluctant and hesitant manner.
>
> During testing, it was evident that Billy was frustrated with many of the reading tasks.
>
> Throughout the assessment, Connie appeared anxious and nervous, as she was biting her nails and always asking whether her answers were correct.

TESTS AND PROCEDURES ADMINISTERED

The next section is called Tests and Procedures Administered. This includes a simple list of the individual tests included in the test battery and any procedures used to enhance the report, e.g., classroom observation, review of records, parent intake. Do not use abbreviations when referring to test names. You may want to add them after the name of each specific test, e.g., Wide Range Achievement Test—3 (WRAT-3). No further explanation is required here other than a list. This section will vary depending upon the professional doing the evaluation. For example, the educational evaluator's list of Tests and Procedures Administered may look like this:

- Wechsler Individualized Achievement Test (WIAT)
- Detroit Tests of Learning Aptitude—Fourth Edition (DTLA-4)
- Gray Oral Reading Test—Fourth Edition (GORT-4)
- Classroom Observation
- Interview with Child
- Parent Interview
- Teacher Conferences
- Review of Cumulative Records

TEST RESULTS

The sixth section, Test Results, is a crucial section because it analyzes the results of each test and looks at the child's individual performance on each measure. There are several approaches to this section, but the two most widely used approaches are the Test-by-Test Analysis and the Content Area-by-Content Area Analysis. The approach chosen is a personal choice and preference of the examiner.

A **Test-by-Test** approach analyzes the child's performance on each test separately. It analyzes the results of the different subtests and provides indications of strengths and weaknesses, manner of approach, and indications of whether or not the scores on the specific test should be considered valid. In this section, the first paragraph of each test analyzed usually contains all the basic score information provided by that specific test—grade levels, age levels, percentiles, stanines, ranges. It should not contain raw scores or other statistical information that has no meaning to the reader. The next several paragraphs under each test normally describe the subtest performance, patterns, strengths and weaknesses, and child's style in handling the task. Information on whether or not the scores should be considered a valid indicator is provided. For example, if a child refuses to do more than two problems and receives a low score, it is important to inform the reader that that score may be misleading and may not reflect the child's true ability due to giving up or an unwillingness to venture a guess.

A **Content Area-by-Content Area** approach takes all the reading, math, spelling, writing, visual, auditory, and motor tests from each evaluation measure and analyzes the results separately by content area. The examiner analyzes each content area in hopes of establishing patterns of strengths and weaknesses. For example, deficient scores on all tests of reading comprehension may establish a pattern of disability, especially if they are discrepant from the child's ability levels. However, extremely high scores on some tests of comprehension and low scores on others need to be explained to the reader.

See the model report in List 4.123 for a comprehensive look at this section.

CONCLUSIONS

The Conclusions section is probably the essence of the report. In this section, the examiner indicates in very simple terms to the reader the trends in the child's testing results that may indicate academic strengths, academic weaknesses, modality strengths, modality weaknesses, process strengths and weaknesses, and overall diagnosis and level of severity of the problem areas indicated. It is not a restatement of the Test Results section but a summary of overall performance.

RECOMMENDATIONS

The eighth section of the report is probably the most valuable section for the reader—Recommendations. It should contain practical recommendations that will bring some hope and direction for the identified problem areas. Keep in mind that the recommendations should be practical enough and explained in such a way so that the reader will have no problem following through. For example, a recommendation to a parent of "Try to spend more time with Brian" is useless. It provides the reader with no direction or specifics. Instead, a recommendation such as, "Read at home with Brian in unison. By this, we mean that both you and Brian should have the same book and read aloud together, so that he receives constant auditory feedback." This more detailed recommendation provides the reader with more direction.

Try to separate the recommendations into the following three sections:

1. *Recommendations to the School*—This section might contain suggestions such as further testing from other professional on staff, vision or hearing tests by the school nurse, a review by the CSE, remedial reading assistance, or an ESL evaluation.

4.122 continued

2. *Recommendations to the Teacher*—This section should contain useful information for the teacher, including an indication of the conditions under which the child learns best. The teacher is probably mainly interested in "what do I do to help the child learn." Keep in mind that even before you begin the evaluation process, you should ask the teacher what he or she has already tried in an attempt to alleviate the problems. This should be done so that your recommendations do not include suggestions already attempted by the teacher. Doing this will avoid having your recommendations being viewed as "nothing I haven't already tried before."

3. *Recommendations to the Parent*—This part should be very practical, direct, and diplomatic. The suggestions should also be inclusive enough to answer the questions "why" and "how" so that parents do not have to interpret them.

Finally, each subsection should contain recommendations in priority order. Try to number each recommendation separately for purposes of clarity. For examples of recommendations to the school, parents, and teachers, see the model report in List 4.123.

EVALUATION SUMMARY TABLE

An Evaluation Summary Table is a useful part of a report in that it summarizes and places all the test scores in one specific area. This type of table can be very useful to other professionals looking for specific test scores or patterns, because they will not have to go through the entire report to find them. It is also a helpful tool to place before parents during a conference so that they can visually see what you are telling them rather than having to memorize everything you say. These types of summary tables may present all the scores from all the evaluations being done at that time, or each evaluation report may have a table that only contains the test scores specific to that evaluation.

4.123   Model Report

The following report shows an example for an elementary school-aged child referred by his teacher for a suspected learning disability.

IDENTIFYING DATA

Name: _____ *Brian Williams* _____
Address: _____ *15 Brewster Street* _____
_____ *Newton, NY 11687* _____
Phone: _____ *546-9864* _____
Date of Birth: _____ *August 10, 1984* _____
Grade: _____ *4* _____
School: _____ *Benton Ave.* _____
Chronological Age: _____ *9.10* _____

Parents' Names: *Jane/Robert* _____
Teacher: _____ *Mrs. Grissom* _____
Referred by: *Teacher* _____
Date of Testing: _____ *June 7, 1993* _____
Date of Report: _____ *June 18, 1993* _____
Examiner: _____ *Sally Jones* _____

REASON FOR REFERRAL

Brian was referred for an educational evaluation as a result of a suspected learning disability.

BACKGROUND HISTORY

Brian is a nine-year-old boy presently living in an intact household with his mother, a teacher; father, an engineer; older brother, age fifteen; and younger sister, age seven. At the present time, no other relatives reside within the home.

According to parent intake, Brian was the result of a full-term pregnancy and normal delivery. According to the mother, Brian was operated on for a hernia but there were no complications. Developmental milestones seem to have been within normal limits except for talking, which the parents indicated was later than expected. Early history indicates normal childhood illnesses, no traumatic experiences, and no long hospital stays. However, Brian had frequent middle ear infections within the first three years. The mother indicated that he has not had his eyesight or hearing checked since last year.

Academic history indicates that Brian seems to have been experiencing difficulties since the early grades. Several teachers, suspecting weaknesses in the reading and language arts areas, have expressed concerns. According to his present and past teachers, Brian's overall performance in the classroom was and still remains poor, despite above-average potential intelligence.

(continued)

His past and present teachers have reported that he does not participate in class, is verbally resistant, has problems remembering and following through on directions, has a short attention span, procrastinates on handing in written assignments, and has difficulty working independently. His present teacher reports that his organizational skills seem weak, and he needs step-by-step instructions from the teacher. She also reported that Brian is having social difficulties and is being isolated by his peers.

Socially, his parents reported that Brian does not seem to have many friends and the ones he does have are much younger. He enjoys collecting stamps and baseball cards and is very involved with the computer.

BEHAVIORAL OBSERVATIONS

Brian entered the testing situation in a relatively guarded manner. He wore a baseball cap pulled down low and made very little eye contact with the examiner. Brian did not initiate conversation, but remained cooperative throughout the sessions. His pattern of performance seemed labored on written tasks and he frequently asked to have the questions repeated.

Brian did briefly comment that he did not like school and wished he didn't have to come. He indicated that he had "a lot of friends" and kept asking how long the testing would take.

Brian is right-handed and holds his pencil with an awkward grasp. He seemed resistant to changing the grip and kept his head fairly close to the paper when writing, slightly tilting his head to the right.

TESTS AND PROCEDURES ADMINISTERED

- *Wechsler Individual Achievement Test (WIAT)*
- *Woodcock-Johnson Cognitive Battery—Revised (WJ-R)*
- *Review of Records*
- *Observation*
- *Parent Intake*

(continued)

TEST RESULTS

Achievement Functioning

Results of the Wechsler Individual Achievement Test indicated the following results:

Reading: *Brian's performance on the WIAT suggests below-average reading skills (Total Reading=4th Percentile). His reading comprehension skills fall in the low-average range (12th Percentile). Brian appeared to be experiencing the most difficulty recognizing stated details and identifying cause-and-effect relationships.*

Brian performed in the below-average range on a task requiring oral reading of visually presented words (5th Percentile). Brian also had difficulty decoding familiar words and seemed unaware of phonemic rules, which added to his inability to decode syllables.

Mathematics: *Relative to other 4th graders, Brian's performance on the WIAT Mathematics section suggests average abilities in mathematics (Total Mathematics Score=46th Percentile). He demonstrated average performance on tasks measuring his understanding of mathematical concepts, vocabulary, and applications. He displayed below-average ability on a paper-and-pencil test of basic numerical operations as well as some difficulty manipulating fractions, decimals, and three-digit numbers.*

Writing: *Brian's performance on sections of the WIAT dealing with written expression indicates below-average skills (Total Writing Score=18th Percentile). His written expression skills were assessed to be in the low-average range (10th Percentile). Although he was cooperative and motivated, Brian had difficulty developing his ideas using appropriate vocabulary. Further, his writing lacked organization and unity. Brian also demonstrated a weak grasp of grammar and sentence structure, which might be hindering his written communication.*

Brian demonstrated below-average (6th Percentile) spelling ability. He was unable to spell even familiar words and relied on basic phonemic rules to attempt spellings. For example, he wrote "easer" for "easier," "wisle" for "whistle," and "being" for "beginning."

Language: *Brian's language performance on the WIAT indicates average skills (Total Language=39th Percentile). He demonstrated average ability to answer questions based upon orally presented stories (39th Percentile). On tasks assessing his ability to orally describe pictures and give directions, Brian again performed in the average range (40th Percentile). His responses were logical and consistent and indicated attention to detail.*

(continued)

Cognitive Functioning

Brian's performance on the Woodcock-Johnson Cognitive Battery placed him in the average range with respect to cognitive ability; Visual Processing—the capability to perceive and think with visual patterns; and Comprehension-Knowledge—a measurement of the breadth and depth of knowledge and its effective application. Brian's scores on tasks measuring short-term memory were within the average range. However, his effectiveness in storing and retrieving information over extended periods of time was in the low-average range.

The area of greatest concern seemed to center on comprehension and synthesis of auditory patterns involved in Auditory Processing (4th Percentile). The skills of auditory closure and sound blending, which comprise this cluster, would impact directly on Brian's word attack skills and spelling.

Further areas of concern appeared in Processing Speed (7th Percentile), which involved the rapid performance of relatively trivial cognitive tasks.

CONCLUSIONS

Brian is a nine-year-old boy presently functioning in the Average range of intellectual ability. Results of testing seem to indicate that Brian presently exhibits adequate skills in areas involving mathematics. However, his most significant weaknesses appear to be in the areas of reading comprehension, reading vocabulary, and auditory processing, which have had a significant impact on his decoding skills in reading and on his ability to spell. Visual-motor integration skills also appear to be of concern and were evident in Brian's written work. Other factors may also be contributing to Brian's overall lack of performance in school. His high level of distractibility, avoidance, procrastination, low self-esteem, and resistance may be symptomatic of secondary tension arising from school frustration.

Analysis of the test results and documented ability levels seem to indicate that Brian's difficulties should be considered moderate-to-severe in nature and his overall pattern fits the criteria for a student with a learning disability.

RECOMMENDATIONS

Results of testing, observation, and intake suggest the following recommendations:

To the School

1. *In view of the nature and severity of Brian's school-related difficulties, a review by the Eligibility Committee is recommended. The Eligibility Committee may want to explore the possibility of resource room assistance.*

(continued)

2. *The school may want to consider placing Brian in remedial reading to increase his ability in decoding.*

To the Teacher

1. *Brian's spelling difficulties may result in resistance to written assignments. The teacher may want to allow Brian the use of a word processor with a spelling checker for written tasks.*

2. *Further, oral spelling tests or spelling tests that require Brian to identify each correctly spelled word from a list of four words may be beneficial. In this way, Brian may gain some confidence in this area.*

3. *Brian will need assistance in the classroom with identifying long vowel sounds, words with the silent "e" spelling pattern, vowel digraphs, and common endings, e.g., ble, dle, tle, ary, ery, cry.*

4. *The teacher may want to seat Brian closer to her desk to increase his attention and focus.*

5. *Further recommendations will be addressed at a meeting with the teacher.*

To the Parent

1. *Mr. and Mrs. Williams may want to set a homework schedule for Brian. In this way, he will have a structured time when homework needs to be addressed. Further, they may want to check his work at the end of the night to make sure it's complete and correct. In this way, Brian can feel more comfortable when he comes to school.*

2. *Unison reading at home is also suggested. Unison reading means that both the parent and the child have the same book and read aloud together, thereby reinforcing the correct pronunciation.*

3. *Further recommendations will be addressed at the meeting with the parent.*

Sally K. Jones, M.S.
Educational Evaluator

PART 5

IEP Information

5.1 New Individualized Education Plan (IEP) Requirements Under IDEA '97

The new IDEA maintains the IEP as a document of central importance and, in the hope of improving compliance, moves all provisions related to the IEP to one place in the law—Section 614(d). (Under the prior law, IEP provisions were found in several different places.)

Modifications have been made to these familiar components to place more emphasis within the law upon involving students with disabilities in the general curriculum and in the general education classroom, with supplementary aids and services as appropriate.

"Present levels of educational performance" must now include a statement of how the child's disability affects his or her involvement and progress in the general curriculum.

Similarly, the IEP must contain a statement of special education and related services, as well as the supplementary aids and services, that the child or youth needs in order to: ". . . be involved and progress in the general curriculum . . . and to participate in extracurricular and other nonacademic activities; and . . . to be educated and participate with other children with disabilities and children who do not have disabilities . . ." [Section 614(d)(1)(A)(iii)]

The IEP must include an explanation of the extent to which the student will not be participating with children who do not have disabilities in the general education class and in extracurricular and nonacademic activities. This explanation of the extent to which the child will be educated separately is a new component of the IEP, yet is clearly in keeping with the changes noted above.

Each student's IEP must now include a statement of how the administration of state or districtwide assessments will be modified for the student so that he or she can participate. If the IEP team determines that the student cannot participate in such assessments, then the IEP must include a statement of (a) why the assessment is not appropriate for the child, and (b) how the child will be assessed.

- Each student must be informed about the transfer of rights as he or she approaches the age of majority.

- Parents will be regularly informed of their child's progress toward meeting the annual goals in the IEP.

- Parents will be informed where services will be delivered to the student.

- Parents will be informed of the transition service needs of the student beginning at age 14.

The new IDEA maintains essentially the same process for developing the IEP—namely, a multidisciplinary team, including the parents, develops the document. However, the new legislation increases the role of the general educator on the IEP team, to include, when appropriate, helping to determine positive behavioral interventions and appropriate supplementary aids and services for the student.

Also added to the IEP process are "special factors" that the IEP team must consider. These factors include:

- Behavior strategies and supports, if the child's behavior impedes his or her learning or that of others

- The child's language needs (as they relate to the IEP) if the child has limited English proficiency

- Providing for instruction in Braille and the use of Braille (unless not appropriate), if a child is blind or visually impaired

- The communication needs of the child, with a list of specific factors to be considered if a child is deaf or hard of hearing

- Whether the child requires assistive devices and services

The language in the new IDEA emphasizes periodic review of the IEP (at least annually, as previously required) and revision as needed. A new, separate requirement exists: Schools must report to parents on the progress of their child with disabilities at least as frequently as the progress of a child who does not have a disability is reported, which seems likely to affect the revision process for IEPs. If it becomes evident that a child is not making "expected progress toward the annual goals and in the general curriculum," the IEP team must meet and revise the IEP.

The new legislation specifically lists a variety of other circumstances under which the IEP team would also need to review and revise the IEP, including the child's anticipated needs, the results of any reevaluation conducted, or information provided by the parents.

The requirements for providing transition services for youth with disabilities have been modified in IDEA '97. Although the definition of transition services remains the same, two notable changes have been made to IEP requirements: (1) Beginning when a student is 14, and annually thereafter, the student's IEP must contain a statement of his or her transition service needs under the various components of that IEP that focus upon the student's courses of study (e.g., vocational education or advanced placement); and (2) beginning at least one year before the student reaches the age of majority under state law, the IEP must contain a statement that the student has been informed of the rights under the law that will transfer to him or her upon reaching the age of majority.

The new law maintains 16 as the age when students' IEPs must contain statements of needed transition services. These two requirements—one for students aged 14 and older and one for students aged 16 and older—seem confusingly similar. However, the purpose of including certain statements for students beginning at age 14, according to the Committee on Labor and Human Resources' Report [to Accompany Section 717], "is to focus attention on how the child's educational program can be planned . . . [and] the provision is designed to augment, and not replace, the separate transition services requirement, under which children with disabilities [who are 16 or older] receive transition services . . ." (p. 22).

5.2   Components to Be Included in the IEP, According to IDEA '97

According to IDEA '97, the components of an IEP must include:

"i. A statement of the child's present levels of educational performance, including—(I) how the child's disability affects the child's involvement and progress in the general curriculum; or (II) for preschool children, as appropriate, how the disability affects the child's participation in appropriate activities;

"ii. A statement of measurable annuals goals, including benchmarks or short-term objectives, related to—(I) meeting the child's needs that result from the child's disability to enable the child to be involved in and progress in the general curriculum; and (II) meeting each of the child's other educational needs that result from the child's disability;

"iii. A statement of the special education and related services and supplementary aids and services to be provided to the child, or on behalf of the child, and a statement of program modifications or supports for school personnel that will be provided for the child—(I) to advance appropriately toward attaining the annual goals; (II) to be involved and progress in the general curriculum in accordance with clause (i) and to participate in extracurricular and other nonacademic activities; and (III) to be educated and participate with other children with disabilities and children who do not have disabilities in the activities described in this paragraph;

"iv. An explanation of the extent, if any, to which the child will not participate with children who do not have disabilities in the regular class and in the activities described in clause (iii);

"v. A statement of any individual modifications in the administration of State or district-wide assessments of student achievement that are needed in order for the child to participate in such assessment; and (II) if the IEP Team determines that the child will not participate in a particular State or district-wide assessment of student achievement (or part of such an assessment), a statement of—(aa) why that assessment is not appropriate for the child; and (bb) how the child will be assessed;

"vi. The projected date for the beginning of the services and modifications described in clause (iii) and the anticipated frequency, location, and duration of those services and modifications;

"vii. Beginning at age 14, and updated annually, a statement of the transition service needs of the child under the applicable components of the child's IEP that focuses on the child's courses of study (such as participation in advanced-placement courses or a vocational education program); (II) beginning at age 16 (or younger, if determined appropriate by the IEP Team), a statement of needed transition services for the child, including, when appropriate, a statement of the interagency responsibilities or any needed linkages; and (III) beginning at least one year before the child reaches the age of majority under State law, a statement that the child has been informed of his or her rights under this title, if any, that will transfer to the child on reaching the age of majority under section 615(m); and

"viii. A statement of—(I) how the child's progress toward the annual goals described in clause (ii) will be measured; and (II) how the child's parents will be regularly informed (by such means as periodic report cards), at least as often as parents are informed of the progress of their children without disabilities, of—(aa) their child's progress toward the annual goals described in clause (ii); and (bb) the extent to which that progress is sufficient to enable the child to achieve the goals by the end of the year." [Section 614(d)(1)(A)(i) through (viii)]

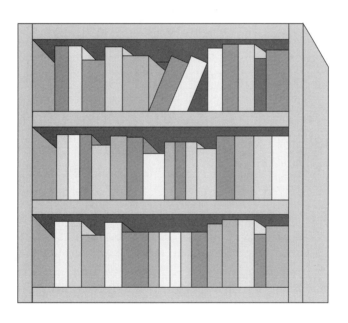

5.3   IDEA '97 and the Development of the IEP

The new law adds specific factors that the IEP team must consider when developing a child's IEP, including, most notably, behavior issues and the specific communication needs of the child if he or she is blind or visually impaired, of limited English proficiency, or deaf or hard of hearing.

"(A) In general.—In developing each child's IEP, the IEP Team, subject to subparagraph (C), shall consider—

"(i)   The strengths of the child and the concerns of the parents for enhancing the education of their child; and

"(ii)   the results of the initial evaluation or most recent evaluation of the child.

"(B) Consideration of special factors.—The IEP Team shall—

"(i)   In the case of a child whose behavior impedes his or her learning or that of others, consider, when appropriate, strategies, including positive behavioral interventions, strategies, and supports to address that behavior;

"(ii)   In the case of a child with limited English proficiency, consider the language needs of the child as such needs relate to the child's IEP;

"(iii) In the case of a child who is blind or visually impaired, provide for instruction in Braille and the use of Braille unless the Eligibility Committee determines, after an evaluation of the child's reading and writing skills, needs, and appropriate reading and writing media (including an evaluation of the child's future needs for instruction in Braille or the use of Braille), that instruction in Braille or the use of Braille is not appropriate for the child;

"(iv) Consider the communication needs of the child, and in the case of a child who is deaf or hard of hearing, consider the child's language and communication needs, opportunities for direct communications with peers and professional personnel in the child's language and communication mode, academic level, and full range of needs, including opportunities for direct instruction in the child's language and communication mode; and

"(v)   Consider whether the child requires assistive devices and services.

"(C) Requirement with respect to regular education teacher.—The regular education teacher of the child, as a member of the Eligibility Committee, shall, to the extent appropriate, participate in the development of the IEP of the child, including the determination of appropriate positive behavioral interventions and strategies and the determination of supplementary aids and services, program modifications, and support for school personnel consistent with paragraph (1)(A)(iii)." [Section 614(d)(3)]

5.4   Sample IEP Form

Section 1—Background Information

School District/Agency: _____Township School District_____

Name and Address: _____Edison Township, VA_____

Individualized Education Plan

Date of Eligibility Committee/CPSE Meeting: _June 12, 2000_

Purpose of Meeting: _____Initial_____

Student Name: _____Ronald Gaines_____

Date of Birth: _2/5/86_   Age: _14_

Street: _13 Benson Ave._

City: _Edison_   Zip: _19876_

Telephone: _675-8976_   County of Residence: _Edison Township_

Male _X_ Female __ Student ID#: _3467H_   Current Grade: _9_

Dominant Language of Student: _English_   Interpreter Needed: Yes __ No _X_

Racial/Ethnic Group of Student:

   (Optional information)

   American Indian or Alaskan Native _NA_

   Black (not of Hispanic origin) _X_

   White (not of Hispanic origin) _NA_

   Asian or Pacific Islander _NA_

   Hispanic _NA_

Date of Initiation of Services: _9/1/2000_   Projected Date of Review: _5/2001_

Date of Eligibility: _5/2000_   Date for Reevaluation: _4/2003_

Medical Alerts: _____ADHD_____

Mother's Name/Guardian's Name: _____Charlat Gaines_____

Street Address: _same_

City: _same_   Zip: _same_

Telephone: _same_   County of Residence: _Wells_

Dominant Language of Parent/Guardian: _English_   Interpreter Needed: Yes__ No _X_

Father's Name/Guardian's Name: _____Malcolm_____

Street Address: _____same_____

City: _____same_____   Zip: _same_

Telephone: _____same_____   County of Residence: _same_

Dominant Language of Parent/Guardian: _English_   Interpreter Needed: Yes__ No _X_

5.4 continued

EXPLANATION OF SECTION 1 OF IEP—
BACKGROUND INFORMATION

Date of the Eligibility Committee/CPSE Meeting: The date the Committee meeting occurred.

Purpose of Meeting: The Eligibility Committee, Subcommittee on Special Education, or Committee on Preschool Education (Eligibility Committee/Committee on Preschool Special Education) meeting may be conducted to address several purposes. The type of meeting may be an initial review, annual review, review of reevaluation results, or request for review by the student's parent or teacher, and should be noted accordingly.

Student Name: The full name of the student should be noted.

Date of Birth: Student's birth date.

Age: The age of the student on the date of the meeting.

Address of Student: Legal address and phone number of the student.

County of Residence: The county in which the student resides.

Gender: Male or female.

Student Identification Number (ID): The ID number may be the student's social security number or a number assigned by the school.

Current Grade Assignment: For school-aged students, the current grade is designated as of the date of the Committee meeting. Students with disabilities who are participating in instruction based on the general education curriculum should have a grade designation that generally is the grade in which the student would be enrolled if the student did not have a disability. For all other students, the term "ungraded" should be noted.

Dominant Language of the Student: For a student who is deaf or hearing impaired or whose native language is other than English, specify the language or mode of communication used with the student. The Committee must arrange for an interpreter if needed for the student to meaningfully participate in developing the Individualized Education Plan (IEP).

Race/Ethnicity: The race/ethnicity of the student is optional.

Date of Initiation of Services: The date when this IEP is to be implemented.

Projected Date of Review: The date when review of this IEP is expected.

Initial Date of Eligibility for Special Education: The date when the student was first identified as a student with a disability and eligible for special education programs and services.

Date for Reevaluation: The date when the next reevaluation of the student is expected to occur. Reevaluations must occur at least every three years.

Medical Alerts/Prescriptive Devices: Include any information that should be readily available to all teachers and other appropriate school personnel, such as medications or specific health-related conditions requiring either constant or intermittent care by a qualified individual, for example: eyeglasses, hearing aids, and allergic reactions.

Parent/Guardian's Name: The names of the parent(s) or the name of a guardian, if appropriate.

Street, City, and Zip: If the address of a parent(s)/guardian is different from the student's address, both addresses should be indicated, when appropriate.

Telephone: If appropriate, the telephone numbers of parent(s)/guardian should be indicated.

County of Residence: The county(ies) in which the parent(s) resides.

Dominant Language of the Parent(s)/Guardian: For parent(s)/guardians who are deaf or hearing impaired or whose native language is other than English, specify the language or mode of communication used by the parent(s). The Committee must ensure that the parent(s)/guardian understand the proceedings of the Committee meeting and must arrange for an interpreter if needed for the parent(s)/guardian to meaningfully participate in developing the IEP.

5.4 continued

Section 2—Present Levels of Performance and Individual Needs

1. **Academic/Educational Achievement and Learning Characteristics:** Address current levels of knowledge and development in subject and skill areas, including activities of daily living, level of intellectual functioning, adaptive behavior, expected rate of progress in acquiring skills and information, and learning style.

Present Levels: Academic development

> *Ronald is currently functioning below his chronological age in the area of academic ability.*

Present Levels: Cognitive ability

> *Ronald is currently functioning at his chronological age in the area of cognitive ability.*

Present Levels: Language ability

> *Ronald is currently functioning below his chronological age in the area of language development.*
>
> *Ronald is currently functioning below his chronological age in the area of receptive development.*
>
> *Ronald is currently functioning below his chronological age in the area of pragmatic/social speech development.*

Abilities: *Ronald understands multistep directions.*

Needs: *None*

Present Levels: Learning style

> *Ronald has a multisensory learning style.*

Present Level: General

> *Given Ronald's functional level, Ronald's disability affects his involvement and progress in the general education program.*
>
> *Ronald models math/goal skills only with teacher support.*
>
> *Ronald is able to independently perform Language Arts goals/skills with minimal support.*

(continued)

Present Level: Rate of Progress

Ronald's rate of progress is below average.

Ronald reads on or above grade level.

Ronald's computational skills impact the ability to perform general education at his grade level.

Abilities: *Ronald is able to read and follow written directions.*

Needs:

Ronald requires an individualized and/or small group approach for instruction in math.

Ronald needs to develop self-monitoring skills as a means of avoiding carelessness and focusing attention to detail (copying homework, completing class work).

2. **Social Development:** Describe the quality of the student's relationships with peers and adults, feelings about self, social adjustment to school and community environment, and behaviors that may impede learning.

Present Levels: Social Interaction with Peers

Ronald is presently functioning below his chronological age in the area of social development.

Abilities: *Ronald has developed some friendships.*

Needs:

Ronald needs to relate appropriately to peers in the classroom.

Ronald needs to relate appropriately to adults in the classroom.

Ronald needs to relate appropriately to adults outside the classroom.

Ronald needs to learn how to communicate effectively in social situations.

Present Levels: *Ronald's Feelings about Self*

Ronald is currently functioning below his chronological age level in regard to feelings about self.

Abilities: *Ronald identifies himself as an individual.*

Needs:

Ronald needs to develop positive self-concept.

Present Levels: School/Community

Ronald is currently functioning below his chronological age level in regard to school and community.

(continued)

Abilities: *Ronald initiates social interactions with adults.*

Needs: *Ronald needs to respond to adult intervention.*
Ronald needs to respond to adult praise.

Present Levels: Adjustment to School/Community
Ronald does not display appropriate social adjustment to school, family, and/or community environment skills.

Abilities: *Ronald can adapt to changes in routine.*

Needs: *Ronald needs guidance to participate in small groups.*
Ronald needs to take initiative in social situations.

3. **Physical Development:** Describe the student's motor and sensory development, health, vitality, and physical skills or limitations that pertain to the learning process.

Present Levels: *Ronald has ADHD medical diagnosis which impacts learning; see health file.*

Abilities: *Ronald may participate in all school activities.*

Needs: *Ronald needs to develop skills required to sit independently.*
Ronald needs to improve attending skills when visual distractions are present.

4. **Management Needs:** Describe the nature and degree to which environmental modifications and human or material resources are required to address academic, social, and physical needs.

A functional behavior assessment should be completed for any student who demonstrates behaviors that impede learning. A functional behavioral assessment becomes the basis for positive behavioral interventions, strategies, and supports for the student.

Present Levels: *Ronald has moderate management needs to address academic goals.*
Ronald has moderate needs to address social goals.

Abilities: *Ronald is able to perform effectively/complete tasks in the classroom environment with additional personnel present.*

Needs: *Ronald needs full-time general education placement with moderate support through special education.*

EXPLANATION OF SECTION 2—PRESENT LEVELS OF PERFORMANCE AND INDIVIDUAL NEEDS

The IEP must describe the student's present levels of educational performance, including the student's abilities and needs. Present levels of performance are based on relevant functional and developmental evaluation information, including information provided by the parent. Many tests and assessment procedures are used to obtain information about a student's present levels of performance.

Present levels of performance must include a statement that explains how the student's disability affects his or her involvement and progress in the general education curriculum. The Committee uses this information to determine a student's eligibility for special education, the specific classification, annual goals and objectives, and the specific type and extent of special education programs and services. The Committee must assess present levels of performance and individual needs in the following areas:

Academic/Educational Achievement and Learning Characteristics: The levels of knowledge and development in subject and skill areas, including activities of daily living, level of intellectual functioning, adaptive behavior, expected rate of progress in acquiring skills and information, and learning style are addressed. Performance in subject areas should be based on the student's ability in relation to the learning standards and performance indicators established for all students.

Social Development: The degree and quality of the student's relationships with peers and adults, feelings about self, and social adjustment to school and community environments are explained.

Physical Development: The degree or quality of the student's motor and sensory development, health, vitality, and physical skills or limitations that pertain to the learning process, including pertinent information from the student's physical examination, are noted.

Management Needs: The nature of and degree to which environmental modifications and human or material resources are required to enable the student to benefit from instruction are discussed.

5.4 continued

Section 3—Long-Term Adult Outcome Statement

Long-Term Adult Outcomes: Beginning at age 14, or younger if appropriate, state long-term adult outcomes reflecting student's needs, preferences, and interests in:

Post-secondary Education/Training:

> Ronald anticipates receiving the following post-secondary education/training:
>   Ronald will attend college.
> The transition service needs of Ronald to meet long-term adult outcomes are:
>   Ronald will receive guidance/career counseling.
>   Ronald will take college entrance courses.
>   Ronald will take regents courses.

Employment: *NA*

Community Living: *NA*

Section 4—Measurable Annual Goals and Short-Term Instructional Objectives

Annual Goal: *Ronald will maintain and improve study skill levels.*

Short-Term Instructional Objective	Evaluation Procedures	Evaluation Schedule
1. *Improve work habits and study skills.*	*classroom teacher contact*	*quarterly*
2. *Organize material including classwork, major assignments, and homework.*		

Annual Goal: *Ronald will successfully complete academic course requirements.*

Short-Term Instructional Objective	Evaluation Procedures	Evaluation Schedule
1. *Incorporate writing process strategies.*		
2. *Improve math computation.*	*quizzes, tests*	*quarterly*

Annual Goal: *Ronald will increase attentiveness and concentration skills.*

Short-Term Instructional Objective	Evaluation Procedures	Evaluation Schedule
1. *Develop necessary behaviors, attitudes, and expectations that will lead to self growth.*	*observation, teacher contact*	*quarterly*
2. *Learn to express feelings both positive and negative.*		

EXPLANATION OF SECTION 3—LONG-TERM
ADULT OUTCOME STATEMENT

Beginning at age 14 and updated annually, the IEP must include a long-term adult outcome statement related to the student's individual needs, preferences, and interests for adult employment, post-secondary education, and community living. At age 14, federal law requires that the IEP include a statement of the transition service needs of the student that focuses on the student's courses of study, such as advanced-placement courses or an occupational education program. By age 15, or earlier as deemed appropriate by the Eligibility Committee, the IEP must reflect the full array of transition service needs in instruction, related services, community experiences, development of employment, and other post-school adult living objectives, including, as appropriate, acquisition of daily living skills and a functional vocational evaluation.

The long-term adult outcome statements establish clear expectations for the school, the student, the student's family, and any agencies participating in planning and implementing the transition programs and services in the IEP. These statements are the basis for planning the student's movement from school to post-school activities and for discussion with appropriate public and private community agencies regarding their contributions to the student's transition process.

Once the statements are established, annual goals and objectives and other activities can be developed to help the student incrementally develop skills, experiences, and contacts with resources—as needed—to work toward these desired adult outcomes. Vocational rehabilitation counselors from the Office of Vocational and Educational Services for Individuals with Disabilities (VESID), in consultation with the student, parents, and school personnel, can provide advice on long-term adult outcomes, including appropriate vocational assessments, post-secondary services, and selection of employment goals for students who meet vocational rehabilitation eligibility criteria.

EXPLANATION OF SECTION 4—MEASURABLE ANNUAL
GOALS AND SHORT-TERM INSTRUCTIONAL OBJECTIVES

Annual goals are statements, in measurable terms, that describe what the student can reasonably be expected to accomplish within a twelve-month period. There must be a direct relationship between the annual goals and the present levels of performance.

Annual goals focus on addressing needs resulting from the disability so that the student can appropriately participate in the general curriculum. The Committee should consider goals from all areas of the student's individual needs, including those associated with behavior and long-term adult outcomes, where appropriate.

The following criteria should be considered:

1. Annual goals should be determined from the abilities and needs of the student as described in the present levels of performance.

2. Annual goals should focus on offsetting or reducing the learning or behavioral problems resulting from the student's disability.

3. Annual goals should focus on meeting the special education needs of the student.

4. Annual goals must be written in measurable terms.

5.4 continued

Short-Term Objectives or Benchmarks: After the Committee has developed measurable annual goals, they must develop short-term objectives or benchmarks relating to each annual goal. Short-term objectives are measurable, intermediate steps between the present levels of performance and the annual goals. Benchmarks are major milestones between the present levels of performance and the annual goals.

Short-term objectives and benchmarks are based on a logical breakdown of the major components of the annual goals and can serve as milestones to determine the extent to which the student is progressing to meet the annual goals. Short-term objectives provide a mechanism to determine the extent of the student's progress during the year, to ensure the IEP is consistent with the student's instructional needs, and to revise the IEP, if appropriate.

The following criteria should be considered:

- Short-term objectives and benchmarks must be written in measurable terms.

- Short-term objectives and benchmarks must include evaluative criteria specified in such a way that they can be measured.

- Short-term objectives and benchmarks must specify evaluation procedures such as systematic observation, teacher-made tests, informal tests, graphs, and work samples.

- Short-term objectives and benchmarks must include a schedule to measure progress toward the annual goal.

Section 5—Special Education Programs and Related Services/Program Modifications

A. Special Education Programs/Related Services	Initiation Date	Frequency	Duration
In-school counseling	*September 2000*	*1x a week*	*45 min.*

B. Extended School Year Services   Yes ___ No _X_
   *Specify group/class size if appropriate:

C. Supplementary Aids & Modifications or Supports for the Student	Initiation Date	Frequency	Duration
Modification of curriculum	*Sept 2000*		
Extra time between classes	*Sept 2000*		
Calculator	*Sept 2000*		

(continued)

D. Describe any assistive technology devices or services needed:

Given Ronald's functional level, Ronald does not need assistive technology services and devices in order to have an equal opportunity to succeed academically.

E. Describe the program modifications or supports for school personnel that will be provided on behalf of the student to address the annual goals and participation in general education curriculum and activities.

School staff will be provided with information on a specific disability and implications for instruction for Ronald.

F. 1. Individual Testing Modification(s):

Ronald requires time and a half to complete standardized tests.

Ronald requires double time to complete classroom tests.

Ronald requires tests to be administered in a small group in a separate location.

Ronald will have tests administered in a location with minimal distractions.

2. State why the student will not participate in a state or districtwide assessment.

NA

3. Explain how the student will be assessed: *Districtwide standardized tests.*

EXPLANATION OF SECTION 5—SPECIAL EDUCATION PROGRAMS AND RELATED SERVICES/PROGRAM MODIFICATIONS

The IEP must indicate the special education programs and related services, supplementary aids and services, assistive technology devices, and program supports or modifications that are to be provided to the student, or on behalf of the student.

Parts A–D. Special Education Programs/Related Services Special education means specially designed individualized or group instruction or special services or programs to meet the individual needs of students with disabilities. Specially designed instruction ensures access of the student to the general curriculum so the student can meet the educational standards that apply to all students.

The IEP must indicate the type of program/service (e.g., special class, consultant teacher, resource room, related service), the initiation date, frequency (i.e., number of times per week a service will be provided), duration (i.e., of minutes per session), and location (e.g., general education class, separate location) for each special education program and service. The IEP must describe the special class size, if appropriate. If the student needs direct and/or indirect consultant teacher services, the IEP should indicate the general education classes, including occupational education, in which the student will receive such

5.4 continued

service. The location where special education and related services will be provided to a student may influence decisions about the nature and amount of these services and when they should be provided. For example, the appropriate location for the related service to be provided may be the regular classroom or a separate location.

The IEP must describe any specialized equipment and adaptive devices needed for the student to benefit from education. IDEA requires each school district to ensure that assistive technology devices and/or services are made available to a preschool or school-aged student with a disability as part of the student's special education, related services, or supplementary aids or services as described in the IEP. Assistive technology devices are any item, piece of equipment, or product system, whether acquired commercially off the shelf, modified, or customized, that is used to increase, maintain, or improve the functional capabilities of a child with a disability.

A school district is not responsible to make available, through purchase or rental, devices that a student would require only for non-school settings or activities. In addition, the district would not, unless specifically stated in the IEP, have to provide items that a student routinely would require for daily life functions regardless of the setting (e.g., wheelchair, hearing aid, or some prosthetic or orthotic devices) that are prescribed by a licensed physician. If a student requires assistive technology to meet the IEP goals and objectives or to participate in the general education curriculum or classes, the Committee must consider who will be responsible for day-to-day maintenance as well as develop a contingency plan to provide repairs, replacements, or back-up equipment.

Part E. Program Modifications/Supports for School Personnel on Behalf of the Student The IEP must describe the program modifications or supports for school personnel that will be provided on behalf of the student to address the student's annual goals and participation in general education curriculum and activities. Examples of modifications or supports that may be provided for school personnel are:

Information on a specific disability and implications for instruction.

Training in use of specific positive behavioral interventions.

Information on the need for special placement of the student within the classroom.

Training in the use of American Sign Language.

Part F. Individual Testing Modifications Required, Nonparticipation in a State or Districtwide Assessment, and How the Student Will Be Assessed

1. *Individual Testing Modifications*—The IEP must indicate the testing modifications. Test modifications must be clearly stated to ensure a consistent understanding by the Committee, the principal, the teacher(s), the student, and the parent(s). Specific test modifications (e.g., use of word processor with spell check function) should be indicated, not generic test-modification categories (e.g., answers recorded in other manner). It is appropriate to indicate the conditions or nature of tests that will require test modifications (e.g., use of a note taker for tests having answer sheets requiring answers to be blackened); however, qualifying terms such as "as appropriate" or "when necessary" should not be used on the IEP.

2. *Statement of Nonparticipation in a State or Districtwide Assessment and How the Student Will Be Assessed*—The Committee must consider the far-reaching effects of nonparticipation in a particular state or districtwide assessment of student achievement (or part of such an assessment) before determining a student will not participate in the assessment. If the Committee determines that the student will not participate in a particular state or districtwide assessment, the IEP must contain a statement of why that assessment is not appropriate for the student. In addition, the IEP must indicate how the student will be assessed.

Section 6—Participation in General Education Classes and Nonacademic and Extracurricular Activities

Explain the extent of participation in general education programs and extracurricular and other nonacademic activities including physical education or adaptive (adapted) physical education and occupational education (if appropriate). Explain the extent, if any, to which the student will not participate with students who do not have disabilities in the regular class and in other activities.

Ronald will participate in all general education classes with support personnel.

If the student is exempt from the second language requirement, explain why.

Ronald will be exempt from foreign language requirements due to the following reasons:

Ronald exhibits a significant discrepancy between verbal and performance areas on IQ testing, where profile suggests significant verbal difficulties. This exempts Ronald from participation in a required second language course.

Section 7—Participating Agencies for Students Who Require Transition Services

Participating agencies that have agreed to provide transition services/supports (before the student leaves the secondary school program):

Agency Name:_____NA_____ Telephone Number: _____
Service: _____

Implementation date if different from IEP implementation date: _____

Agency Name:_____ Telephone Number: _____
Service: _____

Implementation date if different from IEP implementation date: _____

Agency Name:_____ Telephone Number: _____
Service: _____

Implementation date if different from IEP implementation date: _____

5.4 continued

EXPLANATION OF SECTION 6—PARTICIPATION IN GENERAL EDUCATION CLASSES AND NONACADEMIC AND EXTRACURRICULAR ACTIVITIES

IDEA presumes that all students with disabilities are to be educated in general education classes. The IEP must explain both how the student will participate in general education classes, programs, and activities and the extent to which, if any, the student will not participate in such classes, programs, and activities with nondisabled peers. For preschool students, the Committee must explain why the student will not participate in age-appropriate activities with nondisabled peers.

The IEP must specifically indicate how the school-aged student will participate in general education programs, including:

- Physical education or adaptive (adapted) physical education

- Occupational education, if appropriate

- Second language instruction

- Nonacademic activities

- Extracurricular activities

All students are expected to participate in the second language requirement unless specifically exempted by the Committee. The Committee must explain why the student is exempt from the second language requirement.

Students with severe disabilities can also benefit from participation in general education classes and activities with appropriate supports to them and their teachers. In determining the placement of a student with severe disabilities, the Committee must determine whether the assistance of supplementary aids and services is needed. Only upon determining that such goals and objectives cannot be achieved in a general education classroom, with supports and services, should the student be educated in an alternative placement. Moreover, the Committee should also consider the nonacademic benefits to the student (e.g., language development and role modeling) that will result from interaction with students who do not have a disability.

EXPLANATION OF SECTION 7—PARTICIPATING AGENCIES FOR STUDENTS WHO REQUIRE TRANSITION SERVICES

Beginning at age 15, or younger if appropriate, the IEP must reflect the full array of transition programs and services designed to develop post-secondary education, employment, and community living skills. The Committee is responsible for identifying appropriate and necessary participating agencies that will be a part of the student's transition to post-school opportunities.

A "participating agency" is defined as a state or local agency, other than the school district responsible for a student's education, that may have financial and/or legal responsibility for providing transition services to the student. Prior to the Eligibility Committee meeting to determine needed transition services, Eligibility Committee members should have knowledge of both the eligibility criteria and the services provided by agencies that could be expected to send a representative. This will enable the Eligibility Committee to invite appropriate agencies to participate in discussions regarding the provision of transition services for each student. When an agency agrees to provide a service, the IEP must include that service and the implementation date of the service if it is different from the implementation date of the IEP. The Eligibility Committee must document on the IEP these contacts and the services/supports to be provided to the student as he/she transitions from school. The Eligibility Committee must reconvene as soon as possible to consider other strategies to meet the transition objectives should the participating agency fail to deliver agreed-upon services stated in the IEP.

Section 8—Coordinated Set of Activities Leading to Long-Term Adult Outcomes

If any of the following areas are not addressed, explain why.

1. Instruction: *NA*
2. Related Services: *NA*
3. Employment/Post-secondary Education: *NA*
4. Community Experience: *NA*
5. Activities of Daily Living: *NA*
6. Functional Vocational Assessment: *NA*

Section 9—Graduation Information for Secondary Students

Credential/Diploma Sought: *Local Diploma*

Expected Date of High School Completion: *June 2003*

Section 10—Summary of Selected Recommendations

Classification of the Disability: *Other Health Impaired*

Recommended Placement Sept.–June: *Inclusion*

Extended School Year (ESL) Services? Yes _____ No _*X*_

Recommended Placement, July and August: *None*

Transportation Needs: *None*

415

5.4 continued

Section 11—Reporting Progress to Parents

State manner and frequency in which progress will be reported: *Parents/guardians or student over 18 will be informed of the student's progress toward meeting the academic goals and objectives with the same frequency as students without disabilities using the following criteria:*

> *Textbook tests, quizzes, and standardized tests*
>
> *Review of report card grades*
>
> *Contact with classroom teachers on an ongoing basis*

EXPLANATION OF SECTION 8—COORDINATED SET OF ACTIVITIES LEADING TO LONG-TERM ADULT OUTCOMES

For a student aged 14 or older, the IEP, as a whole, must demonstrate the use of a coordinated set of activities as the means by which the student can achieve the long-term adult outcomes. Beginning at age 14, the focus of activity is on instruction. At age 15 and older, the coordinated set of activities must address instruction, related services, community experiences, and the development of employment or other post-school adult living objectives. If one of these activities is not included in the IEP in a particular year, then the IEP must explain why that activity is not reflected in any part of the student's program. Activities of daily living and functional vocational evaluation activities should also be included when appropriate to the student's needs. The coordinated set of activities, in conjunction with the special education programs and services, should incrementally provide the student with skills and experiences to prepare him or her to attain the long-term adult outcomes.

The coordinated set of activities is:

1. *Instruction*—Educational instruction that will be provided to the student to achieve the stated outcome(s) (e.g., general and/or special education course instruction, occupational education, and advanced placement courses).

2. *Related services*—These are specific related services, such as rehabilitation counseling services, which will support the student in attaining the stated outcome(s).

3. *Employment and other post-school adult living objectives*—Educational services that will be provided to the student to prepare for employment or other post-school activity. Post-school activities will determine what other skills or supports will be necessary for the student to succeed as independently as possible. Examples include participation in a work experience program, information about colleges in which the student has an interest, and travel training.

4. *Community experiences*—Community-based experiences that will be offered, or community resources utilized as part of the student's school program, whether utilized during school hours or after school hours, to achieve the stated outcome(s) (e.g., local employers, public library, local stores).

5. *Activities of Daily Living (ADL) skills (if appropriate)*—ADL skills that are necessary to be worked on to achieve the stated outcome(s) (e.g., dressing, hygiene, self-care skills, self-medication).

6. *Functional vocational assessment (if appropriate)*—If the vocational assessment has not provided enough information to make a vocational program decision, additional assessment activities can be performed to obtain more information about the student's needs, preferences, and interests.

EXPLANATION OF SECTION 9—GRADUATION INFORMATION FOR SECONDARY STUDENTS

Credential/Diploma Sought: Students with disabilities must be afforded the opportunity to earn a local high school diploma, if appropriate. Access to required courses, electives, and tests must be provided. This opportunity must be afforded to students regardless of the placement. Not all students with disabilities will pursue a high school diploma. Some students with disabilities will earn an IEP diploma. IEP diplomas are accepted as a minimum requirement by the armed forces to take the Armed Services Vocational Aptitude Battery and by some colleges to take college entrance examinations. However, all of these examinations have set passing scores. Additionally, each college sets its own admission requirements and, therefore, may or may not accept students with disabilities with IEP diplomas.

Expected Date of High School Completion: Indicate the expected date of high school completion.

Credits Earned to Date: Indicate the number of high school units of credit earned.

EXPLANATION OF SECTION 10—SUMMARY OF SELECTED RECOMMENDATIONS

The summary of selected recommendations is completed after the Committee has reviewed the student's present levels of performance and individual needs and has finalized all other components of the IEP.

Classification: The Committee determines a specific disability category based on the definitions of these categories for school-aged students or preschool students.

Recommended Placement: After the completion of all other components of the student's IEP, the Committee determines the recommended placement. The placement of a student with a disability in a special class, special school, or other removal from the general educational environment should occur only when the nature of the disability is such that the student cannot be educated, even with the use of supplementary aids and services, in the general education setting.

Extended School Year Program/Services: The necessity of a July/August program, and where such services will be made available, may be documented in the Summary of Selected Recommendations for convenience in locating this information.

5.4 continued

Transportation: The IEP must document any special transportation to be provided to and from school and/or extracurricular activities. In determining whether to include transportation on a student's IEP, the Committee must consider how the student's disability affects the student's need for transportation, including determining whether the student's disability prevents the student from using the same transportation provided to nondisabled children, or from getting to school in the same manner as nondisabled children.

EXPLANATION OF SECTION 11—
REPORTING PROGRESS TO PARENTS

The IEP must contain a statement of how parents will be regularly informed of their child's progress, at least as often as parents of a child without disabilities are informed of their child's progress. Specifically, the parents must be informed of their child's progress toward the annual goals and the extent to which this progress is sufficient to achieve the child's goals by the end of the year. A parent must be informed of the student's progress toward the IEP goals at least as often as parents of students without disabilities are informed of their child's progress.

5.5   Related Services Available on the IEP

Related services are school-based services that the child with a disability will be receiving that provide support for him or her and that enhance their educational performance. Examples of related services include but are not limited to:

▪ *In-school individual counseling*—When this service is recommended on an IEP, it usually means that the child would benefit from a more intimate therapeutic situation with emphasis on control, insight, cause-and-effect awareness, special attention, and developing a trusting relationship with an authority figure. Although some children only need individual counseling, others might move from individual to group to try out the insights and experiences learned from the individual experience.

▪ *In-school group counseling*—When this service is recommended on an IEP, it means that the child would benefit from a group situation that emphasizes interpersonal relations, social skills, cooperative play and interaction, interdependence, social delay of gratification, peer feedback, and social connections. The group usually meets once or twice a week; many times it may be combined with individual in-school counseling.

▪ *Resource room*—This service is recommended when the Eligibility Committee feels that the child would benefit from extra academic assistance depending upon the recommendations of the diagnostic evaluation, IEP recommendation, and teacher observation. This assistance might involve remediation, compensation, or survival skills depending upon the age and grade of the child. Most children will be recommended for a minimum of three hours per week (divided as needed) to a maximum of 50 percent of the child's school day.

▪ *Speech/language therapy*—This service is recommended when the Eligibility Committee feels that the child's poor performance is directly related to disabilities in language or speech development. The emphasis with this service might include remediation in expressive or receptive language, articulation, voice disorders, fluency disorders, and so on. These services may be administered in small group or individual settings. This recommendation can also be made in conjunction with some other service, such as a resource room, if indicated.

▪ *Physical therapy and occupational therapy*—The Eligibility Committee usually makes this recommendation when the child is suffering from some physical or motor impairment. Physical therapists usually provide exercise therapy and special devices to improve the total physical functioning and strength of a student with a disability. Generally, occupational therapists will focus more on fine-motor skills such as hand control, using the mouth to chew, and any other factor involved in daily living skills.

▪ *Art therapy*—This recommendation, although not as common as some other services, is usually recommended when the Eligibility Committee feels that the production of art in its various forms would have beneficial qualities for students with disabilities. Major factors involved in this recommendation include the opportunity for the child with disabilities to express creativity, to improve fine-motor skills, and to develop appropriate leisure-time activities.

419

5.5 continued

- *Adaptive physical education*—This service is usually recommended when the Eligibility Committee feels that the general physical development of a child with a disability is impaired or delayed. When these programs are instituted, they tend to have a therapeutic orientation. The teachers performing this service must have special training in the use of specialized equipment to improve muscle development and coordination.

- *Music therapy*—This recommendation may be made by the Eligibility Committee when it feels that music and singing can be used with students with disabilities to prompt the development of various functional behaviors such as motivation and improvement of speech, language, and communication skills.

5.6 Extended School-Year Programs/Services Criteria

Some students may require special education services during the months of July and August to prevent substantial regression. Substantial regression means a student's inability to maintain developmental levels due to a loss of skill or knowledge during the months of July and August of such severity as to require an inordinate period of review at the beginning of the school year to reestablish and maintain IEP goals and objectives mastered at the end of the previous school year. The Committee should consider extended school-year programs for:

- Students whose management needs are determined to be highly intensive, who require a high degree of individualized attention and intervention, and who are placed in special classes.

- Students with severe multiple disabilities whose programs consist primarily of rehabilitation and treatment and who are placed in special classes.

- Students who are recommended for home and hospital instruction, whose special education needs are determined to be highly intensive, who require a high degree of individualized attention and intervention, or who have severe multiple disabilities and require primarily rehabilitation and treatment.

- Students whose needs are so severe that they can be met only in a seven-day residential program.

- Students receiving other special education services who, because of their disabilities, exhibit the need for a special service and/or program provided in a structured learning environment of up to 12 months' duration in order to prevent substantial regression.

The Committee must specifically state the initiation date, frequency, duration, and location of services the student is to receive during July and August. In addition, the IEP must indicate the provider of such services.

An IEP developed for an extended school-year program may differ from the IEP developed for the school-year program. The Eligibility Committee determines the type and amount of services that a student needs for an appropriate extended school-year program. The IEP developed for the extended school-year program should focus on the areas in which the student is expected to experience substantial regression. The Eligibility Committee must determine the least restrictive environment required for the student to benefit from special education services during July and August. Extended school-year programs or services may be provided in a location that differs from the one the student attends during the school year, provided the Eligibility Committee determines that the setting is appropriate for the student to benefit from the special education services and to meet the IEP goals.

5.7 Documentation Required for Supplementary Aids and Services, and Program Modifications or Supports

Supplementary aids and services and/or program modifications or supports means aids, services, and other supports that are provided in general education classes or other education-related settings to enable students with disabilities to be educated with students who do not have disabilities to the maximum extent appropriate in the least restrictive environment. Examples of supplementary aids and services include:

- A note taker
- Written materials in Braille format
- Extra time to move between classes
- Modification of curriculum
- Special seating arrangements

Providing modifications to students with suspected disabilities must be substantiated and documented by evidence within the testing results. Although criteria may vary from district to district, examples that may be used to determine the type of modification recommended are listed below.

A. Flexible Scheduling—This modification is usually applied for students who may have problems in the rate in which they process information, e.g., physical disabilities such as motor or visual impairments. Examples of modifications that fall under this category include:

- Extended timed tests.
- Administration of a test in several sessions during the course of the day.
- Administration of a test in several sessions over several days.

The documentation required to make this recommendation should include evidence of:

1. Slow processing speed, or
2. Slow psycho-motor speed, or
3. Severe anxiety.

B. Flexible Setting—This modification allows students with disabilities to take a test in another setting other than a regular classroom. This may become necessary in cases where a child has health impairments and may be unable to leave home or the hospital, where a child's disability interferes with his/her remaining on task, or where a child is easily distracted. In other cases, a student with a disability may require special lighting or acoustics or a specially equipped room. Examples include:

- Individual administration of a test in a separate location.
- Small group administration of a test in a separate location.
- Provisions for special lighting.
- Provisions for special acoustics.

■ Provision for adaptive or special furniture.

■ Administration of test in a location with minimal distractions.

The documentation required to make this recommendation should include evidence of:

1. Students with serious attentional difficulties, or

2. Students who are easily distracted and have difficulty remaining on task because of processing difficulties, anxiety, etc.

C. Revised Test Format—This modification is utilized by students whose disability may interfere with their ability to take a test using the standard test format, e.g., students with visual or perceptual disabilities who may not be able to read regular-sized print. Suggestions include:

■ Use a large print edition.

■ Increase spacing between items.

■ Reduce the number of items per page.

■ Use a Braille edition.

■ Increase the size of answer bubbles on test answer forms.

■ Rearrange multiple-choice items with answer bubble right next to each choice.

The documentation required to make this recommendation should include evidence of visuo-perceptual processing deficits that would cause difficulty transferring answers onto a machine-scorable booklet or sheet.

D. Revised Test Directions—This modification allows students with certain disabilities a greater chance of understanding directions and thereby successfully completing a test.

■ Ability to have directions read to child.

■ Ability to reread the directions for each page of questions.

■ Ability to simplify the language in the directions.

■ Ability to provide additional examples.

The documentation required to make this recommendation should include evidence of:

1. Students who have documented reading comprehension skills below 25th percentile on standardized tests, or

2. Documented language-processing deficits, or

3. Significant receptive language weaknesses.

E. Use of Aids—Some students with disabilities require the use of aids in order to interpret test items, e.g., hearing-impaired children These may include:

■ Auditory amplification devices.

■ Visual magnification devices.

■ Auditory tape of questions.

5.7 continued

- Masks or markers to maintain the student's place on a page.
- Having questions read to the student.
- Having questions signed to the student.

The documentation required to make the recommendation of *use of a word processor or a scribe* (individual who copies notes for the child) should include evidence of:

1. Documented graphomotor deficits, or

2. Documented written language deficits significantly below current grade level.

The documentation required to make the recommendation of the *opportunity to record answers* in any manner should include evidence of:

1. Documented graphomotor deficits, or

2. Documented written language deficits significantly below current grade level.

The documentation required to make the recommendation of *not being penalized for spelling errors* should show evidence of:

1. Below 25th percentile on standardized tests, or

2. Fifty-percent discrepancy between aptitude and spelling achievement score on standardized tests.

F. Revised Format—Some students with disabilities may be unable to record their responses to test questions on conventional answer forms and as a result may require changes in the test format. These may include:

- Ability to record answers directly in the test booklet.
- Ability to increase the spacing between questions or problems.
- Ability to increase the size of the answer blocks.
- Ability to provide cues (stop sign, arrows) directly on the answer form.

The documentation required to make the above recommendations should show evidence of visuo-perceptual processing deficits that would cause difficulty transferring answers onto a machine-scorable booklet or sheet or with other tasks involving visual discrimination or spatial difficulties.

5.8   Considerations for Making Test-Modification Recommendations

When making test-modification recommendations for a student, remember the following:

- Testing modifications are to give students the same opportunities as their peers. They are not designed to achieve the identical result or give an unfair advantage to students with disabilities.

- Testing modifications should NOT be excessive. They should alter standard administration to the least extent possible.

- Testing modifications may allow a student access to higher-level classes.

- Higher scores are NOT reasons for giving test modifications.

- The only students allowed to have modifications are:

  1. Students with disabilities.

  2. Declassified students (until graduation or before if no longer appropriate).

  3. Students (same as classified) with accommodation plans.

  4. Students who acquire short-term disabilities shortly before the test [time, location, note taker, reader (vision impaired; not comprehension), principal's discretion.] Refer to Eligibility Committee or CST for long-term situations.

- Testing modifications are to be specific.

- Students should have to take state exams and the IEP must indicate why a student is exempted from them if necessary. Only IEP diploma-bound students may be exempted from certain tests.

- It is the building principal's responsibility to ensure that test modifications are implemented correctly.

- Diagnostic evaluations (newly referred students) do not require test modifications. Administration of test modifications is at the discretion of the examiner.

- If a student refuses to utilize a test modification, it should be documented and, if necessary, be eliminated from the IEP.

- The principal, as well as all teachers of appropriate students, should receive information on test modifications.

- Students should not be counseled toward more restrictive career objectives because they have disabilities.

- The general education teacher MUST administer test modifications as described in the IEP.

5.9 Student Eligibility and Criteria for Testing Modifications

Alternate testing techniques are modifications that take into account the individual needs of a child with a disability and as a result modify testing procedures or formats. These modifications attempt to provide these students with equal opportunity to participate in testing situations.

These techniques, which must appear on the student's IEP, provide the opportunity to demonstrate mastery of skills by a student with a disability without being unfairly restricted by the presence of that disability.

STUDENT ELIGIBILITY FOR USE OF TESTING TECHNIQUES

Only students who have been identified as having a disability by the Committee on Special Education normally receive alternate testing techniques. However, there are three other possible avenues that can be taken to provide alternate testing techniques without being classified.

1. The law usually allows the school principal the authority to approve a student's need for testing modification that does not alter the intended purpose of a test for a student who may have a disability, but not severe enough to warrant identification by the Eligibility Committee. An example of this may be a student who has ADD (Attention Deficit Disorder) and as a result may have some mild problems but they do not constitute a severe discrepancy in his or her functioning.

2. In cases of certain tests, e.g., college entrance SAT, two pieces of documentation from outside professionals (not working in the same agency) indicating the need for alternate testing techniques, e.g., untimed tests, may allow the student these privileges even though they have not been identified by the Eligibility Committee.

3. Students who receive transitional services (services are provided to students having been declassified by the Eligibility Committee) are entitled to receive services and/or modifications up to one year after declassification.

CRITERIA FOR ALLOWING USE OF TESTING TECHNIQUES

The Eligibility Committee determines alternate testing techniques for a student identified as having a disability. The Committee takes into account several variables when making this determination:

1. The individual needs of the child as determined by evaluation, observation, background history, and other pertinent information presented at the Eligibility Committee meeting.

2. The necessity for modification in light of the student's past academic and test performance without modifications.

3. The student's potential benefit from the modification.

The Eligibility Committee tries to keep in mind that all students could benefit from alternate testing techniques and, as a result, a recommendation based just on potential to enhance performance may be inappropriate. The need for modifications must be substantiated in the evaluation results.

5.10 Special Education Teacher's Role and Responsibilities for Implementation of Alternate Testing Techniques

The special education teacher plays a crucial role in the implementation of alternate testing techniques. This is accomplished in the following ways:

1. A special education evaluator provides a clear understanding of a child's strength and weakness areas, learning style, and the effects of the child's disability upon academic performance. With this information in hand, the special education teacher can analyze the need for specific modifications that can be substantiated by the results of the evaluation.

2. A special education teacher in a self-contained special education classroom comes in direct contact with the student in classroom instruction. This experience provides a strong basis for recommending specific changes or additions to the modifications on a student's IEP.

3. The special education teacher on the Eligibility Committee provides background experience that can assist the committee in recommending appropriate test modifications that may become part of an initial referral IEP, change in an IEP during an annual review, or modification of alternate testing techniques as the result of a report from an outside agency.

4. The special education teacher can also assist the parent of a special education student in understanding alternate testing techniques and available options.

5. The special education teacher may serve as a consultant to teachers, parents, and administrators and offer advice on testing modifications to students.

6. The special education teacher may monitor the implementation of assigned modifications for a particular student to ensure that the student's rights are being respected.

PART 6

Eligibility Committee

Some material in this section is adapted from *Assessment in Special Education: A Practical Approach* by Roger Pierangelo and George A. Giuliani, published by Allyn and Bacon, Boston MA. Copyright © 2002 by Pearson Education. Reprinted by permission of the publisher.

6.1 Responsibilities of the Eligibility Committee

1. Following appropriate procedures and taking appropriate action on any child referred as having a suspected disability.

2. Determining the suitable classification for a child with a suspected disability.

3. Reviewing, at least annually, the status of each child with a disability residing within the district.

4. Evaluating the adequacy of programs, services, and facilities for the children with disabilities in the district.

5. Reviewing and evaluating all relevant information that may appear for each student with a disability.

6. Maintaining ongoing communication in writing to parents with regard to planning, modifying, changing, reviewing, placing, or evaluating the program, classification, or educational plan for a child with a disability.

7. Advising the Board of Education as to the status and recommendations for all children with disabilities in the district.

8. Determining the least restrictive educational setting for any child having been classified as having a disability.

6.2 Eligibility Committee Presentation Checklist

INITIAL REFERRAL

REQUIRED FORMS
- Initial Referral to Eligibility Committee from School Staff, or
- Initial Referral to Eligibility Committee from Parent/Guardian, or
- Parent Consent for Evaluation

EVALUATIONS
- Medical Report
- Classroom Observation
- Psychological Report
- Educational Report
- Speech/Language Report
- Vocational (Secondary Level Only)
- Other (e.g., Occupational Therapist, Physical Therapist, ESL, Reading)—Specify

GUIDANCE MATERIALS
- Child's Schedule
- Transcript of Past Grades
- Latest Report Card
- Teachers' Reports

OTHER
- Social Developmental History Form
- Discipline Information
- Pupil Personnel Team-related Documents (e.g., minutes)
- Standardized Achievement Test Scores
- Report Cards
- Needs (Levels of Development: Social, Physical, Academic, Management)
- Recommended Goals and Objectives (Draft)
- Attendance Records
- Other—Specify

SPECIAL MEETING
- Name of Current/Contact Teacher
- Special Meeting Referral Form
- Current Teacher/s Report
- Recommended Goals and Objectives
- New Evaluations If Completed
- Other Documents—Specify

(continued)

ANNUAL REVIEW

- Prep Sheet
- Current IEP
- Evaluations Completed—Specify
- Needs (e.g., Social, Physical, etc.)
- Recommended Goals/Objectives
- Other Documents—Specify

TRIENNIAL EVALUATION DOCUMENTS

- Parent Notice of Triennial
- Evaluation Form
- Psychological
- Educational
- Speech/Language
- Medical Report
- Social History Update
- Transcript of Grades
- Child's Schedule
- Recent Report Cards
- Teacher Reports
- Other—Specify

Recommended Eligibility Committee Participants:

Case Manager:

Date:

6.3   Annual Review Procedures

Parent Notice: Parents will be notified of date, time, and location of meeting by the Pupil Personnel Office five school days prior to the meeting.

Annual Review Eligibility Committee Membership: The following school/community personnel will comprise the Annual Review Committee: Director of Pupil Personnel Services, Parent, Special Education Teacher, Psychologist, and optional members as needed: Social Worker, Guidance Counselor, Speech Therapist.

Sequence of Discussion:

- Review of current IEP.
- Evaluation of progress (demonstration based on recent tests, grades, observations, and so on).
- Identification of goals and objectives for the upcoming year.
- Determination of the continuation of the child's classification (if a triennial year).
- Determination of program for upcoming year (type of instructional program, Resource Room, self-contained classes, etc.).
- Location of program.
- Related services required for upcoming year (e.g., counseling, speech, etc.).
- Determination of related service provider.
- Testing modifications for upcoming year.

Secondary Students: In addition to the above sequence of discussion, the following areas should be discussed when the annual review involves a student at the secondary level:

- Appropriateness of having the student in attendance at the meeting.
- Student's credits.
- Diploma requirements, including sequences.
- Competency test requirements (if your state requires these tests).
- Development of transitional IEP for any student 15 years or older.

Transportation: The child's transportation needs must be determined by the Annual Review Committee. Any special considerations should be noted (e.g., matrons, wheelchair, two-way radio) as well as necessary information relating to disabilities that would affect the child if an accident occurred (e.g., child has no speech, child is a bleeder). This category should be flagged with a special alert on the necessary forms.

Adaptive Devices/Special Needs: Any device that is required by the child should be discussed and noted.

Levels of Development: The child's academic, social, physical, and management goal areas need to be discussed for the coming year.

6.4 Triennial Review Procedures

One of the responsibilities for the special education teacher may be involvement in the triennial evaluation (a complete and updated evaluation required every three years for all children classified as having a disability by the Committee on Special Education). This is a very important phase of the special education process because it reviews the factors that accounted for the child's classification and placement.

There are several phases to the triennial evaluation that may involve staff members from a variety of disciplines. The objectives for the special education teacher in the triennial evaluation include the following:

1. To retest the child's achievement skill areas.

2. To retest the child's perceptual skill areas.

3. To analyze the results and compare the similarities in patterns to past evaluation results.

4. To write a detailed and comprehensive updated report of the findings that will be shared with the Committee on Special Education as well as the staff and parents.

5. To participate in the annual review meeting (a required yearly meeting for all classified students at which time the child's classification and educational placement are reviewed) and discuss the results in order to help the Committee on Special Education make a decision on continuation of classification and services or declassification (an option by the Eligibility Committee when the classified child no longer requires special education services to maintain success in mainstream classes).

6. To share the results with parents.

7. To help interpret and analyze achievement and perceptual test results that may be submitted from outside agencies or professionals pertinent to the triennial evaluation of a specific child. This can occur if the parent chooses an independent evaluation.

It should be noted that a new release for testing involving a triennial evaluation is not required by law. The school may proceed with this process without a new release, but must inform the parents that the process will be taking place.

6.5   Triennial Review—Required Materials

Evaluations

- New psychological evaluation(s)
- New educational evaluation
- New speech and language evaluation—if applicable
- Outside reports—if applicable
- Medical report—if applicable

Academic data

- Most recent report card
- Classroom teacher's reports
- Student schedule

Developmental data

- New social and developmental history form

Other required information and procedures

- Parent letter of triennial review
- Medical update
- Classroom observation

6.6   Medical Form for the Eligibility Committee

To be completed by the Nurse-Teacher and included in the Eligibility Committee Packet.

Date: _____

Student's Name: _____ Grade _____

Address: _____

_____ State _____ Zip_____

Date of last medical examination _____

Name and address of physician _____

_____

_____

Medical findings (attach copy if pertinent) _____

_____

Last vision exam _____ Results _____

Last hearing exam _____ Results _____

Speech _____

Information that might have implications in determining the outcome of this case:

6.7 Agreement to Withdraw Eligibility Committee Referral

There will be times when the parent and school agree that the evaluation and findings do not seem to substantiate the suspected disability that was originally considered. When this occurs, the school and parent must meet and discuss other methods that will be used to remediate the problem/s. At the time of the meeting, an Agreement to Withdraw the Eligibility Committee Referral form must be filled out and forwarded to the principal and then to the Eligibility Committee chairperson. This will officially withdraw the original referral and stop the Eligibility Committee process.

There are usually time requirements and constraints with this procedure, so check with your district and state policies.

Agreement to Withdraw Eligibility Committee Referral

INITIAL CONFERENCE

Student Name _____ Date of Agreement _____

Date of Birth _____ Date of Current Referral _____

Current Program _____ Name of Referring Party _____

Position of Referring Party _____

Persons Present at Conference _____

The following method(s) will be used to attempt to resolve _____ identified learning difficulties: (attach additional sheets, as needed)

If necessary, a follow-up conference to review the student's progress will be held on

_____

We agree to the above conditions. The referral is hereby withdrawn.

Referring Party Signature _____ Date _____

Parent/Guardian Signature _____ Date _____

CC: Student's Cumulative Educational Record
    Parent/Guardian
    Referring Party

6.8 Eligibility Committee Presentation by the Special Education Teacher as Educational Evaluator

If your role on the Committee has resulted from your educational and perceptual evaluation of the child, then you need to keep the following in mind:

1. Prior to the meeting, you should meet with the parents and go over your results. Follow the procedures outlined in List 4.4, How to Report Test Results to Parents.

2. Make sure that you have your report complete and typed at least seven to ten days prior to the Eligibility Committee meeting. In some districts, the Eligibility Committee requires that the entire packet be forwarded a week in advance.

3. Prior to the meeting, outline the important points of the report that you wish to make. Do not go through the report at the Eligibility Committee meeting looking for the issues that you feel need to be discussed. Preparation will make you look more professional.

4. Make sure you report strengths as well as weaknesses.

5. Even though everyone should have copies of your report in front of them, the length of the report may make it impossible for them to filter out the crucial sections in the time allotted for the meeting. Therefore, you may want to develop a one-page summary sheet that clearly outlines what you will be presenting. This would be handed out as you begin your presentation.

6. Remember that this is not a parent conference to review the entire report. You should have done that earlier, so keep it brief and highlight the important issues. There are several individuals who may need to report results or speak and the Eligibility Committee may have several meetings that day.

7. If you feel that the nature of the case may require more time than that normally set aside by the Eligibility Committee for a review, then call the chairperson and make a request for a longer meeting time. It is very uncomfortable when crucial meetings have to be ended because of time constraints.

8. Be prepared to be questioned about your findings or some aspect of the report by a parent, committee member, lawyer (sometimes brought by the parent), or other attendee. Even though this may not happen, you should be ready to answer without being defensive or anxious. Carefully look over your report and be prepared.

6.9 Eligibility Committee Presentation by the Special Education Teacher as Classroom Teacher

There may be times when you will be asked as the child's classroom teacher to attend an Eligibility Committee meeting either for a review of classification, placement, annual review, change in an IEP, or special meeting requested by the parent. When this occurs, keep the following in mind:

1. The first thing you need to do when you receive a request for your participation at an Eligibility Committee meeting is to find out the reason for the meeting. The material required may vary, but your preparation prior to the meeting is crucial. If the meeting was called by the parents, you may want to have them in for a conference to discuss their concerns.

2. Once you know why the meeting will be held, organize yourself so that you will have information in front of you in the following areas:

   - The child's present academic levels in reading, math, spelling, and writing. These may be available as a result of recent individual or group achievement tests, informal evaluations that you may have administered, observation (although try to be more objective), class tests, etc. Determine grade levels, if possible, and where the child falls in comparison to others in the class.

   - The child's present pattern of classroom behavior. Write this up in behavioral terms (factual, observable, and descriptive notes of behavior that do not include analysis or judgment).

   - The child's present levels of social interaction and social skills.

   - The child's interest areas and areas of strength.

   - The child's present schedule.

   - Samples of the child's work.

   - Outline of parent conferences, phone conversations, or meetings and the purpose and outcome of each. These notes should be kept on an ongoing basis.

   - Your opinion as to whether the child is benefiting from the present placement.

   - Any physical limitations noted and their implication on the learning process.

   - Your opinion of the child's self-esteem.

   - Any pertinent comments made by the child that may have an impact on his or her present situation.

3. You should be well prepared to answer any questions with the above information at hand. When it is your turn to present, do it in an organized manner. Here, too, you may want to provide the participants with an outline of what you will be covering.

4. Try not to be defensive even if the reason for the meeting is the parent's concern over the child's placement in your class, the work load, etc. Try to listen carefully to what the parent is really asking for. It may not be as big of a problem as you think. Try to be solution-oriented, even if the parent is blame-oriented.

6.10   Eligibility Committee Presentation by the Special Education Teacher as Member of the Eligibility Committee

There are times when the special education teacher will be asked to sit on the Eligibility Committee to review a case even though the teacher does not know the child or has not evaluated him or her. The participation of the special education teacher in this situation is for his or her expertise in reviewing academic and perceptual material that may be presented. This material may come from other evaluators within the district, or from an outside agency or professional. If your role involves this aspect, then keep the following in mind:

1. Try to get a copy of the reports prior to the meeting. In some districts, this is the procedure. If not, request it so that you can review the findings and make notes.

2. Your role here is to review and analyze the test results and offer concrete and practical suggestions to the Eligibility Committee in the following ways:

   ▪ Indications of areas of strength and weakness.

   ▪ Level of severity of the problem—mild, moderate, or severe.

   ▪ Educational implications in determining least restrictive placement.

   ▪ Whether or not the recommendations coincide with the test result findings. For example, in some cases, outside agencies or professionals will recommend a resource room even though the child's scores do not reflect a disability.

   ▪ Whether or not the new findings support or disagree with past scores. For this, you should do some research into the child's historical academic patterns by reviewing any prior reports, achievement test scores, report card grades, etc.

   ▪ Whether or not the findings require modifications and which ones they should be, e.g., revised test format, flexible scheduling.

3. Be prepared. Do not wait until the last minute to review reports. It will look more professional if you come with notes, questions, and suggestions.

6.11 Evaluations that May Be Required for Eligibility Committee Presentations

Psychological Evaluation

A full psychological evaluation—including all identifying data, reason for referral, background and developmental history, prior testing results, observations, tests administered, test results (including a breakdown of scaled scores), conclusions, and recommendations—is required. This evaluation must be conducted within one year of the Eligibility Committee meeting. It may also be helpful to include any prior evaluations done over the years.

Educational Evaluation

A psychoeducational evaluation—including identifying data, reason for referral, academic history, prior testing results, observations, tests administered, test results, conclusions, and recommendations—is required. This report should identify achievement strengths and weaknesses and perceptual strengths and weaknesses.

Speech/Language Evaluation

A speech/language evaluation—including identifying data, reason for referral, observations, tests administered, test results, conclusions, and recommendations—should be included, if applicable. A description of the severity of the language deficit should also be included and, if possible, the prognosis.

Reading Teacher's Report

If indicated, a full reading evaluation—including identifying data, reason for referral, observations, prior standardized reading test percentiles, tests administered, test results, conclusions, and recommendations—should be included. A description of the severity of the deficit, which outlines the specific areas in need of remediation, should also be included.

Vocational Evaluation-Aptitude Test Results—Middle School and High School Only (e.g., DAT)

A copy of the child's Differential Aptitude Test results or other measures of vocational aptitude should be included, if applicable.

Outside Reports

From time to time, parents will have a variety of reports from outside agencies, e.g., medical, neurological, psychological, audiological, visual training, etc. These reports should be included only when they are relevant to the possible disability. If outside reports are to be used in lieu of the district's own evaluations, they should be fairly recent, i.e., within the past 6 months to 1 year.

Assessments Related to the Suspected Disability as Required

These measures may include the following areas: communication skills, motor abilities, hearing, vision, gross motor abilities, fine motor abilities, physical therapist's evaluation, occupational therapist's evaluation, adaptive physical education evaluation, i.e., Bruininks-Oseretsky.

441

6.12   Other Information and Procedures Required for Eligibility Committee Presentations

Written Consent for Evaluation

A copy of this signed form by the parents/guardians of the child should be included in the packet so that the Committee has a record of this consent as well as an indication of the 30-day time-limit requirement.

Draft of Recommended Objectives and Goals

Appropriate members of the Pupil Personnel Team (PPT) should develop a draft of initial goals and objectives. These goals and objectives will be used in the development of the Individualized Education Plan (IEP) at the time of the Eligibility Committee meeting. These goals and objectives may be modified at the time of the meeting. The form, specific goals and objectives from which to choose, and other factors may differ from district to district.

Some districts may develop this form at the time of the meeting and may not require a prior draft. However, it is recommended that, if this is the case, prepare yourself anyway with your own recommended goals and objectives so that you can contribute to the IEP at the time of the meeting.

Statement of Least Restrictive Environment

If a PPT is recommending additional services under a classifying condition, state the reasons why additional services or less restrictive environment would be necessary. This statement is also very important if the PPT feels that the child's needs may be better served in an out-of-district placement. While the final decision for placement is up to the Eligibility Committee, the school still needs to substantiate its recommendation.

Parent Given Rights Booklet Prior to Eligibility Committee Meeting

A parent must be given a copy of the state booklet on parents' rights prior to the Eligibility Committee meeting. This will give parents the opportunity to become familiar with the procedure and allow them time to develop any questions that they might have.

Agreement to Withdraw Eligibility Committee Referral

There will be times when the parent and school agree that the evaluation and findings do not seem to substantiate the suspected disability that was originally considered. When this occurs, the school and parent must meet and discuss other methods that will be used to remediate the problem/s. At the time of the meeting, an Agreement to Withdraw the Eligibility Committee Referral form must be filled out and forwarded to the principal and then to the Eligibility Committee chairperson. This will officially withdraw the original referral and stop the Eligibility Committee process. (See List 6.7.)

There are usually time requirements and constraints with this procedure, so check with your district and state policies.

6.13 Procedures for Changing a Student's Classification or Placement

On the Part of the Parent: There may be times when a parent feels that his or her child's present classification or placement needs to be reviewed and possibly changed. When this occurs, *the parent* should follow specific procedures:

1. Although a request for a change of classification or placement can always be made by a parent, there should be some basis for such a request. These may include lack of growth on the part of the child, new diagnostic evaluations indicating another possible cause for the disability, distance from the house if an out-of-district placement, some danger to the child's safety either in transit or at the site, disagreements with the school's educational program, lack of services, and so on.

2. Once you feel that such a meeting is necessary, you should document your reasons carefully. The presentation to the Committee is crucial, especially when you keep in mind that other professionals with a great deal of documentation will be present at the same meeting. Try to keep anecdotal records, papers, work samples, incident reports, calls to administration asking for assistance, and any other records that will present a basis for your request.

3. Once you have developed a packet of information, call the chairperson of the Eligibility Committee and request a special meeting to discuss your concerns about your child's classification or placement.

4. The chairperson may ask you some questions over the phone; if this occurs, a preliminary meeting with him or her is recommended. Many times, a compromise or solution may be obtained by such a meeting. If this does not happen, ask for a meeting of the full Committee. Keep in mind that even if the chairperson agrees with you, any change in an IEP requires a full meeting of the Eligibility Committee.

5. If the Eligibility Committee does not agree with your request, you always have the option of asking for an impartial hearing, which is part of your due process rights. At this meeting, an impartial officer—not an employee of the district—will hear both sides and offer a recommendation, usually within 10 days.

On the Part of the School: There will be times when the school feels that a child's classification or placement needs to be changed. When this occurs, *the school* should follow certain procedures:

1. The reasons for such a request may result from an improvement in a child's performance over a long period of time, possibly indicating declassification, no longer requiring supportive services to maintain adequate school performance, severe difficulties with the present placement and a need for a more restrictive setting, the development of a secondary disability requiring a change to multiply disabled, inability to provide appropriate supportive services within the present placement, and so on.

6.13 continued

2. Once the school feels that such a recommendation is necessary, it should contact the chairperson of the Eligibility Committee and request a special meeting for the purposes of classification or placement review. This usually just requires filling out the necessary form.

3. The school should then call in the parent/s and discuss their concerns and request for a review by the Eligibility Committee. Hopefully, the parents have been involved along the way and such a request will not come as a total surprise.

4. The school should then put together a packet of information including, but not limited to, teacher's comments, work samples, grades, any testing updates, outside evaluations, and so on. This packet should then be sent to the Eligibility Committee with a cover letter, indicating the request for such a meeting and the school's position.

5. The chairperson will then schedule a full meeting of the Eligibility Committee, which is required for any possible change in an IEP.

6. At the meeting, the school should make a very thorough presentation for any change in classification and placement, as this type of change constitutes a very serious modification that may have implications.

7. If the school is recommending declassification, the child will still be able to receive transitional supportive services for one year. The school should be sure that such a recommendation is made on the basis of a historical pattern of success and not on a short-term change. Declassifying and then having to reclassify a student can be traumatic to the student.

8. If the review is based upon the school's feeling that a more therapeutic setting is required, then documentation should indicate what has been tried and why the school feels that the present placement is unsuitable.

9. If the parent disagrees, then the school also has the right to ask for an impartial hearing.

PART 7

Classroom Instruction Techniques for Children with Disabilities and Special Needs

7.1   Mainstreaming Checklist

1. _____The child has become familiar with the rules and routines of the regular class in which he or she will be mainstreamed.

2. _____The student's Individualized Education Plan objectives and modifications have been discussed with the mainstreamed teacher.

3. _____The child has indicated a positive desire to participate in a regular class environment.

4. _____The child has been coached on how to deal with possible reactions and situations presented by other students, both positive and negative.

5. _____The child is capable of remaining focused for appropriate periods of time while in the regular classroom.

6. _____The mainstreamed classroom teacher has been educated on the special needs of the child with disabilities.

7. _____The mainstreamed teacher has been given the proper instruction on the use and purpose of any devices or apparatus used by the student.

8. _____The mainstreamed teacher has been apprised of the student's skill levels.

9. _____The mainstreamed teacher has been apprised of the child's learning style.

10. _____The mainstreamed teacher has been apprised of the child's strength areas and limitations.

11. _____The mainstreamed teacher has been informed of the supportive services provided to the student.

12. _____The mainstreamed teacher has prepared his or her class for the incoming student.

13. _____The mainstreamed teacher has been assigned a specific special service staff member to contact in case of some difficulty.

14. _____The mainstreamed teacher has been given the proper management skills that might be required in dealing with the child while in the mainstreamed class.

15. _____The students in the mainstreamed class have been educated on handicapping conditions and the reasons for mainstreaming.

16. _____The child's parents have met the mainstreamed teacher.

17. _____The child's parents have been involved in the planning of their child's mainstreaming experience.

18. _____The child's parents have been given assistance on parenting techniques that will encourage the child's progress and increase the chances for the success of the mainstreaming experience.

19. _____A member of the mainstreaming team has presented the concept of mainstreaming, its purpose, and what is gained at a PTA meeting for parents of non-disabled children.

20. _____The administrator has been informed of the mainstreaming procedure for this particular child.

7.2   Alternate Learning Activities

audiotapes
brainstorming
chalkboards
community study
debates
discovery
displays
drill and practice
field trips/research
films
flannel boards
games
homework assignments
independent study
investigation/reporting
large group/small group instruction
listening
models
panel discussions
programmed materials
question and answer
real objects
review
simulation
speaking
supervised study
television
verbal illustrations
visual illustrations
writing

bulletin boards
buzz groups
committees
computers
demonstrations
discussions
dramatizations
exhibits
film loops
filmstrips
flip charts
graphics
illustrated talk
information sheets
laboratory work
library research
listing and diagramming
oral recitations
problem solving
projects
reading out loud
resource persons
role-playing
slides
step-by-step procedure panels
team teaching
transparencies
videotapes
work-study

7.3   Key Concepts in Behavior Modification

1. *Baseline data:* A starting point involving frequency and duration in determining a child's behavior change.

2. *Behavior modification:* Classroom management or consequence management.

3. *Continuous Fixed Ratio schedule (CFR):* Reinforcement where every response is reinforced.

4. *Contracting:* A two-way agreement between the student and the teacher.

5. *Differential reinforcement:* Involves two or more different responses, whereby one behavior is reinforced and the other is extinguished.

6. *Discrimination training:* Involves a single behavior that is reinforced in the presence of one stimulus and is extinguished in the presence of other stimuli.

7. *Extinction:* Occurs when a reinforcing event is withdrawn and the behavior that it followed decreases.

8. *Fixed Interval schedule (FI):* Reinforcement follows the first behavior to occur after a fixed period of time has elapsed.

9. *Fixed Ratio schedule (FR):* Reinforcement follows a fixed number of responses.

10. *Fixed schedule:* Reinforcement occurs at a regular interval or after a set number of responses.

11. *Generalization:* The occurrence of a response learned through discrimination training in the presence of a novel or unknown stimulus.

12. *Interval schedule:* Delivers reinforcement after a specified amount of time has elapsed, rather than after a particular number of behaviors.

13. *Modeling:* The use of verbal instructions or initiation to teach a child a new behavior.

14. *Negative reinforcement:* A reinforcement procedure in which something aversive or negative is added to the environment.

15. *Positive reinforcement:* A reinforcement procedure in which something positive or pleasant is added to the environment.

16. *Primary reinforcer:* Some tangible or physical object, such as food or money.

17. *Ratio schedule:* Reinforcement that occurs after a particular number of behaviors.

18. *Reinforcer:* Any event that follows a behavior and that increases the frequency or duration of the behavior and/or increases the chances that the behavior will reoccur.

19. *Secondary reinforcer:* Some social reinforcer that often gains its power from being associated with a primary reinforcer, such as receiving an "A," verbal praise, and so on.

20. *Shaping:* The differential reinforcement of successive approximations of a behavior.

21. *Target behavior:* The behavior identified as needing change.

22. *Token economies:* Settings where the children receive tokens with which they can later buy tangible items or privileges.

23. *Variable Ratio schedule (VR):* Reinforcement that follows an average number of responses.

24. *Variable schedule:* Reinforcement that occurs at irregular intervals or after varying numbers of responses.

7.4 Working with the Child with Learning Disabilities in the Classroom

From time to time, most classroom teachers will come in contact with a child who has been diagnosed as learning disabled. When this occurs, the teacher may be concerned with his or her lack of understanding on how to deal with this child in the classroom. Many times, the teacher may not have the available resources or individuals at hand who can offer practical suggestions and techniques.

There is no doubt that most teachers, given the right preparation, material, and techniques, would be happy to become involved with such a student. However, without these factors, many teachers may feel inadequate and may not want to do anything that might aggravate the situation.

The teacher should be aware that not all techniques would work with all students, but as many of them as possible should be tried. These techniques should create a better learning environment for children with learning disabilities.

Make Adjustments in the Type, Difficulty, Amount, and Sequence of Materials Required

1. Give shorter, but more frequent assignments.

2. Shorten the length of the assignments to ensure a sense of success.

3. Copy chapters of textbooks so that the child can use a highlighter pen to underline important facts.

4. Make sure the child's desk is free from all unnecessary materials.

5. Correct the student's work as soon as possible to allow for immediate gratification and feedback.

6. Allow the student several alternatives in both obtaining and reporting information—tapes, interviews, and so on.

7. Break assignments into smaller units. Allow the child to do five problems or five sentences at a time, so that he or she can feel success, receive immediate feedback, and direct his or her energy to more manageable tasks.

8. Hold frequent, even if short, conferences with the child to allow for questions, sources of confusion, sense of connection, and avoidance of isolation that often occurs if the work is too difficult.

Adjust Space, Work Time, and Grouping

1. Permit the child to work in a quiet corner or a study carrel when requested or necessary. This should not be all the time, as isolation may have negative consequences. This technique depends on the specific learning style of the child who may be less distracted by working under these conditions.

2. At first, you may want to place the child closer to you for more immediate feedback.

3. Try to separate the child from other students who may be distracting.

4. Alternate quiet and active times to maintain levels of interest and motivation.

5. Make up a work contract with specific times and assignments so that the child has a structured idea of his or her responsibilities.

6. Keep work periods short and gradually lengthen them as the student begins to cope.

7. Try to match the student with a peer helper to help with understanding assignments, reading important directions, drilling him or her orally, summarizing important textbook passages, and working on long-range assignments.

Consider Adjusting Presentation and Evaluation Modes

Some students with learning disabilities learn better by seeing (visual learners), some by listening (auditory learners), some by feeling (tactile learners), and some by a combination of approaches. You should make adjustments to determine the best functional system of learning for the child. This will vary from child to child and is usually included in the child's evaluation.

For *auditory learners*, offer adjustments in the mode of presentation by use of the following techniques:

1. Give verbal as well as written directions to assignments.

2. Place assignment directions on tape so that students can replay them when they need.

3. Give students oral rather than written tests.

4. Have students drill on important information by using a tape recorder, i.e., reciting information into the recorder and playing it back.

5. Have students drill aloud to themselves or to other students.

6. Have children close their eyes to try and hear words or information.

For *visual learners*, offer adjustment in the mode of presentation with some of these techniques:

1. Have students use flashcards printed in bold bright colors.

2. Let students close their eyes and try to visualize words or information in their heads, to see things in their minds.

3. Provide visual clues on the chalkboard for all verbal directions.

4. Encourage students to write down notes and memos to themselves concerning important words, concepts, and ideas.

7.5 Working with Children with Emotional Disabilities in the Classroom

Although many problem behaviors may be exhibited by the child with an emotional disabilities, you should try to focus on one target pattern at a time. Patience, fairness, willingness to confront inappropriate behaviors, a sense of conviction in maintaining boundaries, and a fair sense of play in establishing consequences are all aspects required by you in these situations.

Manage Problems of Attendance and Tardiness

- Reward the child for being on time. This reward can be extra free time, a token (if a token economy is being used), a note home, a verbal compliment, and so on.

- Work with the parent on rewarding on-time behavior.

- Plan a special activity in the morning.

- Use a chart to visually project the pattern of punctuality and lateness for the child. This reduces the child's level of denial and may make the child more aware of his or her behavior.

- Encourage and assist the child to start a club in his or her area of greatest interest and make participation contingent upon his or her positive pattern of attendance.

- Use a point system for on-time attendance. These points may be later turned in for class privileges.

- Set up a buddy system if the child walks to school to encourage on-time behavior.

- Set up a nightly contract for the child listing all the things he or she needs to do to make the morning easier to manage. Have the parent sign it, and reward the child when he or she brings it in.

Handle Challenges to Authority, Inappropriate Verbalizations, and Outbursts

- Arrange a timeout area in the classroom. In this case, the amount of time spent in the area is not as significant as the fact that you are able to begin the consequence and end it. Therefore, make the timeout period something you can control.

- Structure a time where the child is allowed to speak to you freely without an audience around. In this way, the child will have an opportunity to speak his or her concerns rather than act them out. It will also allow you to deflect any confrontations to that specific time.

- Approach the child as often as possible and ask him or her if there is anything bothering him or her that the child would like to speak about. Offering the opportunity, even if the child refuses, may reduce the need for "spotlight" behaviors in front of the class.

- Offer an emotional vocabulary so that the child is more able to label feelings. Tension is expressed either verbally or behaviorally. Providing the student with the proper labels may reduce frustration.

- Move the student away from those who might set her or him off.

- Preempt his or her behavior by waiting outside before class and telling the child in private what you expect during class. Also make him or her aware of the rewards and consequences of his or her actions.

- Offer other options and indicate that any inappropriateness is the child's decision. Making the child aware that behavior is his or her responsibility allows the child to realize that not doing something inappropriate is also in his or her control.

- Establish clear classroom rules stating rewards and consequences.

- Praise the student for complying with rules and carrying out directions without verbal resistance.

Deal with Incomplete Class Work

- Work out a contract with the child where he or she can determine the rewards for completion.

- Give shorter but more frequent assignments.

- Do not force the child to write if handwriting is beyond correction. Compensate with a word processor or typewriter.

- Correct assignments as soon as possible and hand them back for immediate gratification.

- Reward the student for handing in neat, completed, and timely assignments.

- Help the student become organized by keeping very little in his or her desk, using a bound book for writing rather than a looseleaf where pages can fall out and add to disorganization, using a large folder for the child to keep work in, and so on.

- Have students mark their own work.

- Be very specific on what you mean by "neat," "organized," and so on. Abstract labels have different meanings to different people. Instead, say "Please be neat and by neat I mean . . . ."

Handle the Child's Difficulty in Remaining Seated

- Try to determine a pattern when the child gets up out of his or her seat. Once this is determined, you can arrange to have him or her run an errand, come up to your desk, and so on. In this way you are channeling the tension and remaining in control.

- Use an external control, such as an egg timer, so that the child has an anchor to control his or her behavior.

- Praise other students or hand out rewards to them for remaining in their seats and following the rules.

- Give the child a written copy of the rules that will result in reward or positive feedback. Also give him or her a list of the behaviors that will lead to consequences.

- Close proximity to the child will assist him or her in staying in his or her seat. Seat the child close to your desk or stand near him or her during a lesson.

7.5 continued

Help the Child Develop Social Relationships

▦ Role-play with another student during private time so that the child can get feedback from a peer.

▦ Provide the child with a "toolbox" of responses and options for typical social situations.

▦ Speak with the school psychologist about including the child in a group.

▦ Arrange for a peer to guide him or her through social situations. The child may be more willing to model peer behavior.

▦ Start the child in a small group activity with only one other child. Slowly increase the size of the group as the child becomes more comfortable.

▦ Arrange for goal-oriented projects where students must work together to accomplish a task. At first, limit this to the student and one other child.

▦ Have the child and a responsible peer organize team activities or group projects. Some children rise to the occasion when placed in a leadership role.

▦ Praise the student as often as is realistic when he or she is not exhibiting aggressive or inappropriate social behavior.

Help the Child Follow Directions and Pay Attention

▦ Use a cue before giving the child directions or important information.

▦ Give one direction at a time and make it as simple as possible.

▦ Have the child chart his or her own patterns of behavior in relation to attention and direction.

▦ Physical proximity may assist the child in focusing on your directions.

▦ Praise the student when he or she follows directions or pays attention. However, be aware that some students with emotional disabilities have a hard time accepting praise, especially in front of a group. In such a case, give the praise in private.

▦ Provide optional work areas that may have less distraction.

▦ Randomly question the child and try to have her or him participate as often as possible to increase her or his interest in the lesson.

▦ Make sure the materials being presented are compatible with the child's learning levels. In this way you can avoid frustration that is also a cause of inattention.

▦ Use a variety of visual and auditory techniques—e.g., overhead projector, tape recorder, or computer—to enhance the lesson and stimulate attention.

7.6 Working with the Child with Developmental Disabilities in the Classroom

A student can be defined as having a developmental disability if he or she exhibits certain learning, social, and behavior patterns to a marked extent and over a prolonged period of time. Such patterns may include:

- A consistently sub-average intellectual level.
- Impaired adaptive functioning in such areas as social skills, communication, and daily living skills.
- Consistently slow rate of learning. As a result, the level of development resembles that of a younger child.
- Delays in most areas of development.

Some common characteristics of a mild developmental disability that you may observe over a period of time include:

- Academic underachievement
- Difficulty with abstract concepts
- Difficulty generalizing learned concepts to new situations
- Social isolation or withdrawal
- Poor social relationships
- Anxiety and worries; excessive fears and phobias
- Easily frustrated even when confronted with a simple task
- Resistance to change
- Short attention span

Students who have mild developmental disabilities learn in the same way as other students. However, adaptations and a variety of techniques need to be utilized. Consequently, certain behaviors should be targeted as priorities when dealing with children with developmental disabilities in the classroom. These target areas include:

- Functional academics
- General work habits
- Career awareness

Although the child with developmental disabilities may exhibit difficulties in many or all of these areas, you should try to focus on one area at a time. Patience, fairness, nurturing, humor, and a sense of conviction in maintaining boundaries are all qualities required by you in these situations.

7.6 continued

STRATEGIES FOR HELPING THE CHILD ATTAIN FUNCTIONAL ACADEMICS

General

▨ Design practice activities in any basic skill that may relate to the child's daily life problems.

▨ Provide materials that are commensurate with the child's skill levels.

▨ Provide activities that will reinforce independent work. If the activity is too hard, the child may become too dependent on teacher supervision.

Reading

▨ Provide activities that focus on reading for information and leisure.

▨ Provide activities that require the child to become more aware of his or her surrounding environment. Having the child list the names of all food stores or all hospitals in the community will increase his or her familiarity with the surrounding environment.

▨ Have the child collect food labels and compare the differences.

▨ Allow the child to look up the names of the other children's families in the phone book. Use the smaller local guide for this activity.

▨ Develop activities that will allow the child to become familiar with menus, bus and train schedules, movie and television timetables, or job advertisements.

Handwriting/Spelling

▨ Have the child make a list of things to do for the day.

▨ Have the child run a messenger service in the classroom so that he or she can write the messages and deliver them from one student to another.

▨ Provide activities for the older child that incorporate daily writing skills necessary for independence, such as social security forms, driver's license application, bank account application, and so on.

Math

▨ Have the child buy something at the school store.

▨ Have the child make up a budget for how he or she plans to use his or her allowance.

▨ Encourage the child to cook in school or at home so that he or she can become more familiar with measurements.

▨ Have the child record the daily temperature.

▨ Involve the child in measuring the height of classmates.

- Have the older child apply for a pretend loan or credit card.

- Show the child how to use a daily planning book.

- Provide activities that teach the child how to comparison-shop.

- Provide the child with a make-believe amount of money and a toy catalog and have the child purchase items and fill out the forms.

STRATEGIES FOR HELPING THE CHILD IMPROVE GENERAL WORK HABITS

This particular area is composed of many skill areas that are necessary to allow the child success in the regular classroom.

Work Completion

- Make reward activities contingent upon successful completion of work.

- Have the child maintain a performance chart on the number of tasks completed each day.

- Evaluate the length and level of an assignment to make sure it is within the ability level of the child.

- Give shorter, but more frequent assignments.

- Build a foundation of success by providing a series of successful assignments. In this way the child can gain a sense of confidence.

Attendance and Punctuality

- Communicate to the child the importance of being on time to class.

- Let the child know your expectations in clear terms concerning attendance and punctuality.

- Have the child maintain a record of attendance and on-time behavior.

- Develop a make-believe time clock that the child has to punch in on when she or he enters the classroom.

- Encourage punctuality by scheduling a favorite activity in the morning.

- Have the child sign a contract establishing the consequences and rewards of on-time behavior.

Working with Others

- Provide the child with small-group activities that are geared to her or his ability levels.

- Utilize peer tutors for the child so that relationships can be established.

- Have the child participate in many group activities that require sorting, pasting, addressing, folding, simple assembly, and so on.

7.6 continued

▦ Provide the child with a simple job that requires the other students to go to him or her. For example, place the child in charge of attendance and have him or her check off the children when they report in.

▦ Help the child start a hobby and then start a hobby club involving other students.

▦ Have the child be part of a team that takes care of the class pets or some other class activity. Calling it a team will make the child feel more connected.

▦ Speak with the school psychologist and see if he or she can run a group in your classroom.

STRATEGIES FOR HELPING THE CHILD
WITH CAREER AWARENESS

Career awareness is a skill that can be part of the classroom curriculum in many ways. Many of the skills mentioned in the preceding list will enhance the child's career skills.

7.7   Subject Areas and Related Goals

Self Help

Advanced Eating
Assistive Devices
Basic Eating
Dressing
Drinking
Grooming
Toileting

Perceptual Motor

Advanced Gross Motor
Basic Gross Motor
Fine Motor
Sensory Awareness
Visual-Perceptual-Motor

Language Development

Early Language
Expressive Language
Language Content
Language Syntax
Receptive Language

Social Skills

Interpersonal Behaviors
Self-related Behaviors
Task-related Behaviors

Communication

Amplification
Articulation
Auditory Training
Fluency
Multisound
Nonverbal Communication
Phonology
Social Communication
Speech-reading
Voice

Visual / Sensory

Advanced Orientation and Mobility
Advanced Special Equipment Utilization
Basic Orientation and Mobility
Basic Special Equipment Utilization
Braille Readiness
Braille Reading and Writing
Low Vision
Touch Typing
Visual Awareness

Reading

Comprehension and Appreciation
Functional Reading
Reading Readiness
Study and Reference Skills
Vocabulary and Word Analysis

Language Arts

Composition and Writing
Cursive Writing
Grammar and Mechanics
Language Arts Concepts and Processes
Literature
Manuscript Writing
Spelling

Math

Advanced Measurement
Advanced Number Systems
Basic Measurement
Basic Number Systems
Math Readiness
Money
Processes and Concepts
Time

7.7 continued

Social Studies

Citizenship and Government
Concepts and Processes in Social Studies
Cultures
Economics
Geography, Maps, and Globes
History

Science

Biological and Environmental Sciences
Earth and Space Sciences
Physical and Chemical Sciences
Scientific Processes and Concepts

Health and Safety

Family Living
Personal Welfare

Arts

Advanced Music Activities
Art Activities
Basic Music Activities
Dance and Movement Activities
Drama Activities

Leisure Time

Leisure Time
Physical Activities

Life Skills

Clothing Care
Computer Applications
Consumer Skills
Cooking
Home Maintenance
Mail
Personal Mobility
Phone
Public Dining

Vocational Training

Advanced Welding
Auto Mechanics
Basic Tool Skills
Basic Welding
Blueprints and Specifications
Career Education
Construction Preparation
Cosmetology
Domestic and Custodial Skills
Exterior and Interior Construction
Food Preparation
Food Service
Manicuring
Office and Clerical
Power Tool Skills
Pre-Vocational Skills
Structure Assembly
Work Habits and Attitudes

PART 8

Transition Services

8.1   Overview of Transition Services

The last two decades have witnessed significant changes for people with disabilities, in large part due to the Disability Rights Movement that in many ways paralleled the Civil Rights Movement. People with disabilities used to be thought of as "the invisible minority." They were overlooked and "hidden away." They were embarrassments, and treated as objects of pity and shame. Now these individuals are taking their place in an inclusive society. Individuals with disabilities are now a presence in all the media, commercial advertising, and many forms of public life. Changes in the laws and progress in technology have helped make these advances possible. Despite these gains, the barriers to acceptance remains in society's myths, fears, and stereotypes about the disabled. Consequently, the efforts for change need to be viewed as an ongoing process. The implementation of transition services is a significant component of this pathway to acceptance.

As most adults know from their own experience, the period in American society known as adolescence is probably the most difficult and unsettling period of adjustment in one's development. It is a time filled with physical, emotional, and social upheavals. Until a child leaves secondary school, parents experience a sense of protective control over their child's life. This protective guidance normally involves educational, medical, financial, and social input to assist their child's growth. When the child leaves this setting, there is a personal struggle on the part of parents in "letting go." There is always a normal amount of apprehension associated with the child's entrance into the adult world. Now the greater responsibility for adjustment falls on the child, and the parent's role diminishes.

However, for the child with a disability, this developmental period can be fraught with even greater apprehension for a variety of reasons. Depending on the nature and severity of the disability, parents may play more of an ongoing role in their child's life even after he or she leaves secondary education. Historically, parents and their children have spent years actively involved in IEP development and meetings, transitional IEP development, and CSE meetings concerning educational and developmental welfare. Depending on the mental competence (the capability to make reasoned decisions) of the child with disabilities, some parents may have to continue to make vital decisions affecting all aspects of their child's life. On the other hand, the parents of such children not affected by diminished mental competence should use all their energies to encourage their child's steps toward independence. Consequently, parents need not shy away thinking that they are being too overprotective if they are involved in their child's life after they leave school.

Because planning for the future of a student with disabilities can arouse fear of the unknown, there may be a tendency for parents to delay addressing these issues and instead focus only on the present. However, it is our belief that working through these fears and thinking about the child's best future interest will ensure a meaningful outcome. Regardless of the nature and severity of a disability, parents will be exposed to a transitional process during their child's school years that will provide a foundation for the adult world. This transitional process will include many facets of planning for the future and should be fully understood by everyone concerned each step of the way. Planning for the future is an investment in a child's well being. The following lists will help you understand all the aspects of this important time.

8.2   Intent of Transition Services

Transition services are aimed at providing students and their families with the practical and experiential skills and knowledge that will assist in a successful transition to adult life. Although transition services are provided in each of the following areas, it is important to understand that not every student with disabilities will need to receive all of these services. The available services included in the transition process involve services and experiences for both students and parents. These may include:

1. Employment services

2. Living arrangements

3. Recreation/leisure

4. Transportation

5. Financial/income

6. Post-secondary/continuing education

7. Assistive technology

8. Medical/health

As an educator working with students with disabilities, it is crucial for you to become familiar with all the aspects of transition so that you can assist both parents and the student in this process toward adulthood. In order to accomplish this, you will need to become familiar with the different areas associated with transition.

8.3 Importance of Keeping Records During the Transition Process

It is extremely important for parents and students to develop a recordkeeping system. This system should encompass three specific categories.

- Official Documents
- Financial Documents
- Chronicle of Information

The first category, *Official Documents*, involves maintaining a file of a child's written official documents. Examples include:

- All high school transcripts
- Evaluations, tests
- Medical records
- Letters of recommendation
- Job coach reports
- On-the-job training reports
- Teacher comments
- Schedules
- Therapist reports
- IEPs
- Transitional IEPs
- End-of-the-year reports

The second category, *Financial Documents*, includes:

- Sources of income and assets (pension funds, interest income, etc.)
- Social security and Medicare information
- Investment income
- Insurance information with policy numbers
- Bank accounts
- Location of safe deposit boxes
- Copies of recent income tax returns
- Liabilities: what is owed to whom and when payments are due
- Credit card and charge account names and numbers
- Property taxes
- Location of personal items

The third category involves an ongoing *Chronicle of Information* gathered as the result of:

- Phone conversations with school or agency officials
- Summaries of meetings
- Copies of letters written by parents
- Copies of letters received by parents
- Brochures handed out by organizations

8.4 Individualized Transitional Education Plan (ITEP)

PLANS THAT ARE AVAILABLE TO HELP STUDENTS TRANSITION FROM SCHOOL TO ADULT LIFE

The IEP, as it has been defined over the years by legislation and court rulings, is not changed by the presence of the transition services section. The IEP is still a contract between the students, the parents, and the school. It is not a performance contract. The IEP spells out what the school will do (services and activities). If it is written on the IEP, the school is responsible for performing this stated service activity.

The IEP should only carry the information about transition services that the school district can provide directly or indirectly (by arranging for another agency to provide services coordinated with the school services).

As in previous interpretations of the IEP, parents cannot be listed as responsible for achieving an outcome or providing a service. The school district is responsible for this.

The ITEP is a part of the overall IEP but represents a very important piece in determining a child's future. The ITEP should include long-term adult outcomes from which annual goals and objectives are defined.

The following should be addressed in the ITEP:

1. A statement of transition services should be responsive to the child's preferences, interests, and needs. The beginning date for the service should be provided.

2. Annual goals and objectives could include the following ten areas:

   - Education, e.g., college
   - Legal/advocacy, e.g., guardianship
   - Independence/residential, e.g., private residence vs. group home
   - Recreation/leisure, e.g., joining sports activities
   - Financial/income, e.g., banking and checking accounts
   - Medical/health, e.g., health insurance, physician selection
   - Employment, e.g., sheltered workshop vs. competitive employment
   - Transportation, e.g., public vs. private
   - Post-secondary/continuing education, e.g., college vs. vocational training
   - Other support needs, e.g., clergy, fraternal organizations

3. Long-term adult outcomes in the IEP should include statements on the child regarding his/her performance in employment, post-secondary education, and community living.

4. A coordinated set of activities must be included on the ITEP. They must demonstrate the use of various strategies, including community experiences, adult living objectives, and instruction. If one of these activities is not included in the IEP in a particular year, then the IEP must explain why that activity is not reflected in any part of the student's program. Activities of daily living and functional vocational evaluation activities should also be included.

5. A list of participants involved in the planning and development of the Individualized Transitional Education Plan should be included.

465

8.5 The Role of the Family in the Transition Process

Listed below are steps that a family can take to assist in the transitional process:

- Explore your community for useful community resources.

- Discuss transition options with other families who have been through this process.

- Seek out information about occupational, educational, and living options.

- Work along with the school to find ways to increase your child's academic, career, and personal independence skills.

- Set achievable goals for your child.

- Help your child develop the ability to communicate his or her needs, preferences, and interests to school staff and other professionals.

- Observe the kinds of things your child can do independently and the areas in which he or she may need assistance.

- Participate actively in meetings with the school and other professionals.

- Make sure you plan and prepare well in advance for your child's future financial, medical, and housing needs, as appropriate, by: (a) assisting with application for Social Security Disability or Supplemental Security Income (SSI) benefits; (b) developing a will; (c) determining guardianship; (d) applying for financial aid for post-secondary education or training. (All of these issues are discussed in other lists in this section.)

- Help your child obtain key identification documents, such as a social security card, driver's license, or non-driver identification card.

- Help your child develop independent decision-making and communication skills.

- Help your child explore options and set realistic goals for the future.

- Enhance your child's positive self-esteem and assist him or her in developing independence, including self-reliance, self-advocacy, and self-management skills.

- Use actual home-life opportunities to teach your child daily living skills, such as, banking, shopping, cooking, cleaning, and laundry.

- Promote good money management, budgeting, and savings.

- Encourage your child to become aware of the world of work.

- Help your child to locate and obtain a part-time job.

- Reinforce work-related behaviors at home (grooming, etiquette, following directions, completing chores, and so on).

- Provide opportunities for leisure-time activities (sports, daily exercise, hobbies).

- Encourage your child to participate in social activities with peers.

- Teach your child how to utilize community-based resources (library, recreation, transportation, stores, and so on).

- Work actively with your Committee for Special Education to make sure the plan is successful.

- Stay in close contact with your child's teachers.

8.6   Transition Planning Timeline

The following is a series of events that needs to be considered during a child's transition process. All items will not be applicable to all students or to all state regulations. The list is provided to serve as an optional planning tool.

Age Range   Action

12–15   _____Initial vocational assessment.

_____Develop and implement strategies to increase responsibilities.

_____Discuss the following curriculum area at CSE meetings:

Academic

Social

Language/communication

Occupational

Self-help skills

Self-advocacy skills

14–16   _____Introduce and discuss transition services.

_____Notify parents that transition services will be incorporated into the IEP beginning at age 15.

_____Assure that copies of work-related documents are available:

Social Security card

Birth certificate

Obtain working papers (if appropriate)

_____Obtain parental consent so that the appropriate adult agency representative can be involved.

_____Develop transition component of IEP and update annually thereafter.

_____Complete periodic vocational evaluations.

15–21   _____Discuss adult transition with CSE.

_____Consider summer employment/volunteer experience.

_____Explore community leisure activities.

_____Consider the need for residential opportunities, including completing applications as appropriate.

_____Complete periodic vocational evaluations.

16–21   _____Obtain personal ID card.

_____Obtain driver's training and license.

_____Develop transportation/mobility strategies such as:

Independent travel skills training

Public or paratransit transportation

Needs for travel attendant

467

8.6 continued

Age Range   Action

_____Investigate SSDI/SSI/Medicaid programs.

_____Consider guardianship or emancipation.

_____Develop and update employment plans.

_____Involve state vocational rehabilitation agencies, as appropriate, within two years of school exit.

_____Research possible adult living situations.

_____Investigate post-school opportunities (further educational vocational training, college, military, etc.)

_____Complete periodic vocational evaluations.

18–21   _____Seek legal guardianship.

_____Apply for post-school college and other training programs.

_____Have male students register for the draft (no exceptions).

_____Register to vote.

_____Review health insurance coverage: inform insurance company of son/daughter disability and investigate rider of continued eligibility.

_____Complete transition to employment, further education or training, and community living, affirming arrangements are in place for the following:

1. Postsecondary/continuing education
2. Employment
3. Legal/advocacy
4. Personal independence/residential
5. Recreation/leisure
6. Medical/health
7. Counseling
8. Financial/income
9. Transportation/independent travel skills
10. Other

8.7 Transition Checklist

The following is a checklist of transition activities that families may wish to consider when preparing transition plans with the IEP team. The student's skills and interests will determine which items on the checklist are relevant and whether or not these transition issues should be addressed at IEP transition meetings. The checklist can also help identify who should be part of the IEP transition team. Responsibility for carrying out the specific transition activities should be determined at the IEP transition meetings.

Four to Five Years before Leaving the School District

- Identify personal learning styles and the necessary accommodations to be a successful learner and worker.
- Identify career interests and skills, complete interest and career inventories, and identify additional education or training requirements.
- Explore options for post-secondary education and admission criteria.
- Identify interests and options for future living arrangements, including supports.
- Learn to help the child communicate effectively his or her interests, preferences, and needs.
- The student should be able to explain his or her disability and the necessary accommodations.
- Learn and practice informed decision-making skills.
- Investigate assistive technology tools that can increase community involvement and employment opportunities.
- Broaden the child's experiences with community activities and help him or her form friendships.
- Pursue and use transportation options.
- Investigate money management and identify necessary skills.
- Acquire identification card and the ability to communicate personal information.
- Identify and begin learning skills necessary for independent living.
- Learn and practice personal health care.

Two to Three Years before Leaving the School District

- Identify community support services and programs (Vocational Rehabilitation, County Services, Centers for Independent Living, etc.).
- Invite adult service providers, peers, and others to the IEP transition meeting.
- Match career interests and skills with vocational course work and community work experiences.
- Gather more information on post-secondary programs and the support services offered. Make arrangements for accommodations to take college entrance exams.

8.7 continued

- Identify health-care providers and become informed about sexuality and family-planning issues.

- Determine the need for financial support (Supplemental Security Income, state financial supplemental programs, Medicare).

- Learn and practice appropriate interpersonal, communication, and social skills for different settings (employment, school, recreation, with peers, etc.).

- Explore legal status with regard to decision-making prior to age of majority, e.g., wills, guardianship, special needs trust.

- Begin a resume and update it as needed.

- Practice independent living skills, e.g., budgeting, shopping, cooking, and house-keeping.

- Identify needed personal assistant services, and, if appropriate, learn to direct and manage these services.

One Year before Leaving the School District

- Apply for financial support programs (Supplemental Security Income, Vocational Rehabilitation, and Personal Assistant Services).

- Identify the post-secondary school plan and arrange for accommodations.

- Practice effective communication by developing interview skills, asking for help, and identifying necessary accommodations at post-secondary and work environments.

- Specify desired job and obtain paid employment, with supports as needed.

- Take responsibility for arriving on time to work, appointments, and social activities.

- Assume responsibility for health-care needs (making appointments, filling and taking prescriptions, etc.).

- Register to vote and, if male, for selective service.

8.8   Sample Transitional IEP

STUDENT TRANSITION ACTION PLAN (page 1)

Descriptive Information   Date plan initiated:

Student name: Age: DOB: Case Coordinator:

Social Security #:   Disability: Phone:

Parent/Guardian name: Home phone #:

Home address: Work #:

Grade: Teacher: County of residence:

Class location: School phone: Social worker:

Vocational Education Placement: Home school district:

Contact Person (Name and Phone):   Contact person (CSE):

Additional Vocational/Technical Placements/Program:

Participants in Transition Planning

Name: Role/Agency   Name: Role/Agency

Additional Services Needed:

(continued)

STUDENT TRANSITION ACTION PLAN (page 2)

Employment	Date	Activities Accomplished	Responsibilities

___Competitive Employment
   (no need for services)
___Competitive Employment
   (time-limited support)
___Supported Employment
   (infrequent support)
___Supported Employment
___(daily support)
___Sheltered Workshop
___Day Treatment
___Volunteer Work
___Summer Employment
___Other
___Not Applicable

**Post-Secondary Education
and Training**
___Community College or University
   (no support needed)
___Community College or University
   (support needed)
___Technical/Trade School
   (no support needed)
___Technical/Trade School
   (support needed)
___Adult Education Classes
___Other
___Not Applicable

Residential
___Parents or Relatives
___Intermediate Care Facility
___Community Residence
___Supervised Apartment
___Supported Apartment
___Independent Living
___Foster Care/Family Care
___Respite
___Section 8 Housing
___Other

(continued)

STUDENT TRANSITION ACTION PLAN (page 3)

	Date	Activities Completed	Responsibilities
Transportation			
___Independent			
___Family			
___Car Pool			
___Public			
___Specialized			
___Agency			
___Other			
___Not Applicable			

Recreation/Leisure
___Independent
___Family Supported
___Church Groups
___Local Clubs
___Community Parks and Recreation
___Specialized Recreation for
   Individuals with Disabilities
___Other
___Not Applicable

Personal/Home/Money Management
___Independent (no support needed)
___Citizenship Skills
___Insurance Coverage
___Money Management
___Use of Community Resources
___Meal Preparation
___Housekeeping Skills
___Self Care
___Other

Advocacy/Legal
___Guardianship
___Wills/Trusts
___Self Advocacy
___Client Assistance Program (CAP)
___Other

(continued)

STUDENT TRANSITION ACTION PLAN (page 4)

Medical	Date	Activities Completed	Responsibilities

___Medical Care, Daily Care

___Intermediate Care

___Medical Services/General Check-ups,

    Specialists, Medical Supervision

___Dental Care

___Use of Free Clinics

___Therapy (OT/PT, Sp./Lang.)

___Family Insurance

___Individual Insurance

___Medicaid

___Visiting Nurse/Home Health

___Aide

___Medication

___Other

Social/Sexual

___Individual Counseling

___Group Counseling/Support

___Family Planning Services

___Other

Financial/Income

___Earned Wages

___Unearned Income (family

    support, gifts)

___SSI/SSDI

___Food Stamps, Housing Subsidy

___Other

Communication

___Braille

___Assistive Technology

___Computer Applications

___Interpreter Services

___Other

8.9   Vocational Assessments

Level I

The Level I assessment takes a look at the child from a vocational perspective. A trained vocational evaluator or knowledgeable special education teacher should be designated to collect the Level I assessment data. The information gathered for analysis should include existing information from:

- Cumulative records
- Student interviews
- Parent/guardian and teachers' interviews
- Special education eligibility data
- A review of child's aptitudes
- Achievements
- Interests
- Behaviors
- Occupational exploration activities

The informal student interview involved in a Level I assessment should consider the child's vocational interest, interpersonal relationship skills, and adaptive behavior.

Level II

A Level II assessment follows and is based upon the analyses obtained from the Level I assessment. This may be recommended by the CSE at any time to determine the level of a student's vocational skills, aptitudes, and interests, but not before the age of 12. The same knowledgeable staff members involved in prior assessments should be used. Collected data should include:

- Writing
- Learning styles
- Interest inventory
- Motor (dexterity, speed, tool use, strength, coordination)
- Spatial discrimination
- Verbal reading
- Perception (visual/auditory/tactile)
- Speaking numerical (measurement, money skills)
- Comprehension (task learning, problem solving)
- Attention (staying on task)

8.9 continued

Level III

A Level III assessment is a comprehensive vocational evaluation that focuses on real or simulated work experiences. This assessment is the basis for vocational counseling. Unlike a Level I and Level II assessment, a trained vocational evaluator should administer or supervise this level of assessment. Level III assessment options include:

- Vocational evaluations including aptitudes and interests that are compared to job performance to predict vocational success in specific areas. Work samples must be valid and reliable.

- Situational vocational assessments that occur in real work settings. This on-the-job assessment considers what has been learned and how.

- Work-study assessments by progress reports from supervisors or mentors that provide information on the child's job performance. A standard observational checklist may be utilized.

8.10 Prevocational Skills

If families have been properly advised through earlier stages of the transition process, their child should have received job-related skills and behaviors, known as prevocational skills, which can be fostered to help him or her be successful in future employment. Examples of these skills include:

- Physical stamina
- Promptness
- Problem solving
- Hygiene
- Ability to follow directions
- Independence in completing assigned tasks
- Ability to establish social relationships with co-workers

Upon graduation from high school or the end of secondary school eligibility, the student will be faced with several options depending upon the nature and severity of his or her disability. Many individuals with disabilities choose to pursue continued employment training in a post-secondary institution while others choose to begin working right away. This direction usually follows along with the student's Vocational Education Plan—sometimes referred to as the Individualized Transitional Education Plan—that was developed while he or she was still in high school. This comprehensive plan should have assisted the student in developing the skills needed to find and keep a job after graduation. Schools may offer a vocational work experience with a job coach. In some schools, a student may have been assigned to a vocationally licensed teacher who operated as the work experience coordinator within the job site. If a school does not have such an individual, then a special education teacher would be responsible for developing the student's vocational goals.

While the student is still in school, the vocational counselor or individual assigned to develop a vocational plan begins to observe and develop a general transition checklist of possible vocational skills. These general observations may change from year to year as the student matures or they may remain the same due to the nature of the disability. Whatever the case, these observations are the beginning of what will be defined as vocational skills and needs. See List 8.11 for a sample checklist. This is not intended to be comprehensive, but merely a beginning tool in assessing the student's needs and skills.

477

8.11   Prevocational Skills Checklist

Domestic skills

Can the student . . .

____prepare a breakfast?
____prepare a lunch?
____prepare a supper?
____prepare a snack?
____pack own lunch?
____clean own room?
____clean own apartment?
____do own laundry?
____use a washer and dryer?
____make own meal plans?
____budget own time?

Vocational skills

Can the student . . .

____get to/from work on time?
____punch/sign in appropriately?
____perform work satisfactorily?
____work cooperatively with
  co-workers?
____take break/lunch appropriately?
____wear suitable clothing?
____use appropriate safety measures?
____follow directions?
____accept supervision?

Recreation/Leisure

Can the student . . .

____use free time for pleasure?
____choose reasonable activities?
____pick a hobby?
____perform required activities?
____use community resources?

Community skills

Can the student . . .

____use public transportation?
____shop for groceries?
____shop for clothing?
____make necessary appointments?
____use the phone?
____use bank accounts?
____be safe in traffic?
____respond appropriately to
  strangers?
____seek help?
____handle money?

Social/Personal skills

Can the student . . .

____supply appropriate personal
  identification, if necessary?
____greet people appropriately?
____use contemporary style of dress,
  hair style, make-up?
____use good grooming/hygiene skills?
____"talk" with friends/co-workers?
____be courteous and friendly?

8.12   Division of Rehabilitation Services (DRS)

At this point, it is necessary to seek out a counselor from Division of Rehabilitation Services (DRS) located within your state. These services are usually well-known to school counselors, who should provide a brochure that is usually put out by this agency.

The counselor from DRS will work with the school, parents, and the student to help plan for employment needs. DRS is an agency that primarily serves adults or individual who have graduated or aged out from secondary education. However, it is important to involve the counselor during the transition process so when the student graduates and enters the work force, the supports are in place that will allow him or her to be successfully employed.

To receive services from DRS, the student must meet certain requirements:

- The student must have a documented physical or mental disability that presents difficulties or barriers to employment.

- There must be a good chance that DRS services will help him or her get and keep a job.

If the student is still being provided public school assistance, then the school will usually make an appointment for DRS involvement somewhere in the transitional process. If the student has more severe limitations, a DRS counselor can become involved during the very early stages of the planning. Also keep in mind that DRS services are time-limited. For example, the agency will:

- Provide job-placement services.

- Ensure that the student with disabilities is satisfactorily employed.

- Provide follow-up services for at least 60 days and up to 18 months after the initial job placement.

Files can be reopened again if the student needs assistance to retain his or her current employment, find a new job, or reestablish a vocational program.

When a DRS agency is contacted, a Vocational Rehabilitation (VR) counselor will be assigned to work closely with the student and the family. The VR counselor will ask for background information that will help him/her work with the student. Questions usually focus on the following:

- Goals
- Interests
- Educational history
- Work history
- Financial situation
- Physical and emotional health

With parental permission, the counselor may want to collect information from the student's doctor, hospital or school, or ask for evaluations at the expense of the DRS agency. The purpose of this gathering process is to give the counselor information about how the student's disability affects his or her ability to work, which is needed to determine whether the student is eligible for services.

8.13 Services Provided by DRS Agencies

Based upon all available information, the DRS counselor will plan a program along with the family. Depending on what the student needs to meet his/her vocational goal, he/she may receive one or more of the following services that the agency buys and provides to the student.

1. A vocational assessment to help identify skills, abilities, interests, possible job goals, and services necessary to get a job and live as independently as possible.

2. A physical and/or psychological examination to help understand how the student's disability affects his or her ability to work.

3. Guidance, counseling, and referral to help the student with problems he or she may have.

4. Vocational counseling and career planning.

5. Short-term medical intervention to improve the student's ability to work (if not covered by family insurance).

6. Training to learn the skills the student will need for the job he or she wants to enter. This may include: on-the-job training, job coach services, college and university programs, trade and business school programs, personal adjustment programs, and work adjustment programs.

7. Transition services.

8. Driver evaluation and training.

9. Homemaker evaluation and training.

10. Services that may assist the student during assessment or training, including special transportation, some maintenance expenses, and attendents, note takers, and interpreters.

11. Supported employment (see List 8.17).

12. Books, tools, and equipment needed for training or employment.

13. Telecommunications aids and adaptive devices the student may need for employment.

14. Assistance with some costs of modifications needed for employment. This may include work site modifications, van or other vehicle modifications, and home modifications.

15. Training in job-seeking skills to learn how to fill out a job application or develop a resume, handle job interviews successfully, and develop other job-related skills.

16. Occupational licenses, tools, initial stock, and supplies for a small business.

17. Job placement services to help the student find suitable work.

18. Follow-up services to make sure of job satisfaction and handle any problems relating to work.

19. Referral to independent living services for peer counseling, advice on other benefits, housing assistance, and training in independent-living skills.

20. Assistance in working with agencies such as the Social Security Administration, Department of Social Services, Office of Mental Health, and Veterans Administration.

Keep in mind that there is no guarantee that all agencies will pay for or provide all of these services. It is strongly suggested that the family investigate the agency in the particular community. While there is usually no cost for such services, sponsorship for some services may be based on the family's income and/or resources.

8.14 Other Assessment Options During the Vocational Transition Phase

Functional Assessment

The purpose of completing a functional assessment is to identify the student's work characteristics, training, and support needs in relation to actual job requirements. Functional assessment information is gathered so that the best job match can be determined for an individual. The information must be interpreted in relation to the actual requirements of the job.

A functional assessment considers a wide variety of individual work characteristics, including:

- Availability to work
- Transportation
- Strength; lifting and carrying
- Endurance
- Orienting
- Physical mobility
- Independent work rate
- Appearance
- Communication skills
- Social skills
- Unusual behaviors
- Attention to task
- Motivation
- Adaptability to change

- Reinforcement needs
- Family support
- Financial situation
- Discrimination skills
- Time awareness
- Functional reading
- Functional math
- Independent street crossing
- Ability to handle criticism
- Ability to handle stress
- Aggressive actions or speech
- Travel skills
- Benefits needed

The rehabilitation counselor, job placement specialist, or employment specialist can use the information from the functional assessment to identify a job in the community with requirements that match the skills, interests, and support needs of the student.

Keep in mind that vocational or situational assessments are only recommended when there is a need to:

- Determine whether the student is an appropriate candidate for supported employment and identify the intensity of support services that he or she will need.
- Clarify inconsistent available information.
- Enhance insufficient information that is required to determine his or her employment needs.

Situational Vocational Assessment

A situational assessment provides a person with a severe disability the opportunity to perform job tasks in real work environments in the community. Usually, a situational

VOCATIONAL EDUCATION PLANNING

Copyright © 2003 by John Wiley & Sons, Inc.

assessment is conducted for a four-hour period in three different types of jobs in the community where the service provider has established a working relationship with the employer. It is important that the jobs selected are representative of the types of jobs found in the local business community, e.g., dishwasher, groundskeeper, grocery clerk.

The information obtained on the student during a situational assessment can assist in identifying the following characteristics about a potential worker:

- Whether support is needed
- The type of support needed
- Individual training needs and effective strategies
- The anticipated level of intervention
- The least restrictive environment
- Other information needed to develop an appropriate individually written rehabilitation program

Actual performance in a job with appropriate training and support is the best predictor of an individual's performance in a supported employment situation. Observing an individual perform real work in multiple environments will provide an indication of the student's work characteristics, interests, skills, abilities, and training needs. For example:

- Does the student seem to show a preference across job types?
- Does the student work more effectively at specific times of the day?
- Does the student respond positively or negatively to factors in the environment (noise, movement, objects, people, amount of space, and so on)?
- What types of prompts does the student respond to and what is the frequency?

Who Conducts a Situational Assessment?

Situational assessments can be requested from a supported employment vendor or a vocational evaluator. The purpose of such an assessment must be to determine the appropriateness of supported employment and/or the extent of supported employment services needed.

What Information Should You Expect to Receive after the Situational Assessment Is Completed?

It is important to obtain a written report from the vendor who completes the situational assessment. The report should include:

- A description of the jobs completed.
- The behavioral data obtained during the assessment process.
- A summary of the student's characteristics.

483

8.15   Training and Work Options

Once the assessment is complete, the student will be presented with a variety of training and work options, depending upon the results of the evaluation. There are many options and directions available.

INTERNSHIPS AND APPRENTICESHIPS

Internships are similar to on-the-job training. They are time-limited, paid or unpaid jobs that permit the intern to sample the type of work available in a general field. Many high school and community transition programs offer individuals the opportunity to participate in an internship prior to competitive employment. By participating in an internship, individuals can learn more about the job and have the opportunity to familiarize themselves with the work environment.

Apprenticeship programs have been an historical means of preparing competent and skilled workers. Apprenticeships offer individuals the opportunity to learn the skills necessary for an occupation by working under the supervision of experienced workers. These programs generally take from three to four years to complete, but participants are paid for their labor. In the beginning, wages may not be more than minimum wage, but by the end of the program, wages are usually nearly those earned by an experienced worker. Generally, the sponsor of the apprenticeship is a company or a group of companies, a public agency, or a union. More than 700 organizations are currently involved in apprenticeship programs.

Local unions, vocational education programs in the community, the State Office of Vocational Rehabilitation, and the State Employment Office are all sources of more information about apprenticeship opportunities; each state also has a State Occupational Informational Coordinating Committee (overseen at the federal level by the National Occupational Informational Coordinating Committee). These committees, to differing degrees in each state, provide systems for individuals to obtain information about apprenticeships. The Bureau of Apprenticeship and Training also has regional offices throughout the United States. To locate the office serving your area, write or call the Bureau of Apprenticeship and Training, 200 Constitution Avenue N.W., Washington, DC 20210, (202) 535-0540.

ADULT EDUCATION

Adult education programs are designed to provide instruction below the college level to any person 16 years of age or older who is no longer being served by the public education system. There are many different programs available, and you can find them in a variety of settings. One setting of importance to youth seeking vocational training is an area vocational center. In many states, area vocational centers operate as part of the public school system. Secondary school students may receive vocational instruction in the area vocational center during the day; instruction for adults in the community would generally be available at night. Vocational courses may include training in such areas as health care, business education, home economics, industrial arts, marketing, or trades such as carpentry or automotive mechanics. The course of study might involve students in apprenticeships, which can lead to certification in a trade or recognized occupation. Adult education programs may also be available to prepare individuals for GED (General Equivalency Diploma) tests or to teach English as a Second Language (ESL). Continuing education programs may also be offered under the auspices of adult education. However, continuing education is generally meant to provide personal enrichment rather than vocational training. For example, continuing education classes may be offered in areas such as cooking, gardening, or sewing.

Information about adult education programs—whether they are intended as vocational training or personal enrichment—can usually be obtained by contacting your local education agency.

TRADE AND TECHNICAL SCHOOLS

These schools are designed to prepare students for gainful employment in recognized occupations. Examples include occupations such as air conditioning technician, bank teller, cosmetologist, dental assistant, data processor, electrician, medical secretary, surveyor, or welder. Vocational training is provided so that an individual can obtain skills in a specific area of interest or increase the level of skills he or she has already achieved. A course of study may take anywhere from two weeks to two years to complete, with the general entrance requirement of a GED or high school diploma. These schools typically place great importance on job placement for their graduates. If students are working with a high school counselor or a vocational counselor at the VR office in or near their community, one of these schools may be recommended to them as a way of getting the training they need.

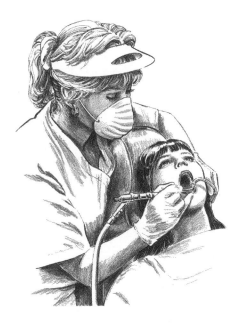

8.16   Competitive Employment

Competitive employment can be defined as full-time or part-time jobs in the open labor market with competitive wages and responsibilities. *Competitive employment* is employment that the individual maintains with no more outside support than a co-worker without a disability would receive. The key word here is "maintains." Although a student may make use of transition services available in the community in order to prepare for and find competitive employment, these services are temporary. Once the individual has the job, support from outside agencies is terminated and the individual maintains, or does, the job on his or her own.

The types of jobs that are normally considered competitive employment are as vast in number as they are varied. Waitresses, service station attendants, clerks, secretaries, mechanics, professional drivers, factory workers, computer programmers and managers, teacher's aides, teachers, health-care workers, lawyers, scientists, and engineers are just some examples of people who are competitively employed. As can be seen by these examples, the amount of training an individual needs varies considerably from job to job. Some jobs are entry-level and require little or no specific training. Other jobs require vocational preparation and training, and still others require extensive academic schooling.

Recently, a training model known as *transitional employment* has been useful in helping many youth prepare for competitive employment. Transitional employment is aimed at those individuals who cannot enter on their own into competitive work. However, with training and support they may be able to handle a full-wage job. Among those who have benefited from transitional employment are individuals who have mental, learning, or developmental disabilities, and persons with hearing and vision impairments.

The important thing to remember about competitive employment, however, is that the assistance and supports offered by a human services agency are time-limited in nature and end once the student has secured employment.

8.17 Supported Employment

There are two aspects to consider when confronted with vocational decisions about finding a job and keeping a job. The student may require little or no help with one or both aspects, or he or she may require a great deal of help. As we have seen, help with finding a job comes from the school system in partnership with the vocational rehabilitation agency.

Employment in which the student will need long-term or ongoing help to keep a job is called *supported employment*. Supported employment is a job with pay at a business in the community. Supported employment is for adults who:

- Traditionally have not been considered part of the workforce.
- Need long-term support to be employed.
- Have one or more disabilities, such as mental retardation, autism, mental illness, traumatic brain injury, physical disabilities, severe learning disabilities, or severe behavioral challenges.
- Require intensive repetitive and/or adaptive assistance to learn new tasks.

How Do Parents Know if Their Children Need Supported Employment?

If the child is already involved in a work situation or has been involved in the past, parents should be aware of several signals that may indicate the need for supported employment services. These include but are not limited to:

- Repeated failures to maintain employment without support.
- Failure or inability to generalize skills from pre-employment training programs.
- Problems acquiring skills.
- Significant communication problems where job-site advocacy would help social integration with co-workers and supervisors.
- The need for extended training and support to develop production rates.

Help for the child is provided by the same companies that specialize in finding employment for adults with disabilities. They can provide a job coach to give help directly to the child with disabilities. Optimally, the job coach will train the child's co-workers and supervisors to provide "natural supports" that are needed to maintain his/her effectiveness on the job. Other services that are provided by job coaches include:

- Travel training
- Task analysis
- Hands-on instruction
- Developing job modifications/accommodations
- Developing visual or other tools to improve productivity
- Training in appropriate job behaviors
- Developing natural supports and social skills
- Employee liaison for problem solving

8.17 continued

- Parent liaison
- Advocating for employee with disability

The amount and kind of help that is provided to find and keep a job should be based on the needs and abilities of the student with disabilities. When parents are involved with an agency that will provide employment services for their child, they will need to learn as much as possible about the agency in order to assess its ability to meet the child's vocational needs and goals. Therefore, parents should ask the following questions:

1. What types of jobs are available?
2. How does the agency select a job for an individual with disabilities?
3. Where are the actual job locations?
4. Does the agency provide individual or group placements?
5. How does the agency promote integration?
6. What are the average wages of employees?
7. What is the average number of hours worked per week?
8. What type of support does the agency provide?
9. Is transportation provided? What type and by whom?
10. What are the average benefit packages available to employees?
11. What provisions does the agency have for employee and parent or family input?

Supported employment is a major avenue to inclusion of persons with disabilities in their communities. As a service, it also reflects the growing conviction by persons with disabilities and their families that they have the right to be involved in decisions affecting the quality of their lives.

Although the transition from high school to adult life is a complex time for all students, it can be especially challenging for young people with disabilities. The goal for parents is to help their child make this transition to the world of work as easily as possible. Being informed and educated as to options, rights, and resources can only enhance the child's transition into the vocational phase of his or her life.

8.18 Sheltered Employment Options

Sheltered employment options are ones in which individuals with disabilities work in a self-contained unit, without integration with workers who do not have disabilities. Sheltered employment options typically range along a continuum from adult day programs to work activity centers to sheltered workshops. In adult day programs, individuals generally receive training in daily living skills, social skills, recreational skills, and prevocational skills. Work activity centers offer individuals similar training but may also include training in vocational skills. In sheltered workshops, individuals perform subcontracted tasks such as sewing, packaging, collating, or machine assembly and are usually paid on a piece-rate basis. Typically, people do not advance to the workshop until they have demonstrated certain mastery levels. Sheltered employment options are generally supported by federal and/or state funds and are operated by private, nonprofit corporations governed by a volunteer board of directors.

Traditionally, sheltered employment options were thought to be the only ones available for individuals with severe disabilities. There is now evidence from supported employment models that individuals with severe disabilities can work in community settings if provided with adequate support. With the emergence of supported employment, many facilities began to modify their sheltered employment programs to provide workers with integrated options Advocates of this trend away from sheltered employment point to the advantages of supported employment, which include higher wages, more meaningful work, and integration with workers who do not have disabilities.

8.19   Centers for Independent Living (CIL)

An important source for information and assistance are the Centers for Independent Living. These centers are programs of services for individuals with significant disabilities or groups of individuals with significant disabilities that promote independence, productivity, and quality of life. The centers are run by people with disabilities who themselves have been successful in establishing independent lives. These people have both the training and personal experience to know what is exactly needed to live independently and may have a deep commitment to assist other people with disabilities in becoming more independent.

These centers are community, consumer-controlled, noninstitutional organizations. They generally offer services free of charge. There are approximately 250 CILs nationally, with at least one in each state.

Funded by the Rehabilitation Services Administration (RSA), CILs may offer a varied combination of independent living services such as:

- Referral services
- Independent living skills training
- Peer counseling
- Individual advocacy
- Counseling services
- Services related to securing housing or shelter
- Rehabilitation technology
- Mobility training
- Life skills training
- Interpreter and reader services
- Personnel assistance services
- Consumer information programs

- Transportation assistance
- Physical rehabilitation
- Therapeutic treatment
- Prostheses
- Individual and group recreational services
- Self-employment skills
- Advocacy skills
- Career options
- Services to children
- Preventive services
- Community awareness programs

8.20 Residential Models

Residential Services

A residential program is a type of housing other than the individuals' natural homes, usually designed for persons with similar needs in terms of age, independence, and/or abilities. A residential program usually provides:

■ A home-like environment, with supervision and guidance as needed;

■ Living experiences appropriate to the functioning level and learning needs of the individual;

■ A location within the mainstream of community life; and

■ Access to necessary supportive, habilitative programs.

The goal of residential programs is to provide access to the highest possible quality of services that a person with certain disabilities needs, while at the same time permitting and encouraging the person to be as independent as possible.

Adult Foster Care

Adult foster care homes are run by families who for altruistic, religious, or monetary reasons provide a home-care environment for the adult with disabilities. In this residential option, the foster-care family receives government reimbursement for this service. Although this living arrangement is meant to be a permanent situation, some factors may prevent this from occurring because no guarantees exist.

Boarding Homes

Boarding homes are residential facilities that provide minimal structure and training for the adult with disabilities. These homes may provide sleeping and meal arrangements and deal with a clientele with a variety of disabilities.

Family Subsidy Program

This program provides financial assistance to families to enable them to care for their children with disabilities up to age 22 at home. The Department of Human Services pays eligible families a monthly allowance for certain home-care costs such as medical equipment, respite care, transportation, and special diets. Eligibility for the program is based on the needs of the family in their ability to provide the necessary level of care in the home. The program is not based on financial need.

Free-Standing Weekend Respite

This is a community-based program for families in need of respite on a planned or emergency basis. The overall objective is to afford families a reprieve from the day-to-day caregiving responsibilities. Respite provides room and board, 24-hour supervision, and appropriate recreational activities to individuals with developmental disabilities.

8.20 continued

Group Homes

The general characteristics of group homes include:

- A home with less than 16 people.
- A family-like structure.
- Similarity to surrounding homes in the community.
- Tasks being accomplished by the residents of the home to the extent of their abilities, e.g., cooking, mowing the lawn, laundry.
- The expectation that the individuals with disabilities will graduate to a more independent situation that will meet their needs and preferences.

The term "group home" has taken on many meanings. As we have seen, this concept has certain general characteristics but these may vary from facility to facility. Group homes are divided into two specific arrangements: Semi-Independent Living Arrangements and Supervised Living Arrangements. These options differ in the following ways:

- Staffing arrangements
- Level of disability
- The need for supervision

Semi-Independent Living Arrangements (SIL). These services provide intensive support and training to persons with disabilities 18 years of age and over to enable them to learn to live independently in the community or to maintain semi-independence. Persons eligible for SIL do not require daily support services, but are unable to live independently without some training or occasional support. SIL recipients live in their own homes or apartments in rooming houses or foster homes. They often share living arrangements with other persons who have disabilities. The key characteristic is that the staff does not live in the facility. In some cases, they may be on-call in case of emergency. *Home Care Attendants* or *Personal Assistant Services* are auxiliary services available to assist consumers in housekeeping and personal care needs. These arrangements are utilized by the consumer in order to live more independently.

Supervised Living Arrangements. These services provide intensive support and training for persons with severe disabilities. Unlike Semi-Independent Living Arrangements, these facilities have full-time residential staff. This type of arrangement is usually provided for individuals who are not able to care for themselves and need full-time supervision.

Because the person with a disability has individual preferences and needs, the family may want to check out a variety of different group living arrangements.

Intermediate Care Facility (ICF/MR)

ICF/MR facilities are specially licensed residential settings for persons who require 24-hour care and supervision. Group homes may range in size from small six-person homes to larger institutions. Most of them are small residences serving fewer than 16 people. This is a Medicaid residential setting for the more severely impaired individual. The ICF provides a full array of direct-care and clinical services within the program model. Clinical services include psychology, social work, speech therapy, nursing, nutrition, pharmacology, and medicine. ICF admission requires participants to be Medicaid eligible, have an IQ below 59, and manifest deficits in basic skills such as grooming and hygiene.

Supportive Living Units (SLU)

SLUs are state-funded small residential sites, typically housing one to three high functioning individuals. These individuals may or may not be Medicaid eligible, are typically competitively employed, and require 21 hours or less per week individual protection and oversight by a direct-care person.

Wavered Services

This service applies to persons with mental retardation who are presently in ICF/MRs or who are at risk of being placed in ICF/MRs unless the wavered services can be provided to them in a home or community setting. The possible living arrangements are intended to be much less restrictive and isolated from the mainstream world than the traditional ICF/MR settings. The new home or community-based residence could include a person's own parental home, a foster home, an apartment, or a small group home. It is believed that through providing an array of wavered services to the individual in his/her home or community-based setting, placement in the more restrictive ICF/MR setting can be avoided. These services are available to individuals who would otherwise qualify for Medicaid only if they were in an out-of-home setting.

Home-Care Attendants

There may be times when an individual with a disability may be able to function independently with only the care of a home-care attendant. This home-care attendant may be paid for by the individual, if economically capable, or by public funds through Medicaid.

8.21   How to Evaluate Residential Programs

There is no substitute for firsthand observation. When you have organized your list of potential residential programs, make appointments to visit each one. Do not hesitate to ask the following questions:

- What are the entry requirements?
- How many people live at the particular residence?
- Is there a waiting list?
- How long is the waiting list?
- What is the staffing pattern?
- What other services are provided at this residence?
- What are the expectations for activities outside the residence? Can the resident go to a day program? Can the resident have a part-time or weekend job?
- What will the costs be for the specific services provided by this residence?
- How is the personal money of the resident monitored?
- Are family visits encouraged?
- What kinds of household chores will the resident be responsible for?
- Are leisure activities part of the resident's program?

Making Your Residence Accessible

Whether you are building a new home or modifying an existing residence, the cost of making the residence accessible can be prohibitive. A home equity or other bank loan may be one financing alternative. Depending upon your circumstances and the nature of the disability, assistance may also be obtained through medical insurance, medical and social services, income support, or vocational services from any of a number of different resources. Consumer-oriented disability organizations and rehabilitation facilities may also provide information resources on funding assistance available in the local community.

8.22   Housing Subsidies

Section 8 Housing

Section 8 refers to rent subsidy payments by the government to allow an individual to secure decent, safe, and sanitary housing in private accommodations. The income limitations for eligibility are determined by the local housing authorities. This program comes under the U.S. Department of Housing and Urban Development (HUD).

The specific steps required in applying for rental assistance are:

1. An application must be completed and filed with the local housing authority.

2. Eligibility is then determined, based on the intended type of occupancy (elderly or disabled) and income.

3. It is up to you or your child to find suitable housing on the open market.

4. This housing must be inspected by the local housing authority and meet demanding quality standards.

5. Once the housing has passed inspection, it must be determined if the landlord is interested in participating in Section 8 housing.

6. If it is determined that rent and utilities do not exceed the fair market rent, and the landlord is in agreement, the housing may be leased.

Section 202 Housing

Section 202 refers to a program that provides direct loans for the construction of housing for three specific populations:

- Individuals with developmental disabilities.
- Individuals with chronic mental illness.
- Individuals with physical disabilities.

These funds are intended for the construction of group facilities for the disabled. You can get further information on this subsidy from your local housing authority.

8.23   Respite Care

What Is Respite Care?

"Respite care" refers to short-term, temporary care provided to people with disabilities so that their families can take a break from the daily routine of care giving. Unlike child-care, respite-care services may sometimes involve overnight care for an extended period of time.

One of the important purposes of respite is to give family members temporary relief from the stress they may experience while providing extra care for a son or daughter with mental retardation or other disability. Respite care enables families to take vacations, or just take a few hours of time off. Respite is often referred to as a gift of time.

Periodic respite care can help parents relax for a while and come back revitalized and better able to care for their son or daughter. Respite care not only provides caregivers a break, but also gives the child a change in his or her daily routine.

Who Provides Respite Services?

Most programs are managed by affiliates or chapters of national organizations such as the American Red Cross (ARC), Easter Seal Society, and United Cerebral Palsy Associations in cooperation with local hotels (US/GAO). Many other programs are provided by local organizations such as churches, schools, and other nonprofit groups.

What Kinds of Services Are Provided?

Services are provided in many ways depending on the provider, the needs of the family, and available funds. Some respite programs send a caregiver to the family's home. Others require that the individual come to a day-care center *or* respite group home.

In some programs, a host family that also has a family member with a disability provides the care. They usually provide respite services in exchange for the same services from another family. These programs are called "host family" or exchange programs.

Emergency respite services are also important. Parents need to be able to access services on short notice in the event that an unexpected family emergency occurs.

Are There Eligibility Requirements for Respite Services?

In almost all state-funded programs, eligibility is based on the child's age and disabilities. Family income is also usually considered.

Some questions to ask about a respite-care program are:

- How are care providers screened?
- What is the training and level of experience of the care providers?
- Will care providers need additional training to meet specific family needs?
- How, and by whom, are the care providers supervised?
- What happens during the time the children are receiving services? Are there organized activities? How are meals handled?

- Does the program maintain current information about each child's medical and other needs? Is there a written care plan?
- What procedures does the program have for emergencies?
- Can parents meet and interview the people who care for the children?
- How far ahead of time do parents need to call to arrange for services?
- Are families limited to a certain number of hours of services?
- Does the program provide transportation?
- Can the provider take care of brothers and sisters as well?
- What is the cost of services? How is payment arranged?

8.24   Travel Training

Travel training is short-term, comprehensive, intensive instruction designed to teach students with disabilities how to travel safely and independently on public transportation. The goal of travel training is to train students to travel independently to a regularly visited destination and back. Specially trained personnel provide the travel training on a one-to-one basis. Students learn travel skills while following a particular route, generally to school or a worksite, and are taught the safest, most direct route. The travel trainer is responsible for making sure the student experiences and understands the realities of public transportation and learns the skills required for safe and independent travel.

The term "travel training" is often used generically to refer to a program that provides instruction in travel skills to individuals with any disability except visual impairment. Individuals who have a visual impairment receive travel training from orientation and mobility specialists, usually under the jurisdiction of the State Commission for the Blind. Travel trainers have the task of understanding how different disabilities affect a person's ability to travel independently, and devising customized strategies to teach travel skills that address the specific needs of people with those disabilities.

A travel trainer usually begins training a student at the student's residence, which allows the trainer to:

- Observe the student in a familiar environment.

- Reassure the family through daily contact.

- Assess the student's home environment at regular travel times for potential problems.

In a quality travel-training program, a travel trainer works with one student at a time. The trainer follows the travel route with the student and instructs the student in dealing with problems, such as getting lost or taking a detour around a construction site. The trainer should teach the student to make decisions, deal with the consequences of decisions, and maintain appropriate safety and behavior standards.

Federal Legislation Supporting the Provision of Travel Training

For many students, transportation is critical to transition, because transportation affects how people live, work, play, and participate in their community. Parents and professionals need to advocate for the inclusion of travel training in the Individualized Education Plan (IEP). Access to transportation and the ability to use it can open doors and provide a means to many otherwise unavailable opportunities to persons with disabilities.

Together, the ADA (Americans with Disabilities Act) and IDEA (Individuals with Disabilities Education Act) provide individuals with disabilities, their families, school systems, service providers, community agencies, and transit systems with compelling incentives to work together to ensure that students learn how to use accessible transportation.

Providing students with travel training can reduce expenses for school districts, local governments, transit providers, agencies, or any organization that provides transportation. The cost of using public transportation is significantly less than the cost of using a contracted private car or private bus service. Although the cost of training a student can be substantial, in the long run that cost is a worthwhile investment, as the student will gain independence and henceforth will assume responsibility for the cost of using public transportation.

When to Enter a Travel-Training Program

Most people enter travel training between the ages of 15 and 21. However, it may be appropriate for some children to be introduced to travel training at an earlier age.

8.25 The Importance of Travel Training

Being able to get around on one's own is an important component of independence; this is as true for people with disabilities as it is for those without disabilities. Almost all people who have disabilities can (with training and the use of accessible vehicles) board, travel on, and exit a public transportation vehicle. However, a certified travel-training program is often needed to teach people who have a disability to do these procedures safely and independently. Programs that maintain high quality procedures for travel training are crucial for helping people who have a disability to develop autonomy and practice their right to move freely through a community.

Who Provides Travel Training?

A logical place to implement travel-training programs is within the public school system. As the primary providers of education for students with a disability, local school districts have a full range of resources available to develop quality travel-training programs. Because students are part of a school system for many consecutive years, educators can plan and deliver a full program of travel instruction. Then, as the students become young adults and are close to exiting the school system, explicit travel training can become part of their education and can form the basis of the transition from school transportation to public transportation. Although the public school system is the optimal environment in which to begin travel training, individuals with disabilities can also get travel training from independent living centers or similar agencies.

Society, too, benefits when people with disabilities participate actively in everyday life. Travel-training programs can enable students with disabilities to become adults who can travel to and from their jobs without support, who are involved citizens of their communities, and who have the opportunity to live independently.

Paratransit Systems

Paratransit systems are shared ride services (van/sedan) in compliance with the Complementary Paratransit Service provisions of the Americans with Disabilities Act of 1990 (ADA).

Although the specific provisions of paratransit systems vary from locality to locality, paratransit usually provides door-to-door transportation for persons with disabilities or mobility impairments who are unable to use public buses. "Door-to-door" usually means transportation from the main entrance to the place of destination. It is, however, the responsibility of the individual to be ready and waiting at the main entrance of the scheduled pickup location.

8.26   Overview of Recreational/Leisure Options for Individuals with Disabilities

Leisure can be defined as an activity that we do by choice for relaxation rather than for money as part of our job. When the student is involved in the transition from school to adult life, a healthy part of this journey should include leisure activities. Parents may generally discover their child's leisure interests by having him or her sample a variety of activities and learning which ones the child is most interested in. Parents of very young children in today's society normally expose them to a wide variety of experiences such as:

- Dance classes
- Little League
- Music lessons
- Scouting
- Sports
- Cultural experiences
- Travel
- Art lessons

As the student without disabilities grows older, this process of sampling leisure interests depends less on the parents and more on their peer group. For young people with disabilities, however, parents and other family members may continue to guide or structure leisure experiences. This extended period of parental guidance and involvement should be considered a realistic part of a student with disabilities' transitional process to adulthood. Learning specific leisure skills can be an important component for successful integration into community recreation programs. Research has shown that leisure skill training contributes to a sense of competence, social interaction, and appropriate behavior.

Advantages of Special Leisure Programs

One of the issues that parents have to address is whether their child should participate in activities designed specifically for people with disabilities or enter activities that are geared for a more mainstreamed population. The advantage of a special program designed for children with disabilities follows:

- It may allow the only opportunity for some children with severe disabilities to participate, e.g., Special Olympics.
- It allows for a sense of group identity.
- It provides a setting for social interaction.
- It creates a more level playing field so that the focus becomes the disabled individual's abilities rather than the disability.

On the other hand, concentrating on "disabled only" activities may unnecessarily exclude individuals from many leisure opportunities and prevent interaction with the nondisabled community.

8.27   Individual Concerns When Faced with Leisure Activities

One of the greatest concerns regarding individuals with disabilities is the problem they may face assimilating into the social world. Many students receive special services while in school that expose them to other children with disabilities. This social interaction and connection provides a foundation for improving social skills. However, once school experience ends and the child is confronted with the mainstream world, many of these social opportunities are not available, and social isolation is often the result. Social isolation is probably the most painful aspect that individuals with disabilities face when they enter adulthood. Therefore, parents play a crucial role in assisting their child by providing the exposure to leisure and recreational activities. Parents may often find themselves the only agent for this particular aspect of life, especially once the child leaves the school setting.

Mastering Leisure Skill Activities

The purpose of mastering a leisure skill activity provides many advantages for the individual with disabilities. This process will:

- Increase the individual's interest level.
- Increase self-esteem and confidence through the mastery of skills.
- Provide the individual with communication topics for social interaction.
- Broaden the individual's knowledge base.

As both the parents and the child investigate opportunities for recreation and leisure, several considerations may arise:

1. What is the experiential and sensitivity level of the people running the program in an integrated activity?

2. How much will the activity/program cost?

3. How will the individual get to the activity?

4. Is the activity integrated?

5. Does the individual need/want to have someone supervise or accompany him or her while participating in the activity?

6. Will the activity/program occur regularly? An optimal leisure plan would include a balance of ongoing and one-time-only activities.

8.28   Exploring Insurance Options for Individuals with Disabilities

The importance of exploring all the available options and avenues of assistance cannot be stressed enough. Being proactive in this area is a valuable activity, as there may be a certain satisfaction that comes from knowing that you, as a parent, have done everything possible to alleviate or reduce the tension of this problem.

The first thing you need to know is the general sources that can be contacted for medical information, financial concerns, and insurance assistance. This process helps you find the best quality health care at the least risk. If cost is a factor, then following this process can help you discover several options that may reduce your costs.

The present state of medical care and insurance has gone through major changes in the last five years with the advent of HMOs (Health Maintenance Organizations). These organizations assist insurance companies by evaluating and authorizing appropriate medical care. Deciding which medical insurance policy will be best for a child with disabilities may already have been determined by your or your spouse's company's insurance carrier. If you do not have an existing policy or are considering changing your current policy, you will be confronted with many different options. There are several individuals and agencies that can be contacted for assistance in making this decision. They include:

- The office of social services in the medical facility where your child is treated or cared for.
- The primary care physician.
- The agent and/or claims representative for the company with which you may have health insurance.
- The billing department for a specific physician or medical facility.
- Your state department of health.

When contacting these individuals or agencies, it may help to develop a script of what you want to say. Keep a piece of paper or notebook handy in which to take notes on each conversation.

You will also need to keep track of offices to which you are referred, insurance policy details, and state support systems.

There are people who can help you identify resources in both your community and state and can help you learn what questions to ask. These are the parents and care providers who have "been there." They can empathize with the complexity of working out all the details—phone calls, correspondence, medical forms, financial forms, and lingering questions. It may be helpful to contact parent groups and disability organizations near you to ask them for help in your research. Associations concerned with specific disabilities can provide helpful information specific to the concerns of their members. Even if there is not an association for your child's needs, another group whose members also have complex medical needs will have information on financing these needs.

When you contact these individuals or agencies, offer the following information so that they may give you the best options for your situation.

- The health care needs of your child
- Your medical insurance situation
- Your outstanding expenses
- What you need

8.29 Types of Insurance Policies

There are three types of policies you may want to consider. However, before choosing one, contact your personnel department, your insurance broker, or your state department of insurance. The three types are:

- A Health Maintenance Organization (HMO)

- An indemnity plan

- Preferred Provider Organization (PPO)

Health Maintenance Organizations represent "pre-paid" or "capitated" insurance plans in which individuals or their employers pay a fixed monthly fee for services, instead of a separate charge for each visit or service. The monthly fees remain the same, regardless of the types or levels of services provided. There is usually a small co-payment required for approved doctor visits. Services are provided by physicians who are employed by, or under contract with, the HMO. HMOs vary in design. Depending on the type of HMO, services may be provided in a central facility or in a physician's own office.

Indemnity health insurance plans are also called "fee-for-service" plans. These are the types of plans that existed before the rise of HMOs. With indemnity plans, the individual pays for services until reaching a defined deductible amount; thereafter, the individual pays a pre-determined percentage of the cost of health-care services, and the insurance company (or self-insured employer) pays the other percentage. For example, an individual might pay 20 percent for services and the insurance company pays the other 80 percent. The fees for services are defined by the providers and vary from physician to physician. The individual also pays the amount, if any, by which the actual fee exceeds the defined fee. Indemnity health plans offer individuals the freedom to choose their health-care professionals.

Preferred Provider Organizations (PPOs) provide that you or your employer receive discounted rates if you use doctors from a pre-selected group. If you use a physician outside the PPO plan, you must pay more for the medical care.

Calculated Decisions

Deciding among an HMO, a PPO, and an indemnity plan is usually based on personal preferences with respect to freedom of choice and one's ability or willingness to pay for that freedom. There are medical factors, however, that may influence an individual's informed decision. In addition to the above information, an individual may also want to consider the following by estimating the expected, predictable health-care needs of each family member over the next year:

1. How many visits to the doctor are expected for such preventive services as childhood immunizations, mammograms, pap tests, or diagnostic procedures?

2. Are you and your family willing to go to new doctors or are you established patients of certain doctors that you prefer?

3. Are you planning to start a family? Will the child be born in the current year or next year?

4. Do you have a chronic condition, such as diabetes, that requires ongoing medication?

5. What is your philosophy about medical services and health-care professionals? Do you tend to go to the doctor for minor problems that in most cases would clear up on their own? Do you practice medical self-care in attempts to avoid going to the physician?

6. What was the average cost for health-care services for you and your family over the past year or several years?

Try to estimate the likelihood of unpredictable health-care needs of each family member over the next year:

1. How healthy have you and your family members been in the past?

2. Do you or a member of the family have a chronic condition that requires sporadic visits to a health-care professional?

3. Do you smoke?

4. Do you consume more than a reasonable amount of alcohol?

5. Are you sedentary or do you exercise regularly?

6. Are you in an occupation that can be hazardous to your health?

Although the answers to the above will not tell you which plan is best for you and your family, they can help you estimate your health-care costs over the next year. Then, you can compare the advantages/disadvantages and estimated costs of the various plans in order to decide which plan is likely to be the best for you.

8.30   Overview of Medicare and Medicaid

Born out of the 1960s, *Medicare* was a result of a response to growing concerns about the high cost of medical care for older Americans. Since that time, however, the program has expanded to include not only older Americans but also millions of adults with disabilities. Unlike in Medicaid (discussed later), which is based solely on financial need, the right to Medicare benefits is established primarily by payroll tax contributions. Medicare is a federal health-care insurance program that provides some medical coverage to people over 65 and also to individuals with disabilities for a limited period of time. Medicare will help meet some bills for long-term care, but will not fund unlimited long-term care. To meet uncovered costs, you may need supplemental or "medigap" insurance policies. Private insurance companies, not the government, offer Medigap insurance. It is not the same as Medicare or Medicaid. These policies are designed to pay for some of the costs that Medicare does not cover.

Medicaid is a federal–state program that helps pay for health care for non-elderly people who are financially needy or who have a disability. Individual states determine who is eligible for Medicaid and which health services will be covered. Most people do not qualify for Medicaid until much of their money has been spent. It is important to realize, however, that some individuals whose incomes are not in the lowest category, but who have substantial medical expenses, do qualify for Medicaid. These individuals—who either have incomes higher than the AFDC (Aid for Families with Dependent Children) cut-off or have very high medical bills that drop their incomes below the level established for "categorically needy"—are termed "medically needy." Once Medicaid covers an individual, he/she is entitled to receive the following minimum services:

- Physician services
- Laboratory and X-ray services
- Outpatient hospital services
- Skilled nursing facilities (SNF) for persons over 21
- Family planning services
- Medical diagnosis and treatment for persons under 21
- Home health services for individuals
- Inpatient hospital service

In many states, Medicaid will also pay for some or all of the following:

- Dental care
- Medically necessary drugs
- Eyeglasses
- Prosthetic devices
- Physical, speech, and occupational therapy
- Private duty nursing
- Care from alternative medicine, e.g., chiropractors, acupuncturists

- Diagnostic, preventive, screening, and rehabilitative services

- Inpatient psychiatric care

Medicaid Waivers

Each state determines which services Medicaid will reimburse. If you have any questions, contact your local social services agency.

Beginning several years ago, states were able to obtain formal permission from the federal Medicaid agency (HCFA—Health Care Financing Administration) to set aside typical Medicaid restrictions. This permission allows for services to be provided in the home or community to certain individuals who would otherwise have to be institutionalized in order to be eligible for Medicaid.

Now, in states with Medicaid waivers, children can stay at home when medically possible and, under certain conditions, not have their parents' income "deemed" (counted as belonging) to them. Also, under some waivers, some "non-medical" services, such as respite care (discussed in List 8.23) may now be covered by Medicaid.

The types of Medicaid waivers include:

Model Medicaid waiver—Under this provision, states apply to the federal government for waivers before they can cover services traditionally covered by the Medicaid program in that state for persons who would have to be institutionalized. The requirement to consider income is waived to allow medically eligible persons to qualify for this program. Each state defines requirements for eligibility.

Home- and community-based medical waiver—Under this provision, states that apply to the federal government for waivers can cover services typically financed under Medicaid (as the Model Medicaid waiver does) and go beyond to cover additional services in the community. These additional services are identified as "wavered services" in the community. Home- and community-based waivers are available for certain categories of individuals who otherwise would be institutionalized and who meet qualifications specified by the state for this waiver.

State Medicaid plan option—Another strategy states can use to help families become eligible for Medicaid is to amend the state plan. With this approach, states can provide, without obtaining special permission from the federal government, medical services to certain designated categories of children who would otherwise be institutionalized or hospitalized. Instead, a state plan, approved by the federal government, certifies categories of children who meet these qualifications.

8.31 Overview of Supplemental Security Income (SSI)

The SSI program is targeted for individuals who are both (a) in financial need, and (b) blind or disabled. People who get SSI usually receive food stamps and Medicaid, too. The evaluation process to determine eligibility varies depending upon whether the applicant is under or over the age of 18. Recently, there have been many significant changes in how the Social Security Administration (SSA) determines the SSI eligibility of individuals under the age of 18. These changes are expected to make it easier for children and youth with disabilities to qualify for SSI benefits. More information about these changes and the specific evaluation process the SSA now uses for individuals under the age of 18 is available by contacting the Social Security Administration directly. When a child reaches the age of 18, the Social Security Administration no longer considers the income and resources of parents when determining if the youth is eligible for benefits.

Under the SSI program, individuals over the age of 18 are eligible to receive monthly payments if they:

- Have little or no income or resources such as savings accounts;
- Are considered medically disabled or blind; and
- Do not work or earn less than a certain amount, defined by the Social Security Administration as Substantial Gainful Activity (SGA).

Individuals who are eligible to receive SSI benefits are eligible in most states for food stamps and Medicaid benefits as well.

Source: U.S. Department of Health and Human Services, July 1990.

8.32   Criteria for Determining SSI Benefits

To determine a person's financial need, the Social Security Administration considers the following:

■ *The person's place of residence*—SSI payments may be reduced by different percentages depending upon the type of residence of your son or daughter. People who live in city or county rest homes, halfway houses, or other public institutions usually cannot get SSI checks. But there are some exceptions. If you live in a publicly operated community residence that serves no more than 16 people, you may get SSI. If you live in a public institution mainly to attend approved educational or job training that will help you get a job, you may get SSI. If you're living in a public emergency shelter for the homeless, you may be able to get SSI checks. If you're in a public or private institution and Medicaid is paying more than half the cost of your care, you may get a small SSI check.

■ *The parents' employment status*—An individual's SSI payments may be determined by parental income and employment status. This is an issue that should be explored fully so that an individual with a disability can receive the proper assistance.

■ *The individual with a disability's income and the things owned*—Whether an individual can get SSI also depends on what he or she owns and how much income he or she has. Income is the money you have coming in such as wages, Social Security checks, and pensions. Income also includes non-cash items you receive, such as food, clothing, or shelter. If you're married, the SSA will also look at the income of your spouse and the things he or she owns. If you're under 18, the SSA may look at the income of your parents and the things they own. And, if you're a sponsored alien, the SSA may also look at the income of your sponsor and what he or she owns.

For specific information and criteria for any of the above factors, contact your local Social Security Administration office.

Before an individual with a disability can get SSI, he or she also must meet other rules.

■ You must live in the U.S. or Northern Mariana Islands.

■ You must be a U.S. citizen or be in the U.S. legally.

■ If you are eligible for Social Security or other benefits, then you must apply for them. (Eligible persons can get both SSI and Social Security checks if eligible for both.) If disabled, you must accept vocational rehabilitation services if they're offered.

8.33   How to Sign Up for SSI Benefits

It's easy. Just visit the local Social Security office or call 1-800-772-1213 for an appointment with a Social Security representative who will help individuals sign up. SSI should be applied for right away because this benefit cannot start before the day one applies. Parents or guardians can apply for children who are blind or disabled under the age of 18.

What to Bring when Signing Up for SSI Benefits

It can be helpful to have the following things before applying for SSI benefits. However, even if applicants don't have all of the things listed, they should sign up anyway. The people in the Social Security office are there to help applicants obtain whatever documentation is needed.

- Social Security card or a record of your Social Security number.
- Birth certificate or other proof of your age.
- Information about residence where you live, such as a home with a mortgage or a lease and landlord's name.
- Payroll slips, bank books, insurance policies, car registration, burial fund records, and other information about income and the things that are owned.
- Medical information supporting the disability.

When signing up for disability, the names, addresses, and telephone numbers of doctors, hospitals, and clinics are required. SSI checks can go directly into an individual's bank, so bring a checkbook or any other papers that show names and account numbers. Many people choose to have their checks sent to the bank because they find it safer and easier than getting their checks by mail.

8.34   Work Incentives

Like nondisabled people, most people with disabilities would rather work than try to live on disability benefits. There are a number of special rules that provide cash benefits and Medicare while they attempt to work. These rules are called "work incentives." You should be familiar with these disability work incentives so that they can be used to your advantage.

If an individual is receiving Social Security disability benefits, the following work incentives apply.

Trial Work Period: For nine months (not necessarily consecutive), individuals may earn as much as they can without affecting their benefits. (The nine months of work must fall within a five-year period before their trial work period can end.) A trial work month is any month in which they earn more than $200. After their trial work period ends, the work is evaluated to see if it is "substantial." If their earnings do not average more than $500 a month, benefits will generally continue. If earnings do average more than $500 a month, benefits will continue for a three-month grace period before they stop.

Extended Period of Eligibility: For 36 months after a successful trial work period, if individuals are still disabled, they will be eligible to receive a monthly benefit without a new application for any month their earnings drop below $500.

Deductions for Impairment-Related Expenses: Work expenses related to the disability will be discounted in figuring whether their earnings constitute substantial work.

Medicare Continuation: Medicare coverage will continue for 39 months beyond the trial work period. If Medicare coverage stops because of work, monthly premiums may be purchased.

Different rules apply to SSI recipients who work. For more information about Social Security and SSI work incentives, ask for a copy of the booklet "Working While Disabled . . . How Social Security Can Help" (Publication No. 05-10095).

8.35 Overview of Social Security Disability Insurance (SSDI)

The SSDI program is a bit different, because it considers the employment status of the applicant's parents. "SSDI benefits are paid to persons who become disabled before the age of 22 if at least one of their parents had worked a certain amount of time under Social Security but is now disabled, retired, and/or deceased" (National Association of State Directors of Special Education, 1990, p. 9). As with SSI, eligibility for SSDI generally makes an individual eligible for food stamps and Medicaid benefits as well.

In the past, the amount of benefits an individual might receive from either or both of these programs would be substantially reduced or even eliminated by income earned at a job. Recent legislation, however, has made major changes in both the SSI and SSDI programs to encourage people receiving these benefits to try to work and become independent. These changes are called *work incentives*, because they make it possible for individuals with disabilities to work without an immediate loss of benefits.

Whatever financial status a family has at the time a child turns 18, a thorough knowledge of his or her financial entitlements should be fully understood by all.

Food Stamps. The Food Stamp program provides financial assistance by enabling recipients to exchange the stamps for food. It is a major supplement for income if an individual with a disability meets the income requirements. This program is federally funded through the Department of Agriculture's Food and Nutrition Service (NFS). It is administered by state and local social service agencies. In most cases, if an individual is eligible for SSI, food stamps will be available too. For more information, contact your local department of social services.

8.36 Helping Individuals with Disabilities Acquire Social Skills

The development of social skills is a process that begins very early. We usually learn these skills from modeling significant individuals in our lives. The road to social skill development is filled with successes and mistakes. When the mistakes occur, parents usually provide us with a clear frame of reference so that we learn from our mistakes. The change in our behavior to more appropriate responses usually results from reward or punishment. Both tend to shape our behavior. Rewards tell us what to do while punishments usually tell us what not to do.

Very important sources of social skill modeling come from friends. If a child is able to maintain a social awareness of other people's reactions, then their responses whether positive or negative affect us and may modify our social responses. However, in the case of individuals with disabilities, this important feedback on performance may be denied (Duncan & Canty-Lemke, 1986). For some, there is a presumption that they cannot learn the basics of social behavior. For others, social isolation plays a key role; how can there be feedback on one's social skills when little socializing takes place?

As previously mentioned, socialization is a process that takes time. In fact, we are always fine-tuning these skills throughout our lives, since we are exposed to many new social situations at different developmental periods. The development of these skills relies on the ability of children and adults to:

- Observe the behavior of others as well as their own.
- Be able to discuss possible behavioral options.
- Practice different skills in a variety of situations to see which ones result in positive feedback.
- Be willing to listen to constructive feedback from individuals whom they trust and respect.

However, individuals with disabilities may have difficulty with many of the skills mentioned above. As a result, they may:

- Have difficulty taking turns during conversations.
- Not be able to maintain eye contact.
- Experience difficulty being polite.
- Have a problem maintaining attention.
- Not know how to repair misunderstandings.
- Not be able to find topics that are of mutual interest.
- Have problems distinguishing social cues (both verbal and nonverbal), e.g., facial expressions, tone of voice.
- Find it hard to express what they mean if language problems exist.
- Have difficulty judging how close to stand to another person.

To compound the problem, many individuals with these deficits are completely oblivious to their social clumsiness. Thus, these individuals do not understand why their social lives are not fulfilling.

8.36 continued

These behaviors, however, can be taught to individuals with disabilities. Teaching can begin at home, with the parents playing a vital role in helping their children socialize. Children should be included in family social activities where they have a part to play in the gatherings. This might include:

- Greeting people at the door,
- Taking their coats,
- Showing them where the chairs are, or
- Offering them food.

Remember, these early interactions lay the foundation for interactions in the future, many of which will take place outside of the home. In many cases, skills will have to be practiced one at a time.

To a certain degree, children may be protected and "saved" from uncomfortable social situations by their parents and teachers throughout school. However, as most children grow older, they interact more and more with people in situations where direct supervision by adults is not possible. One hopes that children learn how to incorporate what they have learned throughout their early years so that they can make friends within their peer group, learn more about socializing, and hopefully refine their social skills as they grow and mature. These friendships are important for all children to develop, because contact, understanding, and sharing with others are basic human needs. As children develop, the natural movement is away from parents and more toward a peer group attachment. Consequently, friends also "serve central functions for children that parents do not, and they play a crucial role in shaping children's social skills and their sense of identity" (Rubin, 1980, p. 12).

Unfortunately, many children with disabilities are socially isolated as a result of several factors.

- The presence of a disability may make peers shy away.
- Transportation to and from social events may be difficult.
- Special health care may be required, e.g., respirator.
- The individual with the disability may be reluctant to venture out socially.

A lack of appropriate social skills may also contribute to a person's social isolation, so an unfortunate spiral gets perpetuated. The current educational trend toward inclusion is an attempt to remedy this social isolation and provide all students with positive social role models.

8.37 How Families Can Help Children with Disabilities with Social Experiences

You must be sensitive to the fact that teaching social skills is one of the most difficult and frustrating experiences confronted by parents and professionals, particularly when the disability is characterized by concrete thinking. What makes it so difficult is that our social behavior varies in different contexts, and children with disabilities may not be able to adjust as quickly as the situation requires.

Parents and professionals can provide a variety of experiences that widen their social circle in a number of ways.

- Emphasize good grooming and personal hygiene, and teach the child the basics of self-care.

- Discuss and explore the characteristics of good friendships—what makes for good friendships, how friendships are formed and maintained, and some reasons why friendships may end.

- Model important social behaviors and then have the individual role-play with parents or other family members any number of typical friendly interactions. Such interactions might include phone conversations, how to ask about another person's interests or describe one's own interests, how to invite a friend to the house, or how to suggest or share an activity with a friend.

- Help the child develop hobbies or pursue special interests.

- Encourage the child to pursue recreational and leisure activities in the community. (See List 8.26.)

- Encourage the child to participate in extracurricular activities at school.

- Help the teenager find employment or volunteer positions in the community. Try not to overprotect. Although it is natural to want to shield a child from the possibility of failure, hurt feelings, and others' rejection, parents must allow their child the opportunity to grow and stretch socially.

8.38 Helping Youth with Disabilities Avoid Social Mistakes

There are two types of social mistakes that many individuals with disabilities need special help to avoid. The first includes those that occur when the person with a disability treats an acquaintance or a total stranger as if he or she were a dear and trusted friend. Individuals with mental retardation are particularly vulnerable to making these kinds of mistakes—for example, hugging or kissing a stranger who comes to the family home.

The second error generally involves doing or saying something in public that society considers unacceptable in that context, such as touching one's genitals or undressing in plain view of others. Committing either type of error can put the person with a disability into a vulnerable position in terms of breaking the law or opening the door to sexual exploitation.

Keep the following in mind:

■ Teach the distinction between public and private through modeling, explanation, and persistence.

■ When a child commits public-private errors, such as touching his or her genitals, immediately and calmly say, "No, that's private. We don't touch ourselves in public." If possible, allow the child to go to a private place.

■ Provide a place of privacy for your child to go. Not only does this allow the child to understand the difference between public and private, but it also acknowledges his or her right as an individual to have and enjoy time alone.

8.39 Fostering Relationships: Suggestions for Young Adults

Young adults with disabilities often think about what it means to have an adult relationship. Some of the normal questions that adolescents and young adults ask themselves are:

- Will I ever have an adult relationship—a boyfriend or girlfriend, a lover, a spouse?
- How will I meet this person?
- What will I talk about?
- What will I say about my disability?
- Will my disability distract the other person from seeing me for the whole and unique person I am?
- What can I do to foster a relationship and help it grow into something strong and meaningful?

Here are some ideas about relationships that can assist young adults in the areas of selfhood, disability, love, sexuality, friendship, patience, hope, and fulfillment.

- Don't ever believe that no one will love you because you have a disability. People with disabilities can both love and be loved. Relationships are based upon friendship, trust, laughter, and respect—all of which combine to spark and maintain the love you find in a relationship.
- Involve yourself in a variety of activities, such as work, community projects, and recreation. These activities will give you the opportunity to meet people. They will also help you grow as a person and avoid boredom and loneliness.
- A relationship is fostered through being a good listener and companion, a person who genuinely cares about others. Build trust and respect between you and the other person. Share activities and ideas. Romance can grow out of such solid ground.
- Keep up on current events. Being able to discuss a variety of topics can help conversations flow.
- Be patient in your search for connection with others. Relationships take time to develop. They cannot be forced. Don't settle for the first person who expresses an interest in you as a woman or a man, unless you are also interested in that person!
- Be open about your disability. Communicate how your disability will affect and might interfere with specific aspects of everyday life. Bring it up yourself, as the other person is often uncomfortable with introducing the topic. The burden of a disability requires that you make other people comfortable with it. How you talk about your disability with openness and humor will set the tone for the relationship.
- Open and frank discussion between you and your partner is the key to solving whatever unique considerations your disability presents. Between loving and trusting partners, mutual pleasure and fulfillment are possible.

8.40 Overview of Assistive Technology

Computers were designed to perform at maximum efficiency when used by the nondisabled. But almost all of us employ some type of adaptive technology when using the computer. Adaptive technology ranges from wearing eyeglasses or wrist supports, to simply adjusting the brightness of the screen display or the height and angle of the monitor. Broadly defined, assistive technology includes any device or piece of equipment that increases the independence of a person with disabilities. Assistive technology for the disabled, of course, is not new. For instance, the wheelchair has long been an indispensable assistive device for those with impaired mobility.

The distinction between adaptive technologies employed by the nondisabled and assistive technologies for the disabled blurs at times. Some of the assistive technologies designed for the disabled have proven so ergonomically sound that they have been incorporated as standard features. One such example is the placement of the keyboard on/off switch, which was designed so that people with motor impairments would not have to reach to the back of the machine to turn the power on and off.

Assistive technology has increased enormously the ability of those with disabilities to lead independent lives. Computer-based environmental control units allow users to turn on lights and appliances and open doors from a wheelchair. Augmentative communication devices enable those who cannot speak to voice thoughts and needs using touch- or light-activated keyboards coupled to synthetic speech systems. Screen reading programs for the blind, screen magnification systems for those with low vision, and special ability switches that permit the mobility-impaired to use a computer are only a few examples of the technology by which the individuals gain access to the computer screen and keyboard.

What Are Assistive Technology Devices?

Assistive technology devices are "any item, piece of equipment, or product system, whether acquired commercially or off the shelf, modified or customized, that increases, maintains, or improves functional capabilities of individuals with disabilities."

"Assistive technology devices can be anything from a simple tool with no moving parts (e.g., a toothbrush with a built-up handle) to a sophisticated mechanical/electronic system (e.g., a robotic arm). Simple, mechanical devices are often referred to as 'low tech' devices while computer-driven or complex assistive technology may be called 'high tech.' However, many people in the assistive technology field have argued that this complexity-based classification is not a useful one as there is no clear division between 'simple' or low-tech and 'complex' or high-tech devices."

Source: Technology-Related Assistance for Individuals With Disabilities Act of 1988 (Public Law 100-407, August 19, 1988).

8.41   Computer-Assistive Technology for the Visually Impaired

The technology available to computer users who are blind or have low vision is extensive. The choice of the appropriate technology depends on a number of factors. Among them are:

- The cause of the visual loss
- The extent of loss of visual acuity
- The quality of peripheral vision
- Any other physical or mental limitations that might affect use of a computer

Following are examples of assistive devices designed to help those with disabilities.

Speech and Braille

Software called outSPOKEN gives audio cues to on-screen visual images such as icons, windows, menus, and cursor location (the numeric keypad replaces the need for a mouse). outSPOKEN is compatible with virtually all Macintosh applications, so people who are blind can use a Macintosh just as sighted people do—in the office, at home, at school, anywhere.

Another program called Duxbury Braille Translator converts text to Braille and formats printing on a Braille embosser.

A synthetic speech system is composed of two parts: the synthesizer, which does the speaking, and the screen access program, which tells the synthesizer what to say. The synthesizers used with PCs are text-to-speech systems.

Magnification

There are several things that can be done to enlarge the images on the screen. One solution, CloseView, is software that magnifies the screen image up to 16 times its regular size. An enhanced version of this software, called inLARGE, is also available as a separate product from Berkeley Access.

Other magnification solutions range from monitors that display images in multiple resolutions to magnification lenses that attach to the outside frame of the monitor. You may also want to consider using software that reads text aloud, so that instead of looking at the words on your computer, you can listen to them.

Persons with considerable vision may not need a screen magnification program. One alternative is a larger monitor, which can provide larger text and graphics while maintaining all the material on the screen. Also, in some applications, the size of the fonts can be increased.

Systems also exist that offer the ability to scan hardcopy text into a PC that then magnifies it on the computer screen. These systems vary in price.

Optical Character Recognition Systems

Optical character recognition (OCR) technology offers blind and visually impaired persons the capacity to scan printed text and then speak it back in synthetic speech or save it to a computer. There are usually three essential elements to OCR technology—scanning, recognition, and reading text. Current generations of OCR systems provide very good accuracy and formatting capabilities at prices that are up to ten times lower than they were a few years ago.

519

8.42 Computer-Assistive Technology for the Hearing Impaired

Alerting Devices/Systems

The various alerting and alarm systems that signal people who are deaf and hard-of-hearing include:

- Security systems
- Baby cry alarms
- Smoke alarm systems
- Doorbell alerting systems
- Paging devices
- Telephone signaling systems
- Wake-up alarms

The signal may be visual (a flashing light), auditory (an increase in amplification), or vibrotactile (a vibrator). For instance, if an alarm clock is wired to a vibrotactile device under the bed pillow, the user is literally shaken awake. Auditory signals are sometimes used in conjunction with either visual or vibratory signals.

Telephone Aids

Amplification devices may include a specially wired telephone handset with portable amplifiers that attach to a phone. Such volume-control handsets may provide up to 30 percent additional power for the listener who has a hearing loss. These devices may be used with or without an individual's hearing aid.

TTYs and TDDs

Text telephones (TTY) and telecommunication devices (TDD) (now called Typed Text QTT) enable people who are deaf and hard-of-hearing to have conversations by typing messages that are sent through the telephone network. Although these devices offer the hearing impaired a major form of communication, they are rather slow devices, especially when compared to computers.

Telecaption Adapters

These devices, sometimes referred to as television decoders, attach to the television and enable people who are deaf and hard-of-hearing to read captions on their television screens.

8.43 Computer-Assistive Technology for Individuals with Mobility Impairments

Many adaptations are available to assist those with impaired mobility to use the computer. Although a standard keyboard and mouse are the input devices of choice for most people, other devices have been developed. Among the most frequently used are modified and alternate keyboards, ability switches, and headpointers and joysticks. Whatever the method, the computer treats the input from these methods as if it had been received through the standard keyboard. Descriptions of several of these follow.

MACINTOSH OPERATING SYSTEM

Keyboards

There are dozens of different kinds of keyboards for the Macintosh. Depending on personal abilities and preferences, any of a number of them may be appropriate. The right keyboard may be the kind that looks like a traditional keyboard, but has large, touch-sensitive keys to help make typing easier. Another has only seven keys and uses a typing technique called "chording," originally designed for one-handed typists.

The Apple Adjustable Keyboard, another possibility, splits into two sections and conforms to the natural position of your arms to make typing comfortable. Other products include switch-operated, on-screen keyboards that let you type with almost any part of your body, and "smart" keyboards that allow you to customize each key's position, size, and function.

Mouse Alternatives

You can fine-tune your mouse's sensitivity by using software that comes with your Macintosh. But this kind of refinement may not adequately address your needs. You may need an altogether different kind of pointing device. If so, there are many from which to choose: head-controlled mice, trackballs (in effect a mouse turned upside down), joysticks, mice of different sizes and speeds, writing pads that function as mice, touch-sensitive screens that act as mice, and even remote-controlled mice. Another solution is Easy Access, a software program that comes with every Macintosh. The MouseKeys feature of Easy Access lets you use the keyboard to control the cursor's movements. How do you determine which pointing device is the most appropriate for your needs? First you need to find out what's available. Try visiting your local newsstand and browsing through a computer magazine devoted to Macintosh technology; there you'll find new and different pointing devices being advertised regularly.

Input Systems

With the right hardware and software, a Macintosh can become a powerful system for learning, working, and playing. But that won't matter to you until you're able to find a way to control the computer . . . your way. Keyboards and mice are traditionally used to control personal computers. Although you may not be able to use these devices, you can choose between a number of alternatives, including a voice recognition system that allows

8.43 continued

you to control the computer by talking to it; an on-screen keyboard that facilitates typing without physically touching the keys; and a head-controlled keyboard/mouse that lets you type using head movements.

PC OPERATING SYSTEM

Keystroke Modification and Mouse Emulation

Keystroke modification and mouse emulation programs provide various combinations of the following utilities:

- Execution of multiple keystroke commands serially rather than simultaneously ("StickyKeys").

- Modification of key repeat function.

- Manipulation of mouse from keypad/keyboard.

- Alternatives to clicking and holding down mouse buttons.

- Provision of visible or audible feedback for keystrokes.

- *Warning:* A problem may occur in accessing the pull-down menus in some programs when using a keystroke modification program. Most application programs require that you hold the Alt at the same time you depress the pull-down menu's appropriate "hotkey" letter. With the "StickyKeys" function on, you can hit them sequentially instead—useful for a one-handed typist, someone using a mouth stick, etc. However, if your program already requires that they be hit sequentially (e.g., WordPerfect 5.1 and earlier versions), the results are unpredictable!

- The key guard is a lightweight overlay, often plastic, that fits over the regular keyboard; holes are punched out of the plastic so that each standard key can be pressed if chosen deliberately, either with the fingers or mouth stick. The key guard cuts down substantially on accidental keystrokes.

- Permanent large-print key labels can be placed on each character, number, and punctuation mark of the standard keyboard. The visually impaired user may benefit from this adaptation, as do children.

- Software exists that will disable the automatic-repeat feature of most keys on the keyboard. Alternate keyboards come in many styles.

8.44 Computer-Assistive Technology for Individuals with Speech, Language, and Learning Impairments

Online computer instruction is a particularly good medium for intensive remedial training. The strengths of the computer in education include its capacity for constant, individual feedback to the student along with an unlimited ability to carry out drill and practice exercises until a subject is mastered. Computer packages have been designed to improve the speech and language capabilities of those with poor hearing and speech, and also to assist those with cognitive injuries or learning disabilities.

Most new computers have speech capability built-in, which means that some notebook computers—in addition to doing everything that a regular computer does—can travel with you, helping you communicate with others. A portable computer is small and lightweight, so it can be carried around in a backpack or easily attached to a wheelchair, making it a versatile communication tool. Using "text-to-speech" software, the computer can create synthetic speech from typed-in words, allowing your computer to speak out loud any word or phrase. Some computers also have the ability to record and play back a person's own voice (somewhat like a tape recorder), which results in a very high-quality sound. Special software can help you manage speech so that you can access the appropriate words on demand. Libraries of pictures, symbols, and graphics are often used to build "picture communication boards," enabling speech samples to be selected quickly and easily.

8.45   Technology and Assistive Technology on the Internet

A number of resources are available today thanks to the development of the Internet. This vast base of knowledge and information is a key resource for parents and individuals with disabilities. In the case of assistive technology, many valuable sites are available to educate, inform, and offer a wealth of guidance on the topic of assistive technology available to individuals with disabilities. The following is a partial list, but contains many of the more complete sites on this topic.

Name of Site: ABLEDATA
Web Address: www.ABLEDATA.com
"ABLEDATA is an extensive and dynamic database listing information on assistive technology available both commercially and non-commercially from domestic and international manufacturers and distributors. The field of assistive and rehabilitation technology holds much promise for people with disabilities. It is one of many keys that can unlock the doors to a life of greater independence for people with disabilities. However, assistive technology is nothing but another unfulfilled promise unless current, usable information on existing assistive devices and services is made available to any and all information seekers."

Name of Site: Access First
Web Address: www.AccessFirst.net
"Access First provides the best in sales, training, and support for the sight impaired, print-handicapped and learning-disabled community. Our main services are that of consultants, instructors, and software developers. We have more than 40 years combined experience in the areas of high technology sales and technical support, applications design, community networking, and funding resources. As end users ourselves, we understand and can address the special needs of the student and professional in the workplace."

Name of Site: Alliance for Technology Access (ATA)
Web Address: www.ataccess.org
". . . providing access to empowering technology for children and adults with disabilities. The Alliance for Technology Access (ATA) helps to enhance the lives of people with disabilities through technology, by raising public awareness, implementing initiatives, and providing information and hands-on exploration at community resource centers."

Name of Site: Apple Computer's Worldwide Disability Solutions Group
Web Address: http://www.apple.com/disability/
"This online version of the Mac Access Passport is a place where you can interactively learn about the kinds of products that make it possible to use a Macintosh computer if you have a disability. You can download the latest version of our product database, link directly with major organizations and manufacturers, find a collection of access software programs from Apple, and more."

Name of Site: The Archimedes Project
Web Address: www.archimedes.stanford.edu//arch
"Project Archimedes seeks to promote equal access to information for individuals with disabilities by influencing the early design stages of tomorrow's computer-based technology."

Name of Site: The Center for Information Technology Accommodation (CITA)
Web Address: www.itpolicy.gsa.gov/cita
A clearinghouse of information about making information systems available to all users. Includes web design guidelines.

Name of Site: DREAMMS for Kids
Web Address: www.dreamms.org
DREAMMS for Kids, Inc. (Developmental Research for the Effective Advancement of Memory and Motor Skills) is a nonprofit parent and professional service agency that specializes in assistive technology-related research, development, and information dissemination. Founded in 1988 by the parents of a Down syndrome child, DREAMMS is committed to facilitating the use of computers, assistive technologies, and quality instructional technologies for students and youth with special needs in schools, homes, and the community. Services include newsletters, individually prepared Tech Paks, and special programs entitled "Computers for Kids" and "Tools for Transition."

Name of Site: Equal Access to Software and Information (EASI)
Web Address: www.rit.edu/~easi
EASI provides online training on accessible information technology for persons with disabilities.

Name of Site: The International Society for Technology in Education
Web Address: www.iste.org
"A nonprofit professional organization dedicated to the improvement of education through computer-based technology."

Name of Site: National Center to Improve Practice
Web Address: www2.edc.org/NCIP/
"The National Center to Improve Practice (NCIP) promotes the effective use of technology to enhance educational outcomes for students with sensory, cognitive, physical and social/emotional disabilities."

Name of Site: Plugged In
Web Address: http://www.pluggedin.org
"Plugged In is a community access and training center for computers and the Internet in East Palo Alto, California. Our mission is to bring the educational and economic opportunities created by new technologies to low income families in our community. We are open 7 days and 70 hours a week. We offer more than 30 classes to kids, teens and adults and work in partnership with more than 10 community agencies."

8.45 continued

Name of Site: Project Pursuit

Web Address: www.rehab.uiuc.edu/archives/ss/9596/pursuit.html

"Here you will find a wealth of resources including: disability information, education accommodation resources, lessons on assistive technology and funding available for this technology, descriptions of careers in science, engineering, and mathematics, high school preparations for these careers, access to countless other information servers, and much more."

Name of Site: WebABLE!

Web Address: http://www.webable.com

"WebABLE! is the World Wide Web information repository for people with disabilities and accessibility solution providers. WebABLE! is dedicated to promoting the interests of adaptive, assistive, and access technology researchers, users, and manufacturers."

8.46 College Responsibilities for Accommodations

In high school, the school district is responsible for providing any or all support services necessary for an individual with disabilities to participate in the educational process. The college or university does not have the same legal obligation. They are required by law to provide any reasonable accommodation that may be necessary for those with disabilities to have equal access to educational opportunities and services available to nondisabled peers, if requested.

Title II of the ADA covers state-funded schools such as universities, community colleges, and vocational schools. Title III covers private colleges and vocational schools. If a school receives federal dollars, regardless of whether it is private or public, it is also covered by the regulation of Section 504 of the Rehabilitation Act requiring schools to make their programs accessible to qualified students with disabilities.

Under the provisions of Section 504, universities and colleges **may not**:

- Limit the number of students with disabilities.
- Make pre-admission inquiries as to whether an applicant is disabled.
- Exclude a qualified student with a disability from a course of study.
- Discriminate in administering scholarships, fellowships, etc., on the basis of a disability.
- Establish rules or policies that may adversely affect students with disabilities.

For college students with disabilities, academic adjustments may include adaptations in the way specific courses are conducted, the use of auxiliary equipment and support staff, and modifications in academic requirements. These modifications may include:

- Removing architectural barriers.
- Providing services such as readers, qualified interpreters, or note takers for students who are deaf or hard-of-hearing.
- Providing modifications, substitutions, or waivers of courses, major fields of study, or degree requirements on a case-by-case basis.
- Allowing extra time to complete exams.
- Using alternative forms for students to demonstrate course mastery.
- Permitting the use of computer software programs or other assistive technological devices to facilitate test taking and study skills.

8.47 Disability-Related College Support Services

Many college campuses have an office for Disabled Student Services or Special Services. Others have designated the Dean of Students or some other administrator to provide this information and to coordinate necessary services and accommodations. At vocational schools or other training programs, the person responsible for disability services can usually provide this information.

There are also many publications that can tell more about the policies and programs that individual colleges and universities have established to address the needs of students with disabilities.

Financial Aid

A major question regarding post-secondary education or training opportunities is the availability of financial aid to help pay for tuition and living expenses. Obtaining financial aid can be a complex process, because laws are amended and eligibility requirements, policies, and disbursement of government funds change each year. Most money called "financial aid" is available to those studying only above the high school level (thus, financial aid is usually not available for Adult Education). The student must usually demonstrate the ability to benefit from the education or training in order to receive traditional financial aid.

The financial aid system is based upon a partnership between the student, parents, post-secondary educational institutions, state and federal government, and available private resources. For a student with a disability, the partnership may be extended to include a Vocational Rehabilitation Agency and the Social Security Administration. Such a partnership requires cooperation of all and an understanding by each of their responsibilities within the financial aid process.

What Is Financial Aid?

Financial aid is a system of financial assistance to help individuals meet their educational expenses when their own resources are not sufficient. Three types of aid are available:

1. **Grants**—gifts and scholarships that do not have to be repaid. (A list of available scholarships and financial aid resources can be found in Appendix 10.7.) Information on financial aid can usually be obtained through the high school guidance counselor.

2. **Loans**—money borrowed to cover school cost that must be repaid (usually with interest) over a specific period of time (usually after the student has left school or graduated).

3. **Work**—employment that enables a student to earn a portion of school costs.

The federal government contributes to all three types of student financial aid. These programs are explained in a booklet called "The Student Guide: Financial Aid from the U.S. Department of Education." The programs described in the booklet are:

1. Federal Pell Grants

2. Federal Supplemental Educational Opportunity Grants (SEOG)

3. Federal Work-Study (FW-S)

4. Federal Perkins Loans

5. Federal Family Education Loans (FFEL) including: Federal Stafford Loans (subsidized and unsubsidized), and Federal PLUS Loans

All of these programs are based upon financial need of the student and his or her family, except the unsubsidized Stafford and PLUS programs.

What Expenses Are Considered Disability-Related?

In addition to the financial aid that one may receive for tuition and room and board, there may be times when additional expenses that may require further financial assistance are incurred. These include:

- Special equipment related to the disability and its maintenance.
- Expenses of services for personal use or study such as readers, interpreters, note takers, or personal-care attendants.
- Transportation necessary to pursue an academic program, if regular transportation is not accessible.
- Medical expenses relating directly to the individual's disability that are not covered by insurance.

Students should be sure to inform the aid administrator of disability-related expenses that may previously have been covered by the family budget. These may include food and veterinary bills for dog guides, batteries for hearing aids, and a Telecommunication Device for the Deaf (TDD) [now called a Typed Text QTT], or the cost of recruiting and training readers or personal-care attendants. Often, leaving home necessitates the purchase of new or additional equipment that will allow the student to be independent at school. Students with disabilities should seek assistance from the Office of Disability Support Services and/or Financial Aid Office to determine disability-related expenses.

Regardless of whether the student is able to obtain any special equipment or services through the institution or elsewhere, it is still important to let the financial aid administrator know of any anticipated expenses. Such information is considered in the determination of the student's financial need, on which all aid decisions are based.

Vocational Rehabilitation and Financial Aid

The local Vocational Rehabilitation Agency has VR counselors who can help a person with a disability determine eligibility for assistance. The VR program is an eligibility program, rather than an entitlement program. To be eligible for services, an individual must have a disability that is a substantial handicap to employment and must have potential for employment as a result of rehabilitation services. The primary goal of a VR counselor is to make the client employable; therefore, the counselor will look closely at a student's educational plans in terms of job potential. While initial counseling and evaluation are open to all, the counselor may determine that a client is not eligible for other services based on state agency policies governing economic need, order of selection, and other policies of the agency.

Among the services that may be provided by VR agencies to a student who is a client are the following:

8.47 continued

- Tuition expenses.

- Reader services for persons who are blind or learning disabled and interpreter services for people who are hearing impaired; individually prescribed aids and devices, which are authorized in advance in an Individualized Written Rehabilitation Program (IWRP) developed jointly by the client and the counselor.

- Telecommunications, sensory, and other technological aids and devices.

- Other goods and services, which help render an individual who is handicapped employable.

The above items may differ from state to state, or be subject to a test of a client's ability to pay or the use of available resources from another social service agency before a commitment of VR funds is made. To understand why there are differences among and between states' VR programs, one needs to know that the U.S. Department of Education's Rehabilitation Services Administration (RSA) administers the Rehabilitation Act, but each participating state administers its own program through the provisions of a state plan that has been developed under the guidelines of the Act and that has been approved by RSA.

8.48 Issues to Consider When Looking into Post-Secondary Education

1. What are admission requirements?

2. What is the required grade point average? ACT? SAT?

3. Are there special accommodations for individuals with disabilities to take entrance exams?

4. Are there special incentive programs?

5. Is there an office for students with disabilities on campus? How do I contact the office? Does it have a full-time or part-time person?

6. What kind of documentation is required to verify disabilities?

7. Is there an organization on campus for students with disabilities? How do I contact the organization?

8. How are the faculty informed of the necessary accommodations, if needed?

9. Is tutoring available? Is it individualized or group? Is there a cost involved?

10. Are note takers and readers available? Is there a cost involved? How are they trained?

11. Is it possible to arrange for tape recorder classes, computers, untimed testing, test readers?

12. Is it possible to relocate classes to more accessible sites?

13. What is the college's policy regarding course substitutes or waiver of curriculum requirements?

14. Are there developmental courses available? In what areas?

8.49   Checklist for Assessing Colleges
for Accessibility

When looking for the right college, make sure to find what services are available through the Office of Services for Students with Disabilities on each campus. The office may be located in the office of Student Affairs, or it may be listed independently. It is essential to obtain as much information as possible about services for students with disabilities, and services that pertain to particular disabilities, before beginning classes. To get ahead, and stay ahead, of the game is imperative!

These are sample questions to consider asking college representatives:

- What services (e.g., readers, note takers, bus service) are offered? Are there fees?

- What are the names of the director and staff people connected to these services? Is there a document that describes the various services?

- Can you introduce me to a student with my disability (or another disability) so I can learn from that person's experience? What arrangements do other students make in the same situation as mine?

- Who is available to assist in finding services (e.g., accessible apartments, restaurants) on and off campus?

- Is there an office for the local Vocational Rehabilitation Agency on campus? If not, where is it?

- What are the local organizations (e.g., Center for Independent Living, Personal Care Association) for individuals with disabilities such as mine? What services can I get through them?

- How many students with disabilities attend this college until graduation? What history is there of my major department making accommodations?

- If accommodations are ever denied, what is the procedure to follow to contest the decision?

- How early does a qualified student have to start to make arrangements for putting textbooks on audiotape?

8.50 College Accommodations for Specific Disabilities

If you have a visual impairment:

- Does the college offer training in finding one's way around campus? If not, how do I get the training? Does the college have a list of qualified instructors?

- Are readers paid or volunteer? Who pays? Whether using a volunteer or paid reader, assess whether my needs are being provided for, and try to find a gracious but clear way to communicate to them if they are not. Ask the office: "Do you help locate readers? Do you have any suggestions for finding them?"

- Are large-print computer programs available to me? What other assistive technology is available? Where is the equipment located? Is there training to help me use the computers and accompanying software?

- What accommodations are there for taking exams? How and where are they usually taken? What responsibility do I have in the whole process—can I work out my own arrangements if I so choose? Can I get the exams in an alternative medium, like large print, or Braille, or recorded?

- Is campus transportation accessible for me? Is there campus or city public transportation and is it accessible to me?

If you have a hearing impairment:

- Will the Office of Services for Students with Disabilities arrange for interpreters? If so, how do I set that up with my class schedule? If not, will they provide assistance in locating them? Who pays?

- Are oral and sign language interpreters available?

- Are note takers available to record lectures for me, or do I have to find my own? Are they paid, and who pays? What is the procedure for payment?

- Does the campus have TDDs (Telecommunication Devices for the Deaf, now called Typed Text QTT)?

- What are the provisions for safety in the dormitory in case of fire or other emergency? Do dormitory telephones have the capacity to have the volume turned up?

- Is captioning of speakers as they are speaking available?

- What amplification equipment is available? Can I borrow any of it for my use?

If you have a mobility impairment:

- What is the accessibility of buildings, classrooms, laboratories, and dormitories? How wide are the residence hall doorways and what is the accessibility of the bathrooms?

- Will there be any special problems or assistance with class registration?

- Will anyone assist me in arranging my schedule to include the required classes and still have enough time to go from one classroom in one building to another classroom in another building?

8.50 continued

- Will I be able to reach and use all the equipment in the laboratory? If not, what arrangements must I make?

- If I need special adaptations to access computers, who will provide them?

- If I need adaptations to access the library catalog system, who will arrange for them?

- If the college has a large campus, is there accessible transportation, such as a lift-equipped van, to get from one area to another? Are there curb cuts and smooth sidewalks that I can manage with a wheelchair?

- Is driver evaluation and training available?

- If my wheelchair needs repair, can I get it done locally?

- Is there a dormitory or other residence that can assist people who require help with daily activities such as eating or dressing?

If you have a learning disability:

- Remember that academic accommodations are based on documented type of learning disability and its severity. Your diagnostic papers need to be written by a licensed medical or psychological examiner. Subtest standard scores need to be listed as legal evidence of severity. Your school skills levels will not be sufficient, nor will an old Individualized Education Plan (IEP).

- There is a high probability that whatever the accommodations recommended by the examiner are, they will not exactly meet your needs in college. In some classes, you will need no accommodations, but in others, you may face demands on your learning disability that no one thought of. For these reasons, it is imperative you understand your learning disability thoroughly enough to explain how it works to a person unfamiliar with learning disabilities.

- Although the laws allow accommodations for diagnosed disabilities, the law does not entitle anyone to misrepresent his/her needs for the purpose of gaining advantage over nondisabled people. The law probably will not protect past accommodations in a different academic circumstance unless the need can be documented. If you should find yourself in a resistant environment within a college or university after you begin attending, you will need to have available your diagnostic papers and the current request for accommodations in order to be successful in advocating for your needs.

- Are academic accommodations (e.g., note takers, extended test time) uniform for everyone, or are they individualized according to the diagnostic papers?

- Are the students with more severe learning disabilities expected to manage their own lives? (For example, getting homework in on time, money management, and school schedules.) Who is available to help when help is needed?

- How early does a qualified student have to start making arrangements for special exam conditions with the professor?

- Can the course load be reworked?

- Are there counseling services available in case I get overwhelmed?

- Can I have additional time for tests? Who arranges for the extra time—me, the professor, the Office of Services for Students with Disabilities, or the Dean?

- May I tape class lectures?

If you have a chronic health condition:

- What medical services are available locally? Are there rehabilitation units in local hospitals?

- How can I arrange my schedule to accommodate fatigue?

- Can arrangements be made for a personal-care attendant if I need one?

The answers to these questions will give you an idea of where college is going to be easy and where it is going to be hard, in terms of accommodations. You may need to change some strategies, and you may need to push for support in areas where the services do not appear to meet your needs. The more you know in advance, the more effectively you will begin, and succeed.

PART 9

Parent Education

9.1 How to Improve a Child's Self-Esteem

1. *Be solution oriented.* An important step in building self-esteem is to teach solutions rather than blame. Teaching children solutions to problems or frustrating situations begins with statements like, "Who's at fault is not important. The more important question is what we can do so that it doesn't happen again."

2. *Allow children the right to make decisions.* Allowing children the right to make decisions that affect their daily life can only enhance their self-esteem. Decisions about clothing, room arrangement, friends to invite to a party, menu for dinner, etc., can help children feel some sense of control in what happens to them.

3. *Offer alternate ways of handling a situation.* Conditioning children to see many alternate ways of handling a situation, obstacle, etc., can also enhance a sense of power and self-esteem. Asking children what they have tried and offering other options to possible solutions increases their "tool box."

4. *Teach children the proper labels when communicating feelings.* When children are unable to label an internal feeling, they become frustrated more quickly. When such feelings go unlabeled, they may become manifested in some negative behavior which will only reduce self-esteem. Parents can offer children the correct labels. Use language like "While the feeling you are expressing sounds like anger, it is really frustration and frustration is. . . . Now that you know this, is there anything that is causing you frustration?"

5. *Allow children the opportunity to repeat successful experiences.* A foundation of positive experiences is necessary for self-esteem. Because the child has mastered skills required for the job, any opportunity to repeat success can only be an ego-inflating experience.

6. *Allow avenues for disagreement.* Children with high self-esteem feel they have an avenue to communicate their concerns. Even though the result may not go in their favor, the knowledge that a situation or disagreement can be discussed with their parents allows the child to feel a sense of power in their destiny rather than feel like a victim.

7. *Help children set realistic goals.* Some children will set unrealistic goals, fall short, and feel like a failure. Repeated over a period of time, the child begins to develop a sense of urgency for success and this in turn may lead to more unrealistic goals. Parents can help children by assisting them in defining their objectives and determining the steps necessary to accomplish the goal. Children should not see one final goal, but a series of smaller goals leading to a final point.

8. *Use a reward system to shape positive behavior.* Punishment tells a child what not to do, while reward informs a child of what is acceptable behavior. Rewarding positive behavior increases self-esteem. Rewards can be in the form of special trips, extra time before bed, special dinners with one parent, a hug, a kiss, or a note in their lunchbox.

9. *Don't pave every road for children.* Some parents or teachers make the mistake of reducing frustration for children to the point where the child receives a distorted view of the world. Children with high self-esteem get frustrated. However, they tend to be more resilient because they have previous success in handling frustrating situations themselves. Teaching children alternate solutions, proper labels for their feelings, to set realistic goals, solution orientation, and techniques to verbalize their disagreements are more productive than "bailing them out" when they are confronted with frustration.

9.2 Possible Causes of Learning Problems

Intellectual Reasons

Limited intelligence—slow learner

Retardation

Emotional Reasons

Consistent school failure

Traumatic emotional development

Separation or divorce

High parental expectations

Sibling performance

Health-related problems

Change in environment, moving

Social Reasons

Peer pressure

Peer rejection

Academic Reasons

Learning disabilities

Poor academic skills—math, reading

Style of teacher vs. style of student

Language difficulties

Be Aware of Avoidance Symptoms Indicating Possible Learning Problems

- Selective forgetting
- Child takes hours to complete homework
- Child can't seem to get started with homework
- Child frequently brings home unfinished class work
- Child complains of headaches, stomach aches, etc.
- Child forgets to write down assignments day after day

Be Aware of Other Symptoms Reflective of Tension, Stress, or Difficulties with Learning

At School

Inability to focus on task

Disorganization

Inflexibility

Irresponsibility

Poor judgment

Denial

At Home

Over-sensitivity

Forgetfulness

Daydreaming

Unwillingness to venture out

Unwillingness to reason

Denial

Social Interaction

Social withdrawal

Finding faults with other children

Low peer status

Unwillingness to try new relationships

Sleep

Trouble falling asleep

Restless sleep

Resistance to rising

Frequent nightmares

Although many of these symptoms may not, by themselves, indicate a major problem, several guidelines should be used in determining the severity of the problem:

1. *Frequency of Symptoms*—Consider how often the symptoms occur. The greater the frequency, the greater chance of a serious problem.

2. *Duration of Symptoms*—Consider how long the symptoms last. The longer the duration, the more serious the problem.

3. *Intensity of Symptoms*—Consider how serious the reactions are at the time of occurrence. The more intense the symptom, the more serious the problem.

If you suspect serious problems, contact the school psychologist, special education teacher, or a private mental health clinic for an evaluation or at least a consultation. The more immediate the response to such symptoms, the greater chance of success with the child.

9.3 How Parents Can Help Their Children with Homework

1. *Set up a homework schedule.* For some children, the responsibility of deciding when to sit down and do homework may be too difficult. Children may decide to do their homework after school or after dinner. This is a personal choice and has to do with learning style. However, once the time is determined, the schedule should be adhered to as closely as possible.

2. *Rank-order assignments.* For some children, the decision as to what to do first becomes a major chore. They may dwell over this choice for a long period of time because everything takes on the same level of importance. Rank-ordering assignments means that the parent determines the order in which the assignments are completed.

3. *Do not sit next to your child while he or she does homework.* Sitting next to your child may create learned helplessness because the same "assistance" is not imitated in the classroom. Parents serve their children better by acting as a resource person to whom the child may come with a problem. After the problem is solved or question answered, the child should return to his or her work area without the parent.

4. *Check correct problems first.* When your child brings you a paper to check, mention to him or her how well he or she did on the correct problems, spelling words, etc. For the ones that are incorrect, say, "If you go back and check these over, you may get a different answer."

5. *Never let homework drag on all night.* The only thing accomplished by allowing a child to linger on her or his homework hour after hour with very little performance is increased feelings of inadequacy. If this occurs, end the work period after a reasonable period of time and write the teacher a note explaining the circumstances.

6. *Discuss homework questions before your child reads the chapter.* Discuss the questions to be answered before the child reads the chapter. In this way he or she will know what important information to look for while reading.

7. *Check small groups of problems at a time.* Many children can benefit from immediate gratification. Have your child do five problems and then come to you to check them. Additionally, if the child is doing the assignment incorrectly, the error can be detected and explained, preventing the child from doing the entire assignment incorrectly.

8. *Place textbook chapters on tape.* Research indicates that the more sensory input children receive, the greater the chance the information will be retained. For instance, parents can place science or social studies chapters on tape so that the child can listen while reading along.

9. *Be aware of negative nonverbal messages during homework.* Many messages, especially negative ones, can be communicated easily without your awareness (e.g., raised eyebrows, inattentiveness). If children are sensitive, they will pick up these messages, which can only add to their tension.

10. *Avoid finishing assignments for your child.* Children tend to feel inadequate when a parent finishes their homework. If children cannot complete an assignment, and they have honestly tried, write the teacher a note explaining the circumstances.

11. *Be aware of possible signs of more serious learning problems.* Parents should always be aware of symptoms indicating the possibility of more serious learning problems. Many of these symptoms may show up during homework. If these symptoms present a pattern, contact the psychologist or resource room teacher for further assistance. Such symptoms may include constant avoidance of homework, forgetting to bring home assignments, taking hours to do homework, procrastination on classwork, low frustration tolerance, labored writing, poor spelling, etc.

12. *Check homework assignments at the end of the night.* This will reduce the child's concerns over the thought of bringing incorrect homework to school. This also offers children a feeling of accomplishment, a source of positive attention, and a sense of security that the work is completed.

9.4 How to Communicate with Your Children

1. *Listen to each other—communication is a two-way street.* Many people feel they are communicating, but in a sense, they never listen. Therefore, use the technique of "I'll talk and you listen, and then you talk and I'll listen" as a first step in developing communication with your child.

2. *Don't attack when communicating your feelings.* When communicating feelings, try using the words "I," "we," or "me" as often as possible and stay away from the word "you." Even if the child has done something to hurt you, focus on your feelings rather than his or her behavior. Inform the child on how the behavior affected you.

3. *Teach children to label feelings properly.* Children may have a very difficult time communicating because they lack the experience in labeling their feelings. Therefore, it is crucial for parents to assist their children in correctly labeling a feeling or emotion. You may want to say, for example, "Although the feeling you are expressing sounds like anger, it is really frustration and frustration is. . . ."

4. *Use connective discussion whenever possible.* When faced with a direct question concerning a feeling or a reason for some behavior, most children will shrug their shoulders in confusion or immediately respond, "I don't know." Instead of this direct communication, try connective discussion. This technique assumes that the parent may be aware of the trigger and connects the feeling and resulting behavior for the child. For example, parents may say, "It seems to me that you are feeling jealous over the attention your new baby brother is getting and that may be the reason for your behavior." At this point, children may have an easier time responding because the foundation and labels have been presented.

5. *Remember that all behavior has a trigger.* If parents can trace back children's responses to the source or trigger, they will have a very good chance of identifying the real problem. Remember that all behavior is a message and, for many children, their behavior is the only means of communicating their frustrations or feelings. The problem is that such behavior is frequently misunderstood and misinterpreted, resulting in more problems.

6. *Be aware of nonverbal misinterpretations.* Children are very prone to nonverbal misinterpretations. They frequently misread a look on a parent's face and personalize it into something negative. If you are upset, angry, or frustrated with something other than your children, let them know that fact in a verbal way. Try, "I am very upset right now about something. But I wanted to tell you that it has nothing to do with you, and after I think for awhile, we will get together."

7. *Use written communication whenever possible.* The use of writing to communicate feelings is an excellent tool in that it allows parents and children to phrase thoughts as desired. Notes thanking a child for some positive behavior or telling the child how proud you are of him/her are just some examples. Notes can also be used to register a complaint without nose-to-nose confrontation.

8. *Try to use direct love as often as possible.* The need to feel loved and cared for is a primary need for any individual at any age. Direct messages of love require no interpretation or assumptions on the part of the child and should be viewed on the same level of importance as gasoline to a car. Examples of direct love include hugging, kissing, cuddling, holding, stroking, etc.

9. *Make yourself as approachable as possible.* The higher the approachability factor on the part of parents, the easier it is for children to express and show direct love. Parents may want to evaluate just how easy their children feel in approaching them with feelings or problems and make adjustments if necessary. In later life, such individuals may have an easier time using direct forms of love in relationships.

9.5　How Parents Can Use Effective Discipline

1. *Use limits and guidelines for a child's emotional development.* For children, realistic, fair, and well-defined limits and guidelines represent a "safety net" within which they can behave. Children will know that any act of poor judgment will be brought to their attention if limits are well-defined. Consequently, they will be brought back to the safety net. Parenting cannot be a popularity contest.

2. *Be sure all behavior has a consequence.* This means appropriate behavior is rewarded and negative behavior is punished. Consistency of consequence, whether reward or punishment, will assist the child in developing a frame of reference on how to behave.

3. *Do not use punishment by itself—it will not work.* Punishment tells children what not to do, but rewards tell children what behavior is acceptable. If long-term changes in behavior are desired, then reward must be included. Rewards need not be monetary. They can include verbal praise, written notes of thanks, extended playtime or TV time, a special trip, or dinner with a parent.

4. *Limit punishment to something you can control.* Quantity or severity of punishment is not always important. The most important thing to remember with discipline is that a parent begins it and the parent ends it. Maintaining both boundaries is crucial. In too many situations, the parent begins the discipline but due to its harshness, unrealistic expectations of time, manipulation by children, or inability of parent to follow through, there is no closure. For young children with no concept of time, 2 minutes in a "timeout" chair (controllable) rather than 30 minutes (uncontrollable) is just as productive.

5. *Never trade a punishment for a reward.* If children do something inappropriate and then something appropriate, the two incidents should be treated separately. If you begin to trade off, children become confused and may be forced to become manipulative.

6. *Focus on inappropriate behavior, not the personality.* Remember, children are not stupid; rather, it's their inappropriate behavior that is unacceptable. You may want to use such phrases as poor judgment, inappropriate behavior, lapse of judgment, acting before thinking, etc., when confronting the act. Focusing on the act allows children to save face. Children who grow up in homes where personalities are attacked frequently tend to model that behavior in their social relationships.

7. *Choose your battles wisely.* Try to view energy like money. In this way, you will be deciding whether an issue is worth $2.00 worth of energy or $200.00. Investing too much energy in situations may lead to early parent "burnout." However, it is very important that both parents agree on the priority of issues, so that the child is not confused.

8. *Try to project a united front.* If one parent should disagree with the other's tactics or reasoning, try to discuss it at a private moment. Open disagreement concerning a disciplinary action can sometimes confuse children and place them in the uncomfortable position of having to choose between parents.

9. *Try to use a forced-choice technique whenever possible.* Choose two options, solutions, or alternatives that are acceptable to you. Then say to the child, "You may do . . . or . . . Which do you prefer?" Using a forced-choice technique allows children to feel that they are making the decision and creates fewer problems than an open-ended question, such as "What would you like?"

10. *Delay a consequence when you are angry.* The use of delay allows for a different perspective from that which is held at the height of anger. Say, "I am so angry now that I don't want to deal with this situation. Go to your room and I'll deal with you in 15 minutes." The use of delay will reduce impractical consequences.

547

9.6 How Parents Can Spot Possible Learning Disabilities in Their Children

1. Intellectual Requirements

Children with learning disabilities usually exhibit intellectual potential within the average range and above. This usually translates into a score of 90 or better. Such potential should only be measured by an individual intelligence test, such as the Wechsler Intelligence Scale for Children—Revised.

2. Academic Requirements

Children with learning disabilities usually exhibit mild academic deficits (6 months to 1 year below grade level), moderate academic deficits (1 to 2 years below grade level), or severe academic deficits (more than 2 years below grade level). These deficits may exhibit themselves in any one of the following areas:

- Decoding (word attack skills)
- Reading Comprehension
- Mathematical Computation
- Mathematical Reasoning
- Written Expression
- Oral Expression
- Listening Comprehension

3. Exclusion Requirements

Children with learning disabilities are not retarded, primarily emotionally disturbed, hearing impaired, visually impaired, slow learners, or the result of inadequate instructional practices or cultural or economic disadvantages.

4. Background Requirements

Children with learning disabilities usually exhibit a history of learning, social, and developmental difficulties dating back to early grades.

5. Behavioral Requirements

Children with learning disabilities usually exhibit several of the following:

Variability in performance across subject areas

Attention problems, e.g., distractibility, poor concentration

Organizational problems with information, space, or time

Poor motivation and attitude due to repeated academic failure

Memory problems

Language deficits in listening, speaking, or writing

Poor motor abilities in fine motor (small muscle) or gross motor (large muscles)

Inappropriate social behavior, e.g., making friends, poor reactions to social situations

6. Processing Requirements

Children with learning disabilities usually exhibit deficits in the learning process. The strengths or weaknesses in this process are usually measured by process (perceptual) tests such as the Slingerland, Woodcock-Johnson, Detroit Tests of Learning Aptitudes, or the ITPA. However, the following list indicates some difficulties exhibited by children with processing problems in selected areas:

Visual-Motor Disability

- Poor motor coordination.
- Poor perception of time and space.
- Gets lost easily.
- Poor handwriting, artwork, drawing.
- Restless, short attention span.
- Awkward, frequent tripping, skipping.

Auditory Association Disability

- Fails to enjoy being read to.
- Has difficulty comprehending questions.
- Slow to respond, takes a long time to answer.
- Relies heavily on picture clues.

Manual Expressive Disability

- Poor handwriting and drawing.
- Poor at game playing, can't imitate others.
- Clumsy, uncoordinated.
- Poor at acting out ideas or feelings.

Auditory Memory Disabilities

- Fails to remember instructions.
- Can't memorize nursery rhymes, poems.
- Doesn't know alphabet.
- Unable to count.

Auditory-Vocal Disability

- Appears not to listen or comprehend.
- Responds with one-word answers.
- May emphasize wrong syllables in words.
- Offers little in group discussions.
- Trouble following directions.
- Trouble with rote memory, e.g., math facts.

Visual Association Disability

- Unable to tell a story from pictures.
- Unable to understand what he/she reads.
- Fails to handle primary workbook.
- Needs auditory cues and clues.

9.6 continued

Verbal Expression Disability

- Mispronounces common words.
- Uses incorrect word endings.
- Difficulty in sound blending.
- Omits correct verbal endings.

Visual Memory Disabilities

- Misspells own name frequently.
- Inconsistent word identification.
- Frequent misspellings, even after practice.
- Can't write alphabet, numbers, etc.

9.7 Frequently Asked Questions about Learning Disabilities

What is a learning disability?

In general, a learning disability is a problem in acquiring and using skills required for listening, speaking, reading, writing, reasoning, and mathematical ability. Such problems in the acquisition of skills cannot be traced to inadequate intelligence, school environment, emotional problems, visual or hearing defects, cultural deprivation, or lack of motivation.

How many children have learning disabilities?

This is somewhat difficult, depending upon the definition used. The U.S. Department of Education reports approximately 5 percent of a school's population may be learning disabled. According to their statistics taken in 1984, this represented 1,811,451 students throughout the country.

What causes learning disabilities?

Several theories have been proposed concerning the cause of learning disabilities. Some of the more widely held theories center around heredity, complications of pregnancy, lag in nervous system development (sometimes referred to as a maturational lag), or some subtle neurological impairment, sort of like crossed wires in a telephone line.

Can a true learning disability show up in later grades with no earlier indications?

This is a widely held misconception. In most cases, a true learning disability has a historical pattern with symptoms appearing as early as a child's first school experience or sooner. A fifth-grade child who is referred by a teacher for suspected learning disabilities and has *no* prior educational difficulties should be considered a low-risk youngster for learning disabilities.

Are dyslexia and learning disabilities the same?

No. Dyslexia is a specific and severe form of a learning disability. Dyslexia refers to a severe problem in learning how to read. All children with learning disabilities are not dyslexic. However, all dyslexic children are learning disabled.

Are reversals an indication of a learning disability?

This symptom has been greatly inflated by the media. Parents should keep in mind that reversal of letters, numbers, etc., may be very common in children up to grade 3 and may not by themselves indicate any learning disability. However, if a child frequently reverses letters, numbers, etc., along with other symptoms or continues after age 8, you should discuss this with a professional as soon as possible.

9.7 continued

Can a child be learning disabled in only one area?

Yes. Some children may have a learning disability in the area of short-term memory, or mathematical computations, or spelling, or reading comprehension, etc. Of course, the more areas affected, the more serious the disability.

What kinds of symptoms signal a possible learning disability?

There are a variety of symptoms that may signal the presence of such a problem. Some of the more common include disorganization, poor muscle coordination, impulsivity, distractibility, short attention span, trouble in completing assignments, poor spelling, poor handwriting, poor social skills, low reading level, difficulty in following directions, discrepancy between ability and performance, and language difficulties.

What is the first thing to do if I suspect that my child may have a learning disability?

Hopefully, the school would have identified this possibility before you. However, if this is not the case, immediately contact the school psychologist, or head of the school's child study team, and make them aware of your concerns. If you do not wish to go through the school, then contact a qualified professional in the field or a clinic that specializes in learning disabilities. They will be happy to evaluate your child. However, keep in mind that such an evaluation can be very expensive, although it is free through the school.

Must my child be referred to the Committee on Special Education if he or she has a learning disability?

The answer in most cases will be yes. It is the legal and moral responsibility of every school district to refer such a child for a review before the Eligibility Committee (Committee on Special Education). A review does not mean immediate classification. It just means that enough evidence exists to warrant a "look" by the district. If the child has a learning disability and is encountering frustration in school, then the services he or she will receive should greatly reduce such problems.

9.8   What Parents Need to Know about Retention

Retention of a student's grade placement is a very difficult decision for both parents and educators. When parents are first presented with this suggestion by the school, they may become very overwhelmed and confused. If parents are presented with this option, then great care should be taken in examining all the variables that will affect the outcome.

Present research seems somewhat divided about the use of such an educational alternative. Some studies have shown that the greatest success for such an action occurs prior to grade 1. The chances for success dramatically decrease as children become older. Other studies seem to indicate that if retention is exercised as an option in kindergarten or first grade, boys seem to benefit more than girls. This result seems to support the developmental pattern of a more advanced social and academic maturity in girls.

Because parents should be involved in the decision of retention, it is important that they become educated in this area. The following factors should be taken into consideration prior to the final action.

1. *Present Grade Placement.* As previously mentioned, the greatest chance for retention to work is in kindergarten and first grade. By the time children are in fourth or fifth grade, the chances for success decrease dramatically.

2. *Immature Behavior Patterns.* The level of interpersonal relations exhibited by children is also a factor to consider. If they tend to play with children much younger than themselves, retention will have fewer consequences. However, if children choose peers who are equal or older in age, retention may have more negative results.

3. *Age of the Child.* Children who are younger than their classmates will experience fewer problems with retention. However, children who are one or two years above their classmates may have more serious adjustments to this action.

4. *Brothers and Sisters.* Children without siblings seem to make a better adjustment when repeating a grade. Others with brothers or sisters in the same grade or one year below find retention much more difficult. Children in this category find the experience ego-deflating and feel a loss of familial status.

5. *Attendance.* The more time a child is out from school, the greater the reason for retention. Children who are ill and miss more than 25 days of school are prime candidates. This is especially important in the early grades where the foundations of reading and basic skills are taught. Some children with excellent attendance are less suitable candidates.

6. *Intellectual Ability.* Children with average intelligence have the better chance of success with retention. However, those with below-average (lower 2–10 percent) or superior ability (upper 2–10 percent) tend to have more difficulty. Children who fall into these categories may be having difficulties in school for other reasons that would not be addressed by retention, e.g., emotional problems, retardation.

7. *Physical Size.* Children who are smaller in stature make better candidates. Those who are physically larger than their present classmates will have more problems when retained.

9.8 continued

8. *Student's Gender.* As previously mentioned, boys in kindergarten and first grade make the best candidates. After fourth grade, both boys and girls will have little chance of success when it comes to retention.

9. *Present Classroom Performance.* Students who are performing one year behind in most academic subjects may find retention a help. Those who are more than two years behind may need an alternate type of program, such as a special education class or a resource room. Children who are functioning on grade level or above should be reviewed carefully.

10. *Present Emotional State.* Children who do not exhibit any signs of serious emotional difficulties, e.g., impulsivity, nervous habits, distractibility, unwillingness to reason, and tantrums, have a better chance when retained. Children who exhibit serious emotional concerns should not be considered for retention. However, other educational options should be explored.

11. *Parent's Attitude About Retention.* This factor is crucial. Children will have the best chance of adjusting to retention when their parents see it as a positive step. Frustrated, angry, and disappointed parents will negate any chance of success.

12. *Number of Schools Attended.* Children who have attended several schools within their first two years of school will have less success with retention.

13. *Student's Attitude.* Children who see retention as an opportunity to "catch up" will have a better chance of success. Children who become very upset, exhibit denial about poor performance, or show indifference may have greater difficulty.

14. *Evidence of Learning Disabilities.* Children with intact learning skills and processes have a greater chance for success when it comes to retention. Children who have been diagnosed as having learning disabilities should receive alternate educational support. In such cases, retention should not be considered as an option.

The above factors are offered as a general guide for parents to follow. There may be other factors that should be considered as well. Regardless, a parent's input into this decision is crucial.

PART 10

Appendices

10.1 Educational Terminology Associated with Special Education

ABILITY GROUPING   The grouping of children based on their achievement in an area of study.

ACCELERATED LEARNING   An educational process that allows students to progress through the curriculum at an increased pace.

ACHIEVEMENT   The level of a child's accomplishment on a test of knowledge or skill.

ADAPTIVE BEHAVIOR   An individual's social competence and ability to cope with the demands of the environment.

ADAPTIVE PHYSICAL EDUCATION   A modified program of instruction implemented to meet the needs of students with special needs.

ADVOCATE   An individual, either a parent or professional, who attempts to establish or improve services for children with special needs.

AGE NORMS   Standards based on the average performance of individuals in different age groups.

AGNOSIA   Inability to recognize objects and their meaning, usually resulting from damage to the brain.

AMPLIFICATION DEVICE   Any device that increases the volume of sound.

ANECDOTAL RECORD   A procedure for recording and analyzing observations of a child's behavior; an objective, narrative description.

ANNUAL GOALS   Yearly activities or achievements to be completed or attained by the child with a disability that are documented on the Individualized Education Plan (IEP).

APHASIA   The inability to acquire meaningful spoken language by the age of 3, usually resulting from damage or disease to the brain.

ARTICULATION   The production of distinct language sounds by the vocal chords.

AT RISK   Usually refers to infants or children with a high potential for experiencing future medical or learning problems.

ATTENTION DEFICIT HYPERACTIVITY DISORDER (ADHD)   A psychiatric classification used to describe individuals who exhibit poor attention, distractibility, impulsivity, and hyperactivity.

BASELINE MEASURE   The level or frequency of behavior prior to the implementation of an instructional procedure that will later be evaluated.

BEHAVIOR MODIFICATION   The techniques used to change behavior by applying principals of reinforcement learning.

BILINGUAL   The ability to speak two languages.

CAREER EDUCATION   Instruction that focuses on the application of skills and content area information necessary to cope with the problems of daily life, independent living, and vocational areas of interest.

CATEGORICAL RESOURCE ROOM   An auxiliary pull-out program that offers supportive services to children who have the same disability.

COGNITION   The understanding of information.

CONSULTANT TEACHER   A supportive teacher of children with disabilities, whose services are provided in the classroom.

CRITERION-REFERENCED TESTS   Tests in which the child is evaluated on his or her own performance to a set of criterion and not in comparison to others.

DECLASSIFICATION   The process in which a student with disabilities is no longer considered in need of special education services. This requires a meeting of the Eligibility Committee and can be requested by the parent, school, or student over the age of 18.

DEFICIT   A level of performance that is less than expected for a child.

DESENSITIZATION   A technique used in reinforcement theory in which there is a weakening of a response, usually an emotional response.

DIAGNOSIS   Specific disorder(s) identified as a result of some evaluation.

DISTRACTIBILITY   Difficulty in maintaining attention.

DUE PROCESS   The legal steps and processes outlined in educational law that protect the rights of children with disabilities.

DYSCALCULIA   A serious learning disability in which there is an inability to calculate, apply, solve, or identify mathematical functions.

DYSFLUENCY   Difficulty in the production of fluent speech, as in the example of stuttering.

DYSGRAPHIA   A serious learning disability in which there is an inability or loss of ability to write.

DYSLEXIA   A severe type of learning disability in which the ability to read is greatly impaired.

DYSORTHOGRAPHIA   A serious learning disability that affects the ability to spell.

ENRICHMENT   Providing a child with extra and more sophisticated learning experiences than those normally presented in the curriculum.

ETIOLOGY   The cause of a problem.

EXCEPTIONAL CHILDREN   Children whose school performance shows significant discrepancy between ability and achievement and as a result require special instruction, assistance, and/or equipment.

FREE APPROPRIATE PUBLIC EDUCATION (FAPE)   Used in P.L. 94-142 to mean special education and related services that are provided at public expense and conform to the state requirements and to the IEP.

GROUP HOME   A residential living arrangement for adults with disabilities, especially the mentally retarded, along with several supervisors who do not have disabilities.

HABILITATION   An educational approach used with exceptional children that is directed toward the development of the necessary skills required for successful adulthood.

HOMEBOUND INSTRUCTION   A special education service in which teaching is provided by a specially trained instructor to students unable to attend school. A parent or guardian must always be present at the time of instruction. In some cases, the instruction may take place on a neutral site and not in the home or school.

HYPERACTIVITY   Behavior characterized by excessive motor activity or restlessness.

IMPULSIVITY   Non-goal-oriented activity that is exhibited by individuals who lack careful thought and reflection prior to a behavior.

10.1 continued

INCLUSION   Returning children with disabilities to their home school so that they may be educated in the same classroom with children who do not have disabilities.

INDIVIDUALIZED EDUCATION PLAN (IEP)   A written educational contract that outlines a child's current levels of performance, related services, educational goals, and modifications. This plan is developed by a team including the child's parent(s), teacher(s), and supportive staff.

INTERDISCIPLINARY TEAM   The collective efforts of individuals from a variety of disciplines in assessing the needs of a child.

INTERVENTION   Preventive, remedial, compensatory, or survival services made on behalf of an individual with disabilities.

ITINERANT TEACHER   A teacher hired by a school district to help in the education of a child with a disability. The teacher is employed by an outside agency and may be responsible for several children in several districts.

LEARNING DISABILITY   Children with average or above-average potential intelligence who are experiencing a severe discrepancy between their ability and achievement.

LEAST RESTRICTIVE ENVIRONMENT   Combining the education of children with disabilities with that of children who do not have disabilities whenever realistic and possible. It is the least restrictive setting in which the child with a disability can function without difficulty.

MAINSTREAMING   The practice of educating exceptional children in the regular classroom.

MENTAL AGE   The level of intellectual functioning based on the average for children of the same chronological age. When dealing with children with severe disabilities, the mental age may be more reflective of levels of ability than the chronological age.

MENTAL DISABILITY   The individual's intellectual level is measured within the subaverage range and there are marked impairments in social competence.

NATIVE LANGUAGE   The primary language used by an individual.

NONCATEGORICAL RESOURCE ROOM   A resource room in a regular school that provides services to children with all types of classified disabilities. The children with these disabilities are able to be maintained in a regular classroom.

NORM-REFERENCED TESTS   Tests used to compare a child's performance with the performance of others on the same measure.

OCCUPATIONAL THERAPIST   A professional who programs and/or delivers instructional activities and materials to assist children and adults with disabilities to participate in useful daily activities.

PARAPROFESSIONALS   A trained assistant or parent who works with a classroom teacher in the education process.

PHYSICAL THERAPIST   A professional trained to assist and help individuals with disabilities maintain and develop muscular and orthopedic capability and to make correct and useful movements.

PINS PETITION   PINS stands for "Person in Need of Supervision." This is a family court referral that can be made by either the school or the parent and is usually made when a child under the age of 16 is out of control in terms of attendance, behavior, or some socially inappropriate or destructive pattern.

POSITIVE REINFORCEMENT   Any stimulus or event that occurs after a behavior has been exhibited and that affects the possibility of that behavior occurring in the future.

PUPIL PERSONNEL TEAM   A group of professionals from the same school who meet on a regular basis to discuss children's problems and offer suggestions or a direction for resolution.

PUPILS WITH HANDICAPPING CONDITIONS (PHC)   Students classified as disabled by the Committee on Special Education.

PUPILS WITH SPECIAL EDUCATIONAL NEEDS (PSEN)   Students defined as having math and reading achievement lower than the 23rd percentile and requiring remediation. These students are not considered disabled but are entitled to assistance to elevate their academic levels.

RELATED SERVICES   Services provided to children with disabilities to assist in their ability to learn and function in the least restrictive environment. Such services may include in-school counseling, speech and language services, and so on.

REMEDIATION   An educational program designed to teach children to overcome some deficit or disability through education and training.

RESOURCE ROOM   An auxiliary service provided to children with disabilities for part of the school day. It is intended to service children's special needs so that they can be maintained within the least restrictive educational setting.

SCREENING   The process of examining groups of children in hopes of identifying potential high-risk children.

SECTION 504   Refers to Section 504 of the Rehabilitation Act of 1973 in which guarantees are provided for the civil rights of children and adults with disabilities. It also applies to the provision of services for children whose disability is not severe enough to warrant classification, but could benefit from supportive services and classroom modifications.

SELF-CONTAINED CLASS   A special classroom for children with specific exceptionalities, usually located within a regular school building.

SHELTERED WORKSHOP   A transitional or long-term work environment for individuals with disabilities who cannot or who are preparing for work in a regular setting. Within this setting, the individual can learn to perform meaningful, productive tasks and receive payment.

SURROGATE PARENT   A person other than the child's natural parent who has legal responsibility for the child's care and welfare.

TOKEN ECONOMY   A system of reinforcing various behaviors through the delivery of tokens. These tokens can be stars, points, candy, chips, and so on.

TOTAL COMMUNICATION   The approach to the education of deaf students which combines oral speech, sign language, and finger spelling.

UNDERACHIEVER   A term generally used in reference to a child's lack of academic achievement in school. However, it is important that the school identify the underlying causes of such underachievement because it may be a symptom of a more serious problem.

VOCATIONAL REHABILITATION   A well-designed program designed to help adults with disabilities obtain and hold a job.

10.2 Psychological Terminology Associated with Special Education

AFFECTIVE REACTION   Psychotic reactions marked by extreme mood swings.

ANXIETY   A general uneasiness of the mind characterized by irrational fears, panic, tension, and physical symptoms including palpitations, excessive sweating, and increased pulse rate.

ASSESSMENT   The process of gathering information about students in order to make educational decisions.

BASELINE DATA   An objective measure used to compare and evaluate the results obtained during some implementation of an instructional procedure.

COMPULSION   A persistent, repetitive act that the individual cannot consciously control.

CONFABULATION   The act of replacing memory loss by fantasy or by some reality that is not true for the occasion.

DEFENSE MECHANISMS   The unconscious means by which an individual protects him- or or herself against impulses or emotions that are too uncomfortable or threatening. *See* DENIAL, DISPLACEMENT, INTELLECTUALIZATION, PROJECTION, RATIONALIZATION, REACTION, FORMATION, REPRESSION, and SUPPRESSION.

DELUSION   A groundless, irrational belief or thought, usually of grandeur or of persecution. It is usually a characteristic of paranoia.

DENIAL   An individual's refusal to admit the reality of some unpleasant event, situation, or emotion.

DEPERSONALIZATION   A nonspecific syndrome in which the person senses that he or she has lost personal identity, that he or she is different, strange, or not real.

DISPLACEMENT   Disguising a motive's goal or intention by substituting another in its place.

ECHOLALIA   Repeating what other people say as if echoing them.

ETIOLOGY   The cause(s) of something.

HALLUCINATION   An imaginary visual image that is regarded as a real sensory experience by the person.

INTELLECTUALIZATION   A defense mechanism in which the individual exhibits anxious or moody deliberation, usually about abstract matters.

MAGICAL THINKING   The primitive and pre-logical thinking in which the child creates an outcome to meet his or her fantasy rather than the reality.

NEOLOGISMS   Made-up words that only have meaning to the individual.

OBSESSIONS   A repetitive and persistent idea that intrudes into a person's thoughts.

PANIC ATTACKS   A serious episode of anxiety in which the individual experiences a variety of symptoms including palpitations, dizziness, nausea, chest pains, trembling, fear of dying, and fear of losing control. These symptoms are not the result of any medical cause.

PARANOIA   A personality disorder in which the individual exhibits extreme suspiciousness of the motives of others.

PHOBIA   An intense irrational fear, usually acquired through conditioning to an unpleasant object or event.

PROJECTION   Disguising a source of conflict by displacing one's own motives to someone else.

PROJECTIVE TESTS   Methods used by psychologists and psychiatrists to study personality dynamics through a series of structured or ambiguous stimuli.

PSYCHOSIS   A serious mental disorder in which the individual has difficulty differentiating between fantasy and reality.

RATIONALIZATION   The interpretation of one's own behavior so as to conceal the motive it expresses by assigning the behavior to another motive.

REACTION FORMATION   A complete disguise of a motive so that it is expressed in a form that is directly opposite to its original intent.

REPRESSION   The psychological process involved in not permitting memories and motives to enter consciousness but rather operating at an unconscious level.

RORSCHACH TEST   An unstructured psychological test in which the individual is asked to project responses to a series of ten inkblots.

SCHOOL PHOBIA   A form of separation anxiety in which the child's concerns and anxieties are centered on school issues, resulting in extreme fear about coming to school.

SUPPRESSION   The act of consciously inhibiting an impulse, affect, or idea, as in the deliberate act of forgetting something so as not to have to think about it.

SYMPTOM   Any sign, physical or mental, that stands for something else. Symptoms are usually generated by the tension of conflicts. The more serious the problem or conflict, the more frequent and intense the symptom.

SYNDROME   A group of symptoms.

THEMATIC APPERCEPTION TEST   A structured psychological test in which the individual is asked to project his or her feelings onto a series of drawings or photos.

WECHSLER SCALES OF INTELLIGENCE   A series of individual intelligence tests measuring global intelligence through a variety of subtests.

10.3 Medical Terminology Associated with Special Education

ALBINISM A congenital condition marked by severe deficiency in or total lack of pigmentation.

AMBLYOPIA A dimness of sight without any indication of change in the eye's structure.

AMNIOCENTESIS A medical procedure done during the early stages of pregnancy for the purpose of identifying certain genetic disorders in the fetus.

ANOMALY Some irregularity in development or a deviation from the standard.

ANOXIA A lack of oxygen.

APHASIA The inability to acquire meaningful spoken language by the age of 3 as a result of brain damage.

APRAXIA Pertains to problems with voluntary, or purposeful, muscular movement with no evidence of motor impairment.

ASTIGMATISM A visual defect resulting in blurred vision caused by uneven curvature of the cornea or lens. Lenses usually correct the condition.

ATAXIA A form of cerebral palsy in which the individual suffers from a loss of muscle coordination, especially those movements relating to balance and position.

ATHETOSIS A form of cerebral palsy characterized by involuntary, jerky, purposeless, and repetitive movements of the extremities, head, and tongue.

ATROPHY The degeneration of tissue.

AUDIOGRAM A graphic representation of the results of a hearing test.

AUDIOLOGIST A specialist trained in the evaluation and remediation of auditory disorders.

BINOCULAR VISION Vision using both eyes working together to perceive a single image.

BLIND, LEGALLY Visual acuity measured at 20/200 in the better eye with best correction of glasses or contact lenses. Vision measured at 20/200 means the individual must be 20 feet from something to be able to see what the normal eye can see at 200 feet.

CATARACT A condition of the eye in which the crystalline lens becomes cloudy or opaque. As a result, a reduction or loss of vision occurs.

CATHETER A tube inserted into the body to allow for injections or withdrawal of fluids or to maintain an opening in a passageway.

CEREBRAL PALSY An abnormal succession of human movement or motor functioning resulting from a defect, insult, or disease of the central nervous system.

CONDUCTIVE HEARING LOSS A hearing loss resulting from obstructions in the outer or middle ear or some malformations that interfere in the conduction of sound waves to the inner ear. This condition may be corrected medically or surgically.

CONGENITAL A condition present at birth.

CRETINISM A congenital condition associated with a thyroid deficiency that can result in stunted physical growth and mental retardation.

CYANOSIS A lack of oxygen in the blood characterized by a blue discoloration of the skin.

CYSTIC FIBROSIS   An inherited disorder affecting pancreas, salivary, mucous, and sweat glands that causes severe, long-term respiratory difficulties.

DIPLEGIA   Paralysis that affects either both arms or both legs.

DOWN SYNDROME   A medical abnormality caused by a chromosomal anomaly that often results in moderate to severe mental retardation. The child with Down syndrome will exhibit certain physical characteristics such as a large tongue, heart problems, poor muscle tone, and a broad, flat bridge of the nose.

ELECTROENCEPHALOGRAM (EEG)   A graphic representation of the electrical output of the brain.

ENCOPRESIS   A lack of bowel control that may also have psychological causes.

ENDOGENOUS   Originating from within.

ENURESIS   A lack of bladder control that may also have psychological causes.

EXOGENOUS   Originating from external causes.

FETAL ALCOHOL SYNDROME   A condition usually found in the infants of alcoholic mothers. As a result, low birth weight; severe retardation; and cardiac, limb, and other physical defects may be present.

FIELD OF VISION   The area of space visible with both eyes while looking straight ahead; measured in degrees.

GLAUCOMA   An eye disease characterized by excessively high pressure inside the eyeball. If untreated, the condition can result in total blindness.

GRAND MAL SEIZURE   The most serious and severe form of an epileptic seizure in which the individual exhibits violent convulsions, loses consciousness, and becomes rigid.

HEMIPLEGIA   Paralysis involving the extremities on the same side of the body.

HEMOPHILIA   An inherited deficiency in the blood-clotting factor that can result in serious internal bleeding.

HERTZ   A unit of sound frequency used to measure pitch.

HYDROCEPHALUS   A condition present at birth or developing soon afterward from excess cerebrospinal fluid in the brain; results in an enlargement of the head and mental retardation. This condition is sometimes prevented by the surgical placement of a shunt that allows for the proper drainage of the built-up fluids. *See* SHUNT.

HYPERACTIVITY   Excessive physical and muscular activity characterized by extreme inattention, and excessive restlessness and mobility. The condition is usually associated with Attention Deficit Disorder or learning disabilities.

HYPEROPIA   Farsightedness; a condition causing difficulty with seeing near objects.

HYPERTONICITY   Heightened state of excessive tension.

HYPOTONICITY   An inability to maintain muscle tone or an inability to maintain muscle tension or resistance to stretch.

INSULIN   A protein hormone produced by the pancreas that regulates carbohydrate metabolism.

IRIS   The opaque, colored portion of the eye.

JUVENILE DIABETES   A children's disease characterized by an inadequate secretion or use of insulin resulting in excessive sugar in the blood and urine. This condition is usu-

10.3 continued

ally controlled by diet and/or medication. However, in certain cases, control may be difficult and, if untreated, serious complications may arise such as visual impairments, limb amputation, coma, and death.

MENINGITIS An inflammation of the membranes covering the brain and spinal cord. If untreated, can result in serious complications.

MENINGOCELE A type of spina bifida in which there is protrusion of the covering of the spinal cord through an opening in the vertebrae.

MICROCEPHALY A disorder involving the cranial cavity characterized by the development of a small head. Retardation usually occurs from the lack of space for brain development.

MONOPLEGIA Paralysis of a single limb.

MULTIPLE SCLEROSIS A progressive deterioration of the protective sheath surrounding the nerves, leading to a degeneration and failure of the body's central nervous system.

MUSCULAR DYSTROPHY A group of diseases that eventually weakens and destroys muscle tissue, leading to a progressive deterioration of the body.

MYOPIA Nearsightedness; a condition that results in blurred vision for distant objects.

NEONATAL The time usually associated with the period between the onset of labor and six weeks following birth.

NEUROLOGICALLY IMPAIRED Individuals who exhibit problems associated with the functioning of the central nervous system.

NYSTAGMUS A rapid, rhythmic, and involuntary movement of the eyes. This condition may result in difficulty reading or fixating upon objects.

OCULAR MOBILITY The eye's ability to move.

OPHTHALMOLOGIST A medical doctor trained to deal with diseases and conditions of the eye.

OPTIC NERVE The nerve in the eye that carries impulses to the brain.

OPTICIAN A specialist trained to grind lenses according to a prescription.

OPTOMETRIST A professional trained to examine eyes for defects and prescribe corrective lenses.

ORGANIC Factors usually associated with the central nervous system that cause a handicapping condition.

OSSICLES The three small bones of the ear that transmit sound waves to the eardrum. They consist of the malleus, incus, and stapes.

OSTENOGENESIS IMPERFECTA Also known as "brittle bone disease," this hereditary condition affects the growth of bones and causes them to break easily.

OTITIS MEDIA Middle ear infection.

OTOLARYNGOLOGIST A medical doctor specializing in diseases of the ear and throat.

OTOLOGIST A medical doctor specializing in the diseases of the ear.

OTOSCLEROSIS A bony growth in the middle ear that develops around the base of the stapes, impeding its movement and causing hearing loss.

PARALYSIS An impairment to or a loss of voluntary movement or sensation.

PARAPLEGIA A paralysis usually involving the lower half of the body, including both legs, as a result of injury or disease of the spinal cord.

PERINATAL Occurring at or immediately following birth.

PETIT MAL SEIZURE A mild form of epilepsy characterized by dizziness and momentary lapse of consciousness.

PHENYLKETONURIA Referred to as PKU, this inherited metabolic disease usually results in severe retardation. However, if detected at birth, a special diet can reduce the serious complications associated with the condition.

PHOTOPHOBIA An extreme sensitivity of the eyes to light. This condition is common in albino children.

POSTNATAL Occurring after birth.

PRENATAL Occurring before birth.

PROSTHESIS An artificial device used to replace a missing body part.

PSYCHOMOTOR SEIZURE An epileptic seizure in which the individual exhibits many automatic seizure activities of which he or she is not aware.

PUPIL The opening in the middle of the iris that expands and contracts and lets in light.

QUADRIPLEGIA Paralysis involving all four limbs.

RETINA The back portion of the eye, on which the image is focused. It contains nerve fibers that connect to the optic nerve.

RETINITIS PIGMENTOSA A degenerative eye disease in which the retina gradually atrophies, causing a narrowing of the field of vision.

RETROLENTAL FIBROPLASIA An eye disorder resulting from excessive oxygen in incubators of premature babies.

RH INCOMPATIBILITY A blood condition in which the fetus has Rh-positive blood and the mother has Rh-negative blood, leading to a build up of antibodies that attack the fetus. If untreated, can result in birth defects.

RHEUMATIC FEVER A disease characterized by acute inflammation of the joints, fever, skin rash, nosebleeds, and abdominal pain. This disease often damages the heart by scarring its tissues and valves.

RIGIDITY CEREBRAL PALSY A type of cerebral palsy characterized by minimal muscle elasticity and little or no stretch reflex, which creates stiffness.

RUBELLA Referred to as German measles, this communicable disease is usually only of concern when developed by women during the early stages of pregnancy. If contracted at that time, there is a high probability of severe handicaps of the offspring.

SCLERA The tough white outer layer of the eyeball that protects as well as holds contents in place.

SCOLIOSIS A weakness of the muscles that results in a seriously abnormal curvature of the spine. This condition may be corrected with surgery or a brace.

SEMICIRCULAR CANALS The three canals within the middle ear that are responsible for maintaining balance.

10.3 continued

SENSORINEURAL HEARING LOSS   A hearing disorder resulting from damage or dysfunction of the cochlea.

SHUNT   A tube that is inserted into the body to drain fluid from one part to another. This procedure is common in cases of hydrocephalus to remove excessive cerebrospinal fluid from the head and redirect it to the heart or intestines.

SPASTICITY   A type of cerebral palsy characterized by tense, contracted muscles, resulting in muscular uncoordination.

SPINA BIFIDA OCCULTA   A type of spina bifida characterized by a protrusion of the spinal cord and membranes. This form of the condition does not always cause serious disability.

STRABISMUS   Crossed eyes.

TREMOR   A type of cerebral palsy characterized by consistent, strong, uncontrolled movements.

TRIPLEGIA   Paralysis of three of the body's limbs.

USHER'S SYNDROME   An inherited combination of visual and hearing impairments.

VISUAL ACUITY   Sharpness or clearness of vision.

VITREOUS HUMOR   The jelly-like fluid that fills most of the interior of the eyeball.

10.4 Terminology Associated with Occupational Therapy

Occupational therapists in an educational setting should communicate their findings in a clear and easy-to-understand manner. The following definitions will help when documenting medically-related terminology for the educational community. A therapist may continue to use medical terminology, but it should be defined in the body of the report. An individual therapist in his or her own words, wherever possible, may write definitions for these terms.

ABDUCTION   Movement of limb outward, away from body.

ACTIVE MOVEMENTS   Movements done without help.

ADAPTIVE EQUIPMENT   Devices used to position or to teach special skills.

ASSOCIATED REACTIONS   Increase of stiffness in spastic arms and legs resulting from effort.

ASYMMETRICAL   One side of the body is different from the other; unequal or dissimilar.

ATAXIC   No balance; jerky.

ATHETOID   A person who has continual uncontrolled and unwanted movements.

ATROPHY   A wasting of the muscles.

AUTOMATIC MOVEMENTS   Necessary movements done without thought or effort.

BALANCE   Not falling over; ability to keep a steady position.

BILATERAL MOTOR   Skill and performance in purposeful movement that requires interaction between both sides of the body in a smooth manner.

CIRCUMDUCTION   To swing the limb away from the body to clear the foot.

CLONUS   Shaky movements of spastic muscle.

COMPENSORY MOVEMENT   A form of movement that is atypical in relation to normal patterns of movement.

CONGENITAL   From birth.

CONTRACTURE   Permanently tight muscle or joint.

COORDINATION   A combination of muscles in movement.

CROSSING THE MIDLINE   Skill and performance in crossing the vertical midline of the body.

DEFORMITY   The body or a limb is fixed in an abnormal position.

DIPLEGIA   The legs are mostly affected.

DISTRACTIBLE   Not able to concentrate.

EQUILIBRIUM   Balance.

EQUILIBRIUM REACTIONS   Automatic patterns of body movements that enable restoration and maintenance of balance against gravity.

EQUINUS   Walking on the toes.

EXTENSION   The straightening of the trunk and limbs.

10.4 continued

EYE–HAND COORDINATION   The eye is used as a tool for directing the hand to perform efficiently.

FACILITATION   Making it possible for a person to move.

FIGURE–GROUND PERCEPTION   The ability to see foreground against the background.

FINE MOTOR   Small muscle movements using the hands and fingers.

FLEXION   Bending of elbows, hips, knees, and so on.

FLOPPY   Soft and flexible; inclined to move around clumsily.

FLUCTUATING TONE   Changing from one degree of tension to another, such as from low to high tone.

FORM CONSTANCY   The ability to perceive an object as possessing invariant properties, such as shape, size, color, and brightness.

GAIT PATTERN   A description of walking pattern including: (1) *swing-to gait*—walking with crutches or walker by moving crutches forward and swinging body up to crutches; and (2) *swing through*—walking with crutches by moving crutches forward and swinging body in front of the crutches.

GENU VALGUS   Knocked-kneed.

GENU VARUM   Bow-legged.

GROSS MOTOR   Coordinated movements of all parts of the body for performance.

GUARDED SUPERVISION   Remaining close to the student to provide physical support if balance is lost while sitting, standing, or walking.

GUARDING TECHNIQUES   Techniques used to help students maintain balance, including contact guarding, when a student requires hands-on contact to maintain balance.

HEAD CONTROL   The ability to control the position of the head.

HEMIPLEGIA   One side of the body is affected.

HYPERTONICITY   Increased muscle tone.

HYPOTONICITY   Decreased muscle tone.

INHIBITION   Positions and movements that stop muscle tightness.

INVOLUNTARY MOVEMENTS   Unintended movements.

KYPHOSIS   Increased rounding of the upper back.

LORDOSIS   A sway back or increased curve in the back.

MANUAL MUSCLE TEST   A test of isolated muscle strength. The ranges are: *normal*, 100%; *good*, 80%; *fair*, 50%; *poor*, 20%; and *zero*, 0%.

MOBILITY   Movement of a body muscle or body part or movement of the whole body from one place to another.

MOTIVATION   Making the person want to move or perform.

MOTOR PATTERNS   Ways in which the body and limbs work together to make movement. *See* PRAXIS.

NYSTAGMUS   A series of automatic back-and-forth eye movements.

ORGANIZATION A person's ability to organize him- or herself in approach to and performance of activities.

ORTHOSIS A brace.

PARAPLEGIC Paralysis of the lower half of the body with involvement of both legs.

PASSIVE Anything that is done to the person without his or her help or cooperation.

PATHOLOGICAL Due to or involving abnormality.

PERCEPTION The organization of sensation from useful functioning.

PERSEVERATION Unnecessary repetition of speech or movement.

POSITION IN SPACE A person's ability to understand the relationship of an object to him- or herself.

POSITIONING Ways of placing an individual that will help normalize postural tone and facilitate normal patterns of movement and that may involve the use of adaptive equipment.

POSTURAL BALANCE Skill and performance in developing and maintaining body posture while sitting, standing, or engaging in an activity.

PRAXIS The ability to think through a new task that requires movement; also known as motor planning.

PRONATION Turning the hand with the palm down.

PRONE Lying on the stomach.

QUADRIPLEGIC Paralysis of all four limbs.

RANGE OF MOTION The full extent over which a joint can move.

REFLEX Stereotypic posture and movement that occurs in relation to specific eliciting stimuli and outside of conscious control.

RIGHT/LEFT DISCRIMINATION Skill and performance in differentiating right from left and vice versa.

RIGHTING REACTION The ability to put the head and body right when positions are abnormal or uncomfortable.

RIGIDITY Very stiff movements and postures.

ROTATION Movement of the trunk; the shoulders move opposite to the hips.

SENSATION A conscious feeling or sense impression.

SENSORY-MOTOR EXPERIENCE The feeling of one's own movements.

SEQUENCING The ordering of visual patterns in time and space.

SCOLIOSIS A curvature of the spine.

SPASM A sudden tightness of muscles.

SPASTICITY Increased muscle tone.

SPATIAL RELATIONS The ability to perceive the position of two or more objects in relation to self and to each other.

STAIR CLIMBING Methods of climbing include: (1) *mark stepping*—ascending or descending one step at a time; and (2) *alternating steps*—step over step.

STEREOGNOSIS Identifying the forms and nature of objects through the sense of touch.

10.4 continued

SUBLUXATION   A partial dislocation where joint surfaces remain in contact with one another.

SUPINATION   Turning the hand with the palm up.

SYMMETRICAL   Both sides are equal.

TACTILE   Pertaining to the sense of touch of the skin.

TANDEM WALKING   Walking in a forward progression, placing heel to toe.

TONE   Firmness of muscles.

VESTIBULAR SYSTEM   A sensory system that responds to the position of the head in relation to gravity and accelerated and decelerated movements.

VISUAL MEMORY   The ability to recall visual stimuli in terms of form, detail, position, and other significant features on both a short- and long-term basis.

VISUAL-MOTOR INTEGRATION   The ability to combine visual input with purposeful voluntary movement of the hand and other body parts involved in the activity.

VOLUNTARY MOVEMENTS   Movements done with attention and with concentration.

10.5 Abbreviations Associated with Special Education

ACLC   Assessment of Children's Language Comprehension

AD/HD   Attention Deficit Hyperactivity Disorder

AE   Age Equivalent

AUD.DIS   Auditory Discrimination

BINET   Stanford-Binet Intelligence Test

BVMGT   Bender Visual-Motor Gestalt Test

CA   Chronological Age

CAT   Children's Apperception Test

CEC   Council for Exceptional Children

CP   Cerebral Palsy

CSE   Committee on Special Education

DAP   Draw-A-Person Test

DB   Decibel—Hearing Measurement

DDST   Denver Developmental Screening Test

DQ   Developmental Quotient

DTLA-3   Detroit Tests of Learning Aptitude—3

ED   Emotionally Disturbed

EMR   Educable Mentally Retarded

FAPE   Free Appropriate Public Education

FQ   Frequency Range—Hearing Measurement

GE   Grade Equivalent

GFW   Goldman-Fristoe-Woodcock Test of Auditory Discrimination

HH   Hard of Hearing

HTP   House-Tree-Person Test

Hz   Hertz—Hearing Measurement

IEP   Individualized Education Plan

IEU   Intermediate Educational Unit

IHE   Institutions of Higher Education

IQ   Intelligence Quotient

ITPA   Illinois Tests of Psycholinguistic Abilities

LA   Learning Aptitude

LD   Learning Disabled

LEA   Local Education Agency

LPR   Local Percentile Rank

MA   Mental Age

10.5 continued

MBD   Minimal Brain Dysfunction

MH   Multiply Handicapped

MMPI   Minnesota Multiphasic Personality Inventory

MR   Mentally Retarded

MVPT   Motor-Free Visual Perception Test

NPR   National Percentile Rank

PHC   Pupils with Handicapping Conditions

PIAT   Peabody Individual Achievement Test

PINS   Person in Need of Supervision

PLA   Psycholinguistic Age

PPVT   Peabody Picture Vocabulary Test

PQ   Perceptual Quotient

PR   Percentile Rank

PS   Partially Sighted

PSEN   Pupils with Special Educational Needs

PTA   Pure Tone Average—Hearing Measurement

SAI   School Abilities Index

SCSIT   Southern California Sensory Integration Tests

SEA   State Education Agency

SIT   Slosson Intelligence Test

SRT   Speech Reception Threshold—Hearing Measurement

TACL   Test for Auditory Comprehension of Language

TAT   Thematic Apperception Test

TMR   Trainable Mentally Retarded

TOWL   Test of Written Language

TWS   Larsen-Hammill Test of Written Spelling

VAKT   Visual/Auditory/Kinesthetic/Tactile

VIS.DIS   Visual Discrimination

VMI   Beery-Buktenica Developmental Test of Visual Motor Integration

WAIS-R   Wechsler Adult Intelligence Scale—Revised

WISC-R   Wechsler Intelligence Scale for Children—Revised

WISC-III   Wechsler Intelligence Scale for Children—III

WPPSI-III   Wechsler Preschool and Primary Scale of Intelligence—III

WRAT-R   Wide Range Achievement Test—Revised

10.6 Publishers of Books and Videos on Special Needs Issues

The publishers* listed here are only some of the many that provide information about issues relating to individuals with disabilities, that is, social skills, sexuality, and sexuality education.

Active Parenting, Inc.   810 Franklin Court, Suite B, Marietta, GA 30067; telephone: (800) 825-0060

ADIS Press   Contact F. A. Davis Company, 1915 Arch Street, Philadelphia, PA 19103-9954; telephone: (215) 568-2270

Albert Whitman & Company   6340 Oakton Street, Morton Grove, IL 60053; telephone: (800) 255-7675 or (708) 647-1355

American Academy of Pediatrics   Committee on Adolescence, Division of Publications, 131 Northwest Point Boulevard, P.O. Box 927, Elk Grove Village, IL 60009-0927; telephone: (800) 433-9016

American Guidance Service   Publishers Building, P.O. Box 99, Circle Pines, MN 55014-1796; telephone: (800) 328-2560; in Minnesota, call (800) 247-5053

Bantam Books   666 Fifth Avenue, New York, NY 10103; telephone: (800) 223-6834

Center for Population Options   1025 Vermont Avenue NW, Washington, D.C. 20005; telephone: (202) 347-5700

Center on Human Policy   School of Education, Syracuse University, 200 Huntington Hall, 2nd Floor, Syracuse, NY 13244-2340; telephone: (315) 443-3851

Channing L. Bete Company   200 State Road, South Deerfield, MA 01373; telephone: (413) 665-7611

Charles C. Thomas   2600 S. First Street, Springfield, IL 62794-9265; telephone: (217) 789-8980

College-Hill Press   c/o Pro-Ed, 8700 Shoal Creek Boulevard, Austin, TX 78758; telephone: (512) 451-3246

Columbia University Press   136 S. Broadway, Irvington-on-Hudson, NY 10533; telephone: (914) 591-9111

Council for Exceptional Children   Division on Mental Retardation, 1920 Association Drive, Reston, VA 22091-1589; telephone: (703) 620-3660

Crown Publishers   c/o Harmony Books Division, 201 East 50th Street, New York, NY 10022; telephone: (212) 751-2600

Department of Health and Human Services   Superintendent of Documents, U.S. Government Printing Office, Washington, D.C. 20402

Ednick Communications   c/o Pro-Ed, 8700 Shoal Creek Boulevard, Austin, TX 78758; telephone: (512) 451-3246

Federation for Children with Special Needs and the Center on Human Policy   Technical Assistance for Parent Programs (TAPP) Project, 312 Stuart Street, Second Floor, Boston, MA 02116; telephone: (617) 482-2915

*At the time of printing, the publishers' addresses and telephone numbers were correct.

10.6 continued

Gallaudet University   Bookstore, 800 Florida Avenue NE, B20E, Washington, D.C. 20002-3695; telephone: (202) 651-5380

Grune and Stratton   c/o Prentice-Hall, Attention: Mail Order Sales, 200 Old Tappan Road, Old Tappan, NJ 07675; telephone: (800) 223-1360

Guilford Press   72 Spring Street, New York, NY 10012; telephone: (800) 365-7006

Harcourt Brace Jovanovich   465 S. Lincoln Drive, Troy, MO 63379; telephone: (800) 543-1918

HarperCollins   Keystone Industrial Park, Reeves & Monahan, Scranton, PA 18512; telephone: (800) 331-3761

Haworth Press   10 Alice Street, Binghamton, NY 13904-1580; telephone: (800) 342-9678

Hazelden   P.O. Box 176, Center City, MN 55012-0176; telephone: (800) 328-9000

Hemisphere Publishing Corporation   1900 Frost Road, Suite 101, Bristol, PA 19007; telephone: (800) 821-8312

Interstate Research Associates   Contact NICHCY, P.O. Box 1492, Washington, D.C. 20013; telephone: (800) 695-0285

James Stanfield Publishing Company   P.O. Box 41058, Santa Barbara, CA 93140; telephone: (800) 421-6534

Johns Hopkins University Press   701 West 40th Street, Baltimore, MD 21211; telephone: (800) 537-5487

March of Dimes   1275 Mamaroneck Avenue, White Plains, NY 10605; telephone: (914) 428-7100

National Association of School Psychologists   Publications, 8455 Colesville Road, Silver Spring, MD 20910; telephone: (301) 608-0500

National Association of Social Workers   P.O. Box 92180, Washington, D. C. 20090-2180; telephone: (800) 752-3590

National Center for Education in Maternal and Child Health   38th and R Street N.W., Washington, D.C. 20057; telephone: (202) 625-8400

National Center for Youth with Disabilities   University of Minnesota, Box 721—UMHC, Harvard Street at East River Road, Minneapolis, MN 55455; telephone: (800) 333-6293

National Down Syndrome Society   666 Broadway, New York, NY 10012; telephone: (800) 221-4602

National Federation of the Blind   1800 Johnson Street, Baltimore, MD 21230; telephone: (301) 659-9314

Norton & Company   c/o National Book Company, 800 Keystone Industrial Park, Scranton, PA 18512-4601; telephone: (800) 223-2584

Paul H. Brookes Publishing Company   P.O. Box 10624, Baltimore, MD 21285-0624; telephone: (800) 638-3775

Plenum Publishing   233 Spring Street, New York, NY 10013-1578; telephone: (800) 221-9369

Pro-Ed   8700 Shoal Creek Boulevard, Austin, TX 78758; telephone: (512) 451-3246

Research Press   2612 North Mattis Avenue, Champaign, IL 61821; telephone: (217) 352-3273

R.R. Bowker   121 Chanlon Road, New Providence, NJ 07974; telephone: (800) 521-8110

St. Martin's Press   175 Fifth Avenue, New York, NY 10010; telephone: (800) 221-7945

St. Paul Ramsey Medical Center   HIHW, 640 Jackson Street, St. Paul, MN 55101; telephone: (612) 221-3569

United Cerebral Palsy Associations, Inc.   UCP/Lancaster County, 1811 Olde Homestead Lane, P.O. Box 10485, Lancaster, PA 17605-0485; telephone: (717) 396-7965

Walker Publishing   720 Fifth Avenue, New York, NY 10019; telephone: (800) 289-25537

Young Adult Institute   460 West 34th Street, New York, NY 10001; telephone: (212) 563-7474

10.7 Scholarships and Financial Aid Resources for Exceptional Children

Scholarships specifically designated for students with disabilities are extremely limited. Listed here are organizations* that offer the few disability-specific scholarships.

Alexander Graham Bell Association of the Deaf   3417 Volta Place NW, Washington, D.C. 20007; telephone: (202) 337-5220 (voice/TT)

American Council of the Blind   1155 15th Street NW, Suite 720, Washington, D.C. 20005; telephone: (800) 424-8666 (3–5:30 P.M.) or (202) 467-5081

American Foundation for the Blind   15 West 16th Street, New York, NY 10011; telephone: (800) 232-5463 or (212) 620-2000

Association for Education and Rehabilitation of the Blind and Visually Impaired   206 North Washington Street, Suite 320, Alexandria, VA 22314; telephone: (703) 548-1884

Blinded Veterans Association   477 H St. NW, Washington, D.C. 20001-2694; telephone: (202) 371-8880; *for children and spouses of blinded veterans*

Bridge Endowment Fund   Scholarship Office, National FFA (Future Farmers of America) Center, P.O. Box 15160, Alexandria, VA 22309-0160; telephone: (703) 360-3600

Central Intelligence Agency (CIA)   Office of Student Programs (Internships), P.O. Box 1925, Department T, Room 220, Washington, D.C. 20013; telephone: (703) 281-8365

Christian Record Braille Foundation   4444 South 52nd Street, Lincoln, NE 68506; telephone: (402) 488-0981

Council of Citizens with Low Vision (CCLV)   5707 Brockton Drive, No. 302, Indianapolis, IN 46220; telephone: (317) 254-0185 or (800) 733-2258

Electronic Industries Foundation (EIF)   Marcie Vorac, 919 18th Street NW, Suite 900, Washington, D.C. 20006; telephone: (202) 955-5814 (TDD 955-5836); *technical or scientific field*

Elks Grand Lodge   telephone: (919) 358-7661

Foundation for Exceptional Children   1920 Association Drive, Reston, VA 22091; telephone: (703) 620-1054

Foundation for Science and Disability, Inc.   Rebecca F. Smith, 115 S. Brainard Avenue, La Grange, IL 60525; *for science students with a disability studying for a Master's Degree*

The Geoffrey Foundation   P.O. Box 1112, Ocean Avenue, Kennebunkport, ME 04046; telephone: (207) 967-5798; *offered to hearing impaired auditory-verbal children and students*

Graduate Fellowship Fund   Gallaudet University, Alumni Association, Alumni Office, 800 Florida Avenue NE, Washington, D.C. 20002; telephone: (202) 651-5060 (Voice/TT); *limited to Ph.D. students who are hearing impaired*

*At the time of printing, the organizations' addresses and telephone numbers were correct.

Immune Deficiency Foundation   3566 Ellicott Mills Drive, Unit B2, Ellicott City, MD 21043; *limited to those with primary genetic immune deficiency*

International Kiwanis Club   Check with local Kiwanis organizations for availability of scholarships; to find a local chapter, telephone: (317) 875-8755

Jewish Braille Institute of America   110 E. 30th Street, New York, NY 10016; *offered to students who wish to become rabbis, cantors, or Jewish educators*

La Sertoma International   1912 E. Meyer Boulevard, Kansas City, MO 64312; telephone: (816) 333-3116; *limited to graduate students who are preparing to assist people who are blind*

Lighthouse, Inc.   800 2nd Avenue, New York, NY 10017; *limited to legally blind students*

National Association of the Deaf   Stokoe Scholarship, 814 Thayer Avenue, Silver Spring, MD 20910; telephone: (301) 587-1788 (voice) or (301) 587-1789 (TT); *supports research related to sign language or deafness*

National Captioning Institute, Inc.   Dr. Malcolm J. Norwood, Memorial Award Panel, 5203 Leesburg Pike, Suite 1500, Falls Church, VA 22041; telephone: (703) 998-2400 (Voice/TT); *limited to students studying for careers in communication and/or media technology*

National Federation of the Blind   1800 Johnson Street, Baltimore, MD 21230; telephone: (410) 659-9314

National Federation of Music Clubs   Music for the Blind, 55 Janssen Place, Kansas City, MO 64109

National 4-H Council   7100 Connecticut Avenue, Chevy Chase, MD 20815; telephone: (301) 961-2800

National Hemophilia Foundation   110 Greene Street, New York, NY 10012; telephone: (800) 42-HANDI

Opportunities for the Blind   P.O. Box 510, Leonardtown, MD 20650

The President's Committee on Employment of People with Disabilities   1331 F Street NW, Washington, D.C. 20004; telephone: (202) 376-6200

Recording for the Blind   20 Rozelle Road, Princeton, NJ 08540; telephone: (609) 452-0606

Rotary Club   Apply for scholarships two years in advance; telephone: (202) 638-3555

Spina Bifida Association of America   4590 MacArthur Boulevard NW, Suite 250, Washington, D.C. 20007; telephone: (800) 621-3141 or (202) 944-3285

Trapshooting Hall of Fame, College Scholarship Fund for Chairshooters   Hugo A. Keim, M.D., 161 Fort Washington Avenue, New York, NY 10032; telephone: (212) 305-5559

Venture Clubs Student Aid Award and Venture Clubs Handicapped Student Scholarship Fund   1616 Walnut Street, Suite 700, Philadelphia, PA 19103; telephone: (215) 732-0512

Very Special Arts Education Office   John F. Kennedy Center for the Performing Arts, Washington, D.C. 20566; *limited to students aged 10–21 studying selected musical instruments*

10.8 Selected Newsletters, Magazines, and Journals on Children with Special Needs

Ability Magazine Jobs Information Business Service, 1682 Langley, Irvine, CA 92714; telephone: (714) 854-8700 or (800) 453-JOBS

ACLD Newsbriefs Learning Disabilities Association of America, 4156 Library Road, Pittsburgh, PA 15234; telephone: (412) 341-1515

ARC's Government Report Association for Retarded Citizens, 1522 K Street NW, Washington, D.C. 20005; telephone: (202) 785-3388

Attention Magazine CH.ADD (Children with Attention Deficit Disorder), 499 NW 70th Avenue, Suite 109, Plantation, FL 33317; telephone: (800) 233-4050; voice mail to request information packet: (305) 587-3700

Case Manager Systemedic Corportion, 10809 Executive Center Drive, Suite 105, Little Rock, AR 72211; telephone: (501) 227-5553

Choice Magazine 85 Channel Drive, Dept. 16, Port Washington, NY 11050; telephone: (516) 883-8280; *free audio anthology, short stories, articles from more than 100 sources, available to visually impaired individuals*

Closing the Gap P.O. Box 68, Henderson, MN 56044; telephone: (612) 248-3294; *assistive technology information*

Dateline on Disability U.S. Department of Housing and Urban Development, Washington, D.C. 20410; telephone: (202) 755-6422

Deaf American National Association of the Deaf, 814 Thayer Avenue, Silver Spring, MD 20910; telephone: (301) 587-1788

Disabilities Resources Monthly Disabilities Resources Inc., Four Glatter Lane, Centereach, NY 11720; telephone: (516) 585-8290

Disabled Outdoors Magazine HC 80, Box 395, Grand Marais, MN 55604; telephone: (218) 387-9100

Exceptional Children Council for Exceptional Children, 1920 Association Drive, Reston, VA 22091; telephone: (703) 620-3660 or (800) 232-7323

Exceptional Parent Magazine 120 State Street, Hackensack, NJ 07601; telephone: (201) 489-0871 or (800) E-PARENT

First DIBS Disability Info. Brokerage System, P.O. Box 1285, Tucson, AZ 85702; telephone: (520) 327-8277; *information resources for the consumer and others on disability topics*

Hobby Newsnote P.O. Box 350073, Elmwood Park, IL 60707; telephone: (708) 622-5996

ILRU Insights ILRU Research/Training Center, Independent Living, 2323 South Shepard, Suite 1000, Houston, TX 77019; telephone: (713) 520-0232; *national newsletter for independent living*

JASH: The Journal of the Association for Persons with Severe Handicaps JASH, 11201 Greenwood Avenue North, Seattle, WA 98133; telephone: (206) 361-8870

Journal of Speech and Hearing Disorders American Speech-Language-Hearing Association, 10801 Rockville Pike, Rockville, MD 20852; telephone: (301) 897-5700

Journal of Visual Impairment and Blindness   American Foundation for the Blind, 15 West 16th Street, New York, NY 10011; telephone: (800) 232-5463 or (212) 620-2000

Kaleidoscope: International Magazine of Literature, Fine Arts & Disability   United Disability Services, 326 Locust Street, Akron, OH 44302; telephone: (216) 762-9755

Life Lines   Life Services for the Handicapped Inc., 352 Park Avenue South, Suite 703, New York, NY 10010; telephone: (212) 532-6740 or (800) 995-0066; *information about long-term care and planning for disabilities*

Life Span   National Council of Community Mental Health Centers, 12300 Twin Brook Parkway, Suite 320, Rockville, MD 20852; telephone: (301) 984-6200; *information on tax tips, insurance, medical care, law, and legislation*

Mainstream Magazine   2973 Beech Street, San Diego, CA 92102; telephone: (619) 234-3138; *reports on employment, education, new products and technology, etc.*

MDC Newsletter   Materials Development Center, School of Education and Human Service, Menomonie, WI 54751; *information on employment and transition services*

NARIC Quarterly   National Rehabilitation Information Center, 8455 Colesville Road, Suite 935, Silver Spring, MD 20910; telephone: (301) 588-9284 or (800) 346-2742; *covers activities, projects, resources, and book reviews*

National Council News   National Council of Community Mental Health Centers, 12300 Twin Brook Parkway, Suite 320, Rockville, MD 20852; telephone: (301) 984-6200; *information on legislation*

National Networker   National Network of Learning Disabled Adults, P.O. Box 32611, Phoenix, AZ 85064; telephone: (602) 941-5112

NCD Bulletin   National Council on Disabilities, 1331 F Street NW, Suite 1050, Washington, D.C. 20004; telephone: (202) 272-2004; *covers latest issues on disabilities*

Newsline   Federation for Children with Special Needs, 95 Berkeley Street, Boston, MA 02116; telephone: (617) 482-2195

NTID Focus   National Technical Institute for the Deaf/RIT, P.O. Box 9887, 1 Lomb Memorial, Rochester, NY 14623; telephone: (716) 475-6400; *research on occupational aspects of deafness*

On Our Own   Vinfen Corporation, Gateway Crafts, 62 Harvard Street, Brookline, MA 02146; telephone: (617) 734-1577; *journal by and for adults with developmental disabilities*

PeopleNet   P.O. Box 897, Levittown, NY 11756; telephone: (516) 579-4043; *information on relationships and sexuality, including personal ads*

Pocket Guide to Federal Help for Individuals with Disabilities   Consumer Information Center, Dept. 114A, Pueblo, CO 81009; telephone: (202) 501-1794; *summary of benefits and services*

Policy Updates   Institute on Community Integration, 86 Pleasant Street, Wulling Hall, Minneapolis, MN 55455; telephone: (612) 626-8200; *information on transition service issues*

Recording for the Blind News   20 Rozelle Road, Princeton, NJ 08540; telephone: (609) 452-0606 or (800) 221-4792

Volta Review   Alexander Graham Bell Association, 3417 Volta Place NW, Washington, D.C. 20007; telephone: (202) 337-5220; *professional journal*

10.9.1 Attention Deficit Disorder

The Attention Deficit Information Network, Inc. (AD-IN)

475 Hillside Avenue
Needham, MA 02194

Phone: (781) 455-9895
Fax: (781) 444-5466
E-mail: adin@gis.net
Internet: http://www.addinfonetwork.com
Newsletters/Publications: Provides audiotapes, videotapes, information booklets, and articles online.
Description: AD-IN is a nonprofit volunteer organization that offers support and information to families of children with Attention Deficit Disorder (ADD), adults with ADD, and professionals through an international network of 60 parent and adult chapters. Contact AD-IN for a list of chapters, as well as to receive cost of information packets specifically designed for adults with ADD, parents, or educators. AD-IN also provides information to those interested in starting a new local chapter and serves as a resource for information on training programs and speakers for those who work with individuals with ADD.

Children and Adults with Attention Deficit Disorder (CH.ADD)

499 Northwest 70th Avenue, Suite 308
Plantation, FL 33317

Phone: (800) 233-4050
Fax: (954) 587-5499
E-mail: national@chadd.org
Internet: http://www.chadd.org
Newsletters/Publications: CH.ADD publishes the newsletter *Chadderbox*, filled with up-to-date information on ADD issues; the quarterly magazine *Attention*; and an educator's manual on ADD.
Description: CH.ADD is a nonprofit, parent-based organization that disseminates information on ADD/ADHD and coordinates more than 500 parent support groups across the country. The Web site also contains extensive practical information for teachers and parents.

National Attention Deficit Disorder Association (NADDA)

9930 Johnnycake Ridge Road, Suite 3E
Mentor, OH 44060

Phone: (800) 487-2282 (to request information packet) or (440) 350-9595
Fax: (440) 350-0223
E-mail: NATLADDA@aol.com
Internet: http://www.add.org
Newsletters/Publications: FOCUS (published quarterly)

Description: NADDA is a national, nonprofit organization that focuses on the needs of adults, young adults, and families with Attention Deficit Disorder. NADDA's mission is to help people with ADD live happier, more successful lives by providing information and resources on treatment and research, as well as workplace, relationship, parenting, and post-secondary educational issues.

10.9.2 Autism/Pervasive Developmental Disability

Autism Network International (ANI)

P.O. Box 448
Syracuse, NY 13210-0448

Phone: (315) 476-2462
Fax: (315) 425-1978
E-mail: jisincla@mailbox.syr.edu
Internet: NA
Newsletters/Publications: ANI's educational materials include the regular newsletter *Our Voice* as well as brochures and audio-visual aids.
Description: ANI is a self-help and advocacy organization dedicated to supporting individuals with autism and helping them to compensate, navigate, and function in the world. The Network provides a forum for people with autism to share information, peer support, and tips for coping and problem solving. In addition to promoting self-advocacy for high-functioning autistic adults, ANI assists people with autism who are unable to participate directly by providing information and referrals to parents and teachers.

Autism Research Institute (ARI)

4182 Adams Avenue
San Diego, CA 92116

Phone: (619) 281-7165
Fax: (619) 563-6840
E-mail: NA
Internet: http://www.autism-society.org/>
Newsletters/Publications: ARI publishes the quarterly newsletter *Autism Research Review International*, and has a publication list of information packets.
Description: ARI is primarily devoted to conducting research, and to disseminating the results of research, on methods of preventing, diagnosing, and treating autism and other severe behavioral disorders of childhood. ARI provides information based on research to parents and professionals throughout the world, and serves as a link between the parents of these children, who are widely scattered geographically, and researchers throughout the world who are in need of carefully diagnosed samples of children for research purposes. Such referrals are made only with the prior consent of the parents. ARI assists families directly by providing information by mail or phone and has made the education of these children one of its priorities.

Autism Society of America (formerly NSAC)

7910 Woodmont Avenue, Suite 650
Bethesda, MD 20814-3015

Phone: (301) 657-0881 or (800) 328-8476
Fax: (301) 657-0869
E-mail: NA

Internet: http://www.autism-society.org

Newsletters/Publications: The American Autism Society publishes a newsletter called *The Advocate*.

Description: The Autism Society of America, a national not-for-profit advocacy organization established in 1965, is dedicated to providing information, assistance, support, and advocacy services to individuals with autism and their families. The Society supports ongoing medical research into the causes, prevention, and treatment of autism; promotes public awareness; and provides information and advocacy services to help affected individuals become fully participating members of their communities. In addition, the Society makes referrals to appropriate sources of support and treatment. The Society's educational materials include newsletters, brochures, and Spanish-language materials.

Families for Early Autism Treatment (FEAT)

P.O. Box 255722
Sacramento, CA 95865-5722

Phone: (916) 843-1536
Fax: NA
E-mail: feat@feat.org
Internet: http://www.feat.org
Newsletters/Publications: FEAT Newsletter
Description: FEAT is a nonprofit organization of parents and professionals, designed to help families with children who have received the diagnosis of Autism or Pervasive Developmental Disorder (PDD NOS). It offers a network of support where families can meet each other and discuss issues surrounding autism and treatment options.

MAAP Services, Inc.

P.O. Box 524
Crown Point, IN 46307

Phone: (219) 662-1311
Fax: (219) 662-0638
E-mail: chart@netnitco.net
Internet: http://www.stepstn.com/nord/org
Newsletters/Publications: The MAAP is a quarterly newsletter that allows subscribers to exchange information, learn about issues related to autism, and share with others who face similar challenges; disseminates specific print materials relevant to high-functioning individuals with autism; and distributes a pamphlet entitled "MAAP Services, Inc."
Description: MAAP Services is a nonprofit organization dedicated to assisting family members of more advanced individuals with autism by offering information and advice on autism and by providing them the opportunity to network with others in similar circumstances. In addition, MAAP Services works to inform professionals and the general public about more advanced individuals with autism and how to meet their needs. The organization conducts conferences, workshops, and meetings of parent groups; supports education; and provides appropriate referrals.

10.9.2 continued

National Alliance for Autism Research (NAAR)

Research Park
414 Wall Street
Princeton, NJ 08540

Phone: (888) 777-NAAR or (609) 430-9160
Fax: (609) 430-9163
E-mail: naar@naar.org.
Internet: http://babydoc.home.pipeline.com/naar/naar.htm
Newsletters/Publications: The Naarrative (published quarterly)
Description: NAAR is a national nonprofit, tax-exempt organization dedicated to finding the causes, prevention, effective treatment, and, ultimately, cure of the autism spectrum disorders.

10.9.3   Hearing Impairment

Alexander Graham Bell Association for the Deaf, Inc.

3417 Volta Place NW
Washington, D.C. 20007

Voice/TTD: (202) 337-5220
Fax: (202) 337-8314
E-mail: agbell@aol.com
Internet: http://www.agbell.org
Newsletters/Publications: The Volta Review (journal) and *Volta Voices* (magazine)
Description: This organization gathers and disseminates information on hearing loss, promotes better public understanding of hearing loss in children and adults, provides scholarships and financial and parent–infant awards, promotes early detection of hearing loss in infants, publishes books on deafness, and advocates for the rights of children and adults who are hard of hearing or deaf.

American Academy of Audiology

8201 Greensboro Drive, Suite 300
McLean, VA 22102

Voice/TTD: (800) 222-2336 or (703) 610-9022
Fax: (703) 610-9005
E-mail: lac@audiology.com
Internet: http://www.audiology.org
Newsletters/Publications: Audiology Today (magazine), *Journal of AAA* (journal), and *Audiology Express* (newsletter)
Description: This is a professional organization of individuals dedicated to providing high-quality hearing care to the public. It provides professional development, education, and research, and promotes increased public awareness of hearing disorders and audiologic services.

ADARA: Professionals Networking for Excellence in Service Delivery with Individuals Who Are Deaf or Hard of Hearing (formerly American Deafness and Rehabilitation Association)

P.O. Box 6956
San Mateo, CA 94403

Voice/TTD: (650) 372-0620
Fax: (650) 372-0661
E-mail: adaraorgn@aol.com
Internet: NA
Newsletters/Publications: JADARA (a journal for professionals) and *ADARA UPDATE* (newsletter)

10.9.3 continued

Description: ADARA promotes and participates in quality human service delivery to deaf and hard-of-hearing people through agencies and individuals. ADARA is a partnership of national organizations, local affiliates, professional sections, and individual members working together to support social services and rehabilitation delivery for deaf and hard-of-hearing people.

American Society for Deaf Children (ASDC)

1820 Tribute Road, Suite A
Sacramento, CA 95815

Voice/TTY: (916) 641-6084
Fax: (916) 641-6085
E-mail: ASDC1@aol.com
Internet: http://www.deafchildren.org
Newsletters/Publication: The Endeavor
Description: ASDC is a nonprofit parent-helping-parent organization promoting a positive attitude toward signing and deaf culture. ASDC also provides support, encouragement, and current information about deafness to families with deaf and/or hard-of-hearing children.

Better Hearing Institute (BHI)

5021-B Backlick Road
Annandale, VA 22003

Voice/TTD: (703) 642-0580 or (800) EAR-WELL (Hearing Helpline)
Fax: (703) 750-9302
E-mail: mail@betterhearing.org
Internet: http://www.betterhearing.org
Newsletter/Publications: Better Hearing News
Description: BHI is a nonprofit educational organization that implements national public information programs on hearing loss and available medical, surgical, hearing aid, and rehabilitation assistance for millions with uncorrected hearing problems. BHI promotes awareness of hearing loss through television, radio, and print media public service messages. BHI maintains a toll-free "Hearing Helpline" telephone service that provides information on hearing loss, sources of assistance, lists of local hearing professionals, and other available hearing help to callers from anywhere in the United States or Canada.

Captioned Films/Videos of National Association of the Deaf

1447 E. Main Street
Spartanburg, SC 29307

Voice: (800) 237-6213
TTD: (800) 237-6819
Fax: (800) 538-5636

E-mail: info@cfv.org
Internet: http://www.nad.org
Newsletters/Publications: A Free-Loan Captioned Films/Videos Catalog is available. Also call for a list of publications.
Description: Free loans of educational and entertainment captioned films and videos for deaf and hard-of-hearing people.

Deafness Research Foundation (DRF)

15 W. 39th Street
New York, NY 10018

Voice/TTD: (212) 768-1181 or (800) 535-3323
Fax: (212) 768-1782
E-mail: drf@drf.org
Internet: http://www.drf.org
Newsletters/Publications: The Hearing Advocate (published twice a year)
Description: The nation's largest voluntary health organization, DRF provides grants for fellowships, symposia, and research into causes, treatment, and prevention of all ear disorders. The DRF also provides information and referral services.

The Ear Foundation

1817 Patterson Street
Nashville, TN 37203

Voice/TTD: (800) 545-HEAR or (615) 329-7809
Fax: (615) 329-7935
E-mail: NA
Internet: http://www.earfound.org
Newsletters/Publications: Otoscope, Steady
Description: A national, not-for-profit organization committed to integrating the hearing- and/or balance-impaired person into the mainstream of society through public awareness and medical education. The Ear Foundation also administers The Meniere's Network, a national network of patient support groups that provides people with the opportunity to share experiences and coping strategies.

Hear Now

9745 E. Hampden Avenue, Suite 300
Denver, CO 80231

Voice/TTD: (800) 648-HEAR or (303) 695-7797
Fax: (303) 695-7789
E-mail: 127737.1272@compuserve.com
Internet: http://www.leisurelan.com~~hearnow/
Newsletters/Publications: Hear Now; also call for list of publications.
Description: Committed to making technology accessible to deaf and hard-of-hearing individuals throughout the United States, Hear Now also provides hearing aids and cochlea implants for very-low-income hard-of-hearing and deaf individuals.

10.9.3 continued

International Hearing Society

20361 Middlebelt Road
Livonia, MI 48152

Voice: (800) 521-5247 or (810) 478-2610
Fax: (810) 478-4520
E-mail: NA
Internet: http:///www.hearingihs.org
Newsletters/Publications: Audecibel
Description: This is a professional association of specialists who test hearing and select, fit, and dispense hearing instruments. The society conducts programs of competence qualifications, education, and training, and promotes specialty-level accreditation. The Hearing Aid Helpline provides consumer information and referral.

League for the Hard of Hearing

71 West 23rd Street
New York, NY 10010-4162

Voice: (212) 741-7650
TTD: (212) 255-1932
Fax: (212) 255-4413
E-mail: postmaster@lhh.org
Internet: http://www.lhh.org
Newsletters/Publications: Hearing Rehabilitation Quarterly (journal); *abc Reports* (newsletter)
Description: The mission of the League is to improve the quality of life for people with all degrees of hearing loss. It offers comprehensive hearing rehabilitation and human service programs for infants, children, and adults and their families, regardless of age or mode of communication. The League promotes hearing conservation and provides public education about hearing.

National Association of the Deaf (NAD)

814 Thayer Avenue
Silver Spring, MD 20910-4500

Voice: (301) 587-1788
TTD: (301) 587-4875
Fax: (301) 587-4873
E-mail: juniornad@juno.com
Internet: http://www.nad.org
Newsletters/Publications: The NAD Broadcaster (published 11 times a year)
Description: The Association develops and promotes citizenship, scholarship, and leadership skills in deaf and hard-of-hearing students (grades 7–12) through chapter projects, national conventions, contests, and other activities. NAD also sponsors a month-long Youth Leadership Camp program each summer in Oregon.

Registry of Interpreters of the Deaf, Inc.

8630 Fenton Street, Suite 324
Silver Spring, MD 20910

Voice/TTD: (301) 608-0050

Fax: (301) 608-0508

E-mail: NA

Internet: http://www.rid,org

Newsletters/Publications: Views (newsletter)

Description: This is a professional organization that certifies interpreters, provides information on interpreting to the general public, publishes a national directory of certified interpreters, and makes referrals to interpreter agencies.

Self Heal for Hard of Hearing People, Inc.

7910 Woodmont Avenue, Suite 1200
Bethesda, MD 20814

Voice: (301) 657-2249

TTD: (301) 657-2249

Fax: (301) 913-9413

E-mail: NA

Internet: http://www.shhh.org/

Newsletters/Publications: Hearing Loss: The Journal of Self Help for Hard of Hearing People.

Description: This organization promotes awareness and information about hearing loss, communication, assistive devices, and alternative communication skills through publications, exhibits, and presentations.

10.9.4   Learning Disabilities

Council for Learning Disabilities (CLD)

P.O. Box 40303
Overland Park, KS 62204

Phone: (913) 492-8755
Fax: (913) 492-2546
E-mail: NA
Internet: http://www1.winthrop.edu/cld/
Newsletters/Publications: Learning Disability Quarterly (4 times/year)
Description: CLD is a national membership organization dedicated to assisting professionals who work in the field of learning disabilities.

International Dyslexia Association (formerly The Orton Dyslexia Society)

8600 LaSalle Road
Chester Building, Suite 382
Baltimore, MD 21286-2044

Phone: (800) ABCD-123 or (410) 296-0232
Fax: (410) 321-5069
E-mail: info@interdys.org
Internet: http://www.interdys.org/
Newsletters/Publications: Contact organization for a list of publications.
Description: The Association is an international scientific and educational organization concerned with the widespread problem of the specific language disability of developmental dyslexia. Local and state chapters serve as literacy resources for dyslexic adults and those who teach or advise them.

Learning Disabilities Association of America, Inc. (LDA)

4156 Library Road
Pittsburgh, PA 15234

Phone: (412) 341-1515
Fax: (412) 344-0224
E-mail: ldanatl@usaor.net
Internet: http://www.ldanatl.org
Newsletters/Publications: The Association prints *LDA Newsbriefs*, a bimonthly newsletter for parents, professionals, and adults with LD. A publications list is available.
Description: LDA is a nonprofit volunteer advocacy organization providing information and referral for parents, professionals, and consumers involved with or in search of support groups and networking opportunities through local LDA Youth and Adult Section Chapters.

Learning Resources Network

1550 Hayes Drive
Manhattan, KS 66502

Phone: (800) 678-5376
Fax: (785) 939-7766
E-mail: hq@lern.org
Internet: www.lern.org
Newsletters/Publications: Several monthly newsletters
Description: Learning Resources Network provides information to practitioners of adult continuing education. It also gives consulting information, takes orders for publications, and provides phone numbers of associations and organizations that deal with learning disabilities.

National Center for Learning Disabilities (NCLD)

381 Park Avenue South, Suite 1401
New York, NY 10016

Phone: (888) 575-7373 or (212) 545-7510
Fax: (212) 545-9665
E-mail: NA
Internet: http://www.ncld.org
Newsletters/Publications: Their World (annual)
Description: NCLD is an organization committed to improving the lives of those affected by learning disabilities. NCLD provides services and conducts programs nationwide, benefiting children and adults with LD, their families, teachers, and other professionals. NCLD provides the latest information on learning disabilities and local resources to parents, professionals, employers, and others dealing with learning disabilities. The Washington office advocates for federal legislation.

Recording for the Blind and Dyslexic (RFBD)

20 Roszel Road
Princeton, NJ 08540

Phone: (800) 221-4792 or (609) 452-0606
Fax: (609) 987-8116
E-mail: webmaster@rfbd.org
Internet: http://www.rfbd.org
Newsletters/Publications: Contact the organization for a catalog.
Description: RFBD is a national nonprofit organization that provides taped educational books, Talking Books, free-on-loan books, books on diskette, library services, and other educational and professional resources to individuals who cannot read standard print because of a visual, physical, or perceptual disability. RFBD provides on-loan recorded books at all academic levels.

10.9.5   Mental Health

American Academy of Child and Adolescent Psychiatry (AACAP)

3615 Wisconsin Avenue NW
Washington, D.C. 20016-3007

Phone: (202) 966-7300
Fax: (202) 966-2891
Internet: http://www.aacap.org
Newsletters / Publications: Call for a list of publications.
Description: The AACAP is the leading national professional medical association dedicated to treating and improving the quality of life for children, adolescents, and families affected by mental, behavioral, and developmental disorders.

American Counseling Association (ACA)

5999 Stevenson Avenue
Alexandria, VA 22304-3300

Phone: (800) 347-6641 or (703) 823-9800
Fax: (703) 823-0252
E-mail: NA
Internet: http://www.counseling.org
Newsletters / Publications: Call for a list of publications.
Description: The ACA is the largest professional organization for guidance counselors.

American Psychiatric Association (APA)

1400 K Street NW
Washington, D.C. 20005

Phone: (202) 682-6326
Fax: (202) 682-6114
E-mail: apa@psych.org
Internet: http://www.psych.org/main.html
Newsletters / Publications: Call for a list of publications.
Description: The APA is the largest professional association for psychiatric professionals.

American Psychological Association (APA)

750 First Street NE
Washington, D.C. 20002

Phone: (202) 336-5500
Fax: NA
E-mail: NA
Internet: http://www.apa.org
Newsletters / Publications: Call for a list of publications.
Description: The APA is the largest scientific and professional association for psychologists.

Center for Effective Collaboration and Practice

American Institute for Research
1000 Thomas Jefferson Street SW, Suite 400
Washington, D.C. 20007

Phone: (888) 457-1551 or (202) 944-5400
Fax: (202) 944-5454
E-mail: center@air-dc.org
Internet: www.air-dc.org/cecp/links/mh.html
Newsletters / Publications: Contact the Institute for a list of publications.
Description: It is the mission of the Center to foster the development and adjustment of children with or at-risk of developing serious emotional disturbance. The Center collaborates at federal, state, and local levels to contribute to and facilitate the production, exchange, and use of knowledge of effective practices. The Center offers publications, teacher training, resources, and links to other mental health agencies and sites. The Center deals with children K–12 and post-secondary education.

Federation of Families for Children's Mental Health

1021 Prince Street
Alexandria, VA 22314

Phone: (703) 684-7710
Fax: (703) 836-1040
E-mail: ffcmh@crosslink.net
Internet: http://www.ffcmh.org
Newsletters / Publications: Call for a list of publications.
Description: The Federation is a not-for-profit, parent-run advocacy organization focused on the needs of children and youth with emotional, behavioral, or mental disorders. The Federation's mission is to provide leadership in the field of children's mental health and develop necessary human and financial resources to meet its goals. The Federation addresses the unique needs of children and youth with emotional, behavioral, or mental disorders from birth through the transition to adulthood. It works to ensure the rights to full citizenship, support, and access to community-based services for all affected children and their families. The Federation also seeks to provide information and engage in advocacy regarding research, prevention, early intervention, family support, education, transition services, and other services.

National Alliance for the Mentally Ill (NAMI)

200 North Glebe Road, #1015
Arlington, VA 22203-3754

Phone: (800) 950-6264 or (703) 524-7600
Fax: (703) 524-9094
TDD: (703) 516-7991
E-mail: membership@nami.org
Internet: http://www.nami.org
Newsletters / Publications: The Advocate (bimonthly newsletter) and *The Decade of the Brain*

10.9.5 continued

Description: NAMI is a not-for-profit, voluntary health organization dedicated to providing mutual support, education, advocacy, and research funding for people affected by mental illness, their families, and their friends. The organization also serves those who have been diagnosed with schizophrenic depression and other related disorders. This self-help organization refers individuals to nationwide support groups, services, and outreach programs.

National Association of School Psychologists (NASP)

4340 East West Highway, Suite 402
Bethesda, MD 20814

Phone: (301) 657-0270
Fax: (301) 657-0275
E-mail: nasp8455@aol.com
Internet: http://www.naspweb.org
Newsletters/Publications: Call for a list of publications.
Description: NASP is an international nonprofit membership association of school psychologists. It provides videos, books, newspapers, and a quarterly *School Psychology Review*.

National Association of Social Workers (NASW)

750 First Street NE, Suite 700
Washington, D.C. 20002-4241

Phone: (202) 408-8600
TTD: (202) 408-8396
Fax: (202) 336-8311
E-mail: NA
Internet: http://www.naswdc.org
Newsletters/Publications: Call for a list of publications.
Description: NASW is the largest professional organization for social workers.

National Institute of Mental Health (NIMH)

6001 Executive Boulevard, Room 8184
Bethesda, MD 20892

Phone: (301) 443-4513
Fax: NA
E-mail: NA
Internet: http://www.ninh.nih.gov
Newsletters/Publications: Contact agency for catalog.
Description: NIMH is the foremost mental health research organization in the world, with a mission of improving the treatment, diagnosis, and prevention of mental disorders such as schizophrenia and depressive illnesses, and other conditions that affect millions of Americans, including children and adolescents.

National Mental Health Association (NMHA)

1021 Prince Street
Alexandria, VA 22314-2971

Phone: (800) 969-6642 or (703) 684-7722

TDD: (800) 433-5959

Fax: (703) 684-5968

E-mail: nmhainfo@aol.com

Internet: http://www.nmha.org

Newsletters/Publications: Educational materials distributed by the Association include the quarterly newsletters *Prevention Update* and *The Bell.*

Description: Established in 1909, NMHA is a not-for-profit, voluntary organization that addresses the mental health needs of individuals throughout the United States. The Association, which has over 300 affiliates in 35 states, has a network of volunteers across the country that works to meet the mental health needs of its communities. Activities include support groups, community outreach and education, information and referral programs, patient advocacy, and a wide array of other services. Nationally, the NMHA works with the media to keep the public informed about mental health and mental illness, and with the Federal government to promote research and services for people with mental health problems. NMHA also works with other major organizations to ensure that the nation's mental health needs are understood and addressed.

10.9.6   Mental Retardation/Developmental Disabilities

American Association on Mental Retardation (AAMR)

444 North Capitol Street NW, Suite 846
Washington, D.C. 20001-1512

Phone: (800) 424-3688 or (202) 387-1968
Fax: (202) 387-2193
E-mail: info@aamr.org
Internet: http://www.aamr.org
Newsletters/Publications: Call for a list of publications.
Description: AAMR is a national membership organization that provides information and services, influences public policy, and advocates for mental retardation.

American Association of University-Affiliated Programs for Persons with Developmental Disabilities (AAUAP)

8630 Fenton Street, Suite 410
Silver Spring, MD 20910

Phone: (301) 588-8252
TTD: (301) 588-3319
Fax: (301) 588-2842
E-mail: info@aauap.org
Internet: http://www.aauap.org
Newsletters/Publications: Call for a list of publications.
Description: AAUAP is a national association that represents three different affiliated programs. AAUAP has sites at major universities and teaching hospitals in all states. These sites target and engage in activities to support the independence, productivity, integration, and inclusion into the community of individuals with developmental disabilities and their families.

The Arc (formerly the Association for Retarded Citizens)

500 East Border Street, Suite 300
Arlington, TX 76010

Phone: (800) 433-5255 or (817) 261-6003
TDD: (817) 277-0553
Fax: (817) 277-3491
E-mail: thearc@metronet.com
Internet: http://thearc.org/welcome.html
Newsletters/Publications: The Arc has a wide variety of publications on topics related to mental retardation, including facts sheets, booklets, Q&As, and position papers. The Arc also hosts an annual conference.
Description: The Arc is a volunteer organization with more than 1,100 affiliated chapters and 140,000 members across the United States. The Arc is the country's largest voluntary organization committed to the welfare of all children and adults with mental retar-

dation and their families. The Arc is committed to securing for all people with mental retardation the opportunity to choose and realize their goals of where and how they learn, live, work, and play. The Arc is further committed to reducing the incidence and limiting the consequence of mental retardation through education, research, advocacy, and the support of families, friends, and community. Through the successful pursuit of quality and justice, The Arc provides leadership in the field of mental retardation and develops necessary human and financial resources to attain its goals.

International Resource Center for Down Syndrome

The Center for Mental Retardation
Keith Building
1621 Euclid Avenue, Suite 514
Cleveland, OH 44115

Phone: (216) 621-5858 or (800) 899-3039 (toll-free in Ohio only)
Fax: (216) 621-0221
E-mail: hf854@cleveland.freenet.edu
Internet: NA
Newsletters/Publications: CMR News (published quarterly)
Description: The Center provides research, information, parent support, and education.

National Down Syndrome Congress (NDSC)

1605 Chantilly Dr. NE, #250
Atlanta, GA 30324-3269

Phone: (800) 232-NDSC or (404) 633-1555
Fax: (404) 633-2817
E-mail: mdsccenter@aol.com
Internet: http://members.carol.net/ndsc
Newsletters/Publications: Down Syndrome News (10 times/year, subscription)
Description: NDSC's mission is to be the national advocacy organization for Down syndrome and to provide leadership in all areas of concern related to persons with Down syndrome. Provides research, education, resources, advocacy, and so on.

National Down Syndrome Society (NDSS)

666 Broadway, #810
New York, NY 10012-2317

Phone: (800) 221-4602 or (212) 460-9330
Fax: (212) 979-2873
E-mail: info@ndss.org
Internet: http://www.ndss.org
Newsletters/Publications: Update (quarterly)
Description: NDSS sponsors research, assists families, increases public awareness, and provides resources and information.

10.9.6 continued

National Institute for People with Disabilities (YAI)

460 West 34th Street
New York, NY 10001-2382

Phone: (212) 563-7474
TDD: (212) 290-2787
Fax: (212) 268-1083
E-mail: link@yai.org
Internet: http://www.yai.org
Newsletters/Publications: Call for a list of publications.
Description: Originally called the Young Adult Institute, YAI is a not-for-profit agency serving children and adults with developmental disabilities in the New York metropolitan area and surrounding counties with a variety of services including information and referral; early intervention and preschool; medical and rehabilitation services; crisis intervention; respite programs; after-school programs; service coordination; residential services; adult day services; home health care; clinical services; parent and family training; employment training and placement; and camping, recreation, and travel. YAI also provides national involvement through staff and management training, development of systems and policies, training resources, and compliance consultations. YAI provides a network of educational videos.

Voice of the Retarded (VOR)

5005 Newport Drive, Suite 108
Rolling Meadows, IL 60008

Phone: (847) 253-6020
Fax: (847) 253-6054
E-mail: vor@compuserve.com
Internet: NA
Newsletters/Publications: VOR publishes *VOR Newsletter* quarterly, which is free to members and any interested parties.
Description: VOR provides information, support, and advocacy services according to individual and group needs; and keeps public officials, legislators, and the general public informed about issues that affect persons with mental retardation. VOR supports alternatives in residential living and rehabilitation systems that best suit the individual needs of a person with mental retardation and his or her family. VOR supports research into causes, prevention, and treatment of mental retardation. VOR maintains state coordinators and a database of organizational members. It welcomes inquiries from parents regarding local parent groups, and has an extensive collection of research files to handle a variety of questions. Copies of material may be requested.

10.9.7   Traumatic Brain Injury

Brain Injury Association (formerly the National Head Injury Foundation)

105 North Alfred Street
Alexandria, VA 22314

Phone: (703) 236-6000

Fax: (703) 236-6001

E-mail: NA

Internet: www.biausa.org

Newsletters/Publications: Brain Injury Source (quarterly)

Description: The mission of the Brain Injury Association is to advocate for and with people with brain injury; to secure and develop community-based services for individuals with brain injury and their families; to support research leading to better outcomes that enhance the life of people who sustain a brain injury; and to promote prevention of brain injury through public awareness, education, and legislation. The site provides a kids corner, national directory, and database.

National Resource Center for Traumatic Brain Injury (NRC TBI)

Department of Physical Medicine and Rehabilitation
P.O. Box 980542
Richmond, VA 23298-0542

Phone: (804) 828-9055

Fax: (804) 828-2378

E-mail: mbking@hsc.vcu.edu

Internet: www.neuro.pmr.vcu.edu

Newsletters/Publications: Call to inquire about a list of publications provided by the agency.

Description: The mission of the National Resource Center for Traumatic Brain Injury is to provide relevant, practical information for professionals, persons with brain injury, and family members. Many of its products are developed by nationally recognized experts. NRC TBI has more than 20 years of experience developing intervention programs and assessment tools, and investigating the special needs and problems of people with brain injury and their families.

10.9.8   Visual Impairment

American Council of the Blind (ACB)

1155 15th Street NW, Suite 720
Washington, D.C. 20005

Phone: (202) 467-5081 or (800) 424-8666 (3–5:30 P.M. Eastern)
Fax: (202) 467-5085
E-mail: ncrabb@access.digex.net
Internet: http://acb.org/
Newsletters/Publications: ACB publishes the monthly magazine *Braille Forum*, subscriptions to which are available free in Braille, large print, cassettes, and DOS diskettes.
Description: ACB is a national organization established to promote the independence, dignity, and well-being of people who are blind or visually impaired. Members are blind, visually impaired, or fully sighted people from all walks of life. ACB helps to improve the lives of the blind by working to enhance civil rights, employment, rehabilitation services, safe and expanded transportation, travel and recreation, Social Security benefits, and accessibility, and works in coalition with other disability groups. The concerns of various professions and special populations are addressed by ACB's many national special-interest affiliates and committees. These affiliates help ACB address the special interests and concerns of women, minorities, students, families, Guide Dog users, Braille readers, and many others.

American Foundation for the Blind (AFB)

11 Penn Plaza, Suite 300
New York, NY 10001

Phone: (800) 232-5463 or (212) 502-7600
TTD: (212) 502-7662
Fax: NA
E-mail: afbinfo@afb.org
Internet: http://www.afb.org/afb
Newsletters/Publications: Call for a list of publications.
Description: A nonprofit organization founded in 1921 and recognized as Helen Keller's cause in the United States, AFB is a leading national resource for people who are blind or visually impaired, the organizations that serve them, and the general public. The mission of AFB is to enable people who are blind or visually impaired to achieve equality of access and opportunity that will ensure freedom of choice in their lives.

American Printing House for the Blind, Inc. (APH)

1839 Frankfort Avenue, P.O. Box 6085
Louisville, KY 40206-0085

Phone: (800) 223-1839 or (502) 895-2405
Fax: (502) 899-2274
E-mail: aph@iglou.com
Internet: http://www.aph.org

Newsletters/Publications: AHP publishes two free, semiannual newsletters: *APH Slate* and *Micro Materials Update.* APH also has brochures including "Wings for the Future," product brochures and catalogs, and a video/brochure package that explores ways that parents and teachers of children with visual impairment can make reading aloud an enjoyable learning experience.

Description: APH promotes independence of blind and visually impaired persons by providing special media, tools, and materials needed for education and life. Its focus is primarily for people who are visually impaired; secondarily for people with learning disabilities and those who are multiply handicapped.

APH manufactures books and magazines in Braille, large type, recorded, and computer disk form. It also manufactures a wide range of educational and daily living aids, such as Braille paper and styluses, talking-book equipment, and synthetic-speech computer products. In addition, APH offers CARL ET AL, an electronic database that lists accessible books in Braille, large type, recorded, computer disk, and tactile-graphic formats.

Blind Children's Fund (formerly known as the International Institute for the Visually Impaired)

4740 Okemos Road
Okemos, MI 48864-1637

Phone: (517) 347-1357
Fax: (517) 347-1459
E-mail: blindchfnd@aol.com
Internet: http://www.blindchildrensfund.org
Newsletters/Publications: Call for a list of publications.
Description: The Blind Children's Fund is an international not-for-profit organization that responds to the special educational and emotional needs of blind children and their families. The Blind Children's Fund represents a network of parents, professionals, and volunteers throughout the United States and the world who are committed to developing, organizing, and disseminating information and materials for affected families. The Fund develops and distributes educational materials and literature; publishes a quarterly newsletter; and distributes national position papers relative to advocacy and program development for affected children. The Fund organizes international symposia, conducts workshops and conferences, provides inservice and consultant services, and offers a slide-and-tape show for UNESCO in four languages that helps train professionals and paraprofessionals who work with infants and young children with blindness.

Foundation Fighting Blindness

Executive Plaza I, Suite 800
11350 McCormick Road
Hunt Valley, MD 21031-1014

Phone: (888) 394-3937 or (410) 785-1414
TDD: (800) 683-5551
Local TDD: (410) 785-9687
Fax: NA

10.9.8 continued

E-mail: NA

Internet: http://www.blindness.org

Newsletters/Publications: Call for a list of publications.

Description: The Foundation Fighting Blindness is a national eye research organization that funds laboratory and clinical research at more than 40 prominent institutions in the United States and abroad. It serves as a source of information for eye-care specialists, professionals, and affected families.

The Lighthouse Inc.

111 East 59th Street
New York, NY 10022

Phone: (212) 821-9200

TTD: (212) 821-9713

Fax: (212) 821-9707

Publications and referrals: (800) 334-5497

E-mail: NA

Internet: http://www.lighthouse.org

Newsletters/Publications: The Lighthouse publishes the newsletter *EnVision* and a variety of other publications.

Description: The Lighthouse works with the families of children who are visually impaired and blind, professionals, and the general public. Its main purpose is to establish connections among the many people who can enhance the early development of the children with these conditions; they work with families, the vision care system, special education programs, and the health and education networks to develop coordinated programs. The Lighthouse staff conducts applied and theoretical research and collaborates with other professionals to develop and share research findings.

National Association for Visually Handicapped (NAVH)

NAVH New York

22 West 21st Street
New York, NY 10010

Phone: (212) 889-3141

Fax: (212) 727-2931

E-mail: staff@navh.org

Internet: http://www.navh.org

Newsletters/Publications: See NAVH San Francisco.

Description: See NAVH San Francisco.

NAVH San Francisco

3201 Balboa Street
San Francisco, CA 94121

Phone: (415) 221-3201
Fax: (415) 221-8754
E-mail: staffca@navh.org
Internet: http://www.navh.org
Newsletters/Publications: Update is the quarterly newsletter available to any interested parties.
Description: NAVH is a national voluntary health agency for the "hard of seeing," not the blind. It supplies services to children and adults in all 50 states and 91 foreign countries. Aside from large print, NAVH offers information, referral, visual aids, and, most important, emotional support.

National Federation of the Blind (NFB)

1800 Johnson Street
Baltimore, MD 21230

Phone: (410) 659-9314
Fax: (410) 685-5653
E-mail: epc@roudley.com
Internet: http://www.nfb.org/
Newsletters/Publications: The Braille Monitor is the leading publication of NFB. It is produced monthly and is available in large print, in Braille, on cassette tape, or in e-mail formats.
Description: NFB's purpose is twofold: to help blind persons achieve self-confidence and self-respect and to act as a vehicle for collective self-expression by the blind. By providing public education about blindness, information and referral services, scholarships, literature and publications about blindness, aids and appliances and other adaptive equipment for the blind, advocacy services and protection of civil rights, job opportunities for the blind, development and evaluation of technology, and support for blind persons and their families, members of NFB strive to educate the public that people who are blind are normal individuals who can compete on terms of equality.

Recording for the Blind and Dyslexic (RFBD)

20 Roszel Road
Princeton, NJ 08540

Phone: (800) 221-4792 or (609) 452-0606
Fax: (609) 987-8116
E-mail: webmaster@rfbd.org
Internet: http://www.rfbd.org
Newsletters/Publications: Contact the organization for a catalog.
Description: RFBD is a national nonprofit organization that provides taped educational books, Talking Books, free-on-loan books, books on diskette, library services, and other educational and professional resources to individuals who cannot read standard print because of a visual, physical, or perceptual disability. RFBD provides on-loan recorded books at all academic levels.

REFERENCES AND SUGGESTED READINGS

Algozzine, B., Christensen, S., and Ysseldyke, J. (1982). "Probabilities associated with the referral-to-placement process." *Teacher education and special education, 5*, 19–23.

Allen, S. G., and Serwatka, T. S. (1994). *Auditory perception tests for the hearing impaired.* East Aurora, NY: Slossen Educational Publications.

American Association on Mental Retardation (1992). *Mental definition, classification, and systems of support* (9th ed.). Washington, DC: Author.

American Psychological Association (1985). *Standards for educational and psychological testing.* Washington DC: Author.

American Psychological Association (1990). *Guidelines for providers of psychological services to ethnic, linguistic, and culturally diverse populations.* Washington DC: Author.

America's Learning Exchange (2002). http://www.alx.org/aboutalx.asp. Telephone: (202) 219-8854.

Anastasi, A. (1998). *Psychological testing.* New York: Macmillan.

Anderson, W., Chitwood, S., and Hayden, D. (1990). *Negotiating special education maze: A guide for parents and teachers* (2nd ed.). Rockville, MD: Woodbine House. [Available from Woodbine House, 6510 Bells Mill Road, Bethesda, MD 20817. Telephone: (800) 843-7323; (301) 897-3570.]

Archibald, D. A.(1991). "Authentic assessment: Principles, practices, and issues." *School psychology quarterly, 6*, 279–293.

Artiles, A. J., and Trent, S. C. (1994). "Overrepresentation of minority students in special education: A continuing debate." *Journal of special education, 27*, 410–437.

Baca, L., and Cervantes, H. T. (1984). *The bilingual special education interface.* Columbus, OH: Merrill.

Baca, L., Escamilla, K., and Carjuzaa, J. (1994). "Language minority students: Literacy and educational reform." In N. J. Ellsworth, C. N. Hedley, and A. N. Baratta (Eds.), *Literacy: A redefinition* (pp. 61–76). Hillsdale, NJ: Lawrence Erlbaum.

Bailey, D. B., and Wolery, M. (1989). *Assessing infants and preschoolers with handicaps.* Columbus, OH: Merrill.

Bailey, D. B., Wolery, M., and McLean, M. (1996). *Assessing infants and preschoolers with special need* (2nd ed.). Englewood Cliffs, NJ: Prentice Hall.

Batzle, J. (1992). *Portfolio assessment and evaluation: Developing and using portfolios in the classroom.* Cypress, CA: Creative Teaching Press.

Bayley, N. (1993). *Bayley scales of infant development—2nd edition (BSID-II).* San Antonio, TX: The Psychological Corporation.

Beaumont, C., and Langdon, H. W. (1992). "Speech-language services for Hispanics with communication disorders: A framework." In H. W. Langdon and L. L. Cheng (Eds.), *Hispanic children and adults with communication disorders* (pp. 1–19). Gaithersburg, MD: Aspen.

Beery, K. E. (1997). *Developmental test of visual motor integration—Fourth edition (VMI-4).* Austin, TX: PRO-ED.

Bellack, L., and Bellack, S. (1974). *Children's apperception test.* Larchmont, NY: C.P.S. Incorporated.

Bender, L. (1938). *Bender visual-motor gestalt test (BVMGT).* New York: The American Orthopsychiatric Association Inc.

Berdine, W. H., and Meyer, S. A. (1987). *Assessment in special education.* Boston: Little, Brown. [Available from HarperCollins, Keystone Industrial Park, Reeves and Monahan, Scranton, PA 18512; (800) 331-3761.]

Bernstein, D. K. (1989). "Assessing children with limited English proficiency: Current perspectives." *Topics in language disorders, 9*, 15–20.

Bigge, J., and Stump, C. (1999). *Curriculum, assessment, and instruction for students with disabilities.* Belmont, CA: Wadsworth.

Bigge, J. L. (1990). *Teaching individuals with physical and multiple disabilities* (3rd ed.). Columbus, OH: Merrill.

Black, J., and Ford, A. (1989). "Planning and implementing activity-based lessons." In A. Ford, R. Schnorr, L. Meyer, L. Davern, J. Black, and P. Dempsey (Eds.), *The Syracuse community-reference curriculum guide for students with moderate and severe disabilities* (pp. 295–311). Baltimore: Paul H. Brookes.

Bloom, L., and Lahey, M. (1978). *Language development and language disorders.* New York: Wiley.

Boehm, A. E. (1986). *Boehm test of basic concepts—Revised (BTBC-R).* San Antonio, TX: The Psychological Corporation.

Bogdan, R., and Knoll, J. (1988). "The sociology of disability." In E. L. Meyen and T. M. Skrtic (Eds.), *Exceptional children and youth* (3rd ed.) (pp. 449–477). Denver: Love Publishing.

Bogdan, R., and Kugelmass, J. (1984). "Case studies of mainstreaming: A symbolic interactionist approach to special schooling." In L. Barton and S. Tomlinson (Eds.), *Special education and social interests* (pp. 173–191). New York: Nichols.

Bracken, B. A. (1984). *Bracken basic concept scale (BBCS).* San Antonio, TX: The Psychological Corporation.

Brigance, A. H. (1991). *Brigance diagnostic inventory of basic skills.* Billerica, MA: Curriculum Associates.

Brown v. *Board of Education* (1954). 347 U.S. 483.

Brown, V., Hammill, D., Larson, S., and Wiederholt, J. L. (1994). *Test of adolescent and adult language—Third edition (TOAL-3).* Austin, TX: PRO-ED.

Brown, V. L., Cronin, M. E., and McEntire, E. (1994). *Test of mathematical abilities—2nd edition.* Austin, TX: PRO-ED.

Brown, V. L., Hammill, D. D., and Wiederholt, J. L. (1995). *Test of reading comprehension—3rd edition.* Austin, TX: PRO-ED.

Bullis, M., and Gaylord-Ross, R. (1991). *Moving on: Transitions for youth with behavioral disorders.* Reston, VA: Council for Exceptional Children. [Available from the Council for Exceptional Children, 1920 Association Drive, Reston, VA 22091-1589. Telephone: (703) 620-3660.]

Burgemeister, B. B., Blurn, L. H., and Lorge, I. (1972). *Columbia mental maturity scale (CMMS).* San Antonio, TX: The Psychological Corporation.

Campione, J. C., and Brown, A. L. (1987). "Linking dynamic assessment with school achievement." In C. S. Lidz (Ed.), *Dynamic assessment: An interactional approach to evaluating learning potential* (pp. 82–115). New York: Guilford.

Carl D. Perkins Vocational Education Act, 20 U.S.C. Sections 2331–2342.

Carlson, J. S., and Wiedl, K. H. (1978). "Use of testing-the-limits procedures in the assessment of intellectual capabilities of children with learning difficulties." *American journal of mental deficiency, 82,* 559–564.

Carlson, J. S., and Wiedl, K. H. (1979). "Toward a differential testing approach: Testing-the-limits employing the Raven Matrices." *Intelligence, 3,* 323–344.

Chalfant, J. C. (1989). "Learning disabilities: Policy issues and promising approaches." *American psychologist, 44*(2), 392–398.

Clark, C. (1994, August). *Exito: A dynamic team assessment approach for culturally diverse students.* Presentation at the BUENO Bilingual Special Education Institute, Boulder, Colorado.

Code of Federal Regulations (CFR): *Title 34; Education; Parts 1 to 499, July 1986.* Washington, DC: U.S. Government Printing Office. [Available from the U.S. Government Printing Office, P.O. Box 371954, Pittsburgh, PA 15250-7954.]

Code of Federal Regulations (CFR): *Title 34; Parts 300 to 399, July 1, 1993.* Washington, DC: U.S. Government Printing Office. [Available from the U.S. Government Printing Office, P.O. Box 371954, Pittsburgh, PA 15250-7954.]

Colarusso, R., and Hammill, D. D. (1996). *Motor Free Perceptual Test—Revised (MVPT-R)*. Novato, CA: Academic Therapy Publications.

Collier, C. (1994). *Multicultural assessment: Implications for regular and special education* (3rd. ed.). Boulder, CO: BUENO Center for Multicultural Education.

Conners, K. C. (1997). *Conners' parent and teacher rating scales*. North Towanaza, NY: Multi-Health Systems Incorporated.

Connolly, A., Nachtman, W., and Pritchett, M. (1997). *Key math diagnostic arithmetic tests—Revised*. Circle Pines, MN: American Guidance Service.

Conoley, J. C., and Kramer, J. J. (Eds.) (1992). *Eleventh mental measurement yearbook*. Lincoln: University of Nebraska Press.

Copenhaver, J. (1995). *Section 504: An educator's primer: What teachers and administrators need to know about implementing accommodations for eligible individuals with disabilities*. Logan, UT: Mountain Plains Regional Resource Center.

Cortâs, C. E. (1986). *The education of language minority students: A contextual interaction model*. In Bilingual Education Office, California State Department of Education (Comp.), *Beyond language: Social and cultural factors in schooling language minority students* (pp. 3–33). Los Angeles: Evaluation, Dissemination, and Assessment Center.

Covarrubias v. San Diego Unified School District (Southern California), No. 70-394-T. S.D., Cal., February, 1971.

Cox, L. S. (1975). "Diagnosing and remediating systematic errors in addition and subtraction computations." *The arithmetic teacher, 22*, 151–157.

Cummins, J. (1986). "Empowering minority students: A framework for intervention." *Harvard educational review, 56*(1), 18–36.

Cummins, J. (1989). "A theoretical framework for bilingual special education." *Exceptional children, 56*(2), 111–119.

Cutler, B. C. (1993). *You, your child, and "special" education: A guide to making the system work*. Baltimore: Paul H. Brookes.

Department of Education (1995). *Seventeenth annual report to Congress on the implementation of the Individuals with Disabilities Education Act*. Washington, DC: Author.

Department of Education (1997). *Nineteenth annual report to Congress on the implementation of the Individuals with Disabilities Education Act*. Washington DC: Author.

DeStefano, L., and Wermuth, T. R. (1992). "IDEA (P.L. 101-476): Defining a second generation of transition services." In F. R. Rusch, L. DeStefano, J. Chadsey-Rusch, L. A. Phelps, and E. Szymanshi (Eds.), *Transition from school to adult life: Models, linkages, and policy* (pp. 537–549). Sycamore, IL: Sycamore Publishing. [Available from Sycamore Publishing Company, P.O. Box 133, Sycamore, IL 60178. Telephone: (815) 756-5388.]

Developmental Disabilities Assistance and Bill of Rights Act, 42 U.S.C. Section 6012.

Diana v. California State Board of Education, No. C-70 37 RFP. District Court of Northern California, February, 1970.

Duffy, J. B., Salvia, J., Tucker, J., and Ysseldyke, J. (1981). "Nonbiased assessment: A need for operationalism." *Exceptional children, 7*, 427–434.

Dunn, L. M., Dunn, L. M., and Williams, K. T. (1997). *Peabody picture vocabulary test—3 (PPVT-III)*. Circle Pines, MN: American Guidance Service.

Durrell, D. O., and Catterson, J. H. (1980). *Durrell analysis of reading difficulty*. San Antonio, TX: The Psychological Corporation.

Elksnin, L., and Elksnin, N. (1990). "Using collaborative consultation with parents to promote effective vocational programming." *Career development for exceptional individuals, 13*(2), 135–142.

Elliott, R. (1987). *Litigating intelligence: IQ tests, special education, and social science in the courtroom*. Dover, MA: Auburn House.

Falvey, M. (Ed.) (1989). *Community-based curriculum: Instructional strategies for students with severe handicaps* (2nd ed.). Baltimore: Paul H. Brookes.

Federal Regulations for Individuals with Disabilities Education Act (IDEA), Amendments of 1997 for Weds. October 22 (1997). [These regulations are available from the Government Printing Office, P.O. Box 371954, Pittsburgh, PA 15250-7954.]

Figueroa, R. A. (1993). "The reconstruction of bilingual special education." *Focus on diversity*, 3(3), 2–3.

Figueroa, R. A., and Ruiz, N. T. (1994). "The reconstruction of bilingual special education II." *Focus on diversity*, 4(1), 2–3.

Figueroa, R., Fradd, S. H., and Correa, V. I. (1989). "Bilingual special education and this issue." *Exceptional children*, 56, 174–178.

First, M. D. (2000). *The diagnostic and statistical manual of mental disorders IV-TR (DSMD-IV-TR).* Washington, DC: American Psychological Association.

Flaugher, R. (1978). "The many definitions of test bias." *American psychologist*, 33, 671–679.

Franklin, M. E. (1992, October/November). "Culturally sensitive instructional practices for African-American learners with disabilities." *Exceptional children*, 59(2), 115–122.

Frostig, M., Lefever, W., and Whittlessey, J. R. (1993). *Marianne Frostig developmental test of visual perception (DTVP).* Austin, TX: PRO-ED.

Fuchs, D., and Fuchs, L. (1989). "Effects of examiner familiarity on Black, Caucasian, and Hispanic children: A meta-analysis." *Exceptional children*, 55, 303–308.

Gardner, M. F. *Tests of auditory perceptual skills—Revised (TAPS-R).* Hydesville, CA: Psychological and Educational Publications.

Gates, A. I., McKillop, A. S., and Horowitz, E. (1981). *Gates-McKillop-Horowitz reading diagnostic tests.* New York: Teachers College Press.

Gearheart, C., and Gearheart, B. (1990). *Introduction to special education assessment. Principles and practices.* Denver: Love Publishing.

General Information About Disabilities Which Qualify Children and Youth for Special Education Services Under the IDEA Act, *News Digest 1995*, National Information Center for Children and Youth with Disabilities (NICHCY), P.O. Box 1492, Washington, DC 20013; (800) 695-0285.

Gilmore, J. V., and Gilmore, E. C. (1968). *Gilmore oral reading test.* San Antonio, TX: The Psychological Corporation.

Ginsberg, H. P., and Baroody, A. J. (1990). *Test of early mathematics ability—2nd edition.* Austin, TX: PRO-ED.

Goldman, R., and Fristoe, M. (1970). *Goldman-Fristoe test of articulation.* Circle Pines, MN: American Guidance Service.

Goodenough, F. L., and Harris, D. B. (1963). *Goodenough-Harris drawing test.* San Antonio, TX: The Psychological Corporation.

Goodman, Y., and Burke, C. (1972). *Reading miscue inventory manual: Procedure for diagnosis and evaluation.* New York: Macmillan.

Graden, J. L. (1989). "Redefining 'prereferral' intervention as intervention assistance: Collaboration between general and special education." *Exceptional children*, 56(3), 227–231.

Graham, M., and Scott, K. (1988). "The impact of definitions of high risk on services of infants and toddlers." *Topics in early childhood special education*, 8(3), 23–28.

Grossman, H. J. (Ed.) (1983). *Manual on terminology and classification in mental retardation* (3rd ed. rev.). Washington, DC: American Association on Mental Deficiency. [No longer available from the publisher.]

Guadalupe Organization Inc. v. *Tempe Elementary School District*, No. CIV 71-435. Phoenix, D. Arizona, January 24, 1972.

Guerin, G. R., and Maier, A. S. (1983). *Informal assessment in education.* Palo Alto, CA: Mayfield.

607

Hager, R. (1999). *Funding of assistive technology. Assistive technology funding and systems change project.* http://www.nls.org/natmain.htm.

Halgren, D. W., and Clarizio, H. F. (1993). "Categorical and programming changes in special education services." *Exceptional children*, *59*, 547–555.

Hammill, D. D. (1998). *Detroit tests of learning aptitudes—Fourth edition (DTLA-4).* Austin, TX: PRO-ED.

Hammill, D. D., Brown, L., and Bryant, B. R. (1992). *A consumer's guide to tests in print.* Austin, TX: PRO-ED.

Hammill, D. D., and Larsen, S. C. (1996). *Test of written language—3.* Austin, TX: PRO-ED.

Hammill, D. D., Pearson, N. A., and Wiederholt, L. (1996). *Comprehensive test of nonverbal intelligence.* Austin, TX: PRO-ED.

Hanson, M., and Lynch, E. (1995). *Early intervention: Implementing child and family services for infants and toddlers who are at risk or disabled* (2nd ed.). Austin, TX: PRO-ED.

Haring, K. A., Lovett, D. L., Haney, K. F., Algozzine, B., Smith, D. D., and Clarke, J. (1992). "Labeling preschoolers as learning disabled: A cautionary position." *Topics in early childhood special education*, *12*(2), 151–173.

Harnisch, D. L., and Fisher, A. T. (Eds.) (1989). *Transition literature review: Educational, employment, and independent living outcomes.* Champaign, IL: Secondary Transition Intervention Effectiveness Institute.

Harry, B. (1992). *Cultural diversity, families, and the special education system: Communication and empowerment.* New York: Teachers College Press.

Hart, D. (1994). *Authentic assessment: A handbook for educators.* Menlo Park, CA: Addison-Wesley.

Hartman, R. C. (Ed.) (1991). *Transition in the United States: What's happening.* Information from *HEALTH*, *10*(3), 1, 4–6.

Hayden, M. F., and Senese, R. (Eds.) (1994). *Self Advocacy Groups: 1994–95 Directory for North America.* This publication lists the addresses and phone numbers of over 700 self-advocacy groups and organizations in the U.S., Canada, and Mexico. [Available from Publications Office, Institute on Community Integration, University of Minnesota, 150 Pillsbury Drive SE, Minneapolis, MN 55455; (612) 624-4512.]

Heiman, G. (1999). *Research methods in psychology* (2nd ed.). Boston: Houghton Mifflin.

Herman, J., Aschbacher, P., and Winters, L. (1992). *A practical guide to alternative assessment.* Alexandria, VA: Association for Supervision and Curriculum Development.

Heward, W. L., and Orlansky, M. D. (1992). *Exceptional children: An introductory survey of special education* (4th ed.). New York: Merrill.

Hodgkinson, L. (1985). *All one system: Demographics of education.* Washington, DC: Institute for Educational Leadership.

Hoover, J., and Collier, C. (1994). *Classroom management and curriculum development* (3rd ed.). Boulder, CO: BUENO Center for Multicultural Education.

Hoy, C., and Gregg, N. (1994). *Assessment: The special educator's role.* Pacific Grove, CA: Brookes/Cole Publishing Company.

Hresko, W. P. (1988). *Test of Early Written Language—2.* Austin, TX: PRO-ED.

IDEA, 1997. Copies of reauthorized IDEA in its entirety are located on the Internet. A Web site providing it is: http://www.ed.gov/offices/OSERS/IDEA. This is the Web address of the Department of Education's Office of Special Education and Rehabilitation Services (OSERS). When you get to the site, select "The Law."

Iliesko, W. P., Reid, D. K., and Hammill, D. D. *Test of early language development—Second edition (TELD-2).* Austin, TX: PRO-ED.

Individuals with Disabilities Education Act (P.L. 101-476), 20 U.S.C. Chapter 33, Sections 1400–1485, 1990.

Jitendra, A. K., and Kameenui, E. J. (1993, September/October). "Dynamic assessment as a compensatory assessment approach: A description and analysis." *Remedial and Special Education, 14*(5), 6–18.

John, J. L. (1985). *Basic reading inventory* (3rd ed.). Dubuque, IA: Kendall-Hunt.

Johnson, B. H., McGonigel, M. J., and Kauffmann, R. K. (1991). *Guidelines and recommended practices for the Individualized Family Service Plan* (2nd ed.). Bethesda, MD: Association for the Care of Children's Health.

Kamphaus, E. W. (1993). *Clinical assessment of children's intelligence.* Boston: Allyn and Bacon.

Kaufman, A. S., and Kaufman, N. L. (1983). *Kaufman assessment battery for children (K-ABC): Mental processing scales.* Circle Pines, MN: American Guidance Service.

Kaufman, A. S., and Kaufman, N. L. (1985). *Kaufman tests of educational achievement.* Circle Pines, MN: American Guidance Service.

Kaufman, A. S., and Kaufman, N. L. (1990). *Kaufman brief intelligence test.* Circle Pines, MN: American Guidance Service.

Keith, T. Z. (1985). "Questioning the K-ABC: What does it measure?" *School psychology review, 14,* 9–20.

Keith, T. Z. (1997). "What does the WISC-III measure? A reply to Carroll and Kranzler." *School psychology quarterly, 12*(2), 117–118.

Keogh, B., and Margolis, T. (1976). "Learn to labor and wait: Attentional problems of children with learning disorders." *Journal of learning disabilities, 9,* 276–286.

King-Sears, M. E. (1994). *Curriculum-based assessment in special education.* San Diego: Singular Publishing Group.

Kirk, S. A., McCarthy, J. J., and Kirk, W. D. (1968). *Illinois Test of Psycholinguistic Abilities (ITPA).* Champaign: University of Illinois Press.

Kozloff, M. (1994). *Improving educational outcomes for children with disabilities: Principles for assessment, program planning, and evaluation.* Baltimore: Paul H. Brookes.

Lambert, W. E. (1977). "The effects of bilingualism on the individual: Cognitive and sociocultural consequences." In P. Hornby (Ed.), *Bilingualism: Psychological, social and educational implications.* New York: Academic Press.

Langdon, H. W. (1992). "Speech and language assessment of LEP/bilingual Hispanic students." In H. W. Langdon and L. L. Cheng (Eds.), *Hispanic children and adults with communication disorders* (pp. 201–265). Gaithersburg, MD: Aspen.

Larsen, S. C., and Hammill, D. D. (1999). *Test of written spelling—4.* Austin, TX: PRO-ED.

Larson, S. L., and Vitali, G. (1988). *Kindergarten readiness test (KRT).* Aurora, NY: Slosson Educational Publications.

Leach, L. N., and Harmon, A. (1990). *Annotated bibliography on transition from school to work* (Vol. 5). Champaign, IL: Transition Research Institute.

Lerner, J. (1991). *Learning disabilities: Theories, diagnosis, and teaching strategies* (7th ed.). Boston: Houghton Mifflin.

Lezak, M. D. (1995). *Neuropsychological assessment* (4th ed.). New York: Oxford University Press.

Lipke, B., Dickey, S., Selmar, J., and Soder, A. (1999). *Photo articulation test—Third edition (PAT-3).* Hydesville, CA: Psychological and Educational Publications.

Luria, A. R. (1980). *The working brain.* New York: Basic Books.

MacGinitie, W., and MacGinitie, R. (1989). *Gates-MacGinitie silent reading tests—Third edition.* Chicago: Riverside.

Maldonado-Colon, E. (1983). "The communication disordered Hispanic child." *Monograph of BUENO Center for Multicultural Education, 1*(4), 59–67.

Markwardt, F. C. (1997). *Peabody individual achievement test—Revised (PIAT-R)*. Circle Pines, MN: American Guidance Service.

Mather, N., Wendling, B. J., and Woodcock, R. W. (2001). *Essentials of WJ III™ tests of achievement assessment*. New York: Wiley.

McCarney, S. B. (1989). *Attention deficit disorders evaluation scale—Revised*. Columbia, MO: Hawthorne Educational Services.

McCarney, S. B. (1995). *The adaptive behavior evaluation scale—Revised*. Columbia, MO: Hawthorne Educational Services.

McCarney, S. B. (1998). *The preschool evaluation scales (PES)*. Columbia, MO: Hawthorne Educational Services.

McCarthy, D. (1972). *McCarthy scales of children's abilities*. San Antonio, TX: The Psychological Corporation.

McGloughlin, J., and Lewis, R. (1994). *Assessing special students* (4th ed.). Columbus, OH: Merrill.

McLean, M., Bailey, D. B., and Wolery, M. (1996). *Assessing infants and preschoolers with special needs* (2nd ed.). Englewood Cliffs, NJ: Merrill.

McLoughlin, J. A., and Lewis, R. B. (1990). *Assessing special students* (3rd ed.). Columbus, OH: Merrill.

McNair, J., and Rusch, F. R. (1991). "Parent involvement in transition programs." *Mental Retardation, 29*(2), 93–101.

Morris, G. (1999). *Psychology: An introduction*. Upper Saddle River, NJ: Prentice Hall.

Murray, H. A. (1943). *Thematic apperception test*. Cambridge, MA: Harvard University Press.

Myers, A., and Hanson, C. (1999). *Experimental psychology* (4th ed.). Belmont, CA: Brookes/Cole Publishing Company.

Naglieri, J. A., McNeish, T. J., and Bardos, A. N. (1991). *Draw-a-person: Screening procedure for emotional disturbance*. San Antonio, TX: The Psychological Corporation.

National Association of School Psychology (1991). *Position statement on early childhood assessment*. Washington, DC: Author.

National Council on Disability (1995). *Improving the implementation of the Individuals with Disabilities Education Act: Making schools work for all of America's children*. Washington, DC: Author.

Newborg, J., Stock, J. R., and Wnek, J. (1984). *The Battelle developmental inventory (BDI)*. Chicago: Riverside.

Newcomer, P. L., and Hammill, D. D. (1997). *Test of language development—Primary: 3 (TOLD-P:3)*. Austin, TX: PRO-ED.

NICHCY (1997). *The education of children and youth with special needs: What do the laws say?* http://www.nichcy.org/pubs/newsdig/nd15txt.htm.

NICHCY (1999). *Questions and answers about IDEA*. http://www.nichcy.org/pubs/newsdig/nd21txt.htm.

Nihira, K., Leland, H., and Lambert, N. (1993). *AAMR Adaptive Behavior Scale—Residential and Community—2*. Austin, TX: PRO-ED.

Nisbet, J. (1992). *Natural supports in school, at work, and in the community for people with severe disabilities*. Baltimore: Paul H. Brookes.

Norris, M. K., Juarez, M. J., and Perkins, M. N. (1989). "Adaptation of a screening test for bilingual and bidialectal populations." *Language, speech, and hearing specialists in schools, 20*, 381–390.

Nurss, J. R., and McGauvran, M. E. (1986). *Metropolitan readiness tests—5th edition (MRT-5)*. San Antonio, TX: The Psychological Corporation.

Office of Special Education and Rehabilitative Services. *Summary of existing legislation affecting persons with disabilities*. Washington, DC: Clearinghouse on Disability Information. [An updated edition of this book is available from the Clearinghouse on Disability Information, Office of Special Education and Rehabilitative Services, 330 C Street SW, Room 3132, Switzer Building, Washington, DC 20202-2319.]

Ortiz, A. (1986). *Characteristics of limited English proficient Hispanic students served in programs for the learning disabled*. Bilingual special education newsletter. Austin: University of Texas, vol. 4.

Ortiz, A. A., and Rivera, C. (1990). *AIM for the BEST: Assessment and intervention model for bilingual exceptional students* (Contract No. 300-87-0131). Washington, DC: Office of Bilingual Education and Minority Languages Affairs.

Otis, A. S., and Lennon, R. T. (1996). *Otis-Lennon school ability test* (Seventh edition). San Antonio, TX: The Psychological Corporation.

Overton, T. (2000). *Assessment in special education: An applied approach* (3rd ed.). Upper Saddle River, NJ: Merrill.

PARC v. *Commonwealth of Pennsylvania* (1972). 343 F. Supp. 279, E.D. PA.

Pase v. *Hannon* (1980). No. 74 C 3586 N.D. Ill.

Paulson, E. L., Paulson, P. R., and Meyer, C. A. (1991). "What makes a portfolio a portfolio?" *Educational leadership*, *48*(5), 60–63.

Pennsylvania Department of Education, Bureau of Special Education (1993, March). *Instructional support*. East Petersburg: Author.

Pierangelo, R., and Giuliani, G. (2000). *The special educator's guide to 109 diagnostic tests*. Paramus, NJ: Center for Applied Research in Education.

Pierangelo, R., and Guiliani, G. (2000). *Assessment in special education: A practical approach* (4th ed.). Boston: Allyn and Bacon.

Public Law 94-142 Education of the Handicapped Act, 1975.

Public Law 99-372, Handicapped Children's Protection Act of 1986.

Public Law 100-407, Technology-Related Assistance for Individuals with Disabilities Act of 1988.

Public Law 101-127, Children with Disabilities Temporary Care Reauthorization Act of 1989.

Public Law 101-336, Americans with Disabilities Act of 1990.

Public Law 101-476, Individuals with Disabilities Education Act, 1990.

Questions and Answers About IDEA, National Information Center for Children and Youth with Disabilities (NICHCY), *News Digest 1991*, P.O. Box 1492, Washington, DC 20013; (800) 695-0285.

Rehabilitation Act of 1973, 29 U.S.C. Section 701-794.

Repetto, J., White, W., and Snauwaert, D. (1990). "Individual transition plans (ITP): A national perspective." *Career education for exceptional individuals*, *13*(2), 109–119.

Reschley, D. (1986). "Functional psychoeducational assessment: Trends and issues." *Special services in the schools*, *2*, 57–59.

Rueda, R. (1989). "Defining mild disabilities with language-minority students." *Exceptional children*, *56*(2), 121–128.

Ruiz, N. T. (1989). "An optimal learning environment for Rosemary." *Exceptional children*, *56*(2), 130–144.

Runyon, R., and Haber, A. (1991). *Fundamentals of behavioral statistics* (7th ed.). New York: McGraw-Hill.

Rusch, F. R., Hughes, C., and Kohler, P. D. (1991). *Descriptive analysis of secondary school education and transition services model programs*. Champaign, IL: Secondary Transition Intervention Effectiveness Institute.

Salvia, J., and Hughes, C. (1990). *Curriculum-based assessment: Testing what is taught*. New York: Macmillan.

Salvia, J., and Ysseldyke, J. (1998). *Assessment* (7th ed.). Boston: Houghton Mifflin.

Sattler, J. (1992). *Assessment of children* (3rd ed.). San Diego: Sattler Publishers.

Schrank, F. A., Flanagan, D. P., Woodcock, R. W., and Mascolo, J. T. (2002). *Essentials of WJ III® cognitive abilities assessment.* New York: Wiley.

Sewell, T. E. (1987). "Dynamic assessment as a nondiscriminatory procedure." In C. S. Lidz (Ed.), *Dynamic assessment: An interactional approach to evaluating learning potential* (pp. 426–443). New York: Guilford.

Shapiro, E. (1989). *Behavioral assessment in school psychology.* Hillsdale, NJ: Lawrence Erlbaum.

Shapiro, E. S. (1989). *Academic skills problems: Direct assessment and intervention.* New York: Guilford.

Skrtic, T. M. (1988). "The crisis in special education knowledge." In E. L. Meyen and T. M. Skrtic (Eds.), *Exceptional children and youth* (3rd ed.) (pp. 415–447). Denver: Love Publishing.

Sleeter, C. E. (1986). "Learning disabilities: The social construction of a special education category." *Exceptional children, 53*(1), 46–54.

Slosson, R. L. (1990). *Slosson oral reading test—Revised.* East Aurora, NY: Slosson Educational Publication.

Slosson, R. L. [Revised by Nicholson, C. L. and Hibpschman, T. L.] (1991) *Slosson intelligence test—Revised (SIT-R).* East Aurora, NY: Slosson Educational Publication.

Smith, D. (1998). *Introduction to special education: Teaching in an age of challenge* (3rd ed.). Boston: Allyn and Bacon.

Smith-Davis, J., and Littlejohn, W. R. (1991). "Related services for school-aged children with disabilities." *NICHCY News Digest, 1*(2), 1–24.

Spache, G. D. (1981). *Spache diagnostic reading scales.* Monterey, CA: CTB Macmillan/McGraw-Hill.

Sparrow, S., Balla, D., and Cicchetti, D. (1984). *Vineland adaptive behavior scale.* Circle Pines, MN: American Guidance Service.

Sprinthall, R. (1994). *Basic statistical analysis* (4th ed.). Boston: Allyn and Bacon.

Stainback, W., and Stainback, S. (1984). "A rationale for the merger of special and regular education." *Exceptional children, 51*(2), 102–111.

Stanovich, K. (1982). "Individual differences in the cognitive processes of reading." *Journal of learning disabilities, 15,* 485–493.

Swanson, H. C., and Watson, B. L. (1989). *Educational and psychological assessment of exceptional children* (2nd ed.). Columbus, OH: Merrill.

Sweetland, R. C., and Keyser, D. J. (Eds.) (1991). *Tests: A comprehensive reference for assessments in psychology, education, and business* (3rd ed.). Austin, TX: PRO-ED.

Taylor, R. (1997). *Assessment of exceptional students: Educational and psychological procedures* (5th ed.). Boston: Allyn and Bacon.

Taylor, R. L. (1991). "Bias in cognitive assessment: Issues, implications, and future directions." *Diagnostique, 17*(1), 3–5.

Terrell, S. L. (Ed.) (1983, June). "Nonbiased assessment of language differences [Special issue]." *Topics in language disorders, 3*(3).

Tharp, R. G. (1989). "Psychocultural variables and constants: Effects on teaching and learning in schools." *American psychologist, 44*(2), 349–359.

Tharp, R. G. (1994, June). *Cultural compatibility and the multicultural classroom: Oxymoron or opportunity.* Paper presented at the Training and Development Improvement Quarterly Meeting, Albuquerque, New Mexico.

The network news, Summer, 1996, National Transition Network, Institute on Community Integration, University of Minnesota, Minneapolis 55455; (612) 626-8200.

The pocket guide to federal help: For individuals with disabilities, (1993). Clearinghouse on Disability Information, Office of Special Education and Rehabilitative Services, U.S. Department of Education, 330 C Street SW, Room 3132, Switzer Building, Washington, DC 20202-2319.

Thorndike, R. L., Hagen, E. P., and Sattler, J. M. (1986). *The Stanford-Binet intelligence scale* (4th ed.). Chicago: Riverside Publishing Company.

Thorndike, R. L., and Lohman, D. F. (1990). *A century of ability testing.* Chicago: Riverside Publishing Company.

Trohanis, P. L. (1995). "Progress in providing services to young children with special needs and their families: An overview to and update on implementing the Individuals with Disabilities Education Act." *NEC*TAS Notes,* no. 7, 1–20.

Turnbull, A., Turnbull, H., Shank, M., and Leal, D. (1995). *Exceptional lives: Special education in today's schools.* Englewood Cliffs, NJ: Merrill.

Turnbull, H. R. (1990). *Free and appropriate public education: The law and children with disabilities* (3rd ed.). Denver: Love Publishing.

Ulrich, D. (1999). *Test of gross motor development—Second edition (TGMD-2).* Austin, TX: PRO-ED.

Vacca, J., Vacca, R., and Grove, M. (1986). *Reading and learning to read.* Boston: Little Brown.

Valles, E. C. (1998). "The disproportionate representation of minority students in special education: Responding to the problem." *Journal of special education, 32,* 52–54.

Vellutino, F. R. (1979). *Dyslexia: Theory and research.* Cambridge, MA: MIT Press.

Venn, J. (2000). *Assessing students with special needs* (2nd ed.). Upper Saddle River, NJ: Merrill.

Wagner, M. (1989, March). *The transition experiences of youth with disabilities: A report from the National Longitudinal Transition Study.* Paper presented at the annual meeting of the Council for Exceptional Children, San Francisco.

Wallace, G., and Hammill, D. D. (1994). *Comprehensive receptive and expressive vocabulary test (CREVT).* Austin, TX: PRO-ED.

Wallace, G., Larsen, S. C., and Elksnin, L. K. (1992). *Educational assessment of learning problems: Testing for teaching.* Boston: Allyn and Bacon.

Walsh, B., and Betz, N. (1985). *Test and assessment.* Englewood Cliffs, NJ: Prentice Hall.

Wandry, D., and Repetto, J. (1993). "Transition services in the IEP." *NICHCY Transition Summary, 1,* 1–28.

Ward, M. J. (1992). "Introduction to secondary special education and transition issues." In F. R. Rusch, L. DeStefano, J. Chadsey-Rusch, L. A. Phelps, and E. Szymanshi (Eds.), *Transition from school to adult life: Models, linkages, and policy* (pp. 387–389). Sycamore, IL: Sycamore Publishing.

Wechsler, D. (1958). *The measurement and appraisal of adult intelligence* (4th ed.). Baltimore: Williams and Wilkins.

Wechsler, D. (1991). *The Wechsler scales of intelligence.* San Antonio, TX: The Psychological Corporation.

Wechsler, D. (1992). *Wechsler individual achievement test-2.* San Antonio, TX: The Psychological Corporation.

Wehman, P. (1992). *Life beyond the classroom: Transition strategies for young people with disabilities.* Baltimore: Paul H. Brookes.

Wepman, J. M., and Reynolds, W. M. (1986). *Wepman test of auditory discrimination—2nd edition (ADT-2).* Los Angeles: Western Psychological Services.

Wiederholt, J. L., and Byrant, B. R. (1992). *Gray oral reading test-3.* Austin, TX: PRO-ED.

Wiggins, G. (1989). "A true test: Toward more authentic and equitable assessment." *Phi Delta Kappan*, *70*(9), 703–713.

Wilkinson, S. (1993). *Wide range achievement test-3.* Wilmington, DE: Jastak Associates—Wide Range Inc.

Williams, R., and Zimmerman, D. (1984). "On the virtues and vices of standard error of measurement." *Journal of experimental education*, *52*, 231–233.

Wilson, A. J., and Silverman, H. (1991). "Teachers' assumptions and beliefs about the delivery of services to exceptional children." *Teacher education and special education*, *14*(3), 198–206.

Wilson, N. O. (1992). *Optimizing special education: How parents can make a difference.* New York: Insight Books.

Wood, J. W., Lazzari, A., Davis, E. H., Sugai, G., and Carter J. (1990). "National status of the pre-referral process: An issue for regular education." *Action in teacher education*, *12*(3), 50–56.

Woodcock, R. (1997). *Woodcock reading mastery tests—Revised.* Circle Pines, MN: American Guidance Service.

Woodcock, R. W., and Johnson, M. B. (1989). *Woodcock-Johnson achievement battery.* Chicago: Riverside.

Woolfolk, E. C. (1999). *Test of auditory comprehension of language—III (TACL-3).* Itasca, IL: Riverside.

Wyatt v. *Stickney* (1972). 344 F. Supp. 387 M.D. Ala.

Yell, M. L. (1995). *The law and special education.* Upper Saddle River, NJ: Prentice Hall.

Ysseldyke, J., and Algozzine, B. (1982). *Critical issues in special and remedial education.* Boston: Houghton Mifflin.

Ysseldyke, J., and Regan, R. (1980). "Nondiscriminatory assessment: A formative model." *Exceptional children*, *46*, 465–466.

Ysseldyke, J., Algozzine, B., Regan, R., and Potter, M. (1980). "Technical adequacy of tests used by professionals in simulated decision making." *Psychology in the schools*, *17*, 202–209.

Zimmerman, I. L., Steiner, V. G., and Evatt, R. L. (1992). *Preschool Language Scale—3 (PLS-3).* San Antonio, TX: The Psychological Corporation.